Microsoft®
SMS Installer

Microsoft®
SMS Installer

Rod Trent

McGraw-Hill

New York   San Francisco   Washington, D.C.   Auckland   Bogotá
Caracas   Lisbon   London   Madrid   Mexico City   Milan
Montreal   New Delhi   San Juan   Singapore
Sydney   Tokyo   Toronto

Contents

v

Preface

SMS Installer is a Microsoft tool that allows the quick creation of redistributable application installations. Microsoft released this tool to provide SMS administrators with the ability to build standard installations that are uniform across all computers in the organization. This aids in reducing the amount of time required to support a user base. It also helps lower the total cost of ownership (TCO) of the company's computer systems.

Who Should Read This Book?

Technical support personnel, SMS administrators, and scripting enthusiasts will all benefit from reading this book. Since the advent of SMS Installer, there has been no easy reference for the product. This book provides detailed references, examples, walk-throughs, tips, and troubleshooting that can be used over and over. SMS Installer will become a frequently used reference book that sits on the shelf of every SMS administrator and user of SMS installer.

This book is written so it can be read anywhere. The text is coupled with screen captures that make the subject at hand easy to understand and simple to follow. Such a setup allows the book to be read away from the SMS Installer interface and still provide concepts and understanding that can be applied later. The book can be read at home, in a car, in an airplane, in a training class, in just about any location, or directly in front of the computer screen while SMS Installer is being used.

What Does This Book Cover?

This book not only covers SMS Installer in its entirety but also explains the general concepts of scripting. Subject matter relates to all levels of experience with the product, from beginning, to intermediate, to advanced.

Beginning concepts: Installation and repackaging.

Intermediate concepts: Watch, run, compile, and script editing.

Advanced concepts: Using the scripting features to customize and create real-world solutions and utilities.

SMS Installer also contains general computer and technology concepts that must be understood to work successfully with SMS Installer. These concepts are insightful to anyone in the computing industry whether or not SMS Installer is being utilized. It provides a methodology for logical thinking that will benefit anyone interested in computer scripting.

Overview of Chapters

Chapter 1 introduces SMS Installer and its features. It provides a list of the benefits for using SMS Installer to repackage applications for small and mass distribution.

Chapter 2 defines the system requirements for running SMS Installer, explains the files that are installed by the product, and leads the reader through a standard SMS Installer installation and the options that it presents.

Chapter 3 takes the reader through repackaging an application to be used for distribution. It also provides explanations for several distribution methods.

Chapter 4 provides detailed reference for all the features of the Installation Expert interface. These references will help the user understand how to customize an installation before it is distributed.

Chapter 5 provides a detailed reference for all the script actions of the Script Editor. It includes descriptions of all the features and also provides an example for using each script action.

Chapter 6 explains some advanced techniques of SMS Installer and leads the reader through the creation of standalone utilities. It also provides reference to some real-world solutions that can be incorporated into standalone utilities of your own.

Chapter 7 describes computer technologies related to SMS Installer that must be understood when the user utilizes SMS Installer so the product can realize its fullest potential. It provides descriptions of the technologies as well as the common methodologies for implementing them.

Chapter 8 contains some quick tips for SMS Installer. These quick tips can help speed up the repackaging and scripting processes by defining some shortcuts and need-to-know information.

Chapter 9 describes the next step in the future of repackaging technology from Microsoft. It provides an overview of the Windows Installer technology currently being implemented in the latest Microsoft products, including Windows 2000.

Finally, the compact disk contains additional reference material for use with SMS Installer, including file-type examples referenced in the book, third-party utilities helpful to SMS Installer, troubleshooting, and additional resources for obtaining more information on SMS Installer and scripting in general.

Microsoft®
SMS Installer

Introduction

Microsoft Systems Management Server (SMS) is a scalable enterprise application that provides systems management support for organizations. It provides tools and processes that lower the total cost of ownership (TCO) by allowing proactive support of systems from the back end all the way to the desktop.

A component of SMS is the ability to distribute software to the client PC, whether as an update to an already installed version or a complete, new installation. It gives the support staff of an organization the ability to distribute timely updates and patches such as virus signature files, patches to the operating system (OS), and critical Y2K software updates. SMS also provides the capability to "advertise" programs to the client PC. These advertisements are software installations that are not considered as critical, so they are just made available for the user to install if the need arises. Both of these components require the creation of "packages" or software installations into the SMS system.

When a package is created in the SMS system, SMS pulls all the files related to the package from a source and places them on a destination share that each client PC has access to. The *destination share* is a common directory structure on a server to which both SMS and the client PC have access. If you are familiar with software installations, you know that installing from CD or diskette media can be cumbersome and not necessarily the most optimum environment to allow the user base to complete on their own. Distribution through SMS to the client PC provides more control and can make the user base more comfortable with the installation. Using this type of software distribution method can also minimize calls to the local help desk. SMS gives the support staff the tools to create successful mass distributions of software, as well as the ability to target specific PCs.

Although SMS provides this functionality, the need for further control of software distribution still exists. Specific settings for a software package may be different from one organization to another or even from one department within the organization to another. Organizations may need to customize software installations across the board in order to standardize what is available in an application or to load only certain components. For instance, an organization may require that the Microsoft Office FindFast utility not be loaded at computer startup. The need exists to be able to install Microsoft Office and to make sure this component is not loaded on all computers. A separate utility is needed to accomplish this task—a utility that is easy to learn and use and still allows complete customization.

To help with this task, Microsoft includes a unique scripting utility called SMS Installer. SMS Installer is, first and foremost, a repackaging utility. *Repackaging* means taking an application installation and recompressing it into a custom installation file. SMS Installer creates self-extracting compressed files used for software installation. The compressed files include everything needed to completely install a software package. It includes the files, the program shortcuts and their icons, and information for modifications to the client PC, such as modifying system files and the registry. SMS Installer takes a "snapshot" of the computer before the software installation, runs the installation, and then takes another snapshot after the software installation completes. Whatever options are selected during the installation, SMS Installer records these verbatim in a standalone script. Just like a movie script, SMS Installer records the steps to complete the custom installation from beginning to end.

SMS Installer provides even further customization of the software package after the snapshot has been taken and recorded. It does this through both an easy-to-use "wizard" (i.e., a set of dialog boxes with easy-to-understand selections) and through a powerful scripting facility.

Repackaging

A repackaging utility allows SMS Installer to watch the installation of a software program, record all the changes to the computer, and then compress the changes into a one-file installation package. These changes include:

1. Modifications made to the boot files (autoexec.bat, config.sys, win.ini, and system.ini)

2. Modifications to the Windows 9x and Windows NT Registry

3. Created icons and program groups

4. Installed application files

5. Installed system files (dll, vxd, etc.)

6. Registered system files

The true value of a repackaging utility such as SMS Installer is the ability to create custom installations. For example, the Microsoft Office toolbar, in some cases, causes problems with software installations because certain system files remain open. The open files are not overwritten by the new application installation, so it may not run as it should or possibly not at all. This happens because the application requires the version it tried to install. If this is already a known issue, the organization may not want the Microsoft Office toolbar installed on the PCs. If the user base is allowed to install Microsoft Office on their own, it is likely that some users will decide to install the Microsoft Office toolbar, thinking it a useful component and not realizing it may cause problems. Using SMS Installer, you deselect the Microsoft Office toolbar during the Microsoft Office installation, and SMS Installer compiles your custom package with your selections.

Powerful Scripting Utility

By "powerful scripting utility" I mean that, using the scripting side of SMS Installer, one can create powerful utilities to help automate processes and produce solutions unique to the environment. An example would be a systemwide security setting that must be set via the Win NT registry. You can create full-featured utilities to accomplish this task, complete with user interaction, or none at all.

Note   Both the repackaging and the scripting include command-line options, one of which is to install the application "quietly" or with no user interaction at all. Installed with the quiet-mode switch, the software installs behind the scenes. This is important when a critical update has to go out, and some users would rather wait until they have more time to click through screens. It is also a great resource for sending updates to Windows NT servers. The servers can be updated without the need for an administrator to be present, sitting at the server console and clicking through installation screens. (For more information on command-line variables see "Command Line QuickList" in Chapter 10.)

SMS Installer Feature Set

Installation Repackaging

One or more application installations can be repackaged into a one-file executable. Wizard-driven, SMS Installer takes a "snapshot" of the computer before the software installation, then takes another snapshot after the software installation and records all changes.

Watch Facility

SMS Installer provides the ability to watch an application running, in order to determine if the application is reliant on other files not included with the original vendor installation. When it finds these files, it adds them to the SMS Installer script.

Intuitive, Easy-to-Use Interface

SMS Installer provides an intuitive interface called the Installation Expert. The Installation Expert is a wizard-based series of dialogs that walk the administrator through the repackaging process.

Powerful Scripting Facility

As mentioned, for those times when more customization is needed, SMS Installer includes a scripting facility. The scripting facility provides the ability to modify the installation in order to produce a more robust installation. It also provides all the scripting features needed to create powerful utilities.

Patching

SMS Installer provides the ability to distribute small changes to applications, files, or operating systems.

Authenticode Technology

SMS Installer fully supports Authenticode technology. Authenticode technology provides a secure method of distributing applications. If a distribution has been signed using Authenticode technology, you can rest assured it is from a trusted source.

Dry-Run Support

SMS Installer provides "dry-run" support, allowing testing of a distribution before it is deployed. This feature can be used to test the interface and debug the installation before a major rollout.

Uninstall and Rollback Support

SMS Installer supports both the standard Windows Uninstall feature and rollback. With the Uninstall feature, software can be removed from the PC when it is no longer needed. The rollback feature provides protection from failed installations by restoring the PC to its original state (before the software was installed). It removes all files and changes, such as those made to the registry, system files, and boot files.

16-Bit and 32-Bit Support

To add continued support for both newer systems and older systems, SMS Installer comes in both 16-bit and 32-bit versions. This allows support for computers with Windows for Workgroups 3.11 and Windows 95/98, and Windows NT installed as the operating system.

Note   Most of the features discussed in this book are geared toward the 32-bit version of SMS Installer. This is due, primarily, to the fact that the majority of computers now run a 32-bit operating system.

Single-File- or Floppy-Based Installations

As well as compiling software installations into a single distribution file, SMS Installer allows distribution via a floppy disk set. SMS Installer will break down the installation into separate files

to fit on floppy diskettes, which can then be installed on a PC
using the floppy disk drive.

Standard User Interface

There is no need to worry about the "look and feel" of the
software installation unless you want to. SMS Installer creates the
installation interface for you with the look and feel of standard
Windows program installations. The installation screens are
familiar, since most applications use the same type of interface for
installation.

Custom Dialogs

For instances where you want to add custom dialogs, SMS
Installer incorporates that ability too. With SMS Installer, you can
even opt to completely discard the standard installation interface
for your own, making the installation a more personal experience
for your organization.

Custom Graphics

Using any standard Windows bitmap, it is easy to incorporate
your own custom graphics, such as company logos, splash
screens, and so on.

Automatic Creation of PDF Files

Microsoft Systems Management Server imports PDF files to
make easier and more rapid package distribution creations. SMS
Installer includes the ability to automatically create the PDF file
at runtime. The PDF is a standard Package Definition File that
contains all the information and instructions about a software
installation.

Automatic Creation of Status MIF Files

SMS Installer includes an interface for creating status Management Information Format (MIF) files. Since the Microsoft Systems Management Server relies on MIF files for reporting and
interaction with the client computer, this allows SMS to report a
success or failure of the software installation. This aids in obtaining a more proactive approach to user support.

Special Support for ODBC and Visual Basic Installations

SMS Installer allows the selection of options to include support for ODBC and the Visual Basic programming system. If the options are selected, SMS Installer will automatically include all the files needed in the distribution package.

Services

SMS Installer provides an easy way to allow the author to create Windows NT and Windows 9x services on the target PC. It allows interaction with the system through a local user account and password or one you specify at runtime.

Password-Protected Installs

The author of an installation can incorporate a password for the installation. The user would be required to enter a password for the installation to complete.

Support for Multiple Languages

Create one installation and include multiple languages, and the user will be able to select which language he or she prefers at runtime.

User Access Customization

SMS Installer provides complete control over the installation of user icons, program groups, file associations, and so on.

Installation Control

SMS Installer includes several options for customizing the installation, such as adjusting the installation speed, choosing standard or maximum compression of the executable, making the executable WinZip-compatible, changing installation screen colors and granularity, and so on.

Note   For this book, we will be referencing the latest version of SMS Installer: SMS Installer version 2.0.91.00. Most of the examples are created with the 32-bit version of SMS Installer. While SMS Installer comes in a 16-bit version, the majority of new applications are created for 32-bit platforms.

System Requirements and Installation

- Windows 9x or Windows NT 4.0
- Minimum 8 MB of RAM
- Approximately 7 MB of free hard disk space
- Microsoft Systems Management Server site server

Installation

SMS Installer is distributed in two ways. It is included on the SMS 2.0 CD and is also available for download from Microsoft's Systems Management Web site:

http://www.microsoft.com/smsmgmt/downloads/default.asp

The downloadable version requires that a SMS site server be present before the installation files will extract from the download. The downloadable file is called SMSIMAIN.EXE.

Shown in Figure 2-1, the SMS Installer installation is straightforward. It can be installed on any Win 9x or Win NT PC. The filename to start the installation is SMSINSTL.EXE. SMS Installer can be distributed and installed in several ways:

- Executed in a local command line on the Primary Site Server and installed onto the Primary Site Server.

- Sent via a Windows NT share created for the executable (with appropriate file and directory rights) to be accessed by others in your organization.

- Copied to a file server. Rights would then be given to others in your organization.

Figure 2-1 *Installation screen 1: Welcome.*

- Copied to floppy disks for installation on standalone or remote computers in your organization.

- Distributed by Microsoft Systems Management Server.

> It is recommended that SMS Installer be installed on a PC that is as close to identical as possible to the PC with the lowest common denominator in your organization. When you create an installation, remember that the installation will be written once and distributed to many computers. For example, if you use SMS Installer on your own PC and your own PC includes the proper Microsoft Foundation Class Library files (MFC), it is possible that some PCs in your organization don't. SMS Installer will only catch the changes on your PC and will not know that the MFC files may need to be included to operate correctly on all other computers. (See "The Methodology of Software Creation/Distribution" in Chapter 07 for more information.)

Note

The installation allows you to change where SMS Installer will be installed, as shown in Figure 2-2. If an existing copy is found in the location you specify, either from a reinstallation of the current version or if you are performing an upgrade to an existing copy, the screen in Figure 2-3 is displayed, prompting you to back up the old files. You can also specify a different directory for the location of the backed-up files (see Figure 2-4).

As shown in Figure 2-5, there are two versions of SMS Installer, a Win16 and a Win32 Integrated Development Environment (IDE). There are some disadvantages to the Win16 version, so it is preferable to install both versions if you know the reference computer supports them. Figures 2-6 and 2-7 show the installation status bar and completion screens, respectively.

If you chose to install both the Win16 and Win32 IDE, two versions of the program are installed, as shown in Figure 2-8.

The shortcuts to the two different programs are installed to START-PROGRAMS-MICROSOFT SMS INSTALLER. Each shortcut points to a different SMS Installer executable. The executable for the 16-bit version is \Microsoft SMS Installer\ SMSINSTL.EXE. The executable for the 32-bit version is \Microsoft SMS Installer\SMSINS32.EXE.

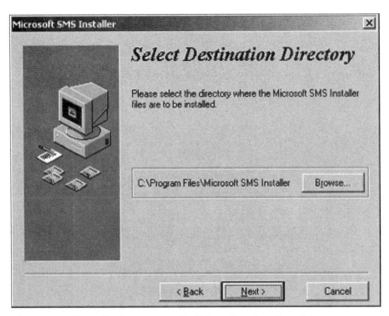

Figure 2-2 *Installation screen 2: Select Destination Directory.*

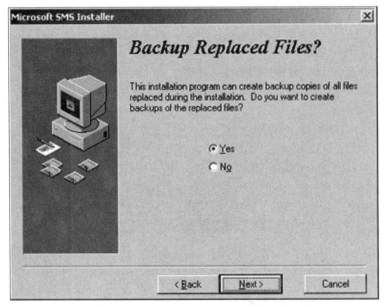

Figure 2-3 *Installation screen 3: Backup Replaced Files.*

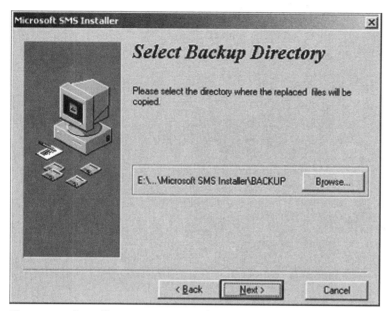

Figure 2-4 *Installation screen 4: Select Backup Directory.*

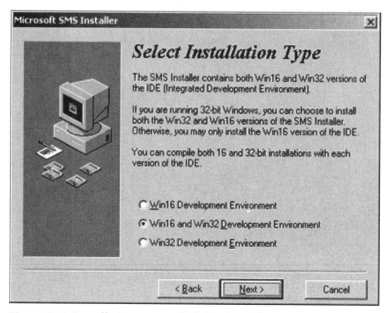

Figure 2-5 *Installation screen 5: Select Installation Type.*

Figure 2-6 *Installation progress dialog box.*

Figure 2-7 *Installation Completed.*

Microsoft SMS   Microsoft SMS
Installer 16   Installer 32

Figure 2-8 *16-bit and 32-bit icons.*

Table 2-1 *Win16/Win32 differences.*

Function	Win16	Win32
Standard Win Search/Index	No	Yes
Compiled Versioning	No	Yes
Context Help Function	No	Yes
Runs on Windows 3.1 and Windows 3.11	Yes	No
Runs on Windows 9x and Windows NT	Yes	Yes

Table 2-1 lists the differences between the Win16 and Win32 versions.

Directory Structure and Files

By default, the SMS Installer is installed to <driveletter>:\Program Files\Microsoft SMS Installer. It is helpful not only to understand the files that are installed, but also to know where files are located, such as the dialog templates and the redistributable files included with SMS Installer (see Figure 2-9). This importance will become clear as this book delves into the customization options of the Installation Expert (see Chapter 04).

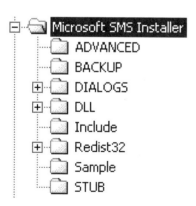

Figure 2-9 *Main directory structure.*

Main Directory

The main Microsoft SMS Installer directory contains the executables and miscellaneous files that run the program. Also included are the help file, the language information file, and the install.log file, which is used to uninstall the program if you so desire. There are also a few Internet shortcuts that the SMS Installer calls from its pull-down Help menu. See Figure 2-10.

Advanced Directory

The Advanced directory, directly under the SMS Installer directory, contains system files and files to help SMS Installer complete tasks such as rebooting Windows NT and registering OCX files. See Figure 2-11.

Dialogs\Template Directory

The Dialogs\Template directory contains the dialog files used in the interface when a repackaged installation is performed.

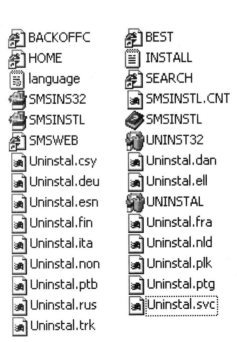

Figure 2-10 *Main directory file.*

Figure 2-11 *Advanced directory.*

These files can be customized through SMS Installer, though it is not recommended to modify these. Alternatively, you can open the files in SMS Installer and save them as a dialog template of your own with its own filename. (See "Dialogs" in Chapter 04 for more information.)

The Wizard.bmp included in the Dialogs directory is the standard Dialog graphic seen during SMS Installer-generated installations. This graphic, shown in Figure 2-12, can also be customized through Microsoft Paint (an accessory included with any Microsoft operating system) or any graphic editing program that can edit bitmap files. You can add a company logo, your name, copyright information, and so on. Using the Wizard.bmp as a template for graphic size, you can create a totally new file and

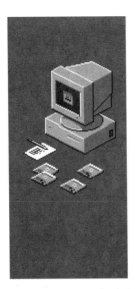

Figure 2-12 *Default Wizard bitmap.*

save it as your Wizard.bmp in the Dialogs\Template directory.
Whenever you author a new installation, the new file you created
will automatically be included on the dialog screens. Figure 2-13
shows the files in the Dialogs\Template directory.

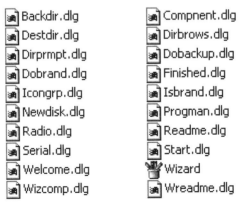

Figure 2-13 *Dialog directory files.*

DLL Directory

As shown in Figure 2-14, the DLL directory contains system files that SMS Installer uses to perform some of its functions. For instance, the Checkvga files allow SMS Installer to determine the VGA properties on the reference computer. The Getcpu32 files determine the central processing unit properties.

DLL\Progress Directory

The DLL\Progress directory contains the files that display the installation progress. This is the small dialog box seen during file installation. It has a number of options (covered later in Chapter

```
Progress
Checkvga.c
Checkvga.def
Checkvga.dll
Checkvga.mak
Getcpu32.c
Getcpu32.def
Getcpu32.dll
Getcpu32.mak
Prompt.c
Prompt.def
Prompt.dll
Prompt.mak
Prompt.rc
Prompt.res
Resource.h
SMSIdll.h
```

Figure 2.14 *DLL directory files.*

04), but it basically shows the overall progress of the installation by percentage. See Figure 2-15.

Include Directory

The Include directory, shown in Figure 2-16, contains SMS Installer script files that are incorporated in an SMS Installer soft-

Figure 2-15 *DLL Progress directory files.*

Figure 2-16 *Include directory files.*

ware installation file. These items include the platform-specific ODBC (Open Database Connectivity) files, the Visual Basic files, the VShare component, the Uninstall script, the software Rollback script, the FoxPro files, and the OLE (Object Linking and Embedding) script. (See "Dialogs" in Chapter 04 for more information on how to select these options.)

Following are descriptions of some of the files in this directory:

Odbc16cr.ipf SMS Installer script that installs the ODBC 16 core files.

Odbc32cr.ipf SMS Installer script that installs the ODBC 3.0 Win32 core files.

Odbc32jt.ipf SMS Installer script that installs the Microsoft Access 97 32-bit ODBC driver.

Ole2.ipf SMS Installer script that installs OLE 2.0 support. Should not be used with VB4 installations.

Rollback.ipf SMS Installer script that performs a rollback if the Backup option is selected and the installation is canceled.

Uninstal.ipf SMS Installer script that installs Uninstall support if that option is selected.

Vb4win16.ipf SMS Installer script that installs VB4 runtime support. *Do not* modify this script, as the order of the files is critical. VB4 is Microsoft's Visual Basic programming language version 4.0.

Vb4win32.ipf SMS Installer script that installs VB4 Win32 support. *Do not* modify this script, as the order of the files and their settings is critical. VB4 is Microsoft's Visual Basic programming language version 4.0.

Vb5.ipf SMS Installer script that installs files to support a Visual Basic 5 installation. It installs the basic components, as well as MS Jet files, ODBC files if required, remote client support, and Crystal Reports OCX. Visual Basic 5 is Microsoft's Visual Basic programming language version 5.0.

Vb5check.ipf SMS Installer script that checks to make sure that the proper OS/service pack is installed for a VB5 application. VB5 is Microsoft's Visual Basic programming language version 5.0.

Vb6.ipf   SMS Installer script that installs files to support a Visual Basic 6 installation. It installs the basic components, as well as MS Jet files, ODBC files if required, remote client support, and Crystal Reports OCX. Visual Basic 6 is Microsoft's Visual Basic programming language version 6.0.

Vb6check.ipf   SMS Installer script that checks to make sure that the proper OS/service pack is installed for a VB6 application. VB6 is Microsoft's Visual Basic programming language version 6.0.

Vfoxpro.ipf   SMS Installer script that installs the Visual Fox-Pro runtime files. FoxPro is a Microsoft database programming language.

Vshare.ipf   SMS Installer script that installs support for VSHARE on Win 9x systems. It installs the vshare.386 file and modifies the System.ini on the target computer.

Redist32\ODBC Directory

The Redis32\ODBC directory contains the ODBC files mentioned previously. It also contains other redistributable files that are included into the SMS Installer script by selection through the Installation Expert interface. (See Figure 2-17.)

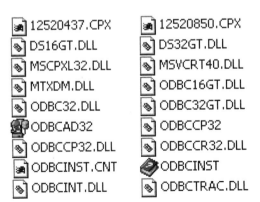

Figure 2.17 *ODBC directory files.*

Sample Directory

Included with SMS Installer are some sample scripts, as shown in Figure 2-18. These samples are "snippets" of script code that can be used to learn basic SMS Installer concepts and can also be copied and pasted into your own scripts. These scripts can be compiled and used as is. Examples of the actual scripts can be viewed in Chapter 10. These script examples are listed in SMS Installer script format. Unless you already understand the SMS Installer script format, you may want to look through Chapter 05 for a better understanding of what is presented.

Following is a breakdown of files in this directory:

Cdrom.ipf   Sample script for creating an SMS Installer installation from a CD or network drive.

Checkvga.ipf   Sample script for checking the VGA configuration. If the VGA settings are 256 colors or better, it displays a message indicating the video is at least 256 colors; if not, the program aborts.

Compar.ipf   Sample script demonstrating the use of variables that can be customized during the script compile stage.

Newdisk.ipf   Sample script demonstrating how to properly script changing floppy disks during installation.

Figure 2-18 *Sample directory file.*

Prompt.ipf   Sample script that points to the prompt.dll file for a dialog box that prompts the user for information during the installation.

Search.ipf   Sample script that searches and finds a file in a path. This shows two different ways to accomplish the task.

Subcomp.ipf   Sample script demonstrating how to use the include components option to use component lists with sub-components.

Textfile.ipf   Sample script that demonstrates working with text files. It shows how to read and update a text file.

Stub Directory

See Figure 2-19.

Backup Directory

If you chose to back up files during the SMS Installer installation and you already had a version of SMS Installer installed, the Backup directory will be created. All files that are overwritten during the SMS Installer installation will be backed up to this directory.

Figure 2-19 *Stub directory files.*

| Repackage | **Repackaging an Application**

Repackaging in SMS Installer means telling SMS Installer to start watching and then run the application's installation program. SMS Installer first takes a look at the local computer and takes a snapshot. It gathers information about the currently installed files and their directory structure, and it looks at the registry. When the information-gathering procedure is complete, it runs the software installation for you. After the software installation is complete, SMS Installer goes back through its information-gathering process again to determine what has been changed. It adds these changes to the script. These changes are commonly referred to as *deltas*.

Note   You should be aware of SMS Installer's repackaging limits. Anything beyond the following values will be ignored:

- Up to 32 levels of directory trees are scanned.
- Up to 64 levels of registry trees are scanned.
- Up to 5888 files can be included.
- Up to 8192 script items can be included.

Also:

- Data conversions or modifications cannot be repackaged. For example, additions to an Access database will not work through SMS Installer.

- SMS Installer does not support hardware installations, which include specific hardware driver files. Examples are a network card or the addition of a printer.

- If a repackage modifies shared files, it could fail.

- Repackaging an application that installs its files to the Program Files directory will result in the application's files being installed there even if the user has the option of installing to a different directory.

- Do not repackage an application that is already Windows Installer–compliant. (See "Windows Installer Technology" in Chapter 09 for more information.)

Before we begin an example of repackaging an application, you must first understand the type of computer on which a repackage should be run. The computer should be of the lowest common denominator of your organization. This means a computer with a configuration that closely matches all the computers in your environment. Many applications share files that may not be picked up in a repackage if the files already exist on the computer. A good example is Microsoft Office products. Microsoft Office products utilize a lot of the same files to perform their functions. If Word is already installed and you want to repackage Excel, some of the DLL files may be missed during the repackage.

A good candidate for a repackaging computer is a PC with similar hardware to the rest that has a minimal OS with patches and nothing else. If Windows NT is the OS of choice for your organization, you should configure the repackaging computer with a minimal installation of Windows NT and with the service pack version that has been displayed. Only install the bare minimum Windows NT accessories, services, and components needed to run the computer.

Follow these guidelines for repackaging the computer.

1. Match the OS version and service packs.

2. Install only the minimum OS requirements to run the PC.

3. Do not use a PC that has hardware that is not installed on the target PCs.

4. Make sure that the repackaging computer does not have a SMS client installed. This could accidentally lead to duplicating the SMS client ID on all computers.

Another important guideline to follow is to reconfigure the computer after every repackage to prepare it for the next repackage. You can use your favorite computer cloning procedure to accomplish this. For more in-depth information, see "The Methodology of Software Creation/Distribution" in Chapter 07.

Running through the Repackage Process

For this example, Adobe Acrobat will be repackaged. When you click on the Repackage button, the properties screen, shown in Figure 3-1, is displayed.

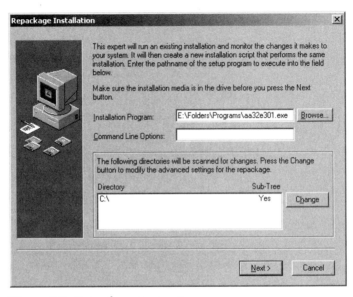

Figure 3-1 *Repackage properties screen.*

The first properties screen allows you to either enter the installation program's setup file or to use the browse button to find it on the local computer's drives. Most applications install from either the CD-ROM drive or the floppy disk drive. The Installation Program entry will accept any valid path. For example, a network drive can also be chosen. Some organizations set up CD towers and connect them to a network in order to make common application installations available. For our example, E:\Folders\Programs\aa32e301.exe was chosen.

The Command Line Options line allows you to enter any known command-line switches. Software vendors sometimes include additional command-line switches, coded into the software installation executable. This enables an additional range of options for the installation. Some software installations, for example, include a / a switch for administrative installations, a / s switch for a silent installation, or a / e switch for extracting the files contained in the installation file. Those command-line switches can be entered here. Check the documentation that comes with the software package to find if the vendor supports additional installation switches in their installation program.

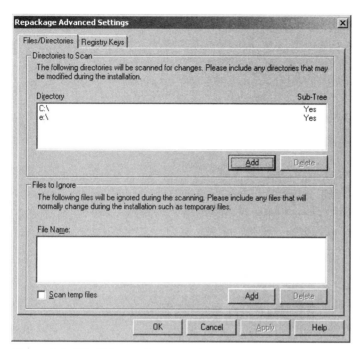

Figure 3-2 *File/Directories, snapshot options.*

The bottom portion of the installation properties is for changing the snapshot options SMS Installer uses to detect changes after the software is installed. Clicking on the Change button brings up the Repackage Advanced Settings dialog screen, shown in Figure 3-2.

Depending on how a software installation operates, it may make modifications to all local drives on the computer. On the Files/Directories tab in the directory box, you can add other drive letters for SMS Installer to watch. If you know what directories will be modified, you can add specific directories. There are instances when you will want to do this (see "Tracking Changes" in Chapter 08 for an example), but generally the root of each local drive will be the correct choice. SMS Installer's default is the root of the C: drive, so you will have to install the application to the C: drive during the repackage unless you change this value. Otherwise, SMS Installer will not pick up the changes.

In the Add dialog box, you pick a local drive or drill down to the specific directory. There is a checkbox for including the subdi-

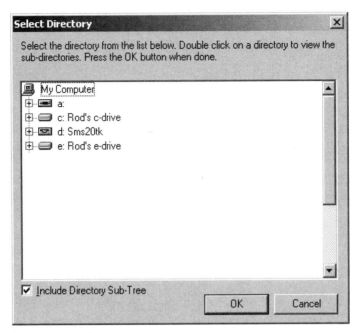

Figure 3-3 *Select Directory.*

rectory structure of a selected directory or drive, as shown in Figure 3-3. This will scan all subdirectories and their files underneath the primary directory selection. This is why it is a good idea to check the root directory of a hard disk drive. If the root is selected, and the subdirectory option is chosen, all file and directory changes will be detected by the repackage.

You can also tell SMS Installer–specific files to ignore during the repackage process. During normal software installations, temporary files can be created and sometimes not deleted correctly. Since SMS Installer does its best to record the changes to the computer verbatim, it will pick up these temporary files and include them in the compiled package unless the references are removed. If you know of other files, such as an e-mail mailbox file that may change during the repackage, exclude those here. See Figure 3-4.

When you click the Add button, a drive and directory dialog box is presented, as shown in Figure 3-5.

Adding exclude information is a little different than is presented. For instance, it is not readily evident that wildcard charac-

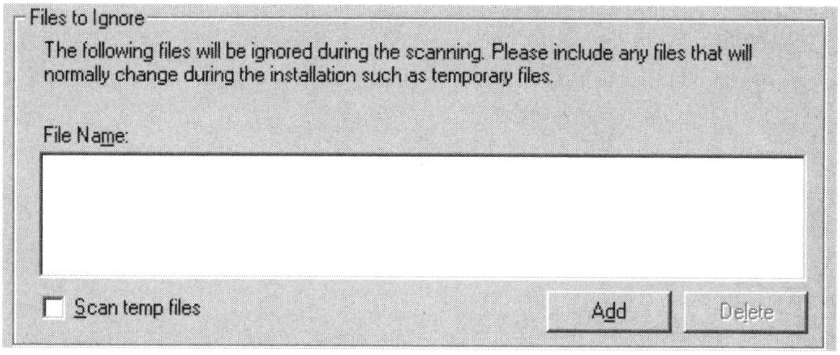

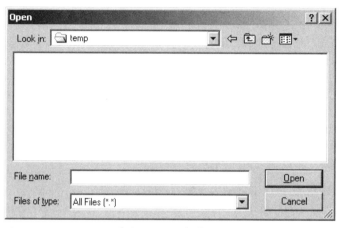

Figure 3-4 *Files to Ignore.*

Figure 3-5 *Drive and directory dialog box.*

ters can or should be used. Use the following procedures for adding specific files, specific directories, and specific types of files:

- To select a specific file, click on it once to highlight it and then click on the Open button. See Figure 3-6.

- To select an entire directory, click on the directory or folder name, type the wildcard characters *.* into the Filename line, and click on Open. See Figure 3-7.

- To select a drive letter and a certain type of file, click on the drive letter, use the wildcard characters with the file extension, and click on Open. See Figure 3-8.

The output of what was just selected is shown in Figure 3-9.

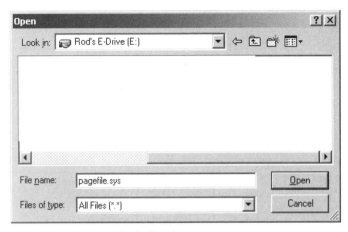

Figure 3-6 *Open File dialog box.*

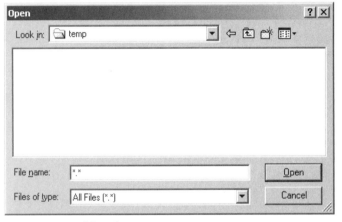

Figure 3-7 *Wildcard entry.*

Note   The Windows NT pagefile.sys file is automatically ignored during
a repackage operation. Windows NT uses the hard disk to simu-
late system RAM. The pagefile.sys file is used to swap data from
RAM to the hard disk and back. Because this is an intensive
process, the file changes rapidly. If SMS Installer did not ignore
this file, it would be picked up every time a repackage process
was initiated.

On the Files/Directories tab, SMS Installer includes a checkbox
to quickly enable scanning of Temp files. As mentioned, some

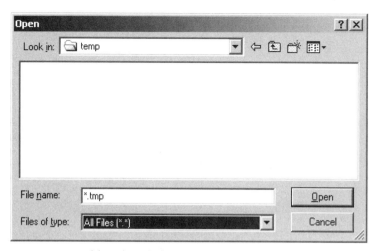

Figure 3-8 *Wildcard with file extension.*

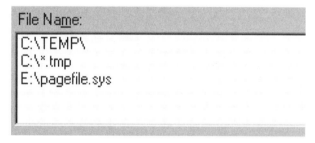

Figure 3-9 *Selection output.*

applications install temporary files. These are not normally needed for a successful repackage, but in the instances where they are needed, be sure to check the box. See Figure 3-10.

The second tab on the Repackage Advanced Settings is the Registry Keys tab, shown in Figure 3-11. It gives you the opportunity to exclude specific registry keys. The registry of the computer is the operating system's database of information. It contains data about the computer's hardware and software, about the OS itself, about the user, and about the user's preferences. This database is critical

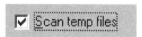

Figure 3-10 *Scan temp files selection.*

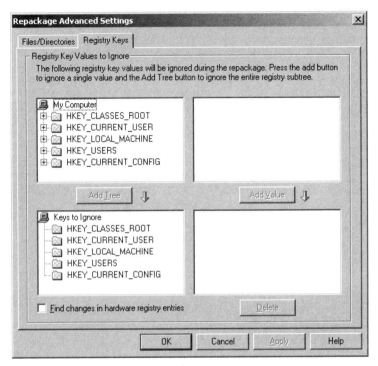

Figure 3-11 *Registry Keys exclusion.*

to the operation of the computer. If the registry were to become
corrupt or if unadvisable changes or additions were made to the
registry, the computer would no longer function (for more information on the registry, see "Registry Overview" in Chapter 07.

Excluding registry keys is good if you know that certain registry entries are updated on a regular basis by the operating system or other applications. Windows NT and Windows 9x make
regular changes to the registry. The registry is very dynamic. It is
a "living" database. If a key is updated during the repackage
process, SMS Installer will see it and record it in the script. If the
item is not removed, it will be populated onto all computers on
which the package is run.

An example of a registry key that could change is in reference
to some of the SMS client components. If a scheduled process
runs, it resets the next schedule date and stores this in the registry.
Repackaging this parameter could set all the computers in the
organization to a previous date every time the package is installed.

The registry exclusion is fairly simple. The top left window lets you navigate the registry keys on the local computer. The Add Tree button is clicked to add the complete registry key. If a registry value (registry key data) is to be excluded, items in the top right window are highlighted and the Add Value button is clicked. If you decide to remove an excluded registry key or value, the Delete button can be clicked on a highlighted item.

In the bottom left of the Registry Keys tab, a checkbox is included to quickly select the option of telling SMS Installer to watch the hardware registry keys. By default this is turned off. As mentioned earlier, SMS Installer does not do a good job of assisting the addition of hardware devices. Unless you know and have tested that a certain hardware component can be repackaged, leave this checkbox unchecked. See Figure 3-12.

> The procedures for customizing the repackage are useful steps to check once you are familiar with SMS Installer. They are not needed to complete a repackage. The repackage process can be as simple or as detailed as you allow. Just clicking the Next button through the repackage process will produce the expected results and should make for a successful SMS Installer package. Again, a straight repackage with SMS Installer is a very simple process. **Note**

If you have chosen to customize the exclusions, click on the OK button. This returns you to the initial Repackage screen where you click the Next button to continue.

As shown in Figure 3-13, SMS Installer scans the local directory structure and registry (observing any exclusions). During this scan, SMS Installer is taking its snapshot of the computer, recording the "before" configuration and preparing for the "after." Once the directory structure and registry have been scanned and the snapshot taken, SMS Installer executes the software setup file (seen here as the Adobe Acrobat Reader 3.01).

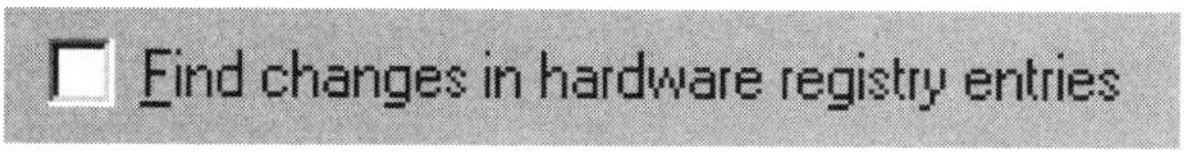

Figure 3-12 *Find changes in hardware registry keys.*

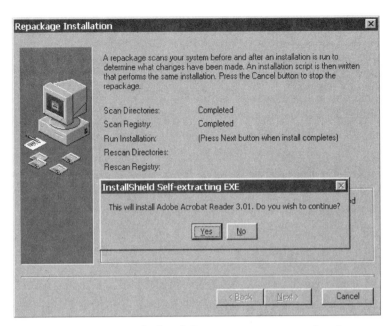

Figure 3-13 *Scanning the local directory structure and registry.*

   Run through the normal software setup, following the prompts
and selecting the software installation preferences. Keep in mind
that whatever preferences are chosen for the application, SMS
Installer will pick these up and they will be populated to any
computer that runs the final SMS Installer package.

Tip   It's a smart idea to plan ahead and become familiar with the software before attempting the repackage. Sit down and install the
software a few times to understand what preferences and components are available. If your company is very structured, it may
also help to sit down with a group to decide what the standards
should be for your organization. If everyone understands how the
software will exist on the computers, the software will be easier to
support once it is installed. It may even help if a user or group of
users acts as a test bed for the application to understand what
components will actually be needed to get the job done. Anything that can be done to ensure a successful software deployment will reflect positively on you and/or your department.

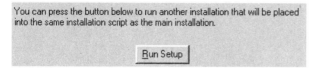

You can press the button below to run another installation that will be placed into the same installation script as the main installation.

Run Setup

Figure 3-14 *Run Setup selection.*

Once the software installation is complete, you have the option of including other applications before continuing. Clicking the Run Setup button, shown in Figure 3-14, will allow the selection of another software setup program. This gives you the ability to include multiple applications in one script. While this is a helpful feature when rolling out multiple applications en masse, it may be a hindrance for future rollouts of the specific applications. If applications are combined, they must always be deployed together. Therefore, it is a better idea to repackage each application separately. Repackaging each application separately also cuts the time needed to ensure that the repackage caught all the changes during the final snapshot.

After the software installation(s) are complete, clicking the Next button will start SMS Installer on its final scan of the computer. This time it checks for all the changes that the software installation made to the computer, compares them to the "before" picture, and records the "after" picture or change in the script. See Figure 3-15.

As shown in Figures 3-16 through 3-20, Adobe Acrobat Reader 3.01 installed 61 files, created 3 icons and/or shortcuts, updated or created 1 INI file, and made 130 registry key modifications or additions. SMS Installer found these changes and recorded them in the script. The repackage process is now complete. You should go ahead and save the new script before continuing.

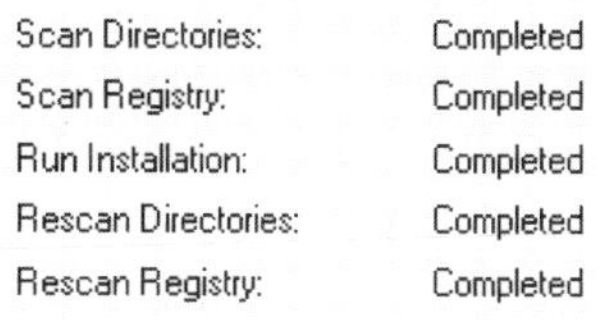

Scan Directories:	Completed
Scan Registry:	Completed
Run Installation:	Completed
Rescan Directories:	Completed
Rescan Registry:	Completed

Figure 3-15 *Before-and-after "snapshot" complete.*

Application Title: Adobe Acrobat 3.01

Figure 3-16 *Application title.*

 Installation Files: 61 selected

Figure 3-17 *Number of files installed.*

 Icons / Shortcuts: 3 created

Figure 3-18 *Number of icons/shortcuts created.*

 INI Files: 1 updated

Figure 3-19 *Number of INI files created or updated.*

 Registry Keys: 130 updated

Figure 3-20 *Number of registry keys updated or added.*

Rebooting During an SMS Installer Repackage

Some software installations are written to reboot the computer after the installation is complete. This does not cause a problem for SMS Installer. SMS Installer marks the progress of the repackage, and once the computer is rebooted, it will start up where it left off. You only need to restart the SMS Installer application and click on the Repackage button for the repackage to continue.

> *Do not* try to accomplish anything else before finishing the repackage after a reboot. This will result in the repackage not resuming. SMS Installer will assume that you have abandoned the Repackage process. The repackaging computer will need to be reconfigured and the repackage process started from scratch.

Note

Watching an Application

<u>W</u>atch

It is useful to watch an application in two instances:

1. Completing a repackage.

2. Creating a package installation for an application that does not have a standard setup program.

First, we will cover completing the repackage. As discussed, the repackaging of an application records all the changes made to the computer by the application's installation program. But what SMS Installer does not "see" it does not record. Application vendors sometimes assume that certain components are already installed on the computer. For example, the Microsoft Foundation Class library files (MFC files) are common components used by many different applications. The MFC files house a large number of "operating system–specific" calls and functions. Since these are already included in the operating system, the vendor will build their application based on the existence of these files and will not include these files in their installation. SMS Installer cannot know the application needs these files to operate. The MFC files are just an example. There are other files that the application may be dependent on, such as ODBC drivers for SQL Server connectivity or Microsoft FoxPro files (see "Data Source Attributes" in Chapter 04 for more information on these components). Having these files included in the SMS Installer package can ensure a successful deployment should the target PC not have these files already installed. Without these files the application could fail to run, thereby frustrating the user base, management, and the staff that supports the implementation. The Watch feature watches the actual program functions and tells SMS Installer to include the additional files that are used or accessed during the application instance.

Clicking on the Watch button brings up the Watch Application dialog box, shown in Figure 3-21. If you know the application path, type it in with the program's filename that runs the application. Or click the Browse button to find the file in the local computer's directory structure. Once the path and file have been selected, click the Run Application button. Clicking this button causes SMS Installer to run the program; in this instance, we're still using the Adobe Acrobat Reader 3.01 from the previous repackage operation. Adobe Acrobat Reader 3.01 is being run while the Repackage script is open.

The purpose of "watching" an application is to put the application through its paces and let SMS Installer monitor and record the file dependencies. Putting the application through its paces involves performing *every* function of the application. For instance, the Adobe Acrobat Reader 3.01 has several file menu options and also several menu buttons that can be clicked to per-

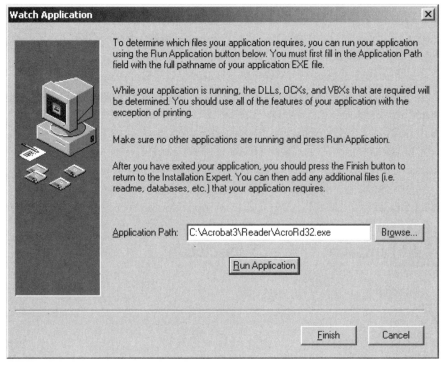

Figure 3-21 *Watch Application dialog box.*

form the file menu functions. Every aspect of the program must be initiated, from opening files, printing files, saving files, browsing through the help features, and so on. If any option is missed, SMS Installer may miss a key dependency needed to complete a successful deployment of the application.

When the application has been completely run through all its features, close the application. This will bring you back to the SMS Installer Watch dialog screen. Click on Finish to return to the SMS Installer Installation Expert.

As previously shown, the repackage process of Adobe Acrobat Reader 3.01 recorded 61 files that were installed during the software's installation. As shown in Figure 3-22, after the watch was complete, SMS Installer recorded an additional 22 files. SMS Installer recorded this information in the Adobe Acrobat Reader 3.01 script. You can see the importance of using the Watch feature to complete a repackage.

In addition to helping complete a repackage, the Watch feature allows SMS Installer to create an installation for an application that does not have a standard setup procedure. An example is the installed utilities that are included with the operating system. When the operating system was installed on the computer, a certain option was not selected. A user needs the additional component, and you want to deploy it; however, there is no common installation. The Watch component of SMS Installer will allow you to do this. In this instance, a package for the Windows Calculator will be created. After clicking the Watch button, you type the application path and filename into the Application Path line, as shown in Figure 3-23.

Installation Files: 83 selected

Figure 3-22 *Number of files after watch is complete.*

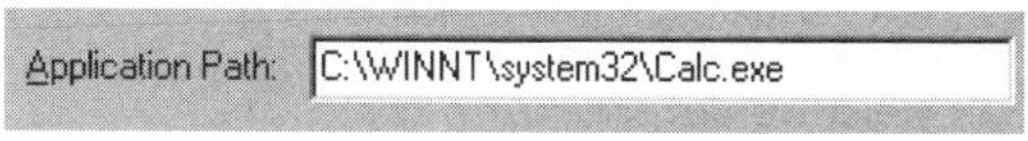

Application Path: C:\WINNT\system32\Calc.exe

Figure 3-23 *Calculator Application Path.*

Figure 3-24 *Microsoft Windows Calculator.*

The application is run. Each function of the Calculator, shown in Figure 3-24, is initiated. Each number button, each arithmetic function, and each menu item (including switching to the scientific calculator and navigating the Help functions) are run.

After the program has been put through its paces, the program is closed and the SMS Installer Watch Finish button is clicked to return to the Installation Expert. With the Watch complete, SMS Installer has recorded three additional files into the Calculator script:

C:\WINNT\system32\Calc.exe

C:\WINNT\system32\Calc.HLP

C:\WINNT\system32\MSVCRT.dll

These are the files that are accessed when using the Windows Calculator utility. SMS Installer records these in the SMS Installer script, allowing the files to be compressed in the compiled executable and installed on the target PC when the installation is run.

Note   The Watch function will not create shortcuts or icons. These must be created manually either by using the customization functions of the Installer Expert or through the Script Editor. For more information on the customization features of Installation Expert, see "Installation Interface Walk-Through" in Chapter 04. For more on the Script Editor, see Chapter 05.

Compiling the Script

Compiling consists of having SMS Installer take the repackage information from the script and compress all the information, the computer changes that were recorded, and the files from the local PC into a one-file executable or a set of floppy diskettes (for more information on creating a floppy disk distribution, see "Media" in Chapter 04). The script must always be compiled on the reference computer with the application installed. This is because SMS Installer looks for the files to include in the compressed file on the local PC in the same directories that were recorded in the script.

SMS Installer automatically names the compressed package with the same name that you used for your script when it was saved. SMS Installer saves the compressed file in the same directory as the script location. It is a good idea to save your script with an easily recognizable name. This makes it easier in the future to go back and find a specific package.

During the compression SMS Installer creates a WSM file, which is a temporary file much like the files created by other Microsoft products. The WSM file is a working file for the compilation and contains the compression information and all the miscellaneous package properties. It is a midpoint between script and executable. This file is not necessary to recompress the installation later. If it is deleted, it will be re-created the next time the script is compiled.

SMS Installer script files can be compiled from the command line without ever opening the SMS Installer program. For more information on compiling from the command line, see "Compiling from the Command Line" in Chapter 10.

Testing the Script

The testing component of SMS Installer allows you to take the new package for a spin. It puts the package through a "dry run," letting you see what the user sees. During the test, the file installation and computer changes don't actually happen. The test is used for viewing the installation to watch the screens. It gives you a chance to make sure the installation is simple but intuitive and that any user will be able to run through the installation without problems. It is recommended that all options are tested, such as the Cancel and Next buttons. Test the package thoroughly so that all possible user scenarios are covered and tested. During the Test mode, try to think like the user. If a certain dialog box is not necessary, take it out. Alternatively, if there is not enough information on a dialog screen, add more information. Again, make the installation as intuitive as possible.

The user's experience during a package installation can make the difference between a successful and unsuccessful deployment. Users don't realize that there are actions going on behind the scenes. All they see are the pretty screens, the easily readable navigation buttons that actually work as displayed, and the end result (the end result being, "The business-critical application I asked for runs when I click on its icon," or perhaps, "We'll have to delay that merger because I couldn't remember if I was supposed to click Next or hit Cancel").

It is a good idea to have other technical support employees run through the Test function to get an understanding of how the package installs. Then, if calls are made to the local help desk concerning the package at deployment time, technical support will already be familiar enough to support the package. Even if a program just "showed up," ready to run on the user's computer, there are those users who will always call with "quick questions." No matter how simple a software package is to install, there will always be the potential for a support burden.

(Testing the package can also be done from the command line. See "Command Line QuickList" in Chapter 10 for more information.)

Running the Installation

The last step in the testing process is actually running the completed package. After the software has been repackaged and completely tested for usability, and the interface has been given the thumbs-up, it is time to become the first user. SMS Installer includes the ability to run the application from within the interface. At this point, the package can be run from any location outside of SMS Installer, but it includes this feature for convenience.

The Run function always compiles the script before executing the package, so the originally compiled executable is not needed, only the script file (IPF).

This is the chance to test the actual package for installation "correctness," the uninstall features, and the fully installed software. It is a smart practice to put the reference computer back to its pristine shape or original configuration a few times and test the installation, the software, and the uninstall each time. See "Cleaning Up the Reference Computer" at the end of this chapter.

Note When testing the uninstall, make sure to check that all components are removed, such as icons, program groups, files, directories, and registry entries. A well-written installation includes a better uninstall path. Some software upgrades require that all previous versions be removed first. If there are lingering files or components, the new version may fail to install on the computer. Another reason for a complete uninstall path is to remove all references that could be used to harm the PC configuration should a user browse the local directory structure and decide to execute the lingering components. A complete uninstall path also helps to free hard disk space should space become a critical issue on the user's computer. Additionally, complete removal of programs can help diagnose other problems should a support issue arise after the software is installed.

To summarize, a complete uninstall path is essential for:

1. Successful upgrades
2. Freeing hard disk space
3. Removing potential support issues
4. Troubleshooting

Distributing the Installation

Note The SMS Installer package adds about 68 KB of overhead on the client during the installation. This overhead is reclaimed once the installation is complete.

After the SMS Installer package has been thoroughly tested, it is time to consider the best vehicles for distribution ("The Methodology of Software Creation Distribution" in Chapter 07 covers this in greater detail). There are several methods for distribution:

1. Microsoft Systems Management Server

2. E-mail

3. Internet/intranet

4. Network share

5. CD-ROM

6. Floppy disk set

Let's look at each of these individually.

Microsoft Systems Management Server (SMS)

Since we're dealing with Microsoft SMS Installer and an SMS Site Server must be installed before SMS Installer will decompress and install, Microsoft Systems Management Server would be the most likely candidate for the distribution of the package. We will not go into the complete scope of SMS in this book, but some understanding of its concepts is pertinent.

Microsoft's SMS is a versatile tool for lowering the total cost of ownership (TCO) of the company's computers. It gives so much in the way of functionality that other tools will not be needed. Many companies try to piecemeal together solutions, which ends up costing the organization more in the long run than if they took a real look at a product like SMS.

Microsoft Systems Management Server version 2.0 is composed of the following features:

1. Software distribution (push technology)

2. Software advertisement (pull technology)

3. Software license metering

4. Auto-discovery of client resources and network components

5. Rich hardware inventory

6. Rich software inventory

7. Help desk tools (such as remote control, remote execute, single file distribution, real-time resource monitoring, remote diagnostics)

8. Queries

9. LAN/WAN bandwidth management

10. Network monitoring

11. Server health monitoring

12. Alerting and thresholds on the SMS system and its clients

13. Alerting and thresholds on network components (routers, switches, etc.)

14. Full-featured reporting on all components

15. Stringent security model

16. Web compatibility

Microsoft has done a great job of providing the tools to support an organization. If each component was researched and then purchased separately, the cost would be incredible. SMS is a relatively low-cost solution that provides everything you will need.

In the scope of SMS Installer, SMS does a wonderful job of not only managing the recording and distribution of packages or applications but also advertising packages for when they are needed. Because of the rich inventory features of SMS, packages can be distributed based on any criteria. Packages can be sent to one user, one user group, an entire site, an entire organization across cities, states, and countries, or any mixture of all these. SMS provides "smart" bandwidth throttling to ensure package delivery. It also provides status on distributions—for instance, whether or not the user has installed the package yet, or whether the installation was successful or a failure. The packages can be distributed as a "run-when-you-can" package or distributed as a mandatory package that must be run before anything else.

In addition to package distribution, SMS also "advertises" packages. Based on the same features as distribution, packages can be advertised to the computers. This is good for letting the user base know a package is available if they need it. It's also good in the event a user uninstalls an application, either because it is no longer needed or to free up disk space until an application is needed again.

E-mail

If the compressed file is small, its transmission via e-mail may be a solution for distribution. If the majority of the user base is mobile or has to dial in to receive e-mail, this may not be a convenient option if a package is over 2 MB. For the distribution to be successful, the vehicle cannot be something that pains the user to install; otherwise, the package will not be installed. Another drawback to e-mail distribution is there is no notification mechanism to report if the package was installed or if the installation was a success or failure. There is, at least, a notification that the e-mail was received and that it was read through return receipt. However, if you are distributing via e-mail to a large enterprise organization, you could expect to be swamped with return receipts when the user receives the message. Used in conjunction with SMS, there are ways of using a status system with e-mail distributions, but e-mail alone does not provide this feature.

Internet/Intranet

Most of the user population is very familiar with the interface given to the Internet. Almost everyone knows how to download files and install them. The Internet has made software distribution easy for the user to understand—almost too easy. Many companies have experienced the woes of diagnosing computer problems related to the freedom of downloading software from the Internet. Not surprisingly, many organizations have written policies against this practice, and some have gone as far as to put technology in place to keep the user base from being able to download files.

Internet technology can be used to an organization's advantage for package distribution. Packages can be placed on an intranet (internal internet) page for download and installation. Since most people are already familiar with the way the Internet works, they should have little trouble downloading and installing the distributions.

As with e-mail for distribution, there is little in the way of distribution status like there is with SMS. Used in conjunction with

SMS, even intranet-based packages can send status information. In addition, since SMS is Web-compatible, SMS can be configured to automatically make the packages available to a common intranet page.

The other caveat with intranet distribution is how the user will be notified that a package is available for installation. E-mail, at least, provides an up-front communication with an attached file. SMS both distributes and advertises to the client PC. More technology would have to go into place to give the intranet technology a notification system.

Network Share

Most companies have a network, and placing the packages on the network is easy to do. A network share is created, and the appropriate security rights are given to the share. The package can be installed on the client computer by a notification through some communication method such as e-mail or offered for installation through login scripts.

Distribution via the network share is good for LAN-locked users but is a poor distribution method for mobile or remote users. It will also be a problem for remote sites that connect through a slow link or modem line to the local network. And, again, there is the problem of not automatically providing a status system.

Making applications available via a network share creates additional administration overhead. Any time a distribution is available, the share has to be created, and the rights have to be assigned and then revoked once the application is completely deployed. Do you want the users to be able to install the application at any time? Server disk space can also become an issue. Eventually, these packages will have to be removed should low server space become a critical concern.

CD-ROM

The package can be distributed by burning the package information to a CD-ROM. The CD can then be handed to an individual to run. Using the CD as the distribution mechanism, the package can also be sent to a client location where several employees are stationed, which allows all employees to insert the

CD and run the installation. An AutoRun feature can be included on the CD so the installation starts automatically when the CD is placed into the CD drive.

As with the previous options, CD distribution provides no status system for success or failure. Another issue may be that not all mobile PCs or laptops have the luxury of a CD drive. For Y2K lockdown some companies have stopped buying CD drives for mobile users or have stopped distributing them to keep unauthorized applications from being installed on the computers. If a noncompliant application were installed on the computer, the entire computer configuration would be forfeited.

Burning CDs for package distributions is a continuing cost. Depending on how many software distributions are conducted each year, this cost could be considerable. There is also the cost of software licenses that could be violated should an employee off-site give the CD to a client to install.

Floppy Disk Set

SMS Installer has an option of creating a floppy disk set for distribution. It compresses the package into several different files that fit on the size of media you choose. Like CD distribution, floppy disk distributions can be handed to a user or a group of users for manual installation.

Also, like the CD distribution, floppy disk distributions can be a continuing cost. The floppy distribution also provides no status mechanism. In addition to these problems, floppy disk media can go bad. Even when putting the package across diskettes, sometimes an error of a disk being bad can present itself only when using the diskette for the installation. If one disk is bad, the whole installation will fail. Floppy disks are lower-cost than CDs and are priced to be throwaway items. And, as with the CD distribution, the floppy disks can be passed along to a nonemployee, which violates the software vendor's license agreement.

Which Should You Use?

Determining which distribution vehicle to use is based on the following considerations, either singularly or in combination:

1. Environment

2. Technology

3. Historical data

4. User base experience

5. Significance

6. Management

Again, let's look at these individually.

Environment

Environment relates to the technological resources in the organization. For instance:

1. Are the LAN or WAN connections fast and capable of handling large packages?

2. Is there a bottleneck that would not be conducive to distribution across the network?

3. Are the users connected to the network 100 percent of the time, or is the environment primarily a mobile workforce?

4. Does the server have enough disk space?

5. If one has been created, is the LAN/WAN administrator group okay with this type of distribution?

6. Does the LAN/WAN group demand to be notified?

7. Are there concessions that have to be taken into account based on communication from remote administrators across a WAN environment?

Technology

Questions you should ask regarding this area are as follows:

1. What types of technology resources are in the organization?

2. Are the computers high- or low-powered?

3. Are CD-ROM drives available?

4. What level of support will the user receive?

5. Is the support staff capable of handling a failed installation?

Historical Data

Questions to ask with regard to historical data include the following:

1. How have past distributions gone?
2. Were they successful?
3. Where did they fail?
4. Have there been lessons learned that should be applied to this instance?

User Base Experience

This area includes such questions as:

1. How capable is the user base?
2. Are they more comfortable with one type of distribution method over another?
3. Have the majority of the users been through a deployment before?
4. Will training be needed or even offered?
5. Is there a regular training plan in place?
6. Is the user base satisfied with the support they are currently receiving?

Significance

Questions to ask in this area include the following:

1. Is the distribution a critical update?
2. Does the distribution need to be completed in hours or days?
3. Is it acceptable for the distribution to take weeks or months?

Tip   It may help to create a rating system for critical updates to determine the required time frame. For instance, based on the following questions, give a "Yes" a value of 1, and a "No" a value of 0.
1. Is the distribution a service pack for an operating system?
2. Does the distribution patch or fix Y2K issues?
3. Is the distribution a new application?

4. Is the distribution a critical patch to fix a software issue?
5. Does the distribution replace a current software package?
6. Does the distribution affect, or provide value to, a large community?

Criticality Scale:

0—2 = Noncritical—Can be rolled out slowly

3—4 = Semicritical—Can be rolled out in a timely manner

5—6 = Critical—Must be rolled out immediately

Your organization could rely on other criteria for proving the criticality of a distribution. Add your criteria to the query and modify the scale accordingly.

Management
Questions include the following:

1. Does management prefer a certain distribution method?

2. Has management made a significant investment in one distribution method?

3. Is management the target of frustrations should a deployment go poorly?

4. Is management support hard to obtain?

Cleaning Up the Reference Computer

After the repackage process is finished and you are satisfied with the results (meaning that all customization is complete and the package is ready to distribute), the reference computer must be set back to its "clean" condition. You could reformat the computer's hard disk and reinstall the operating system and operating system components, but that would take a considerable amount of time. That type of cleaning procedure would take away from the savings realized by creating the custom distribution packages. You should look into some type of "re-imaging" product that can quickly put the computer back to its clean condition. There are several products on the market, both software- and hardware-based, that would do the trick. What could take an hour or more if done manually would take 15 to 20 minutes or less with a re-imaging product. These products do a good job of maintaining a "base" image that can be used to easily reconfigure the computer for you. See "Re-imaging Resources" in Chapter 10 for more information.

04

Installation Expert—
Customizing the Script

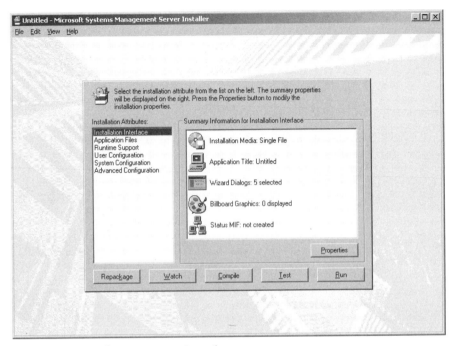

Figure 4-1 *Installation Expert Interface.*

The SMS Installer Installation Expert, shown in Figure 4-1, is a wizard-based entry system that allows quick and easy customization of an installation package. To access a group of items such as the Installation Interface group, you just double-click on the item in the Installation Attributes window. If you want to go straight to a specific item in the group, you should highlight the group in the Installation Attributes window and then double-click on the icon in the Summary Information for Installation Interface window. For instance, if you want to go straight to the Wizard dialogs, click once on Installation Interface then double-click on the Wizard Dialogs icon.

Note   For general reference, customizing an installation via the Installation Expert should be done only after the original repackage program has gone through the testing steps to ensure the base installation will work correctly.

Installation Interface Group

The Installation Interface Group includes five tabs: the Media tab, the Application tab, the Dialogs tab, the Graphics tab, and the SMS tab.

Media Tab

The media screen, shown in Figure 4-2, allows selection of the type of distribution.

Single-File Installation

The single-file installation method compresses all files, instructions, changes to the PC, and so on into a single executable file. Distributing a single file to install an application has several advantages:

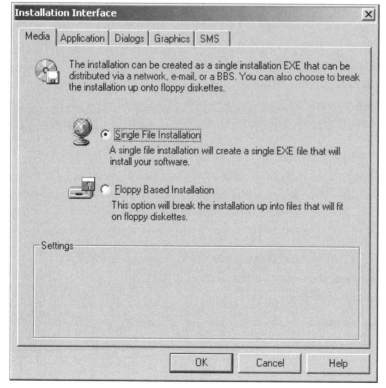

Figure 4-2 *Media tab.*

1. *Less bandwidth*   If distributing is being done via Microsoft Systems Management server, the one-file installation is easier on LAN and WAN bandwidth than a host of files and directory structures.

2. *Easy distribution*   Distributing via e-mail can help remote users receive critical updates. Keep in mind that some installation files can be quite large and the user may not want to receive a 15-MB file over a modem connection.

3. *Easy to update*   A one-file installation can easily be updated through the script to include updated file versions.

4. *Easy to organize*   It's easier to store one file in its own directory on a server or on a CD-ROM.

Floppy-Based Installation

The floppy-based installation method takes the software installation and breaks it down into "chunks" that fit onto floppy diskettes. Floppy size can be selected and even customized, as shown in Figure 4-3. A diskette set can be created and distributed to employees stationed at a client site and then passed from computer to computer. This is a good solution should the installation be too large to distribute via e-mail and distribution via the SMS client is over the slow speed of a dial-in modem connection. The common diskette size is 3.5 inch, but SMS Installer includes the 5.25-inch size and an option box to allow a custom sizing. The chunks are created and placed in the script directory so they can be copied to the media later. They are also available to be copied

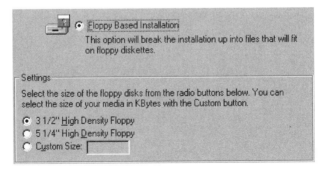

Figure 4-3 *Floppy-based installation.*

at a later time should another copy need to be created. Another option would be to place these chunks on CD-ROM media.

Later we'll see how SMS Installer supports compiling the package into a Zip-compatible format. Creating the chunks adds to the functionality of the Zip option, making it easier to extract files from small chunks rather than a large executable.

Application Tab

The Application tab, shown in Figure 4-4, permits customization of the software title and the default directory in which the program is installed.

Software Title

You can change the software title to whatever you desire. The more descriptive you are with the software title, the easier the installation experience will be for the end user. For instance, to per-

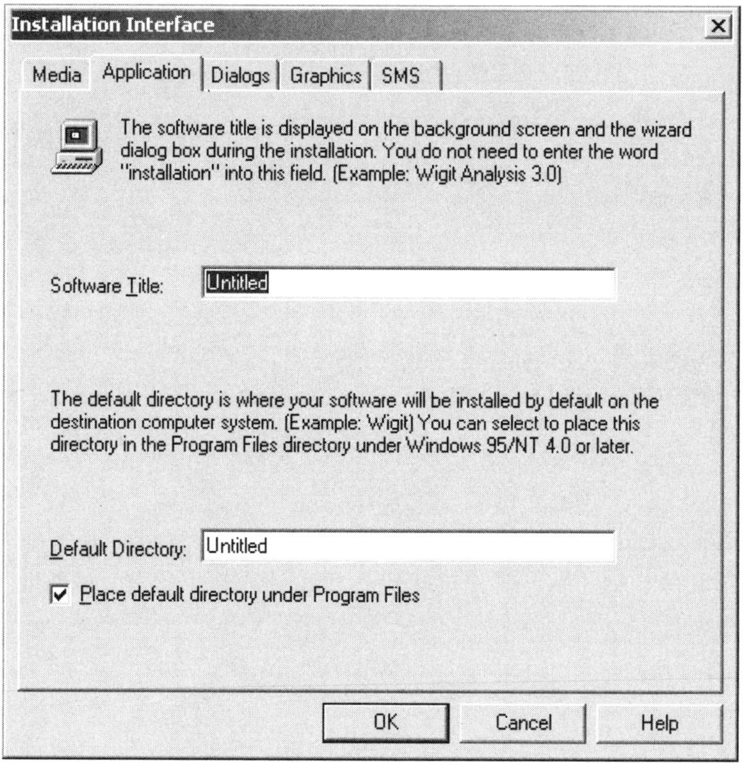

Installation Interface

Media   Application | Dialogs | Graphics | SMS |

The software title is displayed on the background screen and the wizard dialog box during the installation. You do not need to enter the word "installation" into this field. (Example: Wigit Analysis 3.0)

Software Title: Untitled

The default directory is where your software will be installed by default on the destination computer system. (Example: Wigit) You can select to place this directory in the Program Files directory under Windows 95/NT 4.0 or later.

Default Directory: Untitled

☑ Place default directory under Program Files

[OK]   [Cancel]   [Help]

Figure 4-4 *Application tab.*

sonalize Adobe Acrobat to your company, just enter,
`MyCompany's Adobe Acrobat Installation Version 3.01`

Default Directory

You can also change the default directory in which the application is installed. SMS Installer works with installations based on variables. For example, if you change the default directory, SMS Installer will automatically change all program-specific references in the application installation for you. If you have 100 files that are installed, and 10 icons for the executables, SMS Installer automatically informs the installation of the new location if you change the default directory entry. If Adobe Acrobat installs itself into C:\Program Files\Adobe Acrobat, but you have a company-wide standard that all applications must be installed under the D:\Standard Apps\ directory, that change should be made here.

Note   In the Default Directory line, *do not* enter the drive letter; only enter the directory name or directory structure. The default installation drive letter, colon, and backslash (e.g., C:\) is defined elsewhere in the script and placed into a variable. SMS Installer uses the variable and the Default Directory entry to complete the full directory tree information for the installation.

Place Default Directory Under Program Files

In addition to customizing the default directory for the installation files, you can choose whether or not the files are installed under the Program Files directory, as shown in Figure 4-5. Most applications install to the Program Files directory by default. With the release of Windows 95, Microsoft intended to standardize the locations of programs as well as the locations of personal data. Most vendors assume this standard. SMS Installer provides customization to incorporate the same standard in your installations.

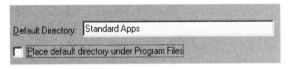

Figure 4-5 *Default directory selection.*

Dialogs Tab

The Dialogs tab, shown in Figure 4-6, is for selecting the dialog boxes that you want the user to see as the installation is being performed. The default dialog boxes are checked in the previous graphic. The Dialogs selection provides a quick way to select the amount of user interaction during the installation.

> The most successful software installations are installations with minimal user interaction. (See "The Methodology of Software Creation/Distribution" in Chapter 07 for more information.) When was the last time you actually read every word of every screen during a software installation? Or better yet, when was the last time you read the software license screen in its entirety? Installations have become so standard in the way that they install; the Next button is clicked without thinking. The general user population operates in the same way.   **Tip**

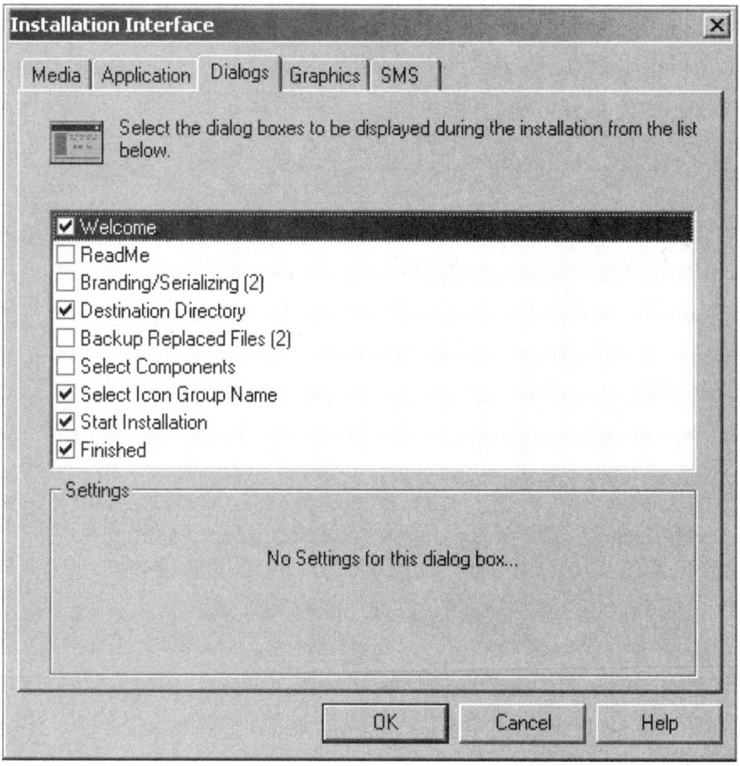

Figure 4-6 *Dialogs tab.*

You also have to take into account that most users are not "power users" or, as technically inclined as you. Minimizing the complexity of the installation gives users the assurance that they are doing the right thing and making the right decisions. It prevents multiple calls to the support help desk.

Welcome Dialog

The Welcome dialog, shown in Figure 4-7, is the first dialog the user sees. This starts the installation, displays the application name that will be installed, and gives directions on how to continue with the installation or cancel or exit the application. Depending on how well the repackage procedure collected the application name, you should see the full application name, on the dialog box. If the application name has not been collected properly, or you would like the installation to be a bit more descriptive, you can always customize the software title by using the Application tab (see the previous section for more information).

Figure 4-7 *Welcome dialog.*

Read Me Dialog

The Read Me dialog allows you to customize the installation even further. It is the only dialog that is customizable from the Dialogs screen. When you click on the Read Me Dialog option, it changes from Figure 4-8 to Figure 4-9.

The Read Me dialog allows you to add custom information to an installation. For instance, if you are creating a package that has been developed in-house, this is where you can include your company's license agreement. Or, suppose you know that if a certain application is open during the installation, then the installation will fail because identified system files are in use. You can create a distinct message, warning the user to make sure the application is closed, and even give them instructions on how to close the particular application.

Here is the procedure:

1. Open Notepad and enter the specific information you want to include, as shown in Figure 4-10 (The Read Me dialog only works with ASCII text files. You can use any text editor to create the information.) Then save the file.

Figure 4-8 *Read Me dialog: Before selection.*

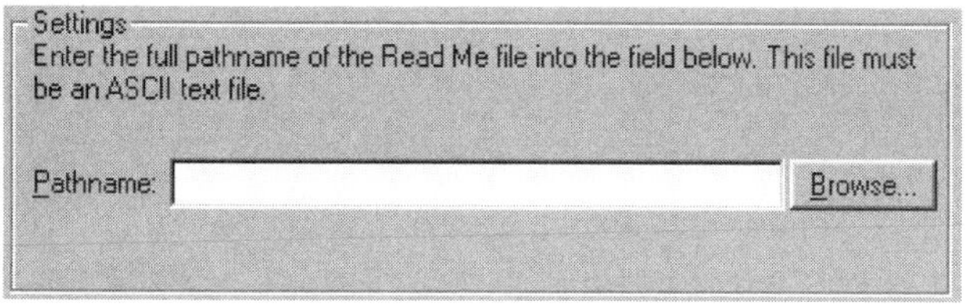

Figure 4-9 *Read Me dialog: After selection.*

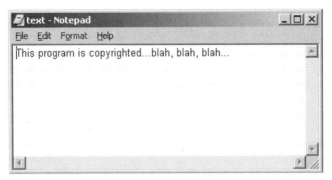

Figure 4-10 *Text file text.*

2. In the settings area of the Dialogs tab, you should either enter the path and filename of the text file or click the Browse button to search for it. See Figure 4-11.

3. After you have saved your customizations, compiled the script, and have either tested or run the installation, the information will display as shown in Figure 4-12.

Note   The Read Me dialog is a read-only field and cannot be edited directly by the user.

Registration Information Dialog

The Registration Information dialog, shown in Figure 4-13, prompts the user to enter the required user and company information. SMS Installer utilizes this information to record that the program has been installed. And, if the program has been installed previously, then subsequent installations will produce the information in Figure 4-14.

```
┌ Settings ─────────────────────────────────────────────────────┐
│ ┌ Enter the full pathname of the Read Me file into the field below. This file must
│   be an ASCII text file.
│
│   Pathname: │C:\text.txt                                    │  [ Browse... ]
│
└────────────────────────────────────────────────────────────────┘
```

Figure 4-11 *Text file pathname.*

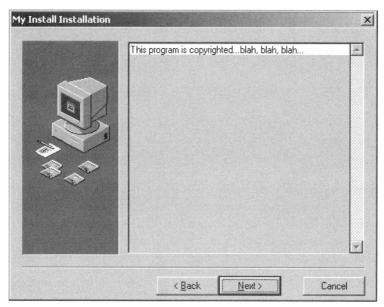

Figure 4-12 *Text file display (Read Me selection).*

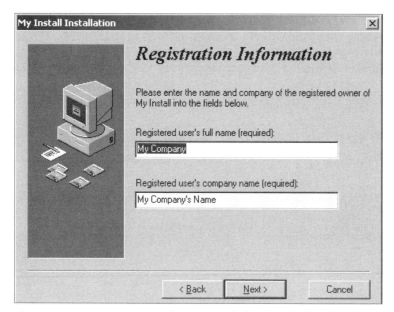

Figure 4-13 *Registration Information dialog.*

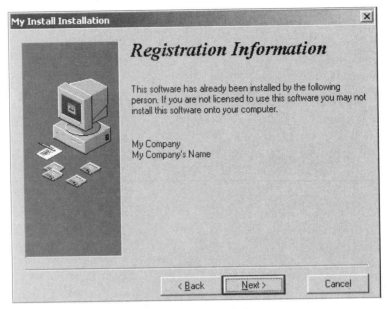

Figure 4-14 *Registration Information dialog.*

The branding/serializing information is stored in a Custdata.ini file on the reference computer in the application's installation directory. Opening the Custdata.ini file reveals the registration information, shown in Figure 4-15.

Select Destination Directory Dialog

The Select Destination Directory dialog, shown in Figure 4-16, is the screen where the user can modify the location where the installation outputs the files, which are identified in the SMS Installer script. While this is a valuable feature, your organization

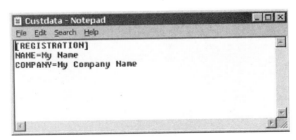

Figure 4-15 *Custdata.ini contents.*

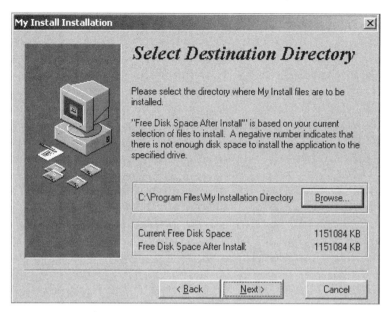

Figure 4-16 *Select Destination Directory dialog.*

may require special directories or may have standardized specific drive letters for programs, so this dialog may not be necessary. Also, while using the Browse button, the user could forget to give a directory path after selecting the drive letter for installation. This will result in the entire program being installed in the root directory of the drive letter.

> Both MS-DOS and Windows 9x have limitations on the amount of **Note** files that can reside in the root directory. If the root directory reaches this limit, the PC will stop functioning. Also, because a lot of programs install similarly named files, required versions could be overwritten if they are being installed to the same place.

This dialog also displays to users the amount of free disk space available on the drive they have selected as the installation drive. It also indicates the amount of hard disk space that will be available after the installation is completed. This enables users to determine the suitable drive to install the application based on hard disk space.

Backup Replaced Files Dialog

As in the SMS Installer installation itself, the Backup Replaced Files dialog, shown in Figure 4-17, allows the backing up of files that are replaced during the installation.

Note   If files are in use when they are replaced and backed up, SMS Installer will direct the user to restart the PC after the installation and will give them the option of doing so after completion.

If "Yes" is selected, the Select Backup Directory dialog, shown in Figure 4-18, is made available. The default location for the Backup directory is underneath the application installation directory. By using the Browse button, you can select a different location for the backed up files.

Select Components Dialog

The Select Components dialog, shown in Figure 4-19, allows the user to choose optional components to install with the application. These components are added to the installation Compo-

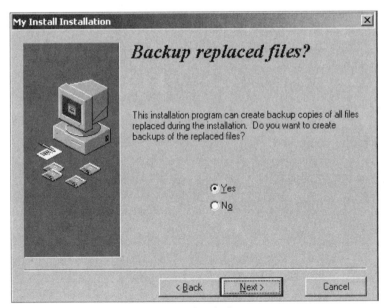

Figure 4-17 *Backup Replaced Files dialog.*

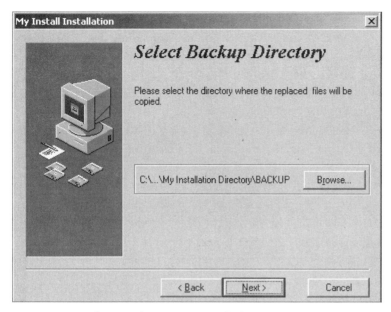

Figure 4-18 *Select Backup Directory dialog.*

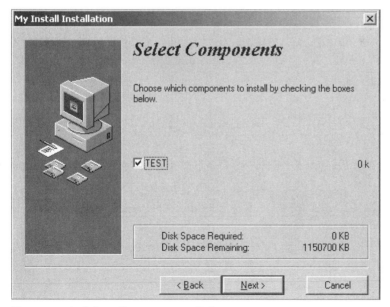

Figure 4-19 *Select Components dialog.*

nents tab of the Application Files group, mentioned later in this chapter. Added components can be predetermined to install automatically or can give the user the choice of which components to install with this dialog.

Start Installation Dialog

After all elements have been configured and selected, and the information has been gathered, the Start Installation dialog, shown in Figure 4-20, is displayed. This means that the installation is now ready to start creating application directories, copying files, creating program groups and their application shortcuts, modifying files, inserting application–specific registry entries, and adding SMS Installer–specific registry information such as the Add/Remove features and versioning.

Installation Completed Dialog

The Installation Completed dialog, shown in Figure 4-21, is the screen that displays after the application has completed the installation. This gives the user the assurance that the installation

Figure 4-20 *Start Installation dialog.*

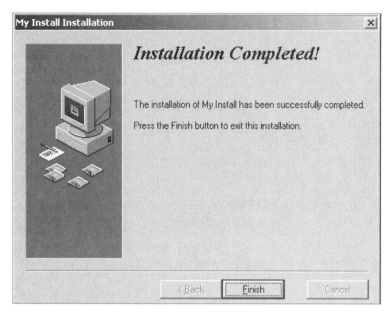

Figure 4-21 *Installation Completed dialog.*

has completed successfully and that the program should now be available to use.

Other Dialogs

There are other dialog screens that are not available through the Installation Expert but can be accessed using the File menu (Edit|Dialog Templates). These dialog screens are utilized more for the scripting facility in SMS Installer. More details on these dialog screens are available in Chapter 05.

Graphics Tab

The Graphics tab, shown in Figure 4-22, allows you to add custom graphics to your installation by clicking the Add button and browsing the computer directories for the desired file. SMS Installer supports Windows bitmap files. These graphic files can help you customize the installation for your company with logos, pictures, and so on. The custom graphic is displayed on the background of the installation screen. When a graphic is added to the list, then the Details, Delete, Move Up, and Move Down buttons will be enabled.

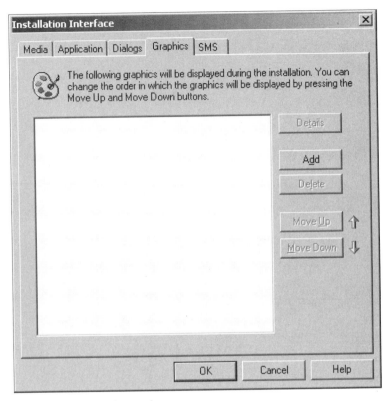

Figure 4-22 *Graphics tab.*

The Delete button deletes a custom graphic from the list. The Move Up and Move Down buttons change the order of the custom graphics should multiple files be added to the list. The Details button brings up the Graphic Settings dialog box shown in Figure 4-23.

In addition to adding the graphics, SMS Installer can help alter the way the graphics are presented during the installation. Each graphic file that you add is separately customizable. If you are familiar with Microsoft PowerPoint, the effects are comparable.

Following is a breakdown of the settings:

- *X-Position* The horizontal location on the installation window for the graphic. Measured in pixels, this coordinate starts from the upper left corner of a 640 × 480 screen.

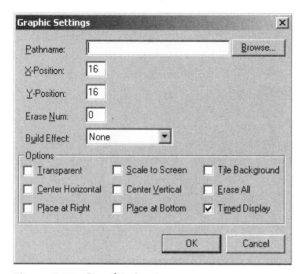

Figure 4-23 *Graphic Settings.*

- *Y-Position* The vertical location on the installation window for the graphic. Also measured in pixels, this coordinate starts from upper left corner of a 640 × 480 screen.

- *Erase Num* Whenever you add custom graphics to your installation, the graphic is assigned a number and recorded in an internal index. This parameter removes the graphic from the index.

- *Build Effect* The Build Effect adds motion to the selected graphic. There are six options:

  - *None*: The graphic appears with the installation screens.
  - *Fade In*: The graphic appears faint and slowly intensifies until it reaches full resolution in the installation screen at the coordinates specified by the X and Y parameters.
  - *From Top*: The graphic slides into view from the top of the installation screen and comes to rest at the coordinates specified by the X and Y parameters.
  - *From Bottom*: The graphic slides into view from the bottom of the installation screen and comes to rest at the coordinates specified by the X and Y parameters.

- *From Left*: The graphic slides into view from the left of the installation screen and comes to rest at the coordinates specified by the X and Y parameters.
- *From Right*: The graphic slides into view from the right of the installation screen and comes to rest at the coordinates specified by the X and Y parameters.

- *Transparent* The custom graphic remains faint during the installation, blending with the background colors.

- *Center Horizontal* The graphic is centered horizontally on the screen at the Y coordinate. When selected, this disables the X-Position entry.

- *Place at Right* The graphic is pushed all the way to the right of the installation screen at the Y coordinate. When selected, this disables the X-Position entry.

- *Scale to Screen* This selection advises the custom graphic to cover the entire installation screen. The graphic is stretched to fit the entire background.

Note   A small custom graphic becomes pixilated when stretched, which can distort the graphic so that it is not easily identified. You may have to work with the graphic to find the optimum size to include with the installation.

- *Center Vertical* The graphic is centered vertically on the screen at the X coordinate. When selected, this disables the Y-Position entry.

- *Place at Bottom* The graphic is placed at the bottom of the installation screen. When selected, this disables the Y-Position entry.

- *Tile Background* Duplicate copies of the graphic are placed end-to-end, horizontal and vertical, until it fills the entire background like a tiled floor.

- *Erase All* All graphic files are removed from the internal index and the SMS Installer background.

- *Timed Display* The Timed Display option calculates the number of custom graphic files selected, with the overall installation time, and then spaces the graphic files to display accordingly throughout the installation.

> Selecting both Center Horizontal and Center Vertical will place the graphic in the very center of the background. Unless you have modified the Progress Dialog Placement (via the Screen tab in the Advanced Configuration group, which is covered later) the custom graphic will be hidden from view by the progress bar.

Note

SMS Tab

The SMS tab, shown in Figure 4-24, offers several fields for enhancing the SMS Installer package when distributed via Microsoft Systems Management Server. When SMS is used to install a package, it creates a status MIF (Management Informa-

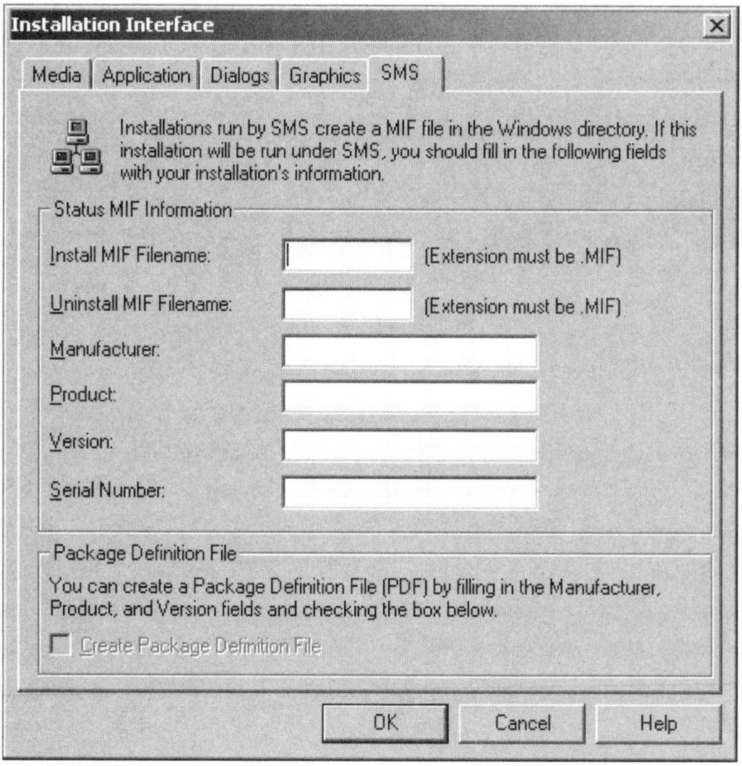

Figure 4-24 *SMS tab.*

tion Format) file. The file is placed in the Windows directory, and SMS finds the file, reads the information from it, and then sends the information back to the SMS site server database (SQL server). This is helpful to the SMS administrator because the package success and failure information is available, allowing the support staff to be proactive in identifying problems with a software distribution.

The information entered on the SMS tab will be incorporated into the status MIF. By entering information such as the manufacturer, product, version, and serial number, the status information is more descriptive and more beneficial to the SMS administrator. You can enter the name of the Install MIF and the name of the Uninstall MIF. Knowing the names of the files will help diagnose problems by enabling you to search on the target computer for the files. It's a good idea to name the file in relation to the software that is being repackaged. For instance, for Adobe Acrobat, you might call the Install MIF: ACROINST.MIF, and the Uninstall MIF: ACROUNST.MIF. Or, alternatively, ACRO301.MIF and UNACRO3.MIF. Find the right fit for your organization and set it as a standard.

Note   You can't just enter the filename of the Install MIF and Uninstall MIF. You must enter the filename *and* the extension. SMS Installer does not enter the extension for you. If the filename does not have a MIF extension, SMS will not recognize that it should act on the file for the status information.

(For an example of a status MIF, see "Example of a Status MIF" in Chapter 10.)

Also, on the SMS tab, you can direct SMS Installer to create a Package Definition File (PDF) along with the compiled script. A PDF file is an ASCII text file with a PDF file extension. The file contains predefined settings for a package. SMS imports PDF files and uses the information to automatically create a distribution package. Many software vendors support and include PDF files with their software. You may want to check the files included with the software for one that has already been created to import into SMS.

(For an example of a PDF file, see "Example of a PDF File" in Chapter 10.)

Application Files Group

The Application Files group includes two tabs: the Components tab and the Files tab.

Components Tab

The Components tab, shown in Figure 4-25, allows you to add other components to the installation. These components could be required shared files like the Microsoft Foundation Class libraries or ODBC drivers.

By clicking the Add button, you add the component name and select whether the user has the option to select the component or if the component is a required installation. If the Install This

Figure 4-25 *Components tab.*

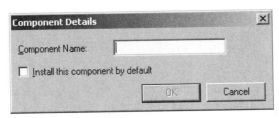

Figure 4-26 *Component Details.*

Component By Default is not checked, users will be prompted to select the components they prefer to install.

Once the component has been added, clicking the Details button brings up the Component Details dialog box shown in Figure 4-26. The Move Up and Move Down buttons allow you to modify the way the component list is displayed on the dialog box. These buttons change the listed position of the components. If you prefer to have the components listed alphabetically or listed in order of importance, indicate that here. The Delete button deletes the highlighted component entry.

The component installation source and component properties are both defined in the scripting facility covered later in Chapter 05. They are also defined on the Files tab if they have available entries.

Files Tab

The Files tab, shown in Figure 4-27, is a useful way to view the files that have been included with the application. The graphical representation displays the local computer window and depicts what the directory structure on the target or destination computer will look like.

In addition to being a viewing screen, it offers the functionality of including other files as needed. Files can be selected from the current computer and placed into the Destination Computer file structure. Used primarily to include files that the repackage operation may have missed, it's also a chance to include other files in the installation that may need distributing. You can "piggyback" other file installations with this tab.

In the Destination Computer window, SMS Installer automatically includes directories common to most computers. The Appli-

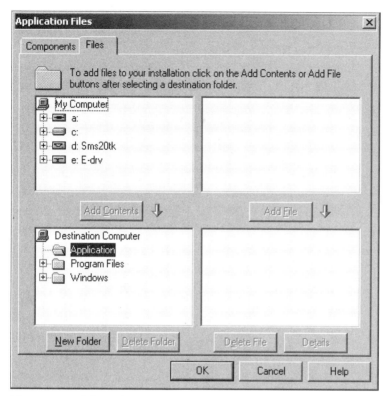

Figure 4-27 *Files tab.*

cation folder is the representation of the %MAINDIR% variable
defined as the application's installation directory (for more information on the %MAINDIR% variable, see Chapter 05, "The Script
Editor"). The Program Files and Windows directories are
included because standard applications tend to install files to
these locations.

Underneath the Program Files directory, the Common Files
directory is included. The Common Files directory is a noncom-
municated standard for shared system files and applications.
Underneath the Windows directory, the Fonts, System, and Sys-
tem32 directories are included.

Windows 3.1 through Windows 9x have the System directory.
Windows NT computers have the System32 directory. This tells
SMS Installer what types of files are being installed based on the
type of system directory they are installed into. Windows 9x com-

puters run 32-bit applications but provide better backward-compatibility for 16-bit applications, in which installations were generally hard-coded to install to the C:\WINDOWS\SYSTEM directory on all computers. This explains why Windows 9x computers do not have a System32 directory. The current standard is 32-bit applications. Windows NT is a complete 32-bit operating system. It includes an entire 16-bit subsystem, enabling it to run 16-bit applications. It cannot, however, run all 16-bit applications.

If components were added in the Components tab, the Destination Computer duplicates the directory structure for each component, allowing the configuration of the component, as shown in Figure 4-28. This is what permits SMS Installer to offer choices to users regarding which components they wish to install. Each component is configured separately in the script. SMS Installer uses logical parameters to distinguish the component installation choices (covered in detail in Chapter 05).

Runtime Support Group

The Runtime Support group contains three items: the Options tab, the Visual Basic tab, and the Visual FoxPro tab.

Options Tab

The Options tab of the Runtime Support group lists the components that are included with SMS Installer that are available for

Figure 4-28 *Duplicated directory structure for Components addition.*

inclusion in the SMS Installer script (the files for these inclusions were listed earlier in Chapter 02). This is the place to tell SMS Installer to include the files with the script. Clicking the box associated with the item will include all the files necessary to install all parts of the component.

Uninstall Support

SMS Installer will include automatic uninstall support if the Uninstall Support box, shown in Figure 4-29, is checked. The Uninstall Support option creates an INSTALL.LOG file and places it in the main application directory. The INSTALL.LOG file is created at the time of the installation, and it records all the valuable information that SMS Installer would need to uninstall the application. When the Uninstall selection is enabled, SMS Installer automatically includes the UNINSTAL.EXE file with the

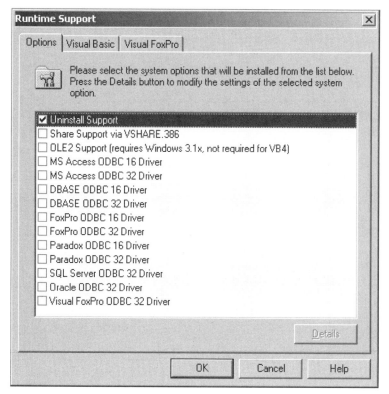

Figure 4-29 *Uninstall Support.*

compiled executable. The UNINSTAL.EXE file is copied to the
main installation directory (%MAINDIR%) by default.
Here is a sample of the Microsoft Calculator log:

```
*** Installation Started 09/24/1999 9:41:55 ***
Title: Microsoft Calculator Installation
Source: C:\WINNT\PROFILES\RTRENT\DESKTOP\CALCUL~1.EXE
File Overwrite: C:\Program Files\Microsoft Calculator\
  Uninstal.EXE
RegDB Key: Software\Microsoft\Windows\CurrentVersion\
  Uninstall\Microsoft Calculator
RegDB Val: Microsoft Calculator
RegDB Name: DisplayName
RegDB Root: 2
RegDB Key: Software\Microsoft\Windows\CurrentVersion\
  Uninstall\Microsoft Calculator
RegDB Val: "C:\Program Files\Microsoft Calculator\
  UNINSTAL.EXE" "C:\Program Files\Microsoft
Calculator\INSTALL.LOG" "Microsoft Calculator Uninstall"
RegDB Name: UninstallString
RegDB Root: 2
File Overwrite: C:\WINNT\System32\Calc.exe
File Overwrite: C:\WINNT\System32\Calc.HLP
File Overwrite: C:\WINNT\System32\MSVCRT.dll
```

Along with this, it enters information into the registry that tells
the operating system the application has a valid uninstall path.
The registry key for registered uninstall applications is as
follows:

```
HKEY_LOCAL_MACHINE\SOFTWARE\Microsoft\
  Windows\CurrentVersion\Uninstall
```

For example, the Microsoft Calculator package created earlier
is registered in this key but under its own name:

```
HKEY_LOCAL_MACHINE\SOFTWARE\Microsoft\
  Windows\CurrentVersion\Uninstall\Microsoft Calculator
```

In the values list for the Microsoft Calculator, the name of the
application is recorded along with the path for the uninstall and
the log filename. The information registered for this application is
as follows:

```
"C:\Program Files\Microsoft Calculator\UNINSTAL.EXE"
"C:\Program Files\Calculator\INSTALL.LOG" "Microsoft
Calculator Uninstall"
```

For those applications that allow an uninstall path, SMS Installer includes the UNINSTAL.EXE file in the script and places it in the application directory with the log. The UNINSTAL.EXE file is capable of reading the log file.

To uninstall an SMS Installer installation, you use the same, standard method as other applications written that support the "Microsoft way" of removal.

For this example, the earlier SMS Installer installation called "My Install" is used. In the control panel of Windows systems there is an Add/Remove icon. When you open this control panel applet, it shows a list of all the applications that have successfully registered uninstall paths. (See Figure 4-30.) If the "My Install"

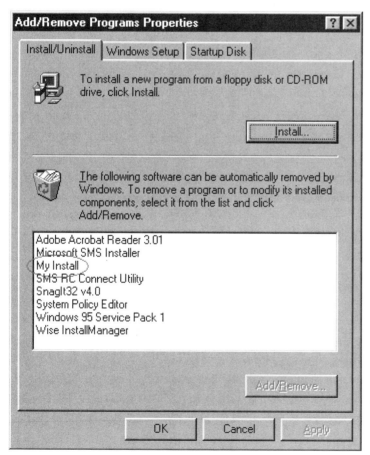

Figure 4-30 *My Install: Add/Remove Programs.*

item is highlighted and the Add/Remove button is clicked, the uninstall procedure will start.

SMS Installer's UINSTALL.EXE command gives the user two options regarding the uninstall procedure. The choices are either an Automatic or a Custom uninstall, as shown in Figure 4-31.

The Automatic uninstall reads the entire INSTALL.LOG file and acts on every item listed. It removes all files and registry entries as they appear in the log. It also removes the application entry contained in the Add/Remove control panel applet.

If the Custom option is selected, the user is prompted to select which files to remove, as shown in Figure 4-32.

Then the user is prompted which directories to remove, as shown in Figure 4-33.

Next, the user is prompted which registry keys to remove, as shown in Figure 4-34.

Not many users will be comfortable with the Custom uninstall, so if the application must be uninstalled, a simple directive to use the Automatic option should be communicated.

No matter which method of uninstall is chosen, the screen in Figure 4-35 will be presented right before SMS Installer begins the uninstall. The user still has a chance to cancel the uninstall

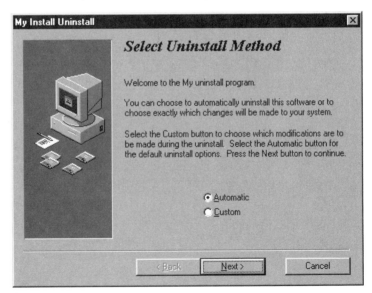

Figure 4-31 *Uninstall methods.*

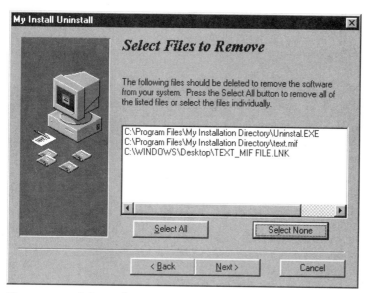

Figure 4-32 *Select Files to Remove.*

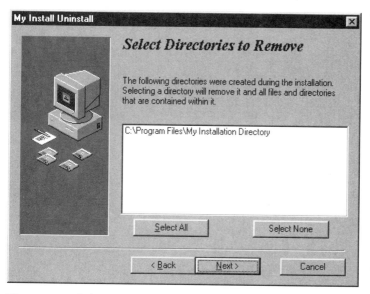

Figure 4-33 *Select Directories to Remove.*

procedure. Clicking the Finish button starts the uninstall process. If the Automatic option is chosen, all files, directories, and registry entries are removed. If the choice is Custom, all custom removal options are flagged and removed. On both options, the

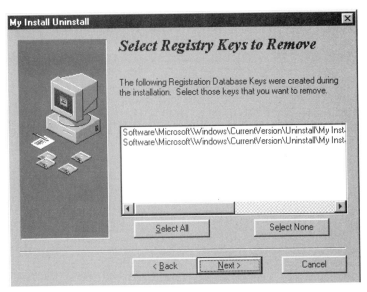

Figure 4-34 *Select Registry Keys to Remove.*

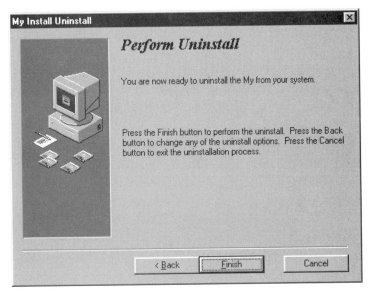

Figure 4-35 *Perform Uninstall.*

Add/Remove Programs list is updated and the application entry is removed. Furthermore, it is removed from the uninstall path in the registry key.

If an Uninstall MIF file was configured on the SMS tab, the MIF file will be placed in the Windows or WinNT directory. SMS will pick this information up and enter it into the SMS database. This gives the SMS administrator the ability to know when an application is uninstalled. Consequently, if a program should not be uninstalled, this form of notification can help an SMS–centric organization proactively support the end user.

> After an uninstall procedure, you may see a lingering directory **Note** structure. SMS Installer will only remove directories during the uninstall if they are empty. If files were created in the application's directories while the application was in use on the computer, these files remain in the directories. SMS Installer only removes the entries listed in the INSTALL.LOG file. These data files keep the directory structure from being removed. This is still considered a successful uninstall. The files, registry entries, and the Add/Remove list are still acted upon.

Additional Include Options

Share Support Via VSHARE.386. VSHARE.386 is an enhanced-mode virtual driver that provides support for 16-bit applications. VSHARE.386 is used with Windows 3.1, Windows 3.11, and Windows for Workgroups for file-sharing and file-locking support. File range locking allows an OLE server application to lock a specific range of a document that contains an OLE object (Object Linking and Embedding, described in the next section). File sharing enables a file to be opened more than once, and in each instance changes can be made and saved. For instance, if an MS Access database was opened in multiple windows and modifications were made to the database in each window, the changes would be saved to the database. This is similar to the way network file sharing works. Generally, 16-bit applications can only have one instance of a program running at a time. In essence, VSHARE simulates 32-bit operations with 16-bit applications and 16-bit operating systems.

The VSHARE.386 option is valid for all instances but should be used in conjunction with choosing a 16-bit SMS Installer script (seen later in this chapter under "Advanced Configuration Group").

Including VSHARE.386 support causes the VSHARE.386 file to install to the C:\WINDOWS\SYSTEM directory and will place a pointer to the file in the SYSTEM.INI under the 386 Enhanced section. The line in the SYSTEM.INI looks like this:

```
[386Enh]
Device=vshare.386
```

Note   Another setting you may want to consider including if you are installing the VSHARE.386 component is the PerVMFiles setting. The PerVMFiles or "private files" is a setting that gives a selected number of file handles to each instance of a program in a 16-bit operating environment. The number of files allocated to the file handles depends on the application you are using. Check the software vendor's documentation for the correct value.

Use the INI Files tab in the User Configuration group (covered later in this chapter) to modify the SYSTEM.INI.

In the SYSTEM.INI the setting would look like this:

```
[386Enh]
PerVMFiles=x
```

The Share support writes an Include Script item to the SMS Installer script facility that includes the VSHARE.IPF script with the current repackage.

OLE2 Support.   OLE2 is version 2.0 of the Object Link and Embedding technology. OLE is a technology that allows one application to share data with another application or control the other application. This is another 16-bit compatibility component. Older versions of applications like MS Word 6.0, for example, use the OLE automation to work with other applications.

Be sure to include this component if you are installing a 16-bit application and you are not sure that OLE is installed on the target computer. See the software vendor's manuals for information on how to find out if it needs OLE to operate. Most of the applications that require this component include it with the installation.

ODBC Data Sources. SMS Installer includes the ODBC (Open dataBase Connectivity) data sources. ODBC adds connection support for database objects that require ODBC connectors.

Each data source available for selection must be configured if it is to be included. The Data Source Name must be entered, the Install Data Source For option must be selected (Win16 or Win32), and the Data Source Attributes must be modified. If ODBC is required by the installation, the repackage should pick it up along with the files and the INI files that are installed or modified. Including ODBC Data Sources is not required, but it is something that can be piggybacked on the current installation if desired.

When ODBC drivers are included with the SMS Installer script, the ODBC.INI on all operating systems is modified with the information; and, on Windows 9x and Windows NT systems, the registry is also updated with the information (see "Example of an ODBC.INI File" in Chapter 10 for an example). The actual ODBC driver must be installed on the target computer. A list of the installed drivers is kept in the ODBCINST.INI file on the target computer (see "Example of an ODBCINST.INI File" in Chapter 10).

> The Data Source Name entry accepts any text up to 255 characters. Remember that if you use the same name as an existing data source name, it will be overwritten along with the custom attributes. So, try to use a different name that differs from those already in use in your organization. **Note**

Shown in Figure 4-36 is the common dialog box for the Configure ODBC Data Source. Each driver uses the same format to modify the information.

Checking the Display Configuration Dialogs checkbox allows the user at the target computer to customize the data source. Checking the System DSN checkbox installs the ODBC driver and attribute for all accounts on the computer to access. This

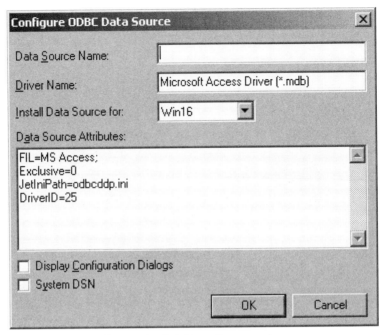

Figure 4-36 *Configure ODBC Data Source.*

means that anyone logging onto the computer would have access to the data source.

Data Source Attributes.   Below are the default data source attributes for each driver. Depending upon the database properties, the attributes must be modified for the driver to install correctly. If the driver, setup, and name attributes are not entered, the script item will fail and display a blank line in the Driver Pathname variable.

Microsoft Access ODBC 16 Driver

```
FIL=MS Access;
Exclusive=0
JetIniPath=odbcddp.ini
DriverID=25
```

Microsoft Access ODBC 32 Driver

```
DBQ=%MAINDIR%\DATABASE.mdb
Description=DESCRIPTION
```

```
Driver=odbcjt32.dll
DriverId=25
FIL=MS Access
ReadOnly=00
SafeTransactions=0
SystemDB=SYSTEM_DB_PATH
ImplicitCommitSync=Yes
MaxBufferSize=512
PageTimeout=5
Threads=3
UserCommitSync=Yes
```

Dbase ODBC 16 Driver

```
Driver=odbcjt16.dll
DefaultDir=%MAINDIR%
Description=Enter description here
DriverId=277
FIL=dBase IV;
JetIniPath=odbcddp.ini
CollatingSequence=ASCII
Deleted=On
PageTimeout=600
Statistics=Truth
```

Dbase ODBC 32 Driver

```
Driver=odbcjt32.dll
DefaultDir=%MAINDIR%
Description=DESCRIPTION
DriverId=533
Exclusive=00
FIL=dBase 5.0;
SafeTransaction=0
UID=
Collating Sequence=ASCII
Deleted=01
ImplicitCommitSync=Yes
PageTimeout=600
Statistics=0
Threads=3
UserCommitSync=Yes
```

FoxPro ODBC 16 Driver

```
Driver=odbcjt16.dll
DefaultDir=%MAINDIR%
Description=Enter description here
DriverId=536
```

```
FIL=FoxPro 2.6;
JetIniPath=odbcddp.ini
```

FoxPro ODBC 32 Driver

```
DefaultDir=%MAINDIR%
Description=DESCRIPTION
DriverId=536
Exclusive=00
FIL=FoxPro 2.6
SafeTransactions=0
UID=
CollatingSequence=ASCII
Deleted=01
ImplicitCommitSync=Yes
PageTimeout=600
Statistics=00
Threads=3
UserCommitSync=Yes
```

Paradox ODBC 16 Driver

```
Driver=odbcjt16.dll
DefaultDir=%MAINDIR%
DriverId=282
FIL=Paradox 4.X;
JetIniPath=odbcddp.ini
UID=
CollatingSequence=ASCII
PageTimeout=600
ParadoxNetPath=
ParadoxNetStyle=4.x
ParadoxUserName=
```

Paradox ODBC 32 Driver

```
DefaultDir=%MAINDIR%
Description=
Driver=odbcjt32.dll
DriverId=538
FIL=Paradox 5.X;
SafeTransactions=0
UID=
CollatingSequence=ASCII
ImplicitCommitSync=Yes
PageTimeout=600
ParadoxNetPath=
ParadoxNetStyle=4.x
ParadoxUserName=
Threads=3
```

```
UserCommitSync=Yes
```

SQL ODBC 32 Driver

```
AnsiNPW=Yes
Database=DATABASE
Description=DESCRIPTION
Driver=sqlsrv32.dll
Language=default
OemToAnsi=No
QuotedId=Yes
Server=local
TrustedConnection=
UseProcForPrepare=Yes
```

Oracle ODBC 32 Driver

```
ConnectString=CONNECT
Description=DESCRIPTION
UID=UID
Buffersize=40000
PWD=
Remarks=0
RowLimit=400
SynonymColumns=1
SystemTable=0
DSN=DSN_NAME
```

Visual FoxPro ODBC 32 Driver

```
BackgroundFetch=Yes
Collate=Machine
Description=DESCRIPTION
Driver=VFPODBC.DLL
Exclusive=No
SetNoCountOn=No
SourceDB=DB_PATHNAME
SourceType=DBC
```

Visual Basic Tab

Visual Basic support can be installed on the target computer by selecting the items on the Visual Basic tab, shown in Figure 4-37. As you no doubt know, Visual Basic is a programming language. The Visual Basic files must be installed on the local computer for SMS Installer to include them in the package. When Visual Basic is installed on a computer, the directory structure is always the same. SMS Installer counts on the files being in the proper directory structure and pulls the files from there.

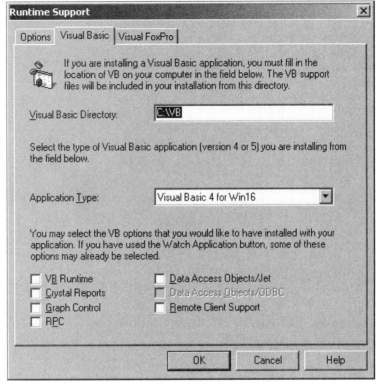

Figure 4-37 *Visual Basic tab.*

Visual Basic Directory

The Visual Basic Directory line tells SMS Installer where Visual Basic is installed on the local computer.

Application Type

SMS Installer also needs to know what version of the Visual Basic files will be installed. In the Application Type drop-down list, the options are as follows:

1. Visual Basic 4 for Win16

2. Visual Basic 4 for Win32

3. Visual Basic 5

4. Visual Basic 6

Specific Visual Basic components can also be selected separately. The available components are shown in Table 4-1.

Table 4-1 *Visual Basic components.*

Component	Description
VB Runtime	Runtime version of Visual Basic. Visual Basic programs require this program be installed on the computer to run properly.
Crystal Reports	Reporting tool developed by Seagate. Visual Basic programs require this program be installed if custom reports are to be used in the application.
Graph Control	Visual Basic component that allows support for data interaction in graphs and charts.
RPC	Remote Procedure Call is a component that allows Visual Basic applications to make communication with remote resources, such as servers and printers. An example of an application that uses RPC heavily is Microsoft Exchange.
Data Access Objects/Jet	Component that allows Visual Basic to communicate with databases.
Data Access Objects/ODBC	Visual Basic files for connecting to different database types.
Remote Client Support	Visual Basic component for network connection support.

Visual FoxPro Tab

SMS Installer gives the option of installing Visual FoxPro files.
Visual FoxPro is a database-programming environment. If an
application was written with Visual FoxPro, it needs certain components installed on the PC in order to run correctly. The Visual
FoxPro tab is shown in Figure 4-38.

As with Visual Basic files, Visual FoxPro files must be installed
on the local computer for SMS Installer to compress them into
the package.

Visual FoxPro Directory

The Visual FoxPro Directory line reveals the location of Visual
FoxPro on the local computer.

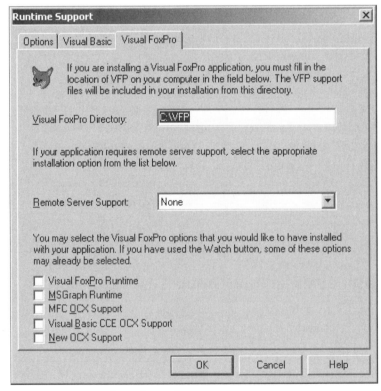

Figure 4-38 *Visual FoxPro tab.*

Table 4-2 *Visual FoxPro files available for installation.*

Files	Description
Visual FoxPro Runtime	The main component that allows the FoxPro application to run.
MSGraph Runtime	A component that allows support for data interaction with graphs and charts.
MFC OCX Support	Support for Microsoft Foundation Class library ActiveX controls.
Visual Basic CCD OCX Support	Support for Visual Basic ActiveX controls.
New OCX Support	Support for self-created ActiveX controls.

Remote Server Support

A Remote Server Support option is also available. It includes:

1. *Remote Server*   The application runs entirely off a remote server.

2. *Remote Server with Local Installation*   The application pulls data from a remote server but runs locally.

Specific Visual FoxPro files, shown in Table 4-2, can be selected to be included in the installation.

User Configuration Group

The User Configuration group contains four items: the Icons tab, the Associations tab, the INI Files tab, and the Registry tab.

Icons Tab

The Icons tab, shown in Figure 4-39, allows you to create icons and groups for the applications. If this is a Repackage, SMS

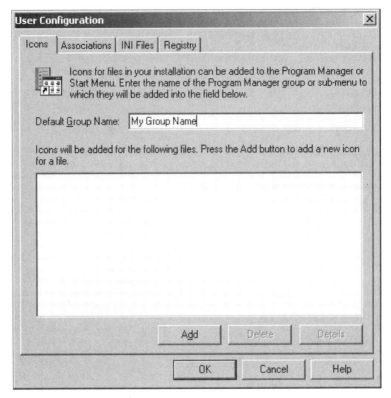

Figure 4-39 *Icons tab.*

Installer will have created these for you and this screen can be
used to modify the SMS Installer–generated icons and groups or
to view what SMS Installer has done. Creating icons and groups
is actually a bit easier using the Script Editor, which is described
later in Chapter 05.

Default Group Name

Immediately, you see the line for the Default Group Name.
This is the Program Manager group name that is applied to the
application installation. When users navigate the Start menu, this
is the group name they will use to find the shortcut to run the
program. If you are creating this from scratch, be very descriptive. If users install Adobe Acrobat Reader 3.01, they expect to be
able to find the application's shortcut easily, and they usually
expect the program group's name to match the name of the installation.

Even if this is a repackage, you can add additional icons. If you are piggybacking other components or applications that have been entered manually after the repackage, you must manually create additional icons.

Click on the *Add* button to add an icon. A directory screen is displayed, as shown in Figure 4-40, that represents the current package. It will only show the directory structure of the current package. In this example, the Microsoft Calculator created earlier will be used.

Clicking on OK adds the new shortcut to the list. Clicking the Details button with the new shortcut highlighted displays the Icon Details screen.

Icon Details

The Icon Details screen shows the information extracted from the entry. The Icon Name shows that SMS Installer will give the icon the name "calc," as shown in Figure 4-41. This is an editable field and you can name the icon anything. For instance, the icon name could be changed to "Microsoft Calculator," and that is what will be displayed for the user.

Command-line options can also be entered on this screen. Some applications have additional switches associated with the programs. These switches can be entered here. Perhaps the icon

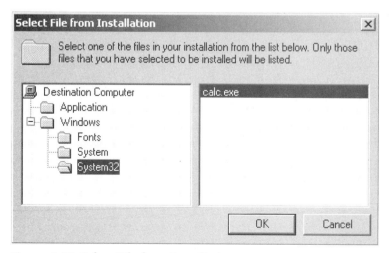

Figure 4-40 *Select File from Installation.*

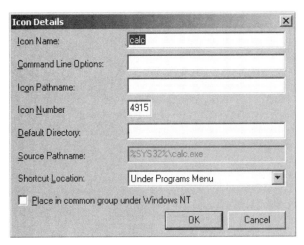

Figure 4-41 *Icon Details.*

will be set up to automatically open an associated data file. For instance, if Notepad was the shortcut that was being added, the Command Line Options line could include a specific text file to open, along with complete drive and pathname. When the user clicks on the shortcut, the text file will open. This feature is useful if you are adding help files to an application installation that can be accessed later for more information.

If you want to add a different icon than the one that SMS Installer has extracted from the program, you can enter the location under Icon Pathname. Of course, this icon would need to be present in the exact path on the target computer. For this case, you will need to include the icon in the distribution by adding it to the Files list.

Many applications' executable files include multiple icons embedded in the compiled file. In the instance of the Microsoft Calculator, the icon number information extracted by SMS Installer is icon number 4915. To find the icon number of a shortcut, simply right-click on the actual shortcut in the file system and then left-click on its properties. Click on the Shortcut tab, and then click on Change Icon. Since Microsoft Calculator only contains one icon, the following example was taken from MS Paint. MS Paint has several different icons embedded in the program, as shown in Figure 4-42.

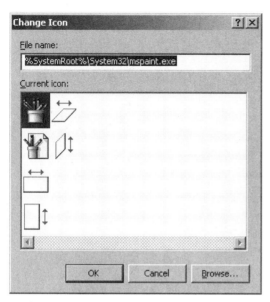

Figure 4-42 *Change Icon.*

Embedded icons are found compressed in EXE and DLL files.   **Note**

Icons are assigned numbers based on an internal index by the software vendor. This index is based on positive integers from 0–9,999.

The Default Directory refers to the local path that the executable runs from. By default, this assumes the program will be run from its current location. Some programs rely on other files to run correctly. If a path variable to the other files is not present in the local environment, you can tell the executable to start running from the location of the other files. The path variable refers to the paths in the file system that all applications have access to when they run. Path variables are usually given to the operating system through the Autoexec.bat; however, additional paths can be given through network login scripts. An example of a path variable in the operating system environment is an MS-DOS prompt. When you type a DOS command like the Windows NT NET.EXE command, you can run the command from any location, even though the command is *actually* located in the C:\WINNT\SYSTEM32 directory.

Note   Alternatively, you can add the specific path variable to the environment by appending the current path in the Autoexec.bat (described later in this chapter) or by using the Add Directory to Path item in the Script Editor (described in detail in Chapter 05).

SMS Installer enters the Source Pathname automatically. This is the location of the executable that was selected during the Add Icon procedure. This is the location from which SMS Installer will pull the local file to place in the compiled script.

The Shortcut Location is the location of the shortcut when the installation is finished. SMS Installer makes it easy to change the shortcut's final destination by providing a drop-down list of the common locations in the operating system. The options are as follows:

1. *Under Programs Menu*   The icon is placed in the group under Start|Programs|Groupname

2. *Startup Group/Menu*   The icon is placed in the Start|Programs|Startup folder. This causes the shortcut's application to automatically start when the computer boots.

3. *Desktop*   This places the icon directly on the Windows desktop along with the other icons such as the My Computer and Recycle Bin shortcuts.

4. *Top of Start Menu*   The icon is placed directly on the start menu above the Programs group.

5. *Directly on Programs Menu*   The icon is placed directly at Start|Programs along with the other group folders. You may notice other applications that take this approach, like Microsoft Office or Visio Professional.

Icons can be placed just about any where in the Windows system. The Create Shortcut script item adds more functionality to this tool, as discussed in Chapter 05.

Associations Tab

The Associations tab, shown in Figure 4-43, allows you to quickly relate certain file types with a program included in the script. File associations on Windows computers causes a file with

Figure 4-43 *Associations tab.*

a certain three-letter extension to open with a specific program. Once the association is made, any file in the system with the exact three-letter extension will always open with the associated program. This enables users to navigate the local directory structure using Windows Explorer; and when they find the file they are looking for, they can open it just by double-clicking on the file. The file will automatically open inside the associated program without the program needing to be opened manually. The icon for the file type will be changed to the same icon as the application. This will make the file easier to find, as well as making its type readily recognizable.

For instance, if a file with the extension of BAK were in the file system without an association, the icon would be the default Windows icon, shown in Figure 4-44.

Figure 4-44 *Default Windows icon.*

Once the file type is associated with Notepad, the icon would display as the icon used for Notepad, as shown in Figure 4-45.

To select an association, click the Add button. Find the file in the installation that should open the file type and enter the three-letter extension in the Three Letter Document Extension line, shown in Figure 4-46.

Clicking on OK places the file in the list. Clicking on the Details button on a currently listed association brings up the screen shown in Figure 4-47.

You can use this screen to modify the current association, changing the Identifier, the Identifier and Identifier Full Name, and the Print Options. SMS Installer already records the Source

Figure 4-45 *Notepad icon.*

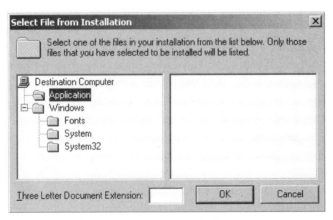

Figure 4-46 *Select File from Installation.*

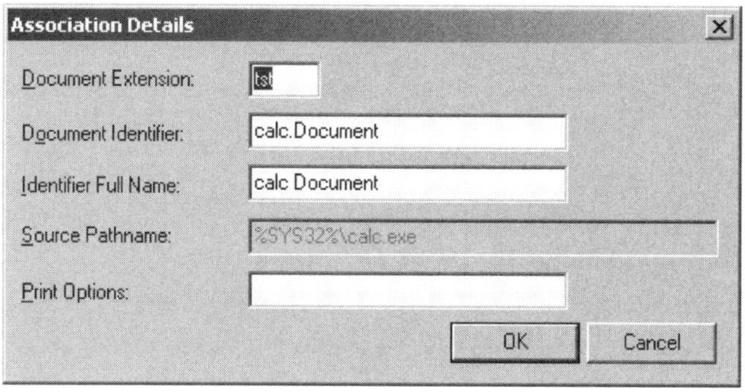

Figure 4-47 *Association Details.*

Pathname from the information provided during the Add procedure or from the repackage if the item already exists.

File associations use the Windows API (Application Programming Interface) built into the operating system to perform actions on the file type. The Windows API is a huge list of operating system-specific functions.

For more information on the Windows API see http://msdn.microsoft.com/library/sdkdoc/portals/win32start_1n6 t.htm.

> File associations can be accessed on the Windows computer by opening My Computer, then clicking on View|Options|File Types. On Windows NT specifically, you can see all the file associations by entering the command ASSOC at the command prompt. For a particular file association, type ASSOC and the three-letter extension.

Note

INI Files Tab

INI files are used by applications to retrieve user- or computer-specific information that is not automatically included in the application itself. In 16-bit computer systems, this allowed the software vendor to provide rich customization features to the user. Currently, 32-bit applications use the Windows Registry to store the customization information. This is a more secure and permanent way of storing the information. INI files can inadvertently be deleted from the file system, consequently removing the application's customized features. See Figure 4-48.

To provide backward-compatibility, Adobe Acrobat Reader 3.01, repackaged previously, included an INI file with one of the installed components. Here is the content of the WebLink.INI:

```
[General]
LinkInfo=1
ToolButton=Y
Application=
Driver=Standard
ProgressDialog=Y

[NoTimeOut]
file=Y
http=Y
mailto=Y
```

Figure 4-48 *INI Files tab.*

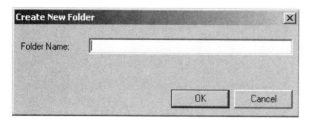

Figure 4-49 *Create New Folder.*

The component reads this information every time it is executed.

If INI files were modified or created during the repackage, SMS Installer will already have those listed here. The INI Files tab allows the user to view the details of the current settings, create or modify new INI files, and delete the entries.

It also allows entering a new folder name to be created by SMS Installer and then placing a new INI file in the folder. Just type in the folder name with the target folder highlighted, and the new folder will be created. See Figure 4-49.

> You do not need to type in the drive letter and path, just the name of the folder you want created. **Note**

To edit an INI file, just enter the pathname and INI filename, and then enter the INI settings that need to be changed or added in the INI File Contents screen, shown in Figure 4-50. Make sure to follow the conventions of the current INI file if editing. Entering the information in the wrong format could cause application errors, or even worse, if editing a file like the WIN.INI or SYSTEM.INI, it could cause an error to be displayed or keep the computer from booting correctly.

Figure 4-50 is an example of the format that would be used to edit the SYSTEM.INI and to add a RESTART variable. For more information on the RESTART variable with SMS Installer, see "The RESTART Variable" in Chapter 08.

> The path to edit an INI file *must* start with a variable. Variables are defined in the Script Editor. For more information on SMS Installer variables, see Chapter 05. **Note**

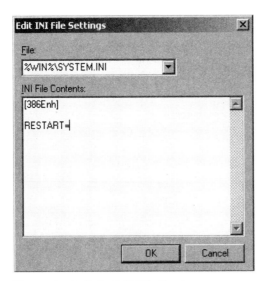

Figure 4-50 *Edit INI File Settings.*

The default directory-specific variables available by default in the drop-down list to the INI File Settings are as follows:

1. %BACKUPDIR%   The backup directory specified if the backup files option is selected

2. %CDESKTOPDIR%   The common user desktop directory

3. %CGROUPDIR%   The common user program group directory

4. %CSTARTMENUDIR%   The common user start menu directory

5. %CSTARTUPDIR%   The common user startup directory

6. %DESKTOPDIR%   The current profile desktop directory

7. %GROUPDIR%   The current profile program group directory

8. %MAINDIR%   The program's main directory

9. %MAINDIR_SAVE%   The program's main save directory

10. %PROGRAM_FILES%   The Program Files directory

11. *%STARTMENUDIR%*   The current profile start menu directory

12. *%STARTUPDIR%*   The current profile startup directory

13. *%SYS%*   The System directory

14. *%SYS32%*   The System32 directory

15. *%SYSWIN%*   The Windows directory

16. *%TEMP%*   The temporary directory specified in the operating system environment

17. *%WIN%*   The Windows directory

You can define your own variables using the Script Editor. Other variables are available in the drop-down list but do not relate to directory structures. INI files exist in the computer directory and file structure.

You may notice that some of the variables are similar, except some have a "C" before the variable name. The "C" stands for "common." When profiles are enabled on a computer, a different directory structure is used. The common directories are locations that are available to anyone who logs on to the computer. The variables without the "C" will only be available to someone that logged on to the computer when the application was installed. Someone else logging on to the computer later will not see the information. For more information on profiles, see "Profiles Overview" in Chapter 07.

The registry uses this profile information as well, putting information in a "common" area and a "profile" area just like the Profiles directories. Specific registry settings are based on the same user profile and common settings.

Registry Tab

The Registry tab, shown in Figure 4-51, is a place to view the registry creations and modifications made by the repackage. Additional keys and values can also be created. For more information on the Windows Registry, see "Registry Overview" in Chapter 07. Clicking the New button brings up the Registry Key Settings dialog box, shown in Figure 4-52.

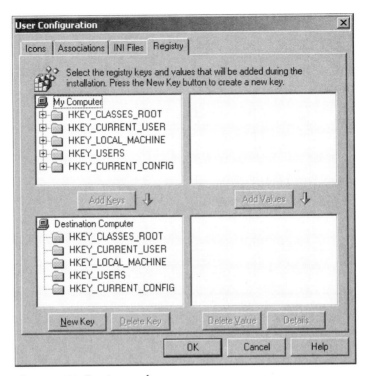

Figure 4-51 *Registry tab.*

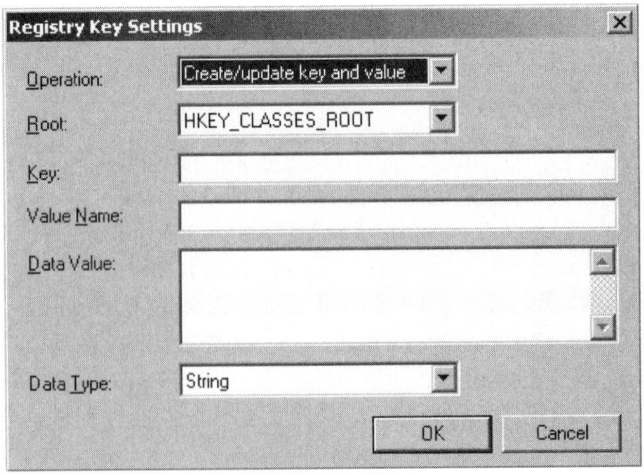

Figure 4-52 *Registry Key Settings.*

The Registry Key Settings also provide manual entry of registry key modifications and additions. If you are not familiar with the structure and the criticality, working with the registry can lead to serious computer problems. Be very careful that you understand the implications of making the wrong modifications and be sure to test the registry modifications on a test PC before trying them on a production computer.

The Registry Key Settings dialog box can be confusing. Even though the New button is clicked, this box can create, modify, and delete registry keys and values. The Operations drop-down box offers the following operations:

1. *Create/update key and value*   Creates a new key and value or modifies or replaces a current key and value

2. *Create empty key*   Creates an empty registry key with no data and no values

3. *Remove key and all subkeys*   Removes an entire key, its sub-keys, and values

4. *Remove value only*   Removes the data and values but leaves the registry key alone

System Configuration Group

The System Configuration group contains four items: the Devices tab, the Services tab, the Autoexec.bat tab, and the Config.sys tab.

Devices Tab

The Devices tab, shown in Figure 4-53, is for adding devices to the 386 Enhanced section of the SYSTEM.INI for Windows 3.x and Windows 9x operating systems. This option is not available for Windows NT because it is primarily for including backward-compatibility for 16-bit systems. For an example of the SYSTEM.INI file and the 386 Enhanced section, see "Example of a System.ini File" in Chapter 10.

The Add button allows you to add devices that have already been selected in the file system of the package. The Delete button

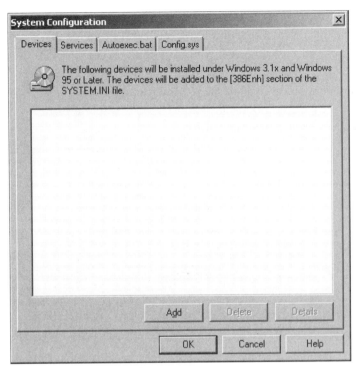

Figure 4-53 *Devices tab.*

deletes a highlighted device. The Details button allows viewing
and modifying of a highlighted device entry.

Note   Adding a device to the SYSTEM.INI causes SMS Installer to add a
RESTART variable to the script. Since the items in the SYSTEM.INI
are loaded at bootup, the computer must be restarted for the
devices to be used by the operating system.

Services Tab

The Services tab, shown in Figure 4-54, allows you to add
Windows NT services. Services are components or programs that
are developed with the ability to run as background processes on
a Windows NT computer. They run in a separate memory space
than the rest of the operating system. This gives performance and
computing power back to the computer. They also run under a
system security context, which is a system account instead of a

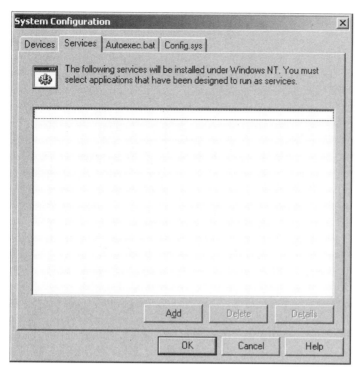

Figure 4-54 *Services tab.*

user account. However, they can be configured to run under a specific local user account for added security.

The Add button allows the user to select executables from the current file list of the package. The Delete button deletes a highlighted service. The Details button allows the user to view or edit a highlighted service.

Autoexec.bat Tab

The Autoexec.bat tab, shown in Figure 4-55, is utilized to quickly add information to the Autoexec.bat file of the target computer. The Autoexec.bat file contains information that Windows 3.x and Windows 9x reads as the computer boots (the Config.sys file, described in the next section, is a file that also provides information for the booting computer). Common information contained in the Autoexec.bat file includes the path information for the computing environment and the commands that need to be loaded before other devices. For an example of an

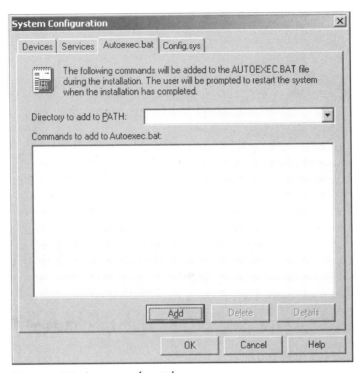

Figure 4-55 *Autoexec.bat tab.*

Autoexec.bat file, see "Example of an Autoexec.bat File" in Chapter 10.

Note   The Autoexec.bat file is recognized on Windows NT, but only if the registry value `ParseAutoexec` is set to 1. If you are modifying information for Windows NT, use the Insert Line Into Text File script item (discussed in Chapter 05 and modify the Autoexec.NT file.

New path information can be quickly added to the current path by entering the path text in the Directory to Add to PATH line. This entry can be both a drive letter and directory and also a variable that is already defined in the script. The drop-down box lists the already-defined variables.

By clicking the Add button, you can add a line of text into the Autoexec.bat. Entries may already exist in the list if the repackage

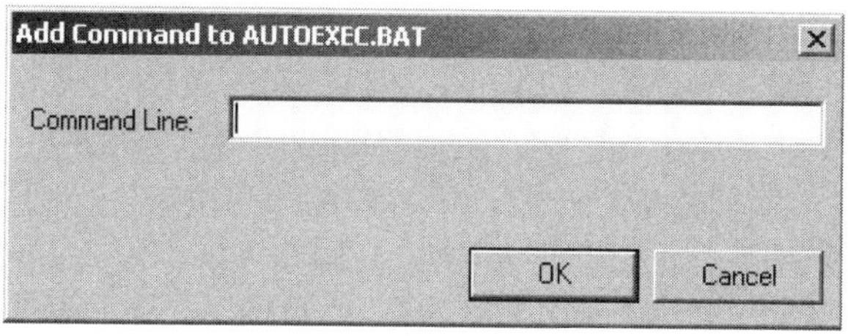

Figure 4-56 *Add Command to Autoexec.bat.*

operation detected modifications to the Autoexec.bat. See Figure 4-56.

The Autoexec.bat line should be entered exactly as it needs to appear in the Autoexec.bat file. The Command Line entry will accept up to 255 characters. If the entry is a command line (entry containing a command to run at bootup), it is imperative to carefully and completely test the entry. Commands placed in startup files can cause the computer not to boot if they are not entered correctly.

Once the entry has been added to the list, the Details button is enabled. Clicking on the Details button brings up the dialog box shown in Figure 4-57.

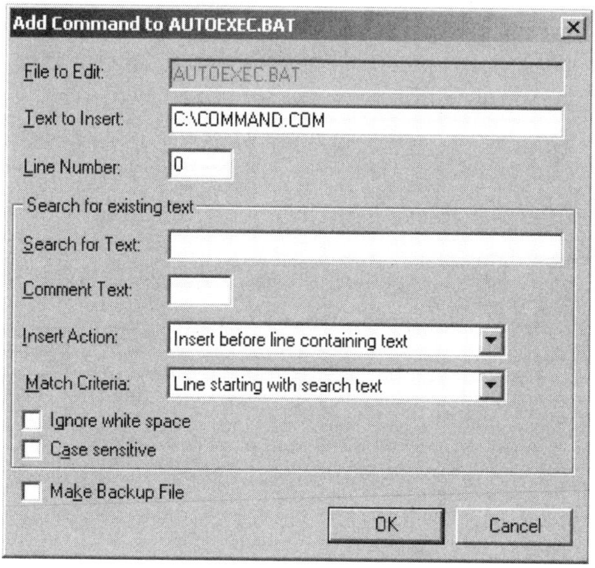

Figure 4-57 *Add Command to Autoexec.bat options.*

The Details dialog box offers several different ways to manage the addition of the line to the Autoexec.bat file. The Text to Insert entry can be modified here in the event the command was entered incorrectly or modifications need to be made (such as adding command-line switches).

The Line Number box gives you the ability to select your preference of line number for the new command line. This value can be any number from 0 to 32,000. A value of 0 instructs SMS Installer to place the line of text at the last line of the Autoexec.bat.

Included with the Autoexec.bat Details dialog box is the ability to perform context searches of the current information in the Autoexec.bat file. This search can help locate current information for deleting, modifying, replacing, or marking. The Search for Text line allows you to input text to search for in the file. Once the text is found, there are several things that can be done with the information.

The Comment Text entry takes the input from here and comments-out the line identified in the search string. This is a good way to replace lines in the Autoexec.bat without deleting them. Commenting-out the line serves as a backup, should the new command line not work properly. The Autoexec.bat can quickly be restored to its original form by removing the comment information from the beginning of the commented line.

Once the search line has been identified, you can choose from the following three actions.

Insert Actions:

1. Insert before line containing text

2. Replace line containing text

3. Insert after line containing text

For the search, you can also define the way it matches information in the Autoexec.bat with the following criteria settings.

Match Criteria:

1. Line starting with search text

2. Line containing search text

3. Line ending with search text

Table 4-3 shows two checkboxes on the Autoexec.bat Details dialog box that relate to the Search function.

One other checkbox, titled Make Backup File, on the Details dialog box tells SMS Installer to make a backup copy of the Autoexec.bat file before the command line(s) are added. The backup file keeps the same name as the original file but changes the extension to .001. Each time the file is updated and a backup is created, the extension will increment by 1. For example, if you see a file extension of .012, you know the Autoexec.bat has been modified 12 times.

> Adding commands to the Autoexec.bat causes SMS Installer to add a RESTART variable to the script. Since the items in the Autoexec.bat are only loaded at bootup, the computer must be restarted for the information to be available to the operating system.

Note

Config.sys Tab

The Config.sys tab, shown in Figure 4-58, allows you to edit the Config.sys file. The Config.sys file, like the Autoexec.bat file, is read by the operating system when the computer boots. DOS mode devices and 16-bit drivers are loaded into the operating environment from the Config.sys. These devices are terminate-and-stay-resident (TSRs) programs that run in background

Table 4-3   *Checkboxes on Autoexec.bat details dialog.*

Checkbox	Description
Ignore White Space	Tells SMS Installer to ignore additional white spaces or blank lines in the Autoexec.bat.
Case Sensitive	Helps maximize the search functionality by making the search case-sensitive. If you know the string you are looking for has a specific letter case, choosing this option will narrow the search.

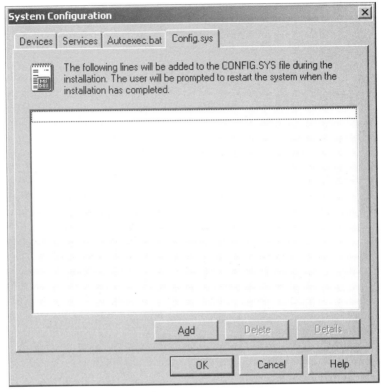

Figure 4-58 *Config.sys tab.*

processes. By loading these in the Config.sys file, the TSRs are available to software written for 16-bit drivers and to applications and processes that run in the MS-DOS prompt. For an example of a Config.sys file, see "Example of a Config.sys File" in Chapter 10.

Note   The Config.sys file is not recognized on Windows NT, only on Windows 3.x and Windows 9x computers. If modifying information for Windows NT, use the Insert Line Into Text File script item (shown in Chapter 05) and alter the Config.NT file.

The Config.sys tab is identical to the Autoexec.bat tab in the way it operates. Enter the command-line string exactly as it needs to appear in the package in order for it to work correctly. As with the Autoexec.bat commands, the lines put into the Config.sys file

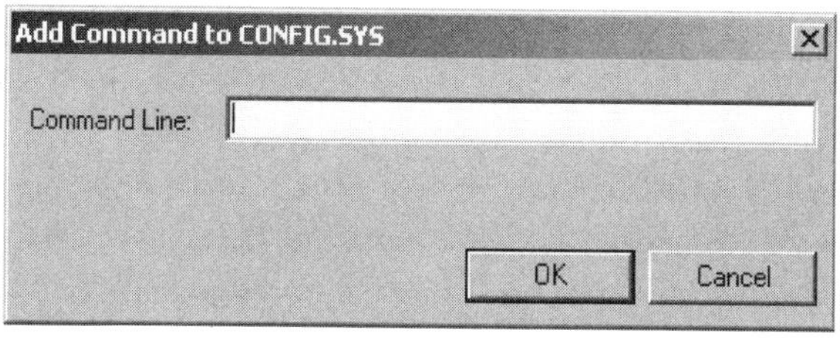

Figure 4-59 *Add Command to Config.sys.*

need to be tested thoroughly before installation on a production environment computer. See Figure 4-59.

Once commands have been entered (some may already exist if this is the customization of a repackage), the Delete button can be used to delete a highlighted item, and the Details button will bring up the dialog box in Figure 4-60 to allow the user to view or modify the command.

The Details dialog box offers many different ways to customize how the lines are inserted into the Config.sys file. The Text to Insert entry can be modified here, in the event the command was entered incorrectly or modifications need to be made, such as adding device switches.

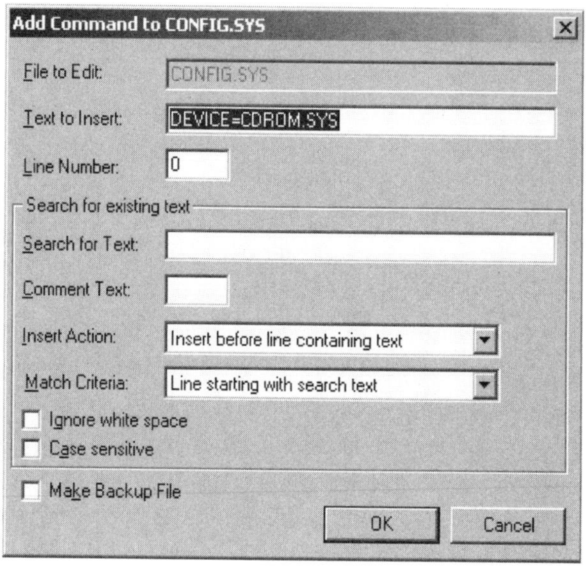

Figure 4-60 *Add Command to Config.sys. options.*

The Line Number box gives you the ability to select your preferred line number for the new command line. This value can be any number from 0 to 32,000. A value of 0 instructs SMS Installer to place the line of text at the last line of the Config.sys.

Included with the Config.sys Details dialog box is the ability to perform context searches of the current information in the file. This search can help locate current information for deleting, modifying, replacing, or marking. The Search for Text line allows you to input text to search for in the file. Once the text is found, several things can be done with the information.

The Comment Text takes the input from here and comments-out the line identified in the search string. This is a good way to replace lines in the Config.sys without deleting them. Commenting-out the line serves as a backup, should the new command line not work properly. The Config.sys can quickly be restored back to its original form by removing the comment information from the beginning of the commented line.

Once the search line has been identified, there are three actions you can choose from:

Insert Actions:

1. Insert before line containing text

2. Replace line containing text

3. Insert after line containing text

You can also define the way the search matches information in the Config.sys with the following criteria settings:

Match Criteria:

1. Line starting with search text

2. Line containing search text

3. Line ending with search text

Table 4-4 shows two checkboxes on the Config.sys Details dialog box that relate to the Search function.

One other checkbox, titled Make Backup File, on the Details dialog box tells SMS Installer to make a backup copy of the Con-

Table 4-4 *Checkboxes on Config.sys details dialog.*

Checkbox	Description
Ignore White Space	Tells SMS Installer to ignore additional white spaces or blank lines in the Config.sys.
Case Sensitive	Helps maximize the search functionality by making the search case-sensitive. If you know the string you are looking for has a specific letter case, choosing this option will narrow the search.

fig.sys file before the command line(s) are added. The backup file keeps the same name as the original file but changes the extension to .001. Each time the file is updated and a backup is created, the extension will increment by 1. For example, if you see a file extension of .012, you know the Config.sys has been modified 12 times.

Note

Adding commands to the Config.sys causes SMS Installer to add a RESTART variable to the script. Since the items in the Config.sys are only loaded at bootup, the computer must be restarted for the information to be available to the operating system.

A script item action titled Set Files/Buffers provides the function of adding the files and buffers values to the Config.sys. This script item is covered in the next chapter.

Advanced Configuration Group

The Advanced Configuration group contains 10 items: the Global tab, the Screen tab, the Font tab, the Languages tab, the Options tab, the Settings tab, the Patching tab, the Compiler Variables tab, the Signing tab, and the Version tab.

Note   Since this group is specific to the compiler, it is also available in the Script Editor by pressing the Ctrl-Z key combination or by selecting Edit|Installation Properties on the File menu.

Global Tab

The Global tab, shown in Figure 4-61, contains custom settings for the SMS Installer package that has an effect on the script as it is being compiled.

Maximum Compression

Checking the Maximum Compression checkbox tells SMS Installer to try to compress the compiled executable even more than normal. This makes the compiled file smaller, which saves

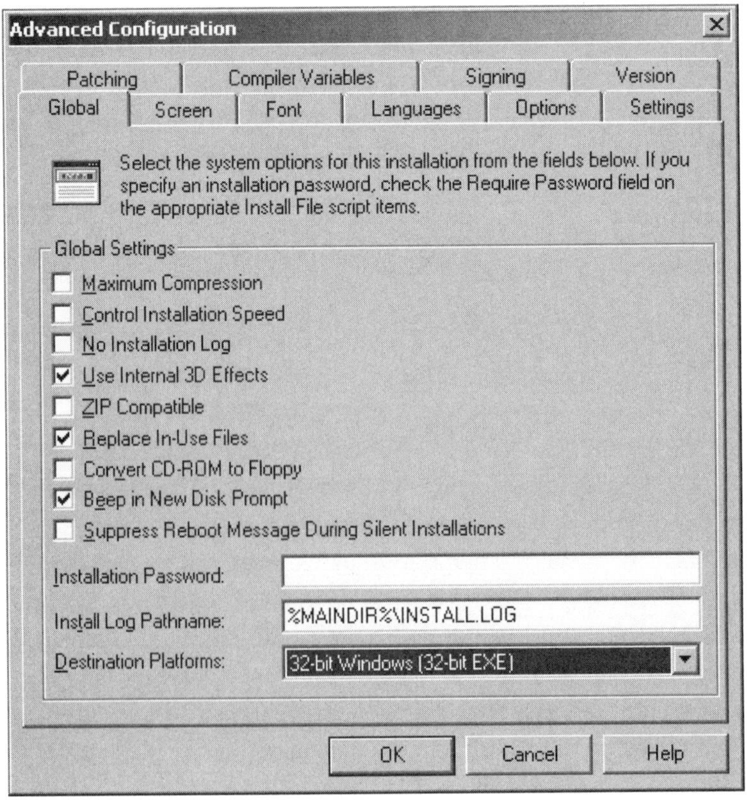

Figure 4-61 *Global tab.*

additional space where the file is stored. Overall distribution of the file is better optimized to save network bandwidth (if distributed via SMS or a network share) and download time (if distributed via e-mail or an FTP or intranet site).

> When the package is compiled with this option turned on, the file takes longer to compile, since SMS Installer must make a more comprehensive check of file structure.   **Note**

Control Installation Speed

Checking the Control Installation Speed checkbox tells the compiled installation to compensate for faster computers by slowing the overall installation speed. Installation dialog boxes such as the file installation descriptions can fly by too quickly on fast computers. Slowing the installation speed will give the user a chance to read all the information during the installation. This does not affect dialog boxes that prompt for information. Test this component thoroughly to make sure slowing the installation speed does not make the installation unbearably slow for the user. If you have a diverse collection of computer speeds in your organization, you may want to think about making separate packages using this component. Make a standard installation for slower computers and a slow installation for faster computers.

No Installation Log

The No Installation Log checkbox tells SMS Installer not to automatically compress the installation log file into the compiled file. If the installation log is not included in the compiled file, the installation cannot be uninstalled. This is primarily for situations where the Uninstall feature is not needed. For instance, if the installation is an operating system patch, or it only replaces one application file with an updated version, the Uninstall feature may not be needed for the installation, and this component would come in handy. Furthermore, if you are creating standalone utilities with the SMS Installer script facility (for an example see "Creating Utilities with SMS Installer" in Chapter 06), the utility itself would not need an Installation log; just the installation that installs the utility on the target computer.

Use Internal 3D Effects

The Use Internal 3D Effects checkbox tells SMS Installer to include the CTL3D.DLL file in the installation file. This DLL file provides buttons and windows that appear to be 3-dimensional. The inclusion of this file adds additional size to the compiled file, but only about 11 KB. This file is generally in use by the operating system itself, since it is a commonly shared system file for providing 3D effects to other applications. If this component is enabled, SMS Installer will successfully update the CTL3D.DLL on the target computer without receiving a file-in-use or sharing error.

Zip Compatible

The Zip Compatible checkbox is a handy feature of SMS Installer. Checking this box tells SMS Installer to give the compiled file compatibility with the standard Zip products on the market. This is particularly useful when a specific file becomes corrupt on a computer and needs to be replaced so that the application can continue to function properly. Using any industry Zip program, the compiled file can be opened with the program and the specific file can be extracted and used. Extraction outside of the installation means the compiled file does not have to be installed for it to be useful. Also, making the file Zip-compatible allows for the use of virus-scanning utilities to safeguard the compiled file and its entire contents against viruses.

Note   If the compiled file is made Zip-compatible, the Installation Password feature cannot be used. Also, the file cannot be split across a floppy disk set; it must remain a one-file executable.

Replace In-Use Files

On Windows systems, Windows will not allow files that are currently being used by other programs or processes to be overwritten. Common files that cannot be overwritten are DLL, OCX, and VBX files. Checking the Replace In-Use Files checkbox tells SMS Installer to note which files are in use during the installation, to compare them to the files that must be installed from its compiled installation, and finally to gather a list of files that cannot be overwritten or replaced. At the end of the installation, SMS Installer requests a reboot of the computer. During the reboot, SMS Installer reads the in-use-files information it gathered and replaces the files before the operating system starts. This option adds 15 KB to the executable.

Convert CD-ROM to Floppy

The Convert CD-ROM to Floppy checkbox automatically directs the Install File(s) action to allow the package to be converted to floppy-drive-size files.

Beep in New Disk Prompt

This checkbox causes the computer to beep during the installation if using a floppy diskette set for installation. This is just an additional notification to the user that it is time to swap to the next installation disk in the set.

Suppress Reboot Message During Silent Installations

During the installation, if in-use files are replaced, or the Autoexec.bat or the Config.sys files are modified, or if a device is added to the System.ini, then SMS Installer will automatically insert a Restart action item in the script. This causes the package to prompt the user to reboot the computer after installation is complete. If a / s switch is used (see "Command Line QuickList" in Chapter 10 for a description of this switch) to make the installation silent (meaning the installation is performed in the background without the user's knowledge), then the installation will still prompt the user to restart the computer. The restart message can be suppressed by clicking this checkbox, forcing the installation to be *completely* silent.

> If the computer must be restarted for an installation to be complete, and it is not, the software package may not work correctly until the computer has been cycled through a restart.

Note

Installation Password

The Installation Password line allows you to enter the password that will protect the installation from being installed by unauthorized users. The password is compiled into the executable. This component must be used with the Set Variable scripting action. The Set Variable action will be discussed in Chapter 05 in more depth.

To set the PASSWORD variable with the SET VARIABLE script item:

1. In the Script Editor, under the Actions list, double-click the SET VARIABLE script item.

2. Complete the Set Variable dialog box by entering the word PASSWORD into the Variable text box and typing the actual password in the Value text box.

3. Click on OK.

4. Place the new SET VARIABLE line toward the beginning of the script before the user dialogs.

Install Log Pathname

The Install Log Pathname line contains the default information for the location of the installation log file. The %MAINDIR%\INSTALL.LOG tells SMS Installer to include the installation log file in the Main Directory path variable, which in most cases, will be the main application directory. As noted in the Adobe Acrobat installation, the main directory path would be the Acrobat3 directory. The INSTALL.LOG file would be installed to this same directory. As mentioned previously, the INSTALL.LOG file contains all the necessary information to uninstall applications. This entry line allows for more control over the location and name of the installation log file.

Note   The installation log file gets installed to a directory that already exists. A directory is not created just for the INSTALL.LOG file alone. If customizing the location of the installation log file, either enter a currently installed directory or create an additional one in which to install the file.

This is helpful when more control over the Uninstall features is needed. For instance, it could become company policy that all installation logs be contained in a single directory. All installation logs could be stored in one directory as long as the INSTALL.LOG file is renamed to match the actual application. This directory could serve as a quick-reference list of applications that have been successfully installed on a computer. And, since the installation log file is deleted as part of the uninstall procedure, this directory could be a record of the applications that have not gone through the uninstall process. SMS provides the ability to not only distribute installations but also to distribute uninstallations. If an uninstall has been distributed, but the installation log remains, this would raise a flag that the remote computer has not processed the uninstall. (For more information on using SMS Installer to uninstall the installation, see "Command Line QuickList" in Chapter 10.)

> **Note** The directory information that contains the installation log file must start with a variable. Use the `SET VARIABLE` script item to give the installation log file's path a variable name. (See Chapter 05 for more information.)

Another compelling reason to use this method is to avoid the installation log file from being deleted. If the log files are stored in one location in a deep directory structure, the user may not find these files to inadvertently delete them. If the installation log file is not present, the application cannot be uninstalled.

> **Tip** If the installation log file cannot be found, the SMS Installer package will not run the uninstall process. An error message will be displayed, and the uninstall will abort. The installation log file can be copied from another computer that has run through the same installation. Place the installation log file into the directory referenced by the installation script, and then rerun the uninstall.

Destination Platforms

The Destination Platforms drop-down list allows you to select the type of operating system that the package will run on. The options are shown in Table 4-5.

Table 4-5   *Destination platform options.*

Option	Description
16/32-bit Windows (16-bit EXE)	Installs on 16-bit operating system such as Windows 3.x, Windows for Workgroups, and Windows 9x.
32-bit Windows (32-bit EXE)	Installs on true 32-bit operating system such as Windows NT and Windows 9x.

Note   Only if the 32-bit Windows is selected will the Versions tab (described later) be available for customization. Versioning the compiled executable allows tracking of multiple versions of a setup program.

Screen Tab

The Screen tab, shown in Figure 4-62, relates directly to the background screen and the progress bar shown during the installation. The custom graphics described in this section relate to the billboard graphics that are added on the Graphics tab of the Installation Interface group, which was discussed earlier.

Progress Bar Section

The first options on the Screen tab deal with the location of the Progress dialog box on the installation screen. The Progress dialog box is the small box that is displayed as the installation files are copied. It contains a percentage bar that gives the user a sense of how close the installation is to completion.

Progress Dialog Placement

The Progress Dialog Placement selection has a drop-down list with multiple options. These options tell the SMS Installer script where the progress dialog box should reside during the entire installation. The options are as follows:

Figure 4-62 *Screen tab.*

1. Top Left
2. Top Center
3. Top Right
4. Middle Left
5. Center (default)
6. Middle Right
7. Bottom Left
8. Bottom Center
9. Bottom Right

The reason for moving the Progress dialog box is in the event that you have included custom graphics to be displayed on the installation's background. For instance, if the company logo were placed in the middle of the background screen, you would want the dialog placed in one of the corners of the screen (Top Left, Top Right, Bottom Left, or Bottom Right).

Progress Bar Based On

The Progress Bar Based On selection provides the ability to change the way the Progress dialog bar displays the progress of the installation. It can be displayed as:

1. *Position in Installation EXE*   SMS Installer calculates the size of the SMS Installer executable and displays the percentage completed.

2. *Position in Installation Script*   SMS Installer calculates the steps in the script and reports based on the percentage of steps completed.

3. *Percentage of Selected Files*   (Default) SMS Installer calculates the number of files that are included in the compiled package and reports on the percentage of total files copied.

All options are based on a 0 to 100 percentile scale. If you are more concerned about the user's perception during the installation, the Percentage of Selected Files may be the best option. The Position in Installation EXE and the Position in Installation Script options do not always offer the user an accurate view of completion. For instance, if customizations have been made to the script to prompt for additional information, the installation actually stops until the user responds.

Custom Progress Bar DLL

The Progress Bar Based On entry allows custom progress bars to be used with the SMS Installer installation. The default progress bar DLL that is used is located in the SMS Installer directory under the \DLL\PROGRESS directory structure. If you are familiar with creating custom DLL files, you can create your own dialog bar, or you can use dialog bar DLLs from other applications. This option also includes a Browse button to help locate the custom DLL files in the local file system.

Center All Dialogs Over Progress Dialog

This checkbox tells SMS Installer to place all dialog boxes over the Progress dialog box. If the Progress Dialog Placement has been used to keep a custom graphic in view during the installation, the other dialog boxes would still cover up the graphic if this option is not enabled. If this option is used, SMS Installer automatically places all other dialog boxes over the Progress dialog box no matter where it is placed.

Background Gradient Section

The Background Gradient section helps you customize how the background screen is displayed. In SMS Installer the gradient is the separation of colors on the background screen.

A real-time view accompanies any modification to this section in the Screen Preview area. **Note**

Background Gradient Size

Although not labeled, this drop-down box changes the size of the Background installation window. The options are as follows:

1. *Full Screen Gradient Window*   (Default) The entire computer screen is covered with the installation background and dialog boxes.

2. *¾ Screen Gradient Window*   Three-quarters of the screen is covered with the installation background and dialog boxes. This option places the background at the top of the screen and leaves 25 percent of space at the bottom of the computer screen.

3. *No Gradient Window*   No background is displayed, only the dialog boxes.

The No Gradient Window option is a better option to use if creating standalone utilities using the Script Editor. It makes the utilities feel more like standalone applications than a standard SMS Installer installation file. For more information on the Script Editor, see Chapter 05. **Note**

Title Bar

The Title Bar checkbox (turned on by default) enables and disables the thin title bar that sits at the top of the installation screen. If this is disabled, the installation title is not shown.

Hide Program Manager

This option is useful for backward-compatibility with Windows 3.x and Windows for Workgroups. Program Manager was the original Windows component that managed the icons, icon groups, task list, services, Run functions, and so on. Windows 9x and later uses the Windows Explorer interface for managing the operating system's interaction with the file structure, directory structure, icons, shortcuts, Run functions, and so on. It replaces the Program Manager.

During a Windows 3.x or Windows for Workgroups installation, SMS Installer opens the Program Manager to install the icons and icon groups. This function leaves the newly created icon group on the screen after the installation is complete, which can be confusing to the user. If this option is selected during an installation on a Window 3.x or Windows for Workgroups computer, the Program Manager remains hidden during the icon and icon group creation.

No Background Gradient

The No Background Gradient turns off the background colors but leaves the background window. This is useful if a large custom graphic is used or if a small custom graphic is tiled across the background. Keep in mind that the more graphics displayed on the background, the slower the video refreshes will perform. When custom graphics are used, turning off the background gradient increases the speed of the installation during screen changes.

Top Color/Bottom Color

The Top Color and Bottom Color buttons select the colors that will be displayed on the gradient window. Depending on the video capabilities of the computer, the gradient separation at the top and bottom of the window can be a smooth transition or a rough one.

> If the video capabilities of the computer are poor, it is sensible to **Tip**
> make both the top and bottom colors the same. Customize the
> background so that it will display correctly on all computers in
> the organization.

The Top Color and Bottom Color buttons use Basic Colors and Custom Colors settings. The Basic Colors dialog box displays the most common colors, as shown in Figure 4-63.

Clicking on the Define Custom Colors button brings up the Custom Colors dialog box, shown in Figure 4-64. Moving the cursor around on the custom pallet screen selects a color. The gradient bar at the far right selects the dark and light versions of the color. Once the color has been selected, click *Add to Custom Colors* and the custom color will be saved for all future SMS Installer scripts.

Font Tab

The Font tab, shown in Figure 4-65, customizes the default font type that is displayed on the dialog and message boxes during the installation.

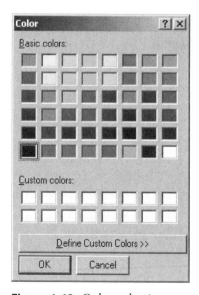

Figure 4-63 *Color selection common dialog box.*

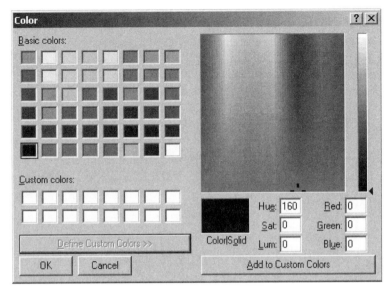

Figure 4-64 *Define custom colors.*

Bold/Light Fonts

The Bold/Light Fonts drop-down list has three options:

1. Bold fonts always

2. Light fonts under Windows 95/NT 4.0 or later

3. Light fonts always (default selection)

On Windows 9x computers, light fonts are the default throughout the operating system.

Message Box Font

The Message Box Font selection selects the font type that is displayed on the message boxes only. The Browse button shows a dialog box to select the preferred font from the font list that is installed on the current computer. Additionally, the preferred font style can be selected (Regular, *Italic*, **Bold**, ***Bold Italic***), the custom font size, and the script type.

Point Size

The Point Size entry box is a quick way of entering the font size. If the Browse button is used on the Message Box Font and a

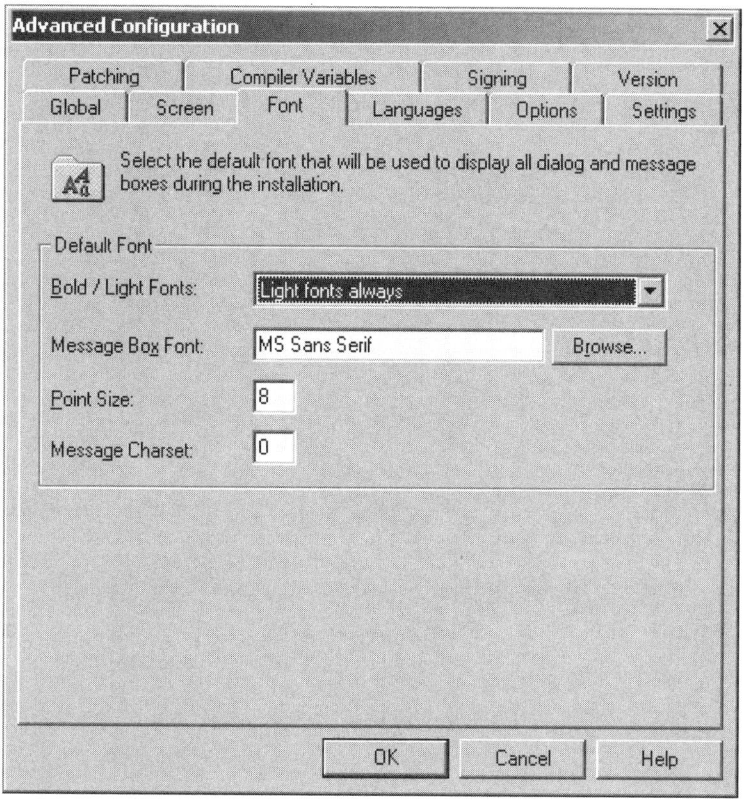

Figure 4-65 *Font tab.*

different font size is selected there, the Point Size entry box value
is automatically updated with the new information.

Message Charset

The Message Charset box is for changing the character set
should the SMS Installer package be translated to another language (shown in the next section).

Languages Tab

The Languages tab, shown in Figure 4-66, allows the selection
of different languages to be included in the SMS Installer package
or multiple languages. The languages that are selected are compiled into the executable. Any changes made to the Languages tab

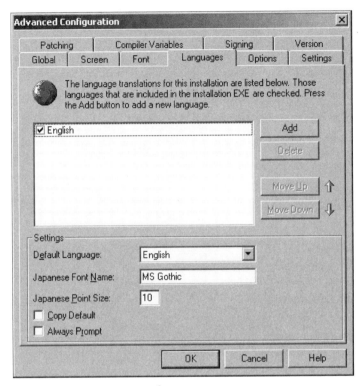

Figure 4-66 *Languages tab.*

are global to SMS Installer. When a new package is started, the Language settings will be retained.

Clicking the Add button pulls up the following list of available languages:

English

Danish

Dutch

Finnish

French

German

Italian

Norwegian

Portuguese

Spanish

Swedish

To create other languages and make them available, you must manually edit the Installer Messages. Clicking on the File menu at Edit|Installer Messages provides access to this. (See Figure 4-67.)

Once a language is selected and added to the list, the Delete button can be used to delete the highlighted entry. The Move Up and Move Down buttons change the position of the highlighted entry in the list of the included languages.

Under the Settings section of the Languages tab there are five available options: Default Language, Japanese Font Name, Japanese Point Size, Copy Default, and Always Prompt.

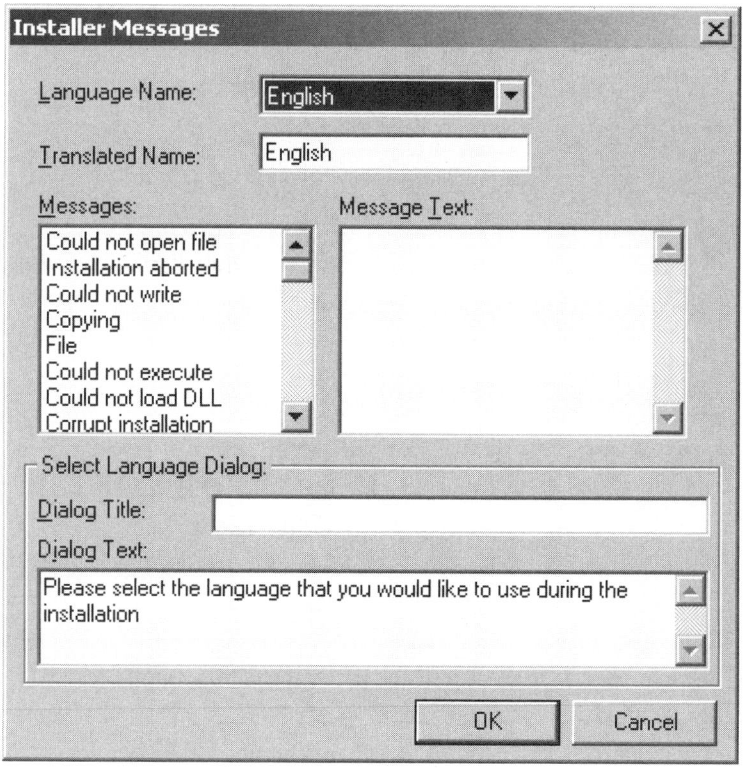

Figure 4-67 *Installer Messages.*

Default Language

The Default Language drop-down list shows the currently selected languages available in the list and allows changing the default language of the SMS Installer package.

Japanese Font Name

The Japanese Font Name shows the default font type that is used when the Japanese language is selected for the SMS Installer package.

Japanese Font Size

The Japanese Font Size shows the point size of the font type that is used when the Japanese language is selected.

Copy Default

If this box is checked, the default font will be copied from the local PC and compiled with the executable during the compile process of the package. This option ensures that the font "look" will be the same across all computers the package is installed on.

Always Prompt

The Always Prompt checkbox always prompts the user to select the language he or she will use for the installation of the SMS Installer package. If this option is left unchecked, the SMS Installer package will automatically check the computer's default language. If multiple languages have been selected and the currently installed language is available in the script, that language will be used for the rest of the installation.

The language selections are placed in a LANGUAGE variable (%LANGUAGE%) in the SMS Installer script. The variable is assigned a three-letter code by SMS Installer from a special INI file. SMS Installer reads these languages from the LANGUAGE.INI file located in the SMS Installer directory. The LANGUAGE.INI file also keeps a list of the unsupported languages.

The related three-letter codes for the supported languages are shown in Table 4-6.

Table 4-6 *Language codes.*

Language	Code
English	ENU
Danish	DAN
Dutch	NLD
Finnish	FIN
French	FRA
German	DEU
Italian	ITA
Norwegian	NON
Portuguese	PTG
Spanish	ESN
Swedish	SVC

Options Tab

The Options tab, shown in Figure 4-68, has three sections dedicated to further customizing the SMS Installer operating environment: the Editor Options, the Compiler Options, and the System DLLs to exclude from the Watch Application. Any changes made to this tab will be saved for all future SMS Installer package or script creations. The changes are global to SMS Installer.

Editor Options

The Editor Options relate directly to the Script Editor. These are the preferences you select based on how you want the Script Editor to function (covered in Chapter 05).

Prompt to Save. If the Prompt to Save checkbox is checked, SMS Installer prompts you to save the current working file when starting a new file. If this is unchecked, SMS Installer automatically saves the current working file and opens a new one.

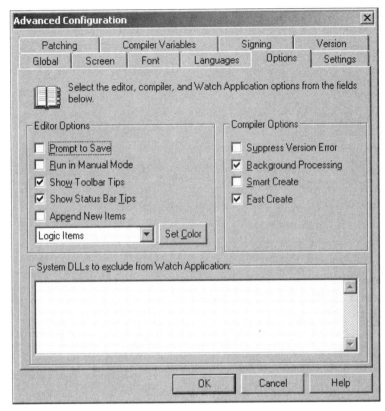

Figure 4-68 *Options tab.*

Run in Manual Mode. The script defines where files are placed. These locations make up the Windows, System, and Installation directories. With this checkbox checked, SMS Installer will prompt you for the preferred location for each file during the installation when run through SMS Installer. This is a good troubleshooting tool to make sure files are being copied into the right directories and with the correct filename.

Show Toolbar Tips. This item is checked by default. This is the option for turning on and off the small help boxes that pop up automatically when the mouse cursor hovers over the toolbar icon.

Show Status Bar Tips. Checked by default, this option is for turning on and off the additional, helpful information tips at the bottom of the Script Editor screen in the status bar area.

Append New Items.   By default, when new action items are added using the Script Editor, they are placed before the high-lighted line. Checking this checkbox puts the new action item after the current highlighted line.

Set Color.   The Set Color option assigns different colors to the common script items. Color coding helps in quickly locating certain areas of the script for troubleshooting. It also helps document the script for reference in the future. The specific items that can be color-coded apply to the Script Editor, which is covered in more detail in Chapter 05. The Set Color button uses the same standard Basic Colors and Custom Colors dialog boxes to set the script item color. Select the specific script item from the drop-down list, and click *Set Color* to set the color for the selected item. This feature is most useful if the colors are standardized across an organization.

Items that can be color-coded are shown in Table 4-7.

Compiler Options

The Compiler Options section relates directly to the compiler itself. The compiler options are the script items that affect how the compiler will function during the compilation of the SMS Installer script.

Suppress Version Error.   SMS Installer uses the internal compiler routines `VerFindFile` and `VerInstallFile` to verify file versions during the file copy process. These methods can be customized using the `Install File(s)` script item covered in Chapter 05. Some files do not contain version resource information and will generate an error message during the installation. Checking the Suppress Version Error checkbox will eliminate this error message.

Background Processing.   When SMS Installer compiles the script into an executable, by default the procedure is processor-intensive. Checking this checkbox causes the compilation to be run as a background task on the computer, which allows other applications to be run during the compile process.

Table 4-7   *Items for color coding.*

Item	Description
Logic Items	Logic items include the branching logic commands such as If/While/Then/Else/End.
Remark Items	Remark items are used to comment-out lines. A valuable use for this item is to document the script in detail within the script structure itself.
Install/Copy File Items	Relates to the areas of the script that do the actual copying of the files compressed into the executable.
Compiler Variable Items	Compiler variables is the logic SMS Installer uses when compiling the script.
Include Script Items	The include item in the script refers to the SMS Installer function of including and running external SMS Installer scripts with the current script.
New Variable Value	New variables placed into the script will be assigned a color.

Note   Running the compile process as a background task makes the compile process take up to 50 percent longer.

Smart Create.   The Smart Create option for the SMS Installer compiler helps automate updating the compiled executable with new file information. With Smart Create enabled, SMS Installer detects file changes such as date and time and file size and includes them in the new executable during the RUN and MAKEDISK actions.

Fast Create.   The Fast Create checkbox speeds up the compile process by copying the old SMS Installer executable into the new one as long as the size or date has not changed. If the size or date has changed, SMS Installer automatically recompresses the file.

System DLLs to Exclude from Watch Application

This section offers a manual entry list for including DLL and VBX files that should be excluded during the SMS Installer watch procedure. This is the chance to exclude common files that should already be on the target computer. Because the target computer may have different versions of certain DLL and VBX files installed (for an application's dependency), adding them to this list will keep the watch procedure from incorporating them into the compiled script. This keeps the necessary files from being overwritten during the installation, which could cause applications to stop functioning.

> The filename, the period, and the extension should be entered, one per line.   **Note**

Settings Tab

The Settings tab, shown in Figure 4-69, deals with the location of additional files and directories for further customizing the compiled executable. If the compile process is completed with the defaults, these defaults are referenced by variables seen on the Compiler Variables tab in this group (seen later). This tab allows the customizing of these variables for the specific script.

Installation EXE Name

The Installation EXE Name changes the path and filename of the compiled executable. Normally, the executable will retain the script name and be saved into the same directory in which the script is saved. The SMS Installer script remains in the directory where it was originally saved.

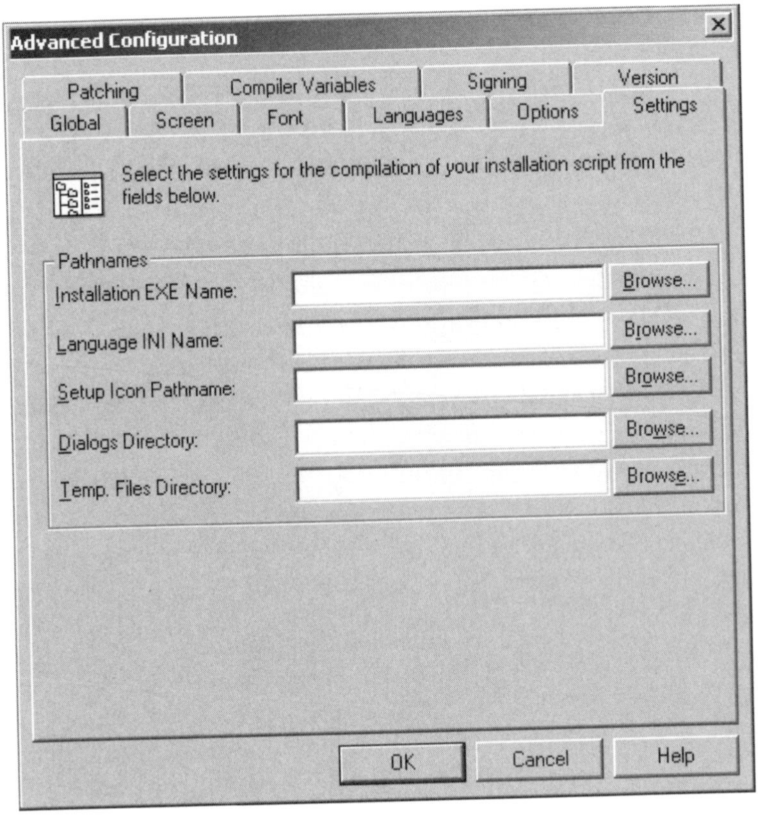

Figure 4-69 *Settings tab.*

Language INI Name

This option references a different location and name for the language information file. The default location is in the root of the SMS Installer directory in the LANGUAGE.INI file.

Setup Icon Pathname

This entry will compile an icon file into the final executable. This function uses standard Windows icon files with the .ICO extension. The new file replaces the original SMS Installer icon. This allows further customization and personalization of the installation. It is beneficial for better identifying repackages by incorporating the original software product icon into the executable. It is also useful for personalizing standalone utilities.

Since this function will accept any standard Windows icon file, it is a smart idea to keep some handy.

Some noteworthy resources for downloading icon file libraries can be found at http://www.zdnet.com. Icon files are generally compiled into an application vendor's executables and DLL files. The files will sometimes hold several different program icons. There are several utilities that will extract the icons from these files. One of interest is IconExplorer. It is a free utility available for download from several Internet locations, but it can also be found at http://www.zdnet.com.

IconExplorer is an easy-to-use utility with a simple, one-screen interface. It allows you to browse the file system for executables and DLL files. When a file is selected, it displays all the icons in the file, along with a checkbox beside each picture. It extracts the icon files and saves them as either a Windows bitmap or an icon file.

Dialogs Directory

The Dialogs Directory entry redirects SMS Installer to a new or alternate location for the dialog box files. The default directory for the dialog boxes is under the SMS Installer directory in a \DIALOGS\Template directory. The files are referenced by a DLG file extension.

Temp. Files Directory

This entry changes the directory that SMS Installer uses to store its temporary files during the compile process. This could be helpful if trying to diagnose compiler problems. Creating a new directory and redirecting the temporary output to this directory will help determine how far the compiler is progressing through the procedure. Using this method is also helpful for redirecting temp file output if one hard disk drive is full and another has enough free space to handle the temporary files.

Patching Tab

SMS Installer provides the feature of being able to patch an application. Patching an application involves replacing only files that have been updated instead of having to reinstall the entire application. SMS Installer compares each file in the original installed version with the upgrade version and creates a new, smaller version with only the changes. The smaller file is much easier to distribute for updates to applications than distributing a full application installation.

The Patching tab, shown in Figure 4-70, provides the following selections for customizing the patching process.

Do Not Create Patching Updates (test mode)/Create Patching Updates
These two options turn Patching mode on and off.

Error Checking
During the compile process of a patch, errors can be defined if matching files and file versions are found. If errors are enabled,

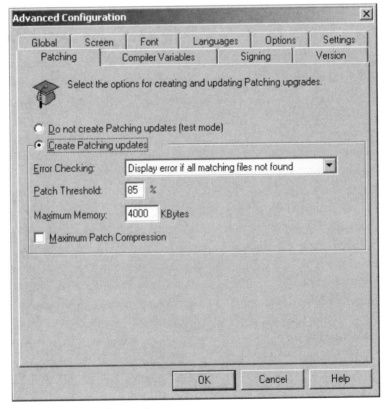

Figure 4-70 *Patching tab.*

the compile process stops without creating the installation file. The drop-down list for Error Checking contains the different options for the error messages:

1. *Do not display errors* Turns off the error messages

2. *Display error if all matching files not found* Displays an error message if all files in the patch are not found

3. *Display error if any matching files not found* Displays an error message if even one matching file is not found

Patch Threshold

During the patch process, SMS Installer compares the old file to the new files that should be included in the patch. If many of the same files are included in the patch but the files have different sizes or different versions, the patching process will include all the files. Eventually, the patching executable could become larger than if a totally new distribution file was created. The Patch Threshold sets the percentage value at which the patching process will stop and a complete distribution file will be created. The default is 85 percent. In this instance, the patching process will compile the patch until it is within 85 percent of the full installation executable size. Depending on the size of the complete installation, you may decide the percentage should be 50 percent.

Maximum Memory

The Maximum Memory entry allows the setting of a threshold on the computer's memory for the patching process. The patching process uses a considerable amount of computer memory for file sizes over about 3 MB. The maximum memory amount should be set to 2 MB less than the total physical memory on the computer.

Maximum Patch Compression

Checking this checkbox tells SMS Installer to use the maximum compression rate to compress the patch executable. This makes the distributable file as small as possible. This does cause the compilation process to take much longer.

Note	To create a successful patched application, the SMS Installer source computer must have both the original installation and the upgrade version installed. These different versions must be installed in different directories so SMS Installer can compare the files. Otherwise, if the upgrade were allowed to install over top of the old version, files with the same name would be overwritten. SMS Installer compares the differences between filenames, file sizes, and file versions.

Compiler Variables Tab

Compiler variables are a bit different than the standard program variables. These are variables that the compiler needs to complete the compile process. The compiler variables look the same as standard variables but must be defined on the Compiler Variables tab. SMS Installer inserts an underscore character (_) at the beginning and end of the variable name for the compiler variables, as shown in Figure 4-71. This is to make the variables easier to identify in the script. You should follow this same convention if adding any new compiler variables. It is also important to use this naming method to keep from duplicating variable names between compiler variables and standard script variables.

Compiler Variables Section

The SMS Installer default compiler variables represents the locations to the System32 directory and the SMS Installer program directory. In this instance:

```
_SYS_ = C:\WINNT\SYSTEM32
```

and

```
_SMSINSTL_ = E:\Program Files\Microsoft SMS Installer
```

Clicking on the Add button includes additional compiler variables. Clicking the Delete button removes the highlighted entry from the list.

Both the Add button and the Properties button bring up the Compiler Variable Settings screen in Figure 4-72.

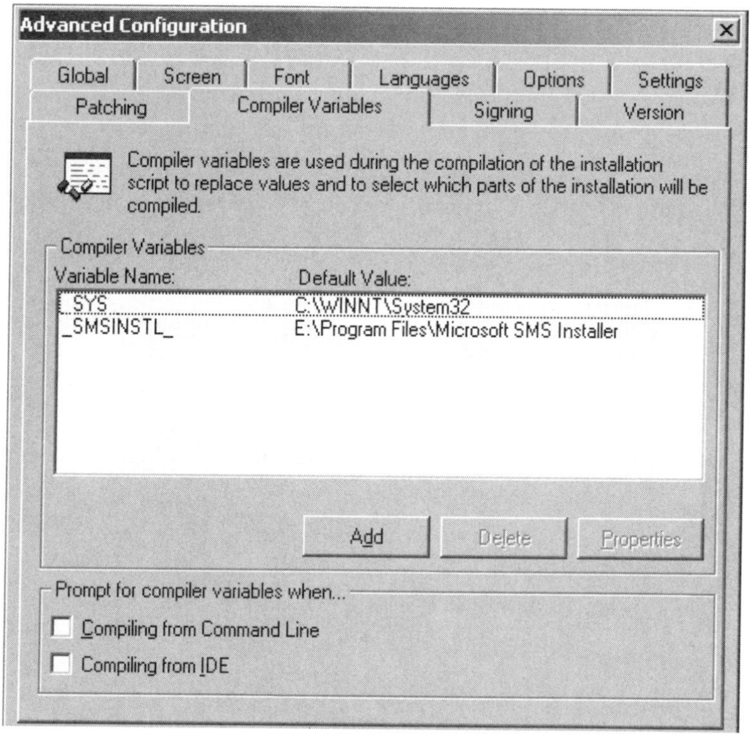

Figure 4-71 *Compiler Variables tab.*

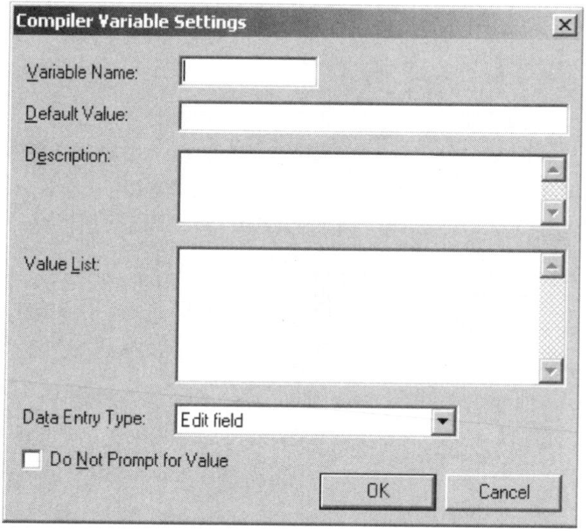

Figure 4-72 *Compiler Variable Settings.*

Variable Name. The Variable Name field is the name you want to give the new compiler variable. Remember, following the SMS Installer convention of placing an underscore character at the beginning and end of the variable name will make it easier to distinguish a compiler variable from a standard script variable. It will also prevent duplicate variable names between the compiler and the script.

Default Value. When the Do Not Prompt for Value checkbox is checked (covered later in this section) or either option from the Prompt for Compiler Variables When...section (also covered later in this section), the value entered into the Default Value line will remain. Otherwise, if these selections are not chosen, the user will be prompted for the specific value, and the default value will be changed to match the user input. The Default Value field should be used to permanently set the value of the compiler variable.

Description

The Description section allows entry of information about the compiler variable. Be as descriptive as possible, since the user will view this information during the compilation process. Give enough information for the user to understand what value to assign the variable.

Value List

If the Data Entry Type is set to List of Values (single-select) or List of Values (multi-select), this entry box contains the values the user has to choose from to assign the value to the compiler variable. The values entered here will be displayed as a radio button dialog box for selecting the value to assign to the variable.

Data Entry Type

The Data Entry Type drop-down box predetermines the way that the user can select the values for the compiler variable. If the Default Value information is entered and the Do Not Prompt for Value checkbox is checked, this selection is ignored.

- *Edit Field* Gives the user a manual entry field for entering which value to assign to the compiler variable

- *Edit Field with Browse Button* Gives the user a manual entry field just as the Edit field, but also displays a Browse button to allow the user to select a file or path from the local PC to place into the compiler variable
- *List of Values (single-select)* Displays a radio dialog box for selecting one of the values referenced in the Value List box
- *List of Values (multi-select)* Displays a radio dialog box for selecting multiple values referenced in the Value List box.

The radio dialog box will be covered in more depth in Chapter 05. The following are examples of what would be displayed at compile time. See Figure 4-73.

Do Not Prompt for Value. Check this checkbox if you do not want the user to be prompted to enter a value for the specific Compiler Variable. The Default Value information must be set.

Prompt for Compiler Variables When...Section

If any of the compiler variables are configured to prompt the user to choose values for the variable, they will not be prompted

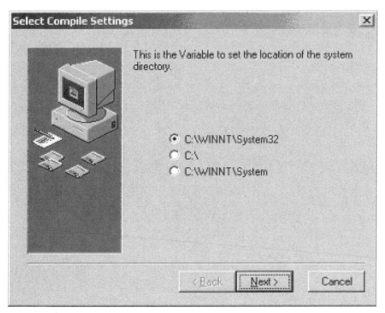

Figure 4-73 *Select Compile Settings.*

unless one or both of the following checkboxes is checked (depending on the compile method—command line or IDE).

Compiling from the Command Line Checkbox.   This option causes SMS Installer to prompt for the compiler variables configured in the Compiler Variables section when the script is compiled using the command-line procedure (see Chapter 10 for more information on compiling from the command line).

Compiling from IDE Checkbox.   This option causes SMS Installer to prompt for the compiler variables configured in the Compiler Variables section. Again, IDE stands for Integrated Development Environment.

Signing Tab

The Signing tab, shown in Figure 4-74, represents the information entered to create a secure installation file. This tab includes the data for location of the secure credentials information. (For more details on signing, see "Authenticode Technology" in Chapter 07.)

Note   Creating a signed installation will produce an executable that can *only* be run under 32-bit Windows operating systems. It will not run on 16-bit operating systems, such as Windows 3.x or Windows for Workgroups.

By default, the code signing is turned off. Clicking in the Create a Code-Signed Installation radio dialog button turns on code signing. Once the code signing is turned on, the other options underneath are enabled.

Web URL

This field is the Web location of the code-signed installation. Use the standard Web format, for example: http://www.URL_Location.com.

Descriptive Name

This entry provides a place to enter details about the Web location that contains the installation. Enter enough information so

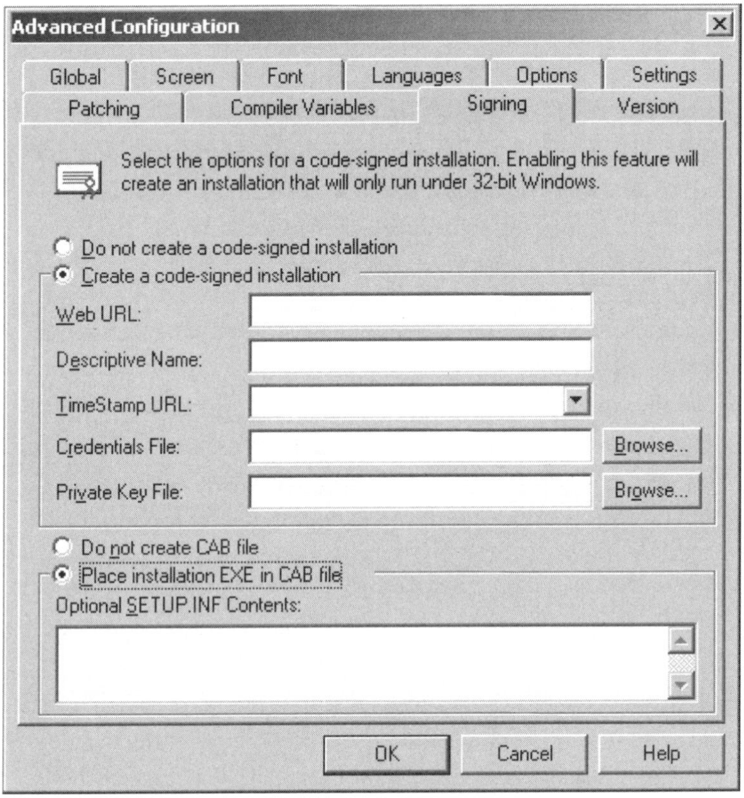

Figure 4-74 *Signing tab.*

that the user will be comfortable downloading and running from the Web.

TimeStamp URL

This field is the Web location that contains the time and date information about the installation file. The timestamp will tell when the file was last updated, giving users a point of reference when checking to see if they have the most current version of the installation.

Credentials File

This field specifies the Software Publishing Credentials file that should be on the local computer to be incorporated into the compiled executable. This is the certificate the user will see when the installation file is executed. A Credentials file is identified by the .SPC file extension.

Private Key File

This field specifies the Private Key file on the local computer that is incorporated into the compiled executable. A Private Key file is identified by the .PVK file extension.

CAB Files

The CAB (or cabinet) file is a Microsoft standard format file for holding files needed for an installation. The CAB file uses a high compression rate to organize the installation files into a smaller format. A Setup.INF file accompanies these CAB files. The Setup.INF file is a setup file with a specific structure that holds all the information for installing the files extracted from the CAB files.

If the Place Installation EXE in CAB File checkbox is enabled, the SMS Installer compiled file will be compressed into a CAB file.

In the Optional SETUP.INF Contents box, you can enter information that the CAB file needs in order to perform the installation. You must have an understanding of the structure of the SETUP.INF file (see "Example of a Setup.INF File" in Chapter 10 for more information).

The CAB file is identified by the .CAB file extension.

Version Tab

You may be familiar with checking version information on a file. If you right-click on a file and choose Properties, you will be presented with specific file data on the Version tab, shown in Figure 4-75. Vendors include header information in their executable files that describe the file type, file version, product associated with the file, specific language, and any legal trademarks.

The Version tab in SMS Installer allows you to add the same type of versioning information to the SMS Installer compiled executable. This is helpful when using the same executable name for future packages. The version information for each different executable can be easily obtained. It is also helpful for users. If they call for support, they can quickly obtain version information on

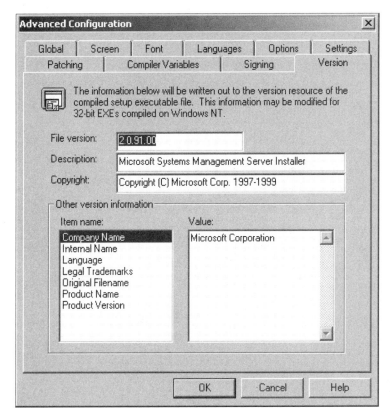

Figure 4-75 *Version tab.*

the executable to help diagnose possible problems. Another reason to use this feature is to enter a company copyright warning to help deter people outside of the organization from installing software not licensed to them. It's a way of tracking the source of the package. In addition, when creating standalone utilities using SMS Installer, this information is valuable in determining different revisions of the utility to make sure the user has the latest update.

SMS 2.0 also uses this information when doing a software inventory. SMS 2.0 "drills down" to the file information header to pull out the file resource information. In the SMS Administrator Console GUI, through the Resource Explorer on a particular computer, this information can be viewed. It can be used to create reports through the Crystal Info MMC snap-in.

Note   The Versioning feature of the SMS Installer–generated executable
can only be used when compiled on a Windows NT computer for
a 32-bit operating system. Because of this, the tab will be enabled
only if the Destination Platforms selection on the Global tab reads
32-bit Windows (32-bit EXE).

File Version

The File Version field is the version number of the executable.
This field uses a format of XXXX.XXXX.XXXX.XXXX, repre-
senting the maximum numeric characters that can be entered. The
total 16 characters do not have to be used, but a character in each
of the dot sections must be used. For instance, the first version of
a utility may be 1.0.0.0 as the File Version. For an update to version 1.0.0.0, the value could be 1.0.0.1. The twenty-fourth revision of the utility could be 1.0000.0000.0024. Do not use
alphanumeric characters in the dot sections, only numeric.

Description

This entry can contain up to 256 characters and should contain as much information as possible about the executable.

Copyright

The Copyright entry lists the copyright information for the
executable.

Other Version Information

This section adds additional information that is compiled into
the executable.

- *Company Name*   This is the company or organization name.
  You can also input specific department information or who
  the target audience should be.

- *Internal Name*   This is generally the internal name of the executable.

- *Language*   This entry is for the languages that are available
  through the Languages tab selections. This field is editable
  only if you switch to the Languages tab, add a language, then

click back to the Versions tab and make the changes. Once the field has been edited and focus has changed to another value, it is disabled until you make another change to the Languages tab.

- *Legal Trademarks* Not editable.

- *Original Filename* This is generally the actual filename of the executable.

- *Product Name* This is the actual name of the executable. For instance, if the executable is an installation file, the entry could be "Adobe Acrobat 3.01 Installation." If the executable is a utility, it could be "My Organization My UtilityName."

- *Product Version* This is the version of the actual product that is being installed. For Adobe Acrobat, the version would be 3.01.00.00 (the Product Version uses the same rules as the File Version when setting the version number). If the executable is a utility, the Product Version should generally match the File Version.

The Script Editor

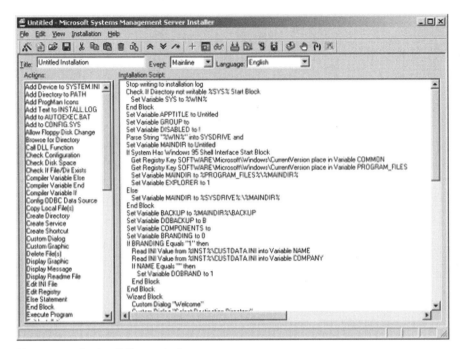

Figure 5-1 *Script Editor window.*

The SMS Installer Script Editor is the "guts" of the program. From the view shown in Figure 5-1, you can see the actual script that is created by the repackage in the Installation Script window, or a blank Installation Script window if starting in Script Editor mode. The Script Editor is made up of two parts: the Actions window and the Installation Script window.

Note   If you create a package starting with the Script Editor then switch to the Installation Expert, some of your script items will be lost. If you create a package starting with the Installation Expert then switch back and forth between the Installation Expert and the Script Editor, your script additions will remain.

Using the Script Editor, you are limited only by your imagination, your familiarity with the script actions, and your understanding of the target operating system. You can script entire solutions, from concept to finished product, using only the Script Editor interface.

The Interface

The SMS Installer Script Editor includes some quick buttons, which allow you to easily edit features of the script.

Installation Expert This quickly switches to the Installation Expert interface.

New This quickly creates a new script, prompting to save if a current script is open and changes have been made.

Open This opens an existing script from the file system.

Save This saves the current script.

Cut This cuts the highlighted script item(s), either for discarding or for pasting to another section of the script.

Copy This copies the highlighted script item(s) in the Windows clipboard. It makes the contents of the clipboard available to copy either into another section of the script or to a standard text file.

Paste This pastes the contents of the Windows clipboard to another part of the script.

Delete This permanently deletes the highlighted script item(s). Similar to the Cut feature, but the deleted item(s) are no longer available to use.

Duplicate This duplicates the currently highlighted item(s). Depending on what option is selected on the Options tab in the Installation Properties, the duplicated items will either be appended to the selection or placed before it.

The Installation Properties of the script is the same information as in the Advanced Configuration group on the Options Tab in the Installation Expert. The Installation Properties can be accessed via

Note

> the Eyeglass icon (upcoming) or by pressing Ctrl-Z simultane-
> ously.

 Move Up   This changes the position of the highlighted script item(s) by moving it up the script.

 Move Down   This changes the position of the highlighted script item(s) by moving it down the script.

 Comment   This comments out a line. SMS Installer skips lines that are commented out. This is similar to the REM (remark) statement in batch files. The comment in SMS Installer is denoted as the symbols /*.

 Add Action   This adds an exact duplicate script action as is highlighted in the script.

 Edit Script Item   This edits the currently highlighted script item in the Installation Script window.

 Installation Properties   This brings up the Advanced Configuration group that is present in the Installation Expert. As mentioned in Chapter 04, these items are specific to the compiled script.

 Compile   This compiles the script into an executable file. This is the same function as the Compile button in the Installation Expert.

 Test   This compiles and tests the current script without running the actual executable files. This is the same function as the Test button in the Installation Expert.

 Run   This compiles the current script and runs the compiled executable file. This is the same function as the Run button in the Installation Expert.

 Make Floppies   This function compiles the script into floppy-sized chunks and prompts for each diskette until the complete installation has been copied to the floppy media.

The other buttons on the SMS Installer Script Editor Toolbar deal with debugging the script.

Debugging the Script

Clicking the Go button starts the debugging procedure. This compiles the script and starts the installation. The Go button must be clicked again, once the script has been started, to continue the debugging process.

Clicking the Set Break Point button places a break point or "bookmark" at specific spots in the script. This gives you the ability to watch sections of the script at a time instead of watching the entire script run through to completion.

When a break point is set, a red circle is placed as a marker. To remove a break point, highlight the marked line and click the Set Break Point button. Clicking the Go button starts the debugger, and it stops at the first break point. The Go button must be clicked again after each set break point to restart the debugger until the next break point is reached.

Clicking the Single Step button compiles the script, starts the installation, and runs the script one line at a time. The script stops after each line and is continued when you press the Single Step button again.

Clicking the Stop Debugging button halts the debugging process completely.

The debugger places the arrow symbol at the beginning of the current line being acted upon.

During the debugging process, the relative variables are listed at the left of the script. The variables can be modified during the debugging process by double-clicking on them. See Figure 5-2.

The Title, shown in Figure 5-3, is the name of the installation that is being created. The SET APPTITLE variable (shown later in this chapter) also sets the installation title.

The Event drop-down box, shown in Figure 5-4, allows selection of the different scripts that are included with the main script. There are three options:

1. *Mainline*   This is the main script.

2. *Exit*   This script can be modified to perform procedures when the user has completed the installation and exited the

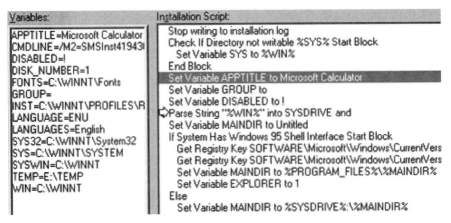

Figure 5-2 *Debugging Processing window.*

Figure 5-3 *The Title of the installation.*

Figure 5-4 *The Event drop-down box.*

setup. A possible procedure could be running the application after the installation is complete.

3. *Cancel*   This script can be modified to perform procedures when the user cancels the installation. Some possible procedures could be cleaning up files or setting the system environment back to its original configuration.

The Language drop-down box, shown in Figure 5-5, allows quick selection of the supported Languages in the script. These are defined on the Languages tab in the Installation Properties.

Figure 5-5 *The Language drop-down box.*

Script Actions Reference

The Script Actions window of SMS Installer is currently composed of 68 items. These 68 items make up the functions of the SMS Installer script. Many of these script items have multiple options and multiple functions built into them.

Each section in the Script Actions Reference follows the same format. It starts with the action description, and then follows with examples of both the Installation Script window and the script sample. For the most part, all script samples are full-featured and can be used in your current scripts. Any other script actions included in the same script for the section are also listed for quick reference. Note also that the script actions are presented in alphabetical order.

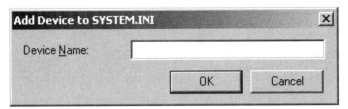

Figure 5-6 *Add Device to SYSTEM.INI dialog box.*

Add Device to SYSTEM.INI

The Add Device to SYSTEM.INI dialog box, as shown in
Figure 5-6, is similar to the Device tab in the System Configuration Group in the Installation Expert. The difference is that the
Device tab allowed selection of a file included in the recorded
repackage. The script action allows only entering the device line
that will be placed at the bottom of the [386Enh] section of the
SYSTEM.INI file. If installing a new device, the device file should
already be referenced in a section of the script. This must be done
using the Install File(s) script action (covered later in this chapter)
before the Add Device to SYSTEM.INI script action is defined.
For an example of a SYSTEM.INI file, see Chapter 10. It's also
possible to add a device to the SYSTEM.INI that is known to
already exist on the local computer, or to use this script action to
force a reboot of the computer as in the RESTART variable in the
following example. For detailed information on using the
RESTART variable, see Chapter 08.

Note   This script action should only be used to add or modify devices in
the SYSTEM.INI file. For other modifications to the SYSTEM.INI file,
such as display drivers, use the Edit INI File script action, described
later in this chapter.

When the Add Device to SYSTEM.INI script action is used
and the specified device does not already exist, the line will be
placed after the last line in the [386Enh] section. If the device is
already present and the values are the same, the line will be left
alone. If the device is already present but the value is different,
the current line will be retained but will be commented-out with a

semicolon as the first character. Then the new device and value will be placed at the end of the [386Enh] section. Using this script action will cause SMS Installer to prompt the user to restart the computer. For information on removing devices from the SYS-TEM.INI, see the Remove from SYSTEM.INI script action in this chapter.

> Before modifying a device, it's a smart practice to check if a device **Tip**
> already exists in the [386Enh] section. You can use the Read INI
> Value script action to verify its existence (described later in this
> chapter).

As with the Device tab in the Installation Expert, this script action is for backward-compatibility with 16-bit applications. The Windows registry, described in Chapter 07, "Registry Overview" replaces the functionality of the SYSTEM.INI file.

> Most device files will be located in the \Windows\System direc- **Note**
> tory on a Win 9x and Win 3.x computer and the \WINNT\
> SYSTEM32 directory on a Windows NT computer. If the device is
> located in any directory other than the default, the full path must
> be included with the device name.

Add Device to SYSTEM.INI Options

Device Name The only available field is the entry of the device that will be added to or modified in the [386Enh] section. This field accepts text strings, predefined variables, or both, up to 255 characters.

Add Device to SYSTEM.INI Example

The following example uses the RESTART variable shown in Chapter 08. It places a RESTART=S variable in the SMS Installer script, which forces the Windows operating system to shut down and restart the computer.

SMS Installer Window:
See Figure 5-7.

Add device RESTART=S to SYSTEM.INI

Figure 5-7 *Add Device to SYSTEM.INI script action window.*

Script:

```
————-Begin Script
item: Add to SYSTEM.INI
  Device=RESTART=S
end
————-End Script
```

Add Directory to Path

The Add Directory to Path dialog box, shown in Figure 5-8, allows you to modify the computer environment at startup. When a path is made available to the operating environment, files contained in the path directory are accessible to all the programs. For instance, some programs install their DLL files in the same directory as the application executable. For the program to run correctly, the operating system must have direct access to the DLL files. This is accomplished by keeping the program's directory path in memory. You can do a quick check to see what is already defined in the PATH environment by opening an MS-DOS prompt, typing PATH, and hitting the Enter key. The contents of the PATH environment variable are displayed in a list with each separate directory entry isolated by semicolons.

Note   The Select Directory field will accept up to 255 characters. Keep in mind that each operating system imposes its own limits on the allowed length of the PATH environment variable. Some applications impose their own PATH limit and will fail to function if the

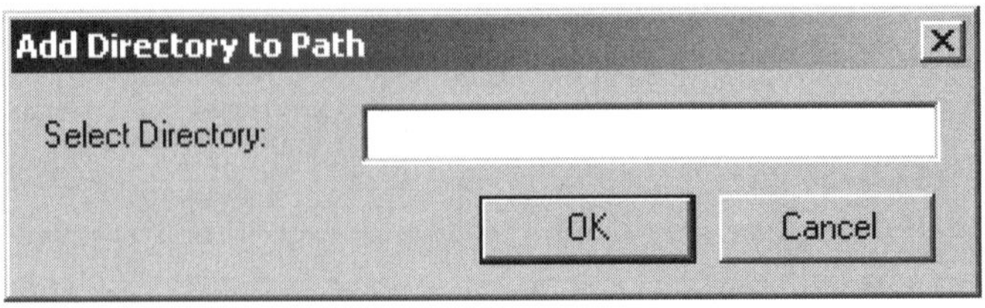

Figure 5-8 *ADD Directory to Path dialog box.*

limit is exceeded. Try to keep the entire PATH environment variable as short as possible. Unless using Windows 3.x, a good rule of thumb to follow is to keep the PATH under 126 characters. If using Windows 3.x, keep the PATH under 64 characters.

The Add Directory to Path entry will accept any string of text (directory path information) or predefined variables, or both. The result will be appended to the computer's current PATH environment variable. In Windows 3.x, the PATH information is contained in the Autoexec.bat file; in Windows 9x and Windows NT, the PATH information is contained in the registry.

If the directory already exists in the path, this script action will be ignored.   **Note**

Add Directory to Path Example

The following example uses the Set Variable script action (described later in this chapter) to set the ROOT variable to equal C:\, and then uses the ROOT variable to place the APPNAME directory into the operating environment.

Other Script Actions Used:

Set Variable

SMS Installer Window:

See Figure 5-9.

Script:

```
————-Begin Script
item: Set Variable
  Variable=ROOT
  Value=C:\
end
item: Add Directory to Path
  Directory=%ROOT%APPNAME\
end
————-End Script
```

```
Set Variable ROOT to C:\
Add %ROOT%APPNAME\ to PATH
```

Figure 5-9 *ADD Directory to Path script action window.*

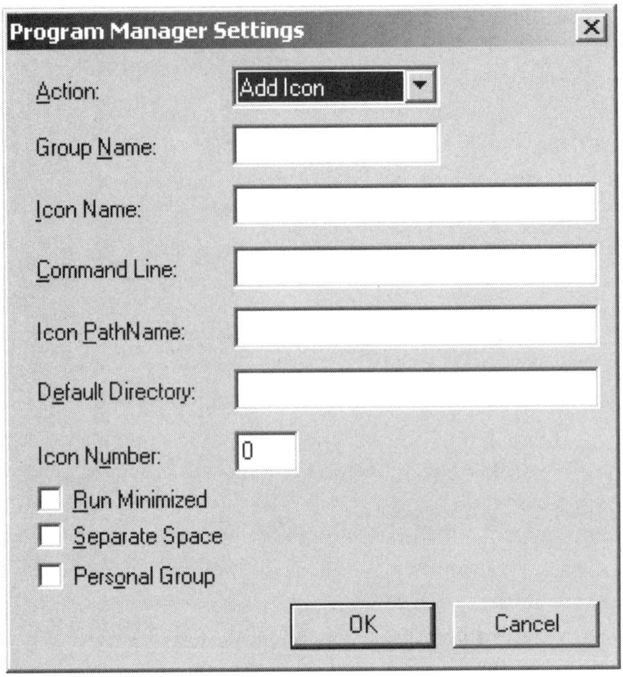

Figure 5-10 *Add ProgMan Icons dialog box.*

Add ProgMan Icons

The Add ProgMan Icons dialog box, shown in Figure 5-10, allows you to do more than the script name suggests. Not only does the script action add icons it also deletes icons and deletes Program Manager program groups. In the Windows 3.x operating system, the Program Manager was the main window that contained all the program icons and icon groups. In Windows 9x and Windows NT, Program Manager refers to the shortcuts and program groups that are accessed by navigating to Start|Programs.

Note   For Windows 9x and Windows NT operating systems, it is much better to use the Create Shortcut script action. The Add ProgMan Icons script action communicates with the older DDE (Dynamic Data Exchange) Windows technology. Though this method will work with both 16-bit and 32-bit operating systems, using the Create Shortcut item does not invoke the DDE, but rather creates links inside the Explorer shell. This way takes less operating over-head because the program can be run from its exact location instead of being managed by a background process. Also, when using this script action, icons and groups can only be created under the Programs menu on Windows 9x and Windows NT com-puters. Icons and groups cannot be created directly on the Start menu as with the Create Shortcut script action.

Add ProgMan Icons Options

Action　The Action drop-down list has three options that specify how the Start menu or Program Manager should be modified:

- *Add Icon*　Adds an icon in the specified group name. If an icon with the same name exists, it is overwritten with the new one.
- *Delete Icon*　Deletes an icon from the specified group name.
- *Delete Group*　Deletes the entire group and its contents (icons).

Add Group is not an option in the Action drop-down list. The group is created automatically when an icon is added. All program groups must have contents. You cannot create an empty group.

Note

Group Name　Group Name is a required field. The name entered here will be the group name that is created by the script action.

Icon Name　The information entered into the Icon Name field will be used to name the icon that is created. Input descriptive information, since this will be what the user sees when accessing the program. If the field is left blank, the Icon Name will default to the actual program executable name.

Selecting the Delete Icon action makes the Icon Name a required field. The icon's exact name must be input, or the Delete Icon action will fail.

Note

Command Line   The Command Line field contains the directory path information (including executable name and extension) that points to the program file.

Icon PathName   The Icon PathName field contains the location (directory and filename) of the icon file on the local computer. If this field is left blank, the icon will default to the first icon contained in the executable specified in the Command Line field. If selecting a different icon, other than the one that was included with the program, enter that information here as well. This field can point to any icon file. Icons can be used from DLL files, executables, and icon files (ICO).

Default Directory   This optional field configures the new icon to point to another location when running the executable. This is useful when the program is reliant on files in other directories that are not part of the PATH environment variable.

Icon Number   The Icon Number relates to icons contained in DLL or executable files. Icons are assigned numbers based on an internal index by the software vendor. This index is based on positive integers from 0-9999.

Run Minimized   This option configures the new icon to open the program in minimized mode on the Windows 9x and Windows NT taskbar and as an icon in Windows 3.x. Normally, a program will open in full screen or in a window size specified by the vendor. This option overrides the program's default.

Separate Space   This option configures the new icon to run in its own memory space on a Windows NT computer. Windows NT is a true 32-bit operating system and must use a 16-bit subsystem for running 16-bit applications. This subsystem runs outside the normal Windows NT memory space. If the Separate Space option is selected, 16-bit applications will be given their own memory space in which to run. This enables crash protection for Windows NT should the 16-bit application not be completely compatible.

Personal Group   The Personal Group option enables the Add ProgMan Icons action to employ user profiles (described in detail

Add Icon "MyGroupIcon" to Program Manager Group "MyGroup"

Figure 5-11 *Add ProgMan Icons script action window.*

in "Profiles Overview" in Chapter 07) for Windows 9x and Windows NT computers. If this checkbox is not selected, the icon(s) will be created for all users of the computer instead of just the user who is currently logged on.

Add ProgMan Icons Example

The following script examples show the different options for this script action. All the information stays the same except for the modification of the Flags information. These flags tell SMS Installer which options have been selected in the script action.

For this example, the Windows Calculator is the target of the icon.

SMS Installer Window:
See Figure 5-11.

Add Icon Script:

```
————-Begin Script
item: Add ProgMan Icon
  Group=MyGroup
  Icon Name English=MyGroupIcon
  Command Line=C:\WINNT\SYSTEM32\CALC.EXE
  Icon Pathname=C:\WINNT\SYSTEM32\CALC.EXE
  Default Directory=C:\WINNT\SYSTEM32\
end
————-End Script
```

```
Delete Icon Script:
————-Begin Script
item: Add ProgMan Icon
  Group=MyGroup
  Icon Name English=MyGroupIcon
  Command Line=C:\WINNT\SYSTEM32\CALC.EXE
  Icon Pathname=C:\WINNT\SYSTEM32\CALC.EXE
  Default Directory=C:\WINNT\SYSTEM32\
  Flags=00000001
end
————-End Script
```

```
Delete Group Script:
————-Begin Script
item: Add ProgMan Icon
  Group=MyGroup
  Icon Name English=MyGroupIcon
  Command Line=C:\WINNT\SYSTEM32\CALC.EXE
  Icon Pathname=C:\WINNT\SYSTEM32\CALC.EXE
  Default Directory=C:\WINNT\SYSTEM32\
  Flags=00000010
end
————-End Script
```

```
Add Icon to Personal Directory Script:
————-Begin Script
item: Add ProgMan Icon
  Group=MyGroup
  Icon Name English=MyGroupIcon
  Command Line=C:\WINNT\SYSTEM32\CALC.EXE
  Icon Pathname=C:\WINNT\SYSTEM32\CALC.EXE
  Default Directory=C:\WINNT\SYSTEM32\
  Flags=01000000
end
————-End Script
```

Add Text to INSTALL.LOG

The Add Text to INSTALL.LOG dialog box (see Figure 5-12) directs SMS Installer to write custom information to the INSTALL.LOG file. The INSTALL.LOG file is the file that is created during the installation that records all physical changes to the target computer. These changes include files copied, icons and icon groups that are created, and registry additions and modifications. This information is used when the uninstall procedure is performed. Adding custom information to the INSTALL.LOG file is useful for separating the different installation procedures. For instance, you may want to separate the file copy section from the registry modifications section for troubleshooting purposes.

The input of this script action will accept 255 characters, but you may want to shorten this to 60 characters to make sure the information is readable in the log. If more characters are required, use multiple instances of this script action.

Before this script action can be used, the INSTALL.LOG file must be opened. Therefore, the Add Text to INSTALL.LOG script action must be used in conjunction with the Open/Close

Figure 5-12 *Add Text to INSTALL.LOG dialog box.*

INSTALL.LOG script action (covered later in this chapter). The example below shows the best practice for this procedure. If the INSTALL.LOG file does not already exist, it will be created.

Add Text to INSTALL.LOG Example

The example listed below sets the log file to be created in the root of the C:\ drive by first setting the %ROOT% variable. The rest of the log file information is contained in the Installation Properties dialog shown in Figure 5-13.

The example uses the Open/Close INSTALL.LOG script action to open the log file, and then it writes several lines of information to clearly separate the file copy section and the registry modification section from the rest of the script. The log file output is also listed. The log file reports the time and date that it was modified/created, the title of the installation, and the information added by the script action.

Other Script Actions Used:

1. Check Disk Space
2. Set Variable
3. Open/Close INSTALL.LOG

Install Log Pathname:	%ROOT%INSTALL.LOG

Figure 5-13 *Install Log Pathname entry.*

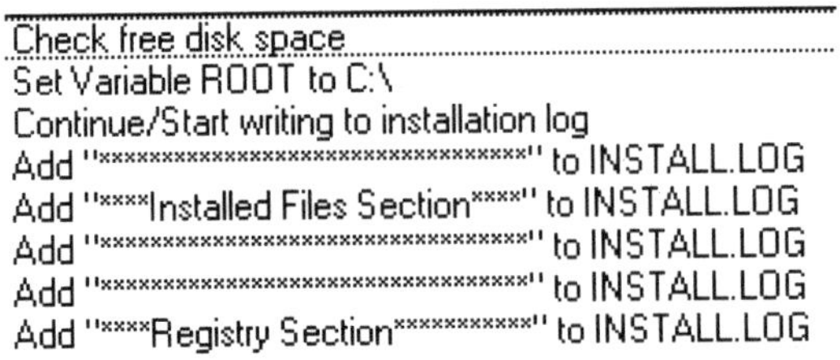

```
Check free disk space
Set Variable ROOT to C:\
Continue/Start writing to installation log
Add "xxxxxxxxxxxxxxxxxxxxxxxxxxxxxxxxx" to INSTALL.LOG
Add "****Installed Files Section****" to INSTALL.LOG
Add "xxxxxxxxxxxxxxxxxxxxxxxxxxxxxxxxx" to INSTALL.LOG
Add "xxxxxxxxxxxxxxxxxxxxxxxxxxxxxxxxx" to INSTALL.LOG
Add "****Registry Section***********" to INSTALL.LOG
```

Figure 5-14 *Add Text to INTALL.LOG script action window.*

SMS Installer Window:

See Figure 5-14.

Script:

```
————-Begin Script
item: Check Disk Space
end
item: Set Variable
  Variable=ROOT
  Value=C:\
end
item: Open/Close INSTALL.LOG
end
item: Add Text to INSTALL.LOG
  Text=*********************************
end
item: Add Text to INSTALL.LOG
  Text=****Installed Files Section****
end
item: Add Text to INSTALL.LOG
  Text=*********************************
end
item: Add Text to INSTALL.LOG
  Text=*********************************
end
item: Add Text to INSTALL.LOG
  Text=****Registry Section***********
end
————-End Script
```

Script Output to the INSTALL.LOG File:

```
*** Installation Started 10/20/1999 2:44:53 ***
Title: Test INSTALL.LOG
Source: C:\Packages\ ADD.EXE
*********************************
```

```
****Installed Files Section****
*********************************
*********************************
****Registry Section***********
```

Add to AUTOEXEC.BAT

The Add to AUTOEXEC.BAT dialog box, shown in Figure 5-15, is very similar to the Autoexec.bat tab in the Installation Expert (covered in Chapter 04). This script action requires better understanding of the Autoexec.bat file. The Autoexec.bat file contains information that Windows 3.x and Windows 9x read as the computer boots (the Config.sys file, described in the next section, is a file that also provides information for the booting computer). Common information contained in the Autoexec.bat file includes the path information for the computing environment and the commands that need to be loaded before other devices. For an example of an Autoexec.bat file, see "Example of an Autoexec.bat File" in Chapter 10.

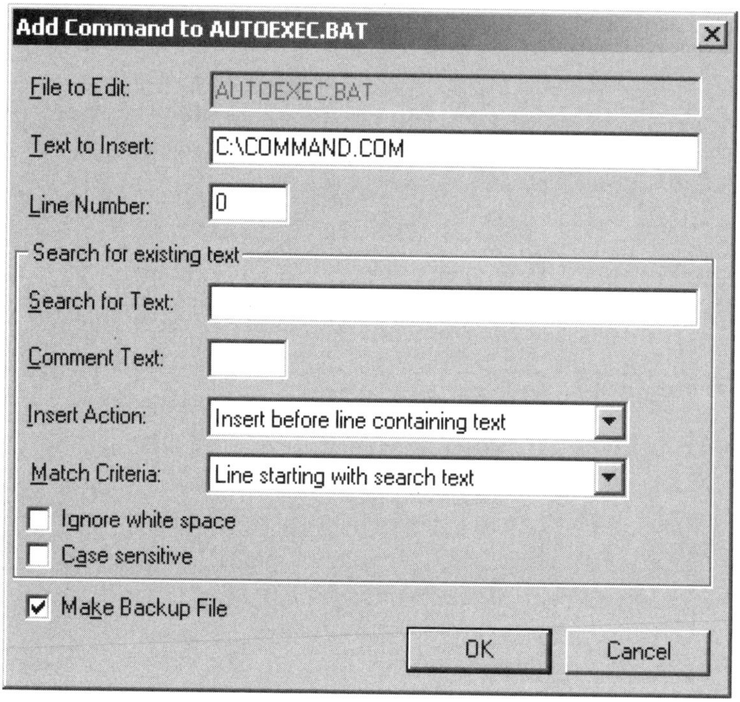

Figure 5-15 *Add to AUTOEXEC.BAT dialog box.*

Note   The Autoexec.bat file is recognized on Windows NT, but only if the registry value `ParseAutoexec` is set to one. If you are modifying information for Windows NT, use the Insert Line Into Text File script item (discussed later in this chapter) and modify the Autoexec.NT file.

The Add Command to Autoexec.bat dialog box offers several different ways to manage the addition of information to the Autoexec.bat file.

Add to AUTOEXEC.BAT Options

Text to Insert   The Text to Insert can be modified here in the event the command was entered incorrectly or modifications need to be made (such as adding command-line switches).

Line Number   The Line Number box gives you the ability to select your preference of line number for the new command line. This value can be any number from 0 to 32,000. A value of 0 instructs SMS Installer to place the line of text at the last line of the Autoexec.bat.

Search for Existing Text Section

- *Search for Text*   Included with the Autoexec.bat Details dialog box is the ability to perform context searches of the current information in the Autoexec.bat file. This search can help locate current information for deleting, modifying, replacing, or marking. The Search for Text line allows you to input text to search for in the file. Once the text is found, there are several things that can be done with the information.

- *Comment Text*   The Comment Text option takes the input from here and comments-out the line identified in the search string. This is a good way to replace lines in the Autoexec.bat without deleting them. Commenting-out the line serves as a backup, if the new command line does not work properly. You can quickly restore the Autoexec.bat to its original form by removing the comment information from the beginning of the commented line.

- *Insert action*   Once the search line has been identified, there are three actions you can choose from:
  1. Insert before line containing text
  2. Replace line containing text
  3. Insert after line containing text

- *Match Criteria*   For the search, you can also define the way SMS Installer matches information in the Autoexec.bat with the following criteria settings:
  1. Line starting with search text
  2. Line containing search text
  3. Line ending with search text

- *Checkboxes*   There are three quick checkboxes on the Autoexec.bat Details dialog box that relate to the Search function.

Table 5-1   *Autoexec.bat Details Checkboxes.*

Checkbox	Description
Ignore White Space	Tells SMS Installer to ignore additional white spaces or blank lines in the Autoexec.bat.
Case Sensitive	Helps maximize the search functionality by making the search case-sensitive. If you know the string that you are looking for has a specific letter case, choosing this option will narrow the search.
Make Backup File	Tells SMS Installer to make a backup copy of the Autoexec.bat file before the command line(s) are added. The backup file keeps the same name as the original file but changes the extension to .001. Each time the file is updated and a backup is created, the extension will increment by 1. For example, if you see a file extension of .012, you know the Autoexec.bat has been modified 12 times.

Note   Adding commands to the Autoexec.bat causes SMS Installer to
            add a RESTART variable to the script. Since the items in the
            Autoexec.bat are only loaded at bootup, the computer must be
            restarted for the information to be available to the operating
            system.

Add to Autoexec.bat Example

SMS Installer Window:
See Figure 5-16.

Script:

```
————-Begin Script
item: Add to AUTOEXEC.BAT
  New Text=C:\COMMAND.COM
  Line Number=0
  Flags=00000100
end
————-End Script
```

Add to CONFIG.SYS

The Add to CONFIG.SYS dialog box, shown in Figure 5-17, is
very similar to the Config.sys tab in the Installation Expert (covered in Chapter 04). The script action requires better understanding of the Config.sys file. The Config.sys file, like the
Autoexec.bat file, is read by the operating system when the computer boots. DOS-mode devices and 16-bit drivers are loaded into
the operating environment from the Config.sys. These devices are
terminate-and-stay-resident (TSRs) programs that run in background processes. By loading these in the Config.sys file, the
TSRs are available to software written for 16-bit drivers and to
applications and processes that run in the MS-DOS prompt. For
an example of a Config.sys file, see "Example of a Config.sys
File" in Chapter 10.

Add "C:\COMMAND.COM" to AUTOEXEC.BAT

Figure 5-16 *Add to AUTOEXEC.BAT script action window.*

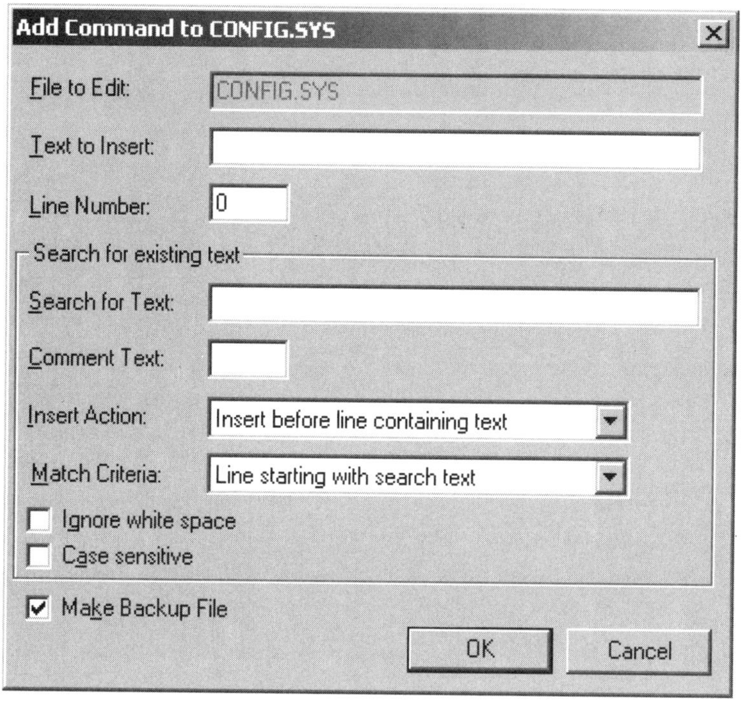

Figure 5-17 *Add to CONFIG.SYS dialog box.*

The Config.sys file is not recognized on Windows NT, only on Windows 3.x and Windows 9x computers. If modifying information for Windows NT, use the Insert Line Into Text File script item (discussed later in this chapter) and alter the Config.NT file.

Note

The Add to Config.sys script action is identical to the Add to Autoexec.bat script action in the way it operates. Enter the command-line string exactly as it needs to appear in the package in order for it to work correctly. As with the Autoexec.bat commands, the lines put into the Config.sys file need to be tested thoroughly before installation on a production environment computer.

The Add Command to Config.sys dialog box offers many different ways to customize how the lines are inserted into the Config.sys file.

Add to CONFIG.SYS Options

Text to Insert   The Text to Insert can be modified here, in the event the command was entered incorrectly or modifications need to be made, such as adding device switches.

Line Number   The Line Number box gives you the ability to select your preferred line number for the new command line. This value can be any number from 0 to 32,000. A value of 0 instructs SMS Installer to place the line of text at the last line of the Config.sys.

Search for Existing Text Section

- *Search for Text*   Included with the Add to Config.sys dialog box is the ability to perform context searches of the current information in the file. This search can help locate current information for deleting, modifying, replacing, or marking. The Search for Text line allows you to input text to search for in the file. Once the text is found, there are several things that can be done with the information.

- *Comment Text*   The Comment Text option takes the input from here and comments-out the line identified in the search string. This is a good way to replace lines in the Config.sys without deleting them. Commenting-out the line serves as a backup, if the new command line does not work properly. The Config.sys can quickly be restored back to its original form by removing the comment information from the beginning of the commented line.

- *Insert Action*   Once the search line has been identified, there are three actions you can choose from the following:
  1. Insert before line containing text
  2. Replace line containing text
  3. Insert after line containing text

- *Match Criteria*   You can also define the way the search matches information in the Config.sys with the following criteria settings:
  1. Line starting with search text
  2. Line containing search text
  3. Line ending with search text

Table 5-2 *Config.sys Detail checkboxes.*

Checkbox	Description
Ignore White Space	Tells SMS Installer to ignore additional white spaces or blank lines in the Config.sys.
Case Sensitive	Helps maximize the search functionality by making the search case-sensitive. If you know the string you are looking for has a specific letter case, choosing this option will narrow the search.
Make Backup File	One other checkbox, titled Make Backup File, on the Details dialog box tells SMS Installer to make a backup copy of the Config.sys file before the command line(s) are added. The backup file keeps the same name as the original file but changes the extension to .001. Each time the file is updated and a backup is created, the extension will increment by 1. For example, if you see a file extension of .012, you know the Config.sys has been modified 12 times.

- *Checkboxes* There are three quick checkboxes on the Config.sys Details dialog box that relate to the Search function.

Note Adding commands to the Config.sys causes SMS Installer to add a RESTART variable to the script. Since the items in the Config.sys are only loaded at bootup, the computer must be restarted for the information to be available to the operating system.

There is a script action titled Set Files/Buffers that provides the function of adding the Files and Buffers values to the Config.sys. This script item is covered later in this chapter.

Add to CONFIG.SYS Example

The following example adds the line `DEVICE=CDROM.SYS` to the Config.sys file. It first checks the current Config.sys file for the possible existence of the statement. If it finds the statement, it is commented-out using the REM (remark) line, and then it adds the specified line below the current one.

Add "DEVICE=CDROM.SYS" to CONFIG.SYS

Figure 5-18 *Add to CONFIG.SYS script action window.*

SMS Installer Window:
See Figure 5-18 here.

Script:

```
————-Begin Script
item: Add to CONFIG.SYS
 New Text=DEVICE=CDROM.SYS
 Search Text=CDROM.SYS
 Comment Text=REM
 Line Number=0
 Flags=00110110
end
————-End Script
```

Allow Floppy Disk Change

The Allow Floppy Disk Change script action does not have an associated dialog box for editing its properties. Double-clicking on this script action places it in the currently highlighted script position. When SMS Installer reaches this script action, the current executable file is closed, the computer prompts for another floppy disk, and the next consecutive executable is opened and run.

This script action is mainly for use when running an SMS Installer–generated installation from a floppy diskette set, but it can be used to simply close the current SMS Installer executable and call another one from the local file system. The called executable can be an SMS Installer–generated file that is distributed with the compressed file, but it can also be *any* local file executable file (.exe, .com, .bat, .cmd, etc.). The example in this section shows using this script action for running external programs.

Allow Floppy Disk Change Example

The following example pulls in the WINDIR environment variable to be used to set the SMS directory variable. On Windows 9x computers, this directory is normally C:\WINDOWS; on Windows NT computers, this is normally C:\WINNT. It then checks for the existence of the Sinv.exe (SMS Software Inventory executable) in the file system. If it does not find the file, the program exits. If the file is found, the script combines the WINDIR variable with the location of the SMS client directory and then uses the Allow Floppy Disk Change script item to stop the current process and start the SMS software inventory process.

> On Windows 9x computers, the WINDIR environment variable is set in the [Paths] section of the MSDOS.SYS file in the root of the C: drive. The MSDOS.SYS file is a read-only (+r)/system (+s)/hidden (+h) file. On Windows NT computers, the WINDIR environment variable is set through System Properties|Environment Variables. This can be accessed through the System Control Panel applet. These variables are user-chosen options defined during the initial setup of the operating system.
>
> **Note**

Other Script Actions Used:

1. Check Disk Space
2. Get Environment Variable
3. Check If File/Dir Exists
4. Set Variable
5. Else Statement
6. Exit Installation
7. End Block

SMS Installer Window:
See Figure 5-19.

```
Check free disk space
Get Environment Variable WINDIR into Variable WINDIR
Check If File exists sinv.exe Start Block
    Set Variable SMSDIR to %WINDIR%\MS\SMS
    Allow Floppy Disk Change / Close Install File
    Execute %SMSDIR%\clicomp\sinv\sinv32.exe
Else
    Exit Installation
End Block
```

Figure 5-19 *Allow Floppy Disk Change script action window.*

Script:

```
--------Begin Script
item: Check Disk Space
end
item: Get Environment Variable
  Variable=WINDIR
  Environment=WINDIR
end
item: Check if File/Dir Exists
  Pathname=sinv.exe
  Flags=01000100
end
item: Set Variable
  Variable=SMSDIR
  Value=%WINDIR%\MS\SMS
end
item: Allow Floppy Disk Change
end
item: Execute Program
  Pathname=%SMSDIR%\clicomp\sinv\sinv32.exe
  Default Directory=%SMSDIR%\CORE\BIN\
end
item: Else Statement
end
item: Exit Installation
end
item: End Block
end
--------End Script
```

Note   The Allow Floppy Disk Change script action does not include a message prompting the user to switch disks. If using this script action to swap floppy diskettes for an installation, use a Display Message script action after setting the floppy swap. This will inform the user it is time to change diskettes. The following script shows this example:

```
--------Begin Script
item: Allow Floppy Disk Change
end
item: Display Message
  Title English=Floppy Disk Change
  Text English=Please remove the current floppy disk,
insert disk 2, and click OK to continue...
  Flags=00001000
end
--------End Script
```

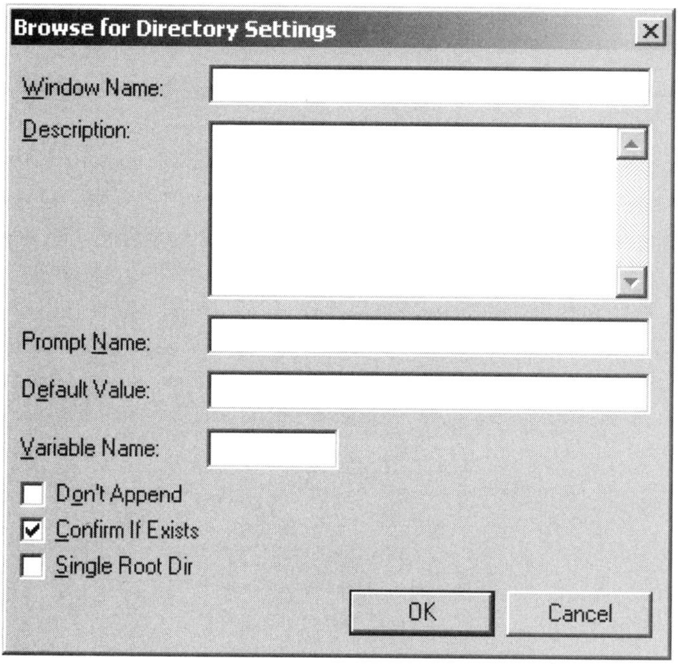

Figure 5-20 *Browse for Directory dialog box.*

Browse for Directory

The Browse for Directory dialog, shown in Figure 5-20, enables you to prompt the user for a directory location during an installation or during the execution of a utility. The script action can be used to allow the user to customize the location of files copied by the SMS Installer script or to tell the SMS Installer script where to find specific local files. The location is placed into a variable that can be used by the rest of the script.

Browse for Directory Options

Window Name   The information entered into the Window Name field will be displayed on the Browse for Directory window title. The window title is displayed in the thin blue bar at the top of the dialog box. This entry will identify what function the Browse window is providing. It will allow a string of text, a predefined variable, or both. Be attentive to the length of the title. The field accepts up to 64 characters, but anything past 40 characters will be truncated because of the window size.

Description   The Description field allows you to enter context information that describes the function of the Browse window. The field can also be used to give the user any other information. For example, the information can include instructions on how to use the Browse window, what the Browse window function will do, or even to describe the next steps in the script. The Description field can accept 511 characters, but because of the text window size, only six lines will be displayed. The field can accept text strings, predefined variables, or both.

Prompt Name   The Prompt Name field gives the directory entry field a title on the script's dialog box output. This field accepts text strings, predefined variables, or both. The field can accept up to 255 characters, but because of the size of the dialog box, anything over 35 characters will be wrapped underneath the directory entry field instead of immediately underneath the title line.

Default Value   The Default Value field is used to display a default directory or starting point when the Browse for Directory dialog box is presented to the user. This field can accept text strings, predefined variables, or both. If this field is left blank, the boot drive of the computer (generally, C:\) will be displayed as the default directory starting point. And if the entered directory is not found on the local computer, the default will be used. This field can accept up to 255 characters.

Note   The Don't Append checkbox must be included with the Default Value field if you want the browse directory list to start in the entered directory path. If it is not, the browse list will open in the root of the specified drive.

Variable Name   The Variable Name field allows you to create a new variable based on the directory selection in the Browse dialog box. Whatever selection is made, the drive letter and path are automatically stored in the new variable value. The new value can be used with the rest of the script. The Variable Name is a required field. If no value is entered, the Browse dialog box will not display correctly and the directory information will not be stored.

> When assigning new variable names, make sure the variable name does not already exist somewhere in the script. Always create a brand-new variable name. If a variable name is used that already exists, the variable contents will be changed to the new value and the rest of the script could fail. Also, when creating new variables, the names should be entered as standard text without percent symbols (%). When using variables, you must use the percent symbols. The percent symbol tells SMS Installer that a variable has been previously defined and that it should use the contents of the variable to perform the function.
>
> *Example*:
> Creating Variables: `DEFAULT_DIR`
> Using Variables: `%DEFAULT_DIR%`

Note

Don't Append   The Don't Append checkbox tells SMS Installer not to append the Default Value field to every selection. For instance, when this checkbox is not selected, if the Default Value has been set to D:\MyApp and the user selects the Program Files directory, the output in the directory field will be D:\Program Files\MyApp. Checking this box will allow the user more control over the destination of the installed files. Also, this checkbox *must* be selected if the Default Value field is set to open at a location lower than the root directory.

Confirm If Exists   This checkbox, if selected, warns users that their selection already exists if they select a directory that is already present in the file system. If they choose to continue, the directory will be overwritten with the new files. If they choose not to continue, the script will return to the directory selection dialog box to try again.

Single Root Dir   Even though this checkbox is available in SMS Installer, Microsoft has no future plans to enable it.

See Figure 5-21 for Directory Selection dialog.

Browse for Directory Example

The following example creates a standard Browse for Directory dialog box. It places the directory selection in the `DIRLOC`

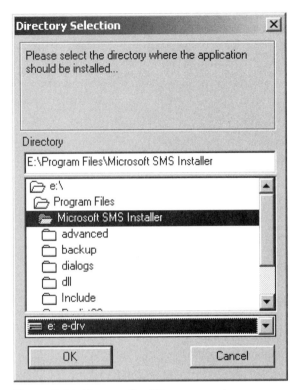

Figure 5-21 *Browse for Directory script output.*

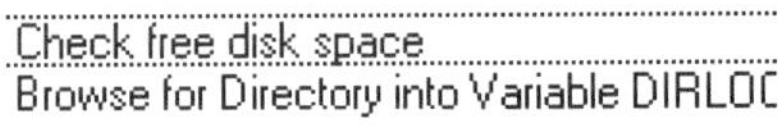

```
Check free disk space
Browse for Directory into Variable DIRLOC
```

Figure 5-22 *Browse for Directory script action window.*

variable and presents the user with quick direction on using the dialog box.

Other Script Actions Used:

Check Disk Space

SMS Installer Window:
See Figure 5-22.

Script:

```
————-Begin Script
item: Check Disk Space
end
```

```
item: Browse for Directory
  Variable=DIRLOC
  Flags=0
  Window Name English=Directory Selection
  Prompt Description English=Please select the directory
where the application should be installed...
  Prompt Name English=Directory
end
———-End Script
```

Call DLL Function

The Call DLL Function dialog, shown in Figure 5-23, allows you to use the functions of other system files with the SMS Installer script. This provides additional functionality to SMS

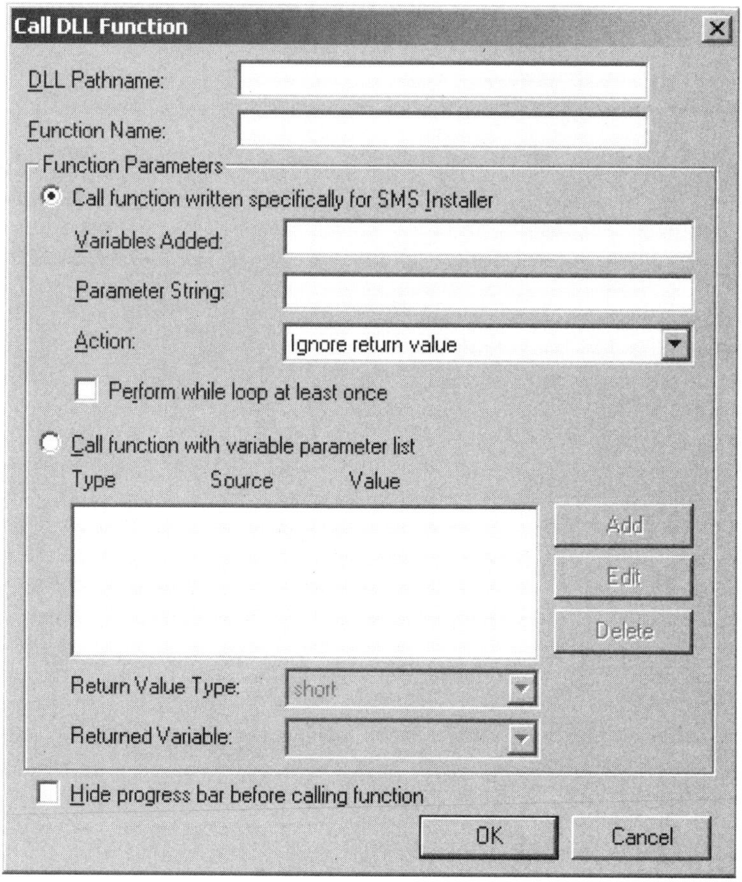

Figure 5-23 *Call DLL Function dialog box.*

Installer that would otherwise not be available. To use the DLL files, you need to know what functions they provide. For the most part, Microsoft details their own DLL files through a variety of channels. One location to find these references is in the manuals of a programming language such as Visual Basic or Visual C++. Microsoft also provides information on these references through their Microsoft Developer Network (MSDN) Web site: http://msdn.microsoft.com. Along with the MSDN Web site, Microsoft sells subscriptions to the Microsoft Developer Network service. This allows you direct and full access (depending on the level of subscription) to Microsoft's developer information. For information on pricing and features, see http://msdn.microsoft.com/subscriptions/prodinfo/overview.asp. Other vendors provide much the same information through various means. Check with the vendor to see if access to their developer functions is available.

The Call DLL Function script action accepts both 16-bit and 32-bit DLL files; however, the 16-bit version of SMS Installer accepts both 16-bit and 32-bit DLL files, but the 32-bit version only accepts 32-bit DLL files. The DLL files can be part of the current installation or already installed on the target computer. If you are not sure if the DLL exists on the target system or if the location of the DLL is in question, it is wise to always include the referenced DLL in the compiled package.

Note   If including the DLL in the compiled package for referencing with this script action, don't forget to use the Install Local File(s) script action *before* calling the file.

If the DLL is included with the installation, make sure not to leave the file on the target computer. The best method is to install the file, use the Call DLL Function script action, then delete the file. One way of doing this is to use the Get Temporary Filename script action. See the corresponding topic later in this chapter for information on this method.

SMS Installer includes some sample DLLs and their source in the \Microsoft SMS Installer\DLL directory. Other DLL files can be used from third-party vendors, or you can create your own DLL files with the functions you specify.

If creating your own DLL files, keep in mind that each DLL must have a defined DEF file. If one is not present, SMS Installer will display an error message: "Unable to load DLL." SMS Installer reserves 5 KB of stack space for calling the DLL functions. Make sure that all functions of your DLL can be removed from memory when the script function is complete.

Call DLL Function Options

DLL Pathname   The DLL Pathname is a required field that records the location of the DLL file. This field *must* start with a predefined variable, but it can include text to finish the location of the file. It is limited to 255 characters, including both the variable and the text.

Function Name   This required entry is the actual DLL function you want to call. This can be a string of text, a variable, or both, up to 255 characters.

Call Function Written Specifically for SMS Installer   This selection tells SMS Installer that you will be calling a specific function inherent to the SMS Installer DLL files.

- *Variables Added*   The Variables Added entry allows entering of a list of variables, separated by commas. These variables will be passed on to the DLL function. The field accepts up to 1900 different variable names. Once the variable has been set, it is still available to the SMS Installer script after the DLL function is complete.

- *Parameter String*   The Parameter String entry accepts text up to 30 KB long. The string is used by the function but is not available after the DLL function is complete.

- *Action*   The Action entry has four selections that tell SMS Installer what to do after the DLL function is called:
  1. *Ignore Return Value*   If the return value does not apply to the script's logic or is not intended to return a value, choose this option.
  2. *Exit If Function Returns True*   If you want to exit the installation should the return value equal TRUE, select this option.

3. *Start Block If Function Returns True*   Use this option if the return value is TRUE or FALSE and you want to use the if/else script logic to perform different functions based on the value.

4. *Loop While Function Returns True*   If the return value equals TRUE and you want to start a loop until the return value equals FALSE, choose this option. The script will continue to call the DLL until the FALSE value is given.

- *Perform While Loop at Least Once*   If you have chosen the Loop While Function Returns True option, selecting this checkbox will cause the function to loop at least once even if the return value is FALSE.

Call Function with Variable Parameter List   This selection is used when calling DLL functions outside of SMS Installer's knowledge. If DLLs are used from other vendors, select this option. The following options are presented:

- *Add*   The Add button brings up the dialog box shown in Figure 5-24. It allows adding of a specific DLL function call with parameter type, value source, and variable name or constant value.

- *Edit*   The Edit button brings up the dialog box shown in Figure 5-24 for the highlighted call function.

- *Delete*   The Delete button removes the highlighted call function.

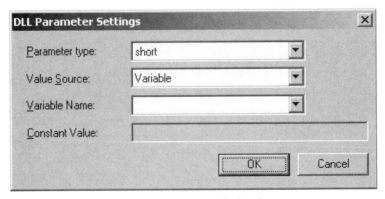

Figure 5-24 *DLL Parameter Settings dialog box.*

- *Return Value Type*   The Return Value Type specifies what format the returned data will be. There are five options:
  1. *Short*   Returns a 16-bit signed integer value (+/-).
  2. *Word*   Returns a 32-bit signed integer value (+/-).
  3. *Long*   Returns a 16-bit unsigned value (>=0).
  4. *Dword*   Returns a 32-bit unsigned value (>=0).
  5. *String Pointer*   Returns a pointer to a memory address that includes a string.

- *Returned Variable*   The drop-down list allows selecting of a predefined variable that is returned by the function call.

Hide Progress Bar Before Calling Function   This checkbox suppresses the installation progress bar when the Call Function section starts. This is useful for hiding the Installing <filename>...message as the DLL file is temporarily installed. This keeps the user from seeing the temporary file location and possibly retaining the file before it can be deleted.

The DLL Parameter Settings dialog box, shown in Figure 5-24, is used by both the Add and Edit buttons of the Call Function with Variable Parameter List option. When adding a new DLL parameter, the following options are available:

- *Parameter Type*   The Parameter Type has the following nine options available in the drop-down list:
  1. *Short*   Returns a 16-bit signed integer value (+/-).
  2. *Word*   Returns a 32-bit signed integer value (+/-).
  3. *Long*   Returns a 16-bit unsigned value (>=0).
  4. *Dword*   Returns a 32-bit unsigned value (>=0).
  5. *String Pointer*   Returns a pointer to a memory address that includes a string.
  6. *Short Pointer*   Returns a pointer to a memory address that includes a 16-bit signed integer value (+/-).
  7. *Word Pointer*   Returns a pointer to a memory address that includes a 32-bit signed integer value (+/-).
  8. *Long Pointer*   Returns a pointer to a memory address that includes a 16-bit unsigned value (>=0).
  9. *Dword Pointer*   Returns a pointer to a memory address that includes a 32-bit unsigned value (>=0).

- *Value Source*   This drop-down list depicts the type of the originator of the value. It has four options:
  1. *Variable*   This identifies the value source as a variable.
  2. *Constant*   This identifies the value source as a constant.
  3. *Constant with NULL Value*   This identifies the value source as a constant with a NULL or "0" value.
  4. *Constant with Window Handle*   This identifies the value source as a constant that returns window or screen values.

- *Variable Name*   If variables have been defined, they will be available in this drop-down list. If defining a new variable name to accept the return value, enter that here. If the Constant value is selected in the Value Source, this option is not available.

- *Constant Value*   If the Constant value is selected in the Value Source, this field is available. This is a manual entry and allows you to create a Constant value.

Call DLL Function Example

The following example is from the Prompt.Ipf file that is installed with SMS Installer in the \Microsoft SMS Installer\Samples directory. It has been modified to work with all instances. It calls the Prompt.DLL file from the \Microsoft SMS Installer\DLL directory. The example uses the DLL file to ask users what level of installation they prefer: Complete Installation, Network Installation, or Minimum Installation. For an additional example of the Call DLL Function script action, see the LockWorkstation script in Chapter 06.

Other Script Actions Used:

1. Check Disk Space

2. Set Variable

3. Get Temporary Filename

4. Install File(s)

5. Display Message

6. End Block

SMS Installer Window:
See Figure 5-25.

```
Check free disk space
Set Variable ROOT to C:\
Get Temporary Filename into DLLPATH
Install File C:\Program Files\Microsoft SMS Installer\DL_\Prompt.dll to %TEMP%\%DLL^ATII%
Call DLL %TEMP%\%DLLPATH% Function Prompt
Call DLL Block %TEMP%\%DLLPATH% Function CheckType
  Display Message "Complete Installation"
End Block
Call DLL Block %TEMP%\%DLLPATH% Function CheckType
  Display Message "Network Installation"
End Block
Call DLL Block %TEMP%\%DLLPATH% Function CheckType
  Display Message "Minimum Installation"
End Block
```

Figure 5-25 *CALL DLL Function script window.*

Script:

```
————Begin Script
item: Check Disk Space
end
item: Set Variable
  Variable=ROOT
  Value=C:\
end
item: Get Temporary Filename
  Variable=DLLPATH
end
item: Install File
  Source=E:\Program Files\Microsoft SMS
Installer\DLL\Prompt.dll
  Destination=%TEMP%\%DLLPATH%
  Flags=0000000000000010
end
item: Call DLL Function
  Pathname=%TEMP%\%DLLPATH%
  Function Name=Prompt
  Variables Added=SMSINSTL, TYPE
  Parameter English=C:\PROMPT
  Return Variable=0
  Flags=00000001
end
item: Call DLL Function
  Pathname=%TEMP%\%DLLPATH%
  Function Name=CheckType
  Parameter English=C
  Return Variable=0
  Flags=00000010
end
```

```
item: Display Message
  Title English=Complete Installation
  Text English=You have selected a complete installation to
the %SMSINSTL% directory. The script items in this block
would execute.
end
item: End Block
end
item: Call DLL Function
  Pathname=%TEMP%\%DLLPATH%
  Function Name=CheckType
  Parameter English=N
  Return Variable=0
  Flags=00000010
end
item: Display Message
  Title English=Network Installation
  Text English=You have selected a network installation to
the %SMSINSTL% directory. The script items in this block
would execute.
end
item: End Block
end
item: Call DLL Function
  Pathname=%TEMP%\%DLLPATH%
  Function Name=CheckType
  Parameter English=M
  Return Variable=0
  Flags=00000010
end
item: Display Message
  Title English=Minimum Installation
  Text English=You have selected a minimum installation to
the %SMSINSTL% directory. The script items in this block
would execute.
end
item: End Block
end
————-End Script
```

Output:

See Figure 5-26.

Check Configuration

Check Configuration, the dialog box for which is shown in
Figure 5-27, provides built-in system checking for quick output.

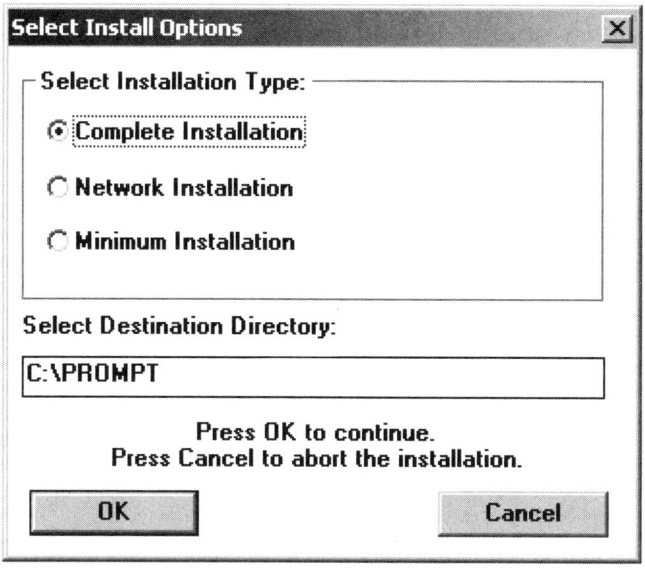

Figure 5-26 *Call DLL Function example output.*

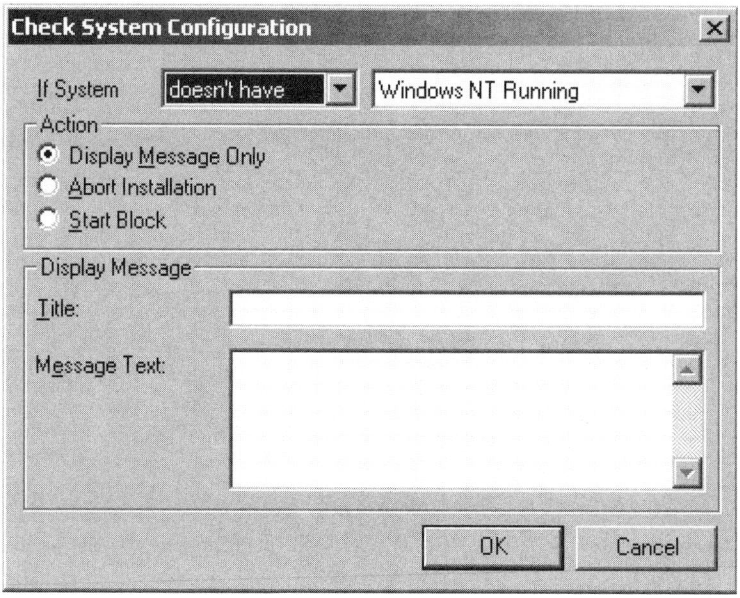

Figure 5-27 *Check Configuration dialog box.*

The output can be used to determine if the minimum requirements are met on the target computer before the installation continues. It offers several methods of exiting the installation
gracefully and provides a dialog box for communication to the
user. Based on the return values, the Check Configuration contains a set of actions that can be performed.

This script action can also be used to write one script for many
different types of computer operating environments. For instance,
SMS Installer can check if Windows NT is installed on the computer. If Windows NT is the operating system, the installation
continues installing Windows NT–specific files. If it is not, a
whole separate set of files are installed based on the script logic of
the If/Else statement.

Check Configuration Options

If System   The If System option has two items in the drop-down
list:

1. *Does Have*   Checks to see if the requirement is met. Returns
   a TRUE value if it is found, a FALSE value if it is not.

2. *Doesn't Have*   Checks to see if the requirement is not met.
   Returns a TRUE value if it is not found, a FALSE value if it is.

Configurations   The configurations drop-down list displays SMS
   Installer's built-in checking functions. Most of the configurations are self-explanatory, but it helps to know what is available since this selection includes numerous options. For the
   most part, the items in the drop-down list follow no logical
   order. Table 5-3 separates the options into categories of configurations.

Note   The Check Configuration script action does not include a cate-
   gory to check disk space thresholds. This function is included in
   its own script action covered in this chapter.

Table 5-3   *Configuration categories.*

Category	Options	Description
Operating System	Windows NT Running, Windows 95 or Later Running, 32-bit Windows Running, Windows 95 Shell Interface	The Operating System category checks to see what operating system is installed on the computer.
Video	256 Color or Better Graphics, VGA or Better Graphics, 800 x 600 Graphics or Better, 1024 × 768 Graphics or Better	The Video category checks the computer's video capabilities. The VGA or Better Graphics option checks to see that the computer has at least a 640 × 480 resolution.
Processor	286 Processor or Better, 386 Processor or Better, 486 Processor or Better	The Processor category checks the computer's processor information.
Memory (RAM)	At Least 1 MB Free Memory, At Least 2 MB Free Memory, At Least 3 MB Free Memory, At Least 4 MB Free Memory, At Least 5 MB Free Memory, At Least 6 MB Free Memory, At Least 7 MB Free Memory, At Least 8 MB Free Memory, At Least 9 MB Free Memory, At Least 10 MB Free Memory, At Least 11 MB Free Memory, At Least 12 MB Free Memory	The Memory category checks the available amount of memory (RAM) on the computer when the installation is run. If the specified amount is not available, you may want to use the display message to notify the user to shut down some applications before continuing.

Table 5-3   *Configuration categories (Continued)*.

Category	Options	Description
Security	NT Administrator Rights	Some applications and installations require the currently logged on user to have local administrator rights if using Windows NT. The Security category checks for the proper security rights.
Sound	WAV File Playback Support, MIDI File Playback Support, WAV and MIDI Playback Support	The Sound category checks not only the computer's sound capabilities but also the installed driver for playing WAV and MIDI files (standard multimedia format files).
Paging	Paging Enabled	The Paging category checks the computer for the availability of paging services. Paging services set up temporary file storage on the computer to allow data to be swapped in and out of RAM.
Share	Share Loaded	The Share category verifies the existence of file sharing. It checks for the availability for all versions: DOS Share, Windows VSHARE, Windows NT, or Windows 9x.
Operating Mode	386 Enhanced Mode, Standard Mode Running	The Operating Mode category checks the computer's mode of opera-

Table 5-3   *Configuration categories (Continued)*

Category	Options	Description
Operating Mode (Continued)	386 Enhanced Mode, Standard Mode Running	tion. This category is for with Windows 3.x and Windows for Workgroups operating systems. Enhanced mode allows application multitasking, whereas Standard mode does not.
Math Capability	Math Coprocessor	The Math Capability category checks the computer to verify that it is capable of math calculations. This is extremely useful when distributing math-intensive applications such as AutoCAD.

Action   The Action section sets the steps that are performed depending on the result of the If System section. There are three options:

- *Display Message Only*   When the If System result is returned, SMS Installer can display a message to the user. If this option is selected, only a message is displayed and then the installation continues. This is useful for informing the user that the minimum requirements have been met.

- *Abort Installation*   When the If System result is returned, and the minimum requirement has not been met, the installation can be terminated by selecting this option. If text has not been entered into the Display Message section the installation will close immediately. Entering information into the Display Message section will display a message to the user before the installation exits. This is useful for providing information to the user concerning why the installation cannot complete and what steps can be taken to ensure the installation is successful next time.

- *Start Block*   When the If System result is returned, a logic block (If/Then/Else) can be started. This is useful for installing different sets of files based on the returned operating system value. If text has been entered into the Display Message section, a message will be presented to the user before the script continues.

Display Message   The Display Message section allows entering of information that will be displayed to the user at the end of the Check Configuration script action. Two fields are presented in this section:

- *Title*   This is the information displayed at the top of the message dialog box. It gives a brief description of the window. The Title field can accept up to 255 characters, but keep in mind that any text beyond the width of the dialog box will not be displayed. The text will stop at the window size and will be enclosed in ellipses.

- *Message Text*   This is the actual message that the user will see, so be as descriptive as possible. This field accepts up to 511 characters. Pressing Ctrl-Enter starts a new line of text.

Check Configuration Example 1

There are two examples in this section. The first shows how to display a dialog box to inform the user that the installation is exiting because the requirements have not been met. The second shows how to use script logic to install separate file sets based on different operating systems.

The following example checks to see if the Windows 95 shell is loaded. If it is not, it displays a message to the user and exits the installation.

Other Script Actions Used:

Check Disk Space

SMS Installer Window:
See Figure 5-28.

```
Check free disk space
If System Doesn't Have Windows 95 Shell Interface
```

Figure 5-28 *Check Configuration script action window.*

Script:

```
————-Begin Script
item: Check Disk Space
end
item: Check Configuration
  Message English=This PC is not running Windows 95. Win-
dows 95 is required for this installation. If you feel this
message is in error, please contact your technical support.
The installation will now exit.
  Title English=Windows 95 Required...
  Flags=01011011
end
————-End Script
```

Output:
See Figure 5-29.

Check Configuration Example 2

The following example uses script logic to determine if Windows NT is installed. If it is, a Windows NT.txt file is installed to the root of the C: drive. If the OS is not Windows NT, it installs a Windows 95.txt file to the root of the C: drive.

Other Script Actions Used:

1. Check Disk Space

2. Set Variable

3. Install File(s)

Figure 5-29 *Check Configuration example output.*

```
Check free disk space
Set Variable ROOT to C:\
If System Has Windows NT Running Start Block
  Install File C:\Windows NT.txt to %ROOT%Windows NT.txt
Else
  Install File C:\Windows 95.txt to %ROOT%Windows 95.txt
End Block
```

Figure 5-30 *Check Configuration script action window.*

4. Else Statement

5. End Block

SMS Installer Window:

See Figure 5-30.

Script 2:

```
————-Begin Script
item: Check Disk Space
end
item: Set Variable
  Variable=ROOT
  Value=C:\
end
item: Check Configuration
  Flags=10100000
end
item: Install File
  Source=C:\Windows NT.txt
  Destination=%ROOT%Windows NT.txt
  Flags=0000000000000010
end
item: Else Statement
end
item: Install File
  Source=C:\Windows 95.txt
  Destination=%ROOT%Windows 95.txt
  Flags=0000000000000010
end
item: End Block
end
————-End Script
```

Check Disk Space

The Check Disk Space dialog box, shown in Figure 5-31, allows you to check for available hard disk space on the target computer. Through the dialog box, you can also set additional

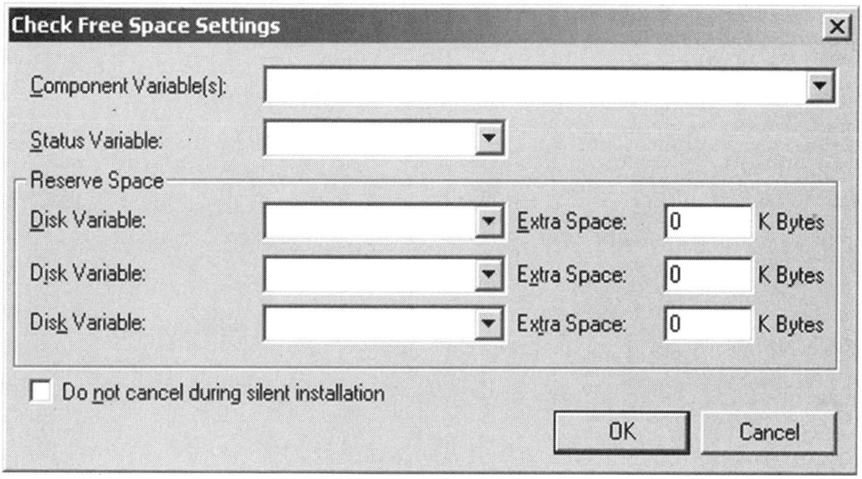

Figure 5-31 *Check Disk Space dialog box.*

space allocations if you know that certain data created with the application will add additional requirements after the program has been in use. It is also wise to set the space allocation higher when the installed application opens temp files during its use.

> Because SMS Installer's primary function is to repackage and install applications, the Check Disk Space script action is required by default in all fully functional scripts. Even if creating standalone utilities with SMS Installer, the script will not compile without this script action being present somewhere in the script. You can suppress this error message by changing the Progress Bar configuration in the Installation Properties. To do this:
>
> 1. Press *Ctrl-Z* to bring up the Installation Properties screen.
> 2. Click on the Screen tab.
> 3. In the Progress Bar Based On drop-down box, select either *Position in Installation EXE* or *Position in Installation Script*.
>
> The Percentage of Selected Files option requires the Check Disk Space script action be present before the SMS Installer script will compile.

Note

The Check Disk Space script action does not necessarily check the currently available hard disk space, but rather, it verifies the amount of hard disk space available after the installation is complete.

Check Disk Space Options

Component Variables   The Component Variables drop-down box allows selecting of the additional defined components included with the installation. These additional components are defined through the Components tab in the Application Files group of the Installation Expert. The components are a combined set of files available for installation that the user can choose to install. Entering the components in this field automatically retrieves their installation size and conveys the information to the Check Disk Space script action. This field is only required if you are using a component-based installation. If you are including more than one component, you should use commas to separate the entries. If no components are being used, you should leave this field blank.

Status Variable   When the sufficient disk space requirements are not met for the installation, the user is prompted with an error message that displays the amount of disk space needed (see Figure 5-32). When a STATUS variable is entered and the user chooses to retry the operation, SMS Installer places an "R" in the variable. The Retry selection allows the user to clear disk space and retry the installation. If the user chooses to ignore the error, SMS Installer places an "I" in the variable. The Ignore selection tells SMS Installer to ignore the fact that there is not enough disk space and continue the installation anyway. If the user chooses to cancel the installation, no value is placed into the variable and the installation stops. SMS Installer uses these values to continue the script logic and can be used later in the script.

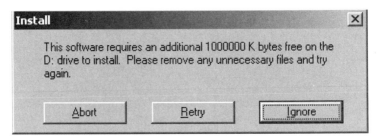

Figure 5-32 *Inadequate disk space error message.*

Reserve Space   The Reserve Space section includes line items for specifying up to three different hard drives to check for required space. Some computers have multiple disk drive partitions or multiple, physical hard disk drives. If installing the application to a network drive, one of the following line items can be used to check the network for available space:

- *Disk Variable*   This entry takes a predefined drive letter variable and calculates the drive space for current and proposed available space. It uses the Extra Space field for the calculation. Defining the drive letter variable is shown in the example in this section.

- *Extra Space*   The Extra Space field allows entering of the amount of disk space that should be available after the installation. The format is in kilobytes (i.e., 1000 KB = 1 MB). This field only accepts values up to 999,999. If this value is exceeded an error will be generated. See Figure 5-33.

Do Not Cancel During Silent Installation   If the installation has been distributed in silent mode (i.e., with the / s switch), this checkbox allows the script to continue without user intervention. If the disk space requirements are not met, the user will not be warned if this checkbox is selected, and the installation will not abort. If this is left unchecked and the disk space requirements fail, the installation will abort and will give the user no indication of why the program did not complete.

Figure 5-33 *Value exceeded error message.*

Check Disk Space Example

The following example sets the variable for the two installed drives on the computer and then uses the Check Disk Space script action to verify the amount of available hard disk space.

Other Script Items Used:

Set Variable

SMS Installer Window:

See Figure 5-34.

Script:

```
————-Begin Script
item: Set Variable
  Variable=CDRIVE
  Value=C:
end
item: Set Variable
  Variable=DDRIVE
  Value=D:
end
item: Check Disk Space
  Space1=999999
  Variable1=CDRIVE
  Space2=999999
  Variable2=DDRIVE
  Space3=0
  Status=DISKSTATUS
end
————-End Script
```

Check If File/Dir Exists

The Check If File/Dir Exists dialog box, shown in Figure 5-35, allows you to check for the existence or nonexistence of specified files and directories on the target computer. The script action will check for each (file or directory) or both in combination. It also includes the ability to determine if a 16-bit application or module is loaded into the computer's memory and a check to establish if a certain directory is writable. This script action

```
Set Variable CDRIVE to C:
Set Variable DDRIVE to D:
Check free disk space
```

Figure 5-34 *Check Disk Space script action window.*

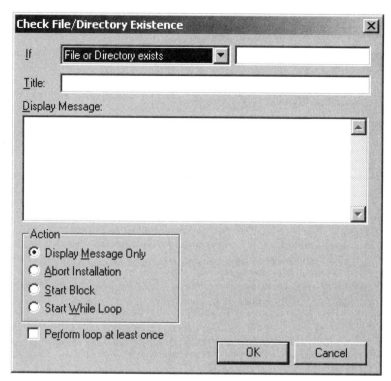

Figure 5-35 *Check If File/Dir Exists dialog box.*

includes several script logic actions that can be used with the return values.

Check If File/Dir Exists Options

If   The If section sets the file and directory existence state, as well as the file and directory location and name.

- *File/Dir State*   The File/Dir State includes six file state options:
  1. *File or Directory Exists*
  2. *File or Directory Doesn't Exist*
  3. *File Exists*
  4. *Directory Exists*
  5. *Directory Not Writable*   Determines if a directory path, specified in the File/Dir Condition, allows files to be copied to it. Some directories may not be writable due to a security context set by an administrator.

6. *Module Loaded in Memory*   This option is limited to only checking for 16-bit programs loaded in memory.

- *File/Dir Condition*   This editable text field tells SMS Installer what directory, file, or directory and file to verify the condition. It accepts any predefined variable, string of text, or both. It supports up to 255 characters. If Module Loaded in Memory is selected from the File/Dir State option, only enter the filename with extension in this field. The directory is not needed.

Title   The Title field displays a title for the Message window that the user sees when presented with a message dialog box. Even though this field will accept up to 255 characters, it should be used as a brief description of the displayed message. If the text exceeds the dialog window width, the text will stop at the window size and will be enclosed in ellipses.

Display Message   This is the actual message that the user will see so be as descriptive as possible. This field accepts up to 511 characters. Pressing Ctrl-Enter starts a new line of text. If this text box is left blank, no display message window will be presented to the user.

Action   The Action section tells SMS Installer what to do with the results of the Check If File/Dir Exists script action. It has four options:

- *Display Message Only*   If this option is selected, the message dialog box will be displayed as entered in the Display Message text box, but no further action will be taken.

- *Abort Installation*   If the Abort Installation option is selected, the installation will stop. In this instance the installation just exits without notifying the user. If you are concerned with communicating to the user what has transpired, you may consider using the Start Block action instead. Then use the Display Message script action with the Exit Installation.

- *Start Block*   This option starts a script logic block. This can be used to install the necessary file(s) or create the necessary

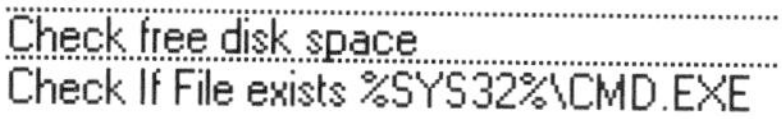

```
Check free disk space
Check If File exists %SYS32%\CMD.EXE
```

Figure 5-36 *Check If File/Dir Exists script action window.*

directory(ies) if it is determined they do not exist by the File/Dir State. This can also be used to utilize third-party programs to remove modules loaded in memory before continuing (see "Building the SMS Installer Toolkit" in Chapter 10 for more information). If the Display Message field has information in it, a message dialog box will be displayed to the user with its contents.

- *Start While Loop* If the return value equals TRUE and you want to start a loop until the return value equals FALSE, choose this option. This is useful if a loaded module takes several attempts to be removed from memory or you want to use the Create Directory script action to modify the local directory structure before continuing.

Perform Loop at Least Once If you have chosen the Start While Loop option, selecting this checkbox will cause the function to loop at least once even if the return value is FALSE.

Check If File/Dir Exists Example

The following example uses the SMS Installer internal %SYS32% variable to check for the existence of the Windows NT Command Interpreter (CMD.EXE) file. When it finds the file in the specified location, it displays a message to the user.

Other Script Actions Used:

Check Disk Space

Windows Installer Window:
See Figure 5-36.

Script:

```
————-Begin Script
item: Check Disk Space
end
item: Check if File/Dir Exists
  Pathname=%SYS32%\CMD.EXE
```

```
   Message English=The Windows NT Command Interpreter was
found on this computer. The installation may continue nor-
mally.
   Title English=Windows NT Command Interpreter...
   Flags=01000000
end
───────-End Script
```

Compiler Variable Else

The Compiler Variable Else script action has no associated dialog box. It must be used with the Compiler Variable If script action. This script action provides much the same feature as the Else statement, except that the variables are defined in the Installation Properties on the Compiler Variables tab, accessed by pressing Ctrl-Z simultaneously.

Compiler Variable End

The Compiler Variable End has no associated dialog box. It must be used with the Compiler Variable If script action. This script action provides much the same feature as the End Block, except that the variables are defined in the Installation Properties on the Compiler Variables tab accessed by pressing Ctrl-Z simultaneously.

Compiler Variable If

The Compiler Variable If script action (see the associated dialog box in Figure 5-37) must be used in conjunction with the

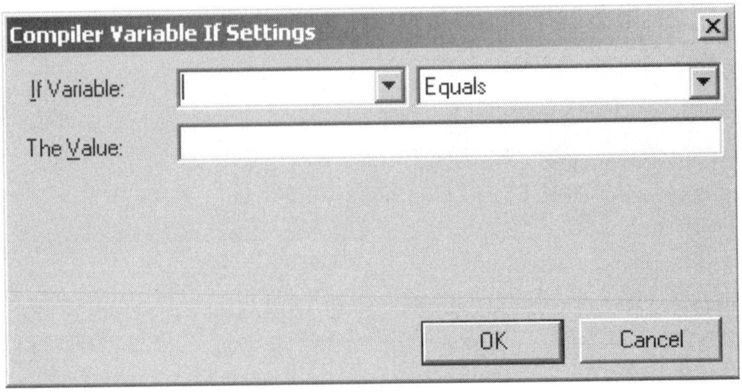

Figure 5-37 *Compiler Variable If dialog box.*

Compiler Variable End. The Compiler Variable Else script action can be used to perform branching script logic to provide different actions based on a specified value. The values that are used with this script action are set on the Compiler Variables tab or the Installation Properties. Ctrl-Z brings up the Installation Properties dialog box. Variables added to this tab are global to the SMS Installer script. For a review, see "Compiler Variables Tab" in Chapter 04.

Compiler Variable If Options

If The If section provides the data and condition for the script action to continue. It has the following options:

- *Compiler Variable* This drop-down list will display all the compiler variables defined in the Installation Properties. This field must contain a selection from the drop-down list. New compiler variables are only created through the Installation Properties. They cannot be created in the script as with some of the other script actions.

- *Condition* The Condition drop-down list, contains five different states with which to create the script logic:

  1. *Equals* Compares the Value data against the variable. This is a case-sensitive comparison that returns a TRUE value if the data and variable match.

  2. *Not Equals* Compares the Value data against the variable. This is a case-sensitive comparison that returns a FALSE value if the data and variable do not match.

  3. *Contains Any Letters In* Compares the Value data against the variable. This is a case-sensitive comparison in which it checks for *any* similar alphanumeric characters between the data and variable. It returns a TRUE value if it finds a match and a FALSE value if it does not.

  4. *File Exists* Checks for the existence of the file specified in the Value field. It returns a TRUE value if the file is found and a FALSE value if it is not.

  5. *Contains* Compares the Value data against the variable. This is a case-sensitive comparison that checks for the existence of the *entire* string between the data and variable.

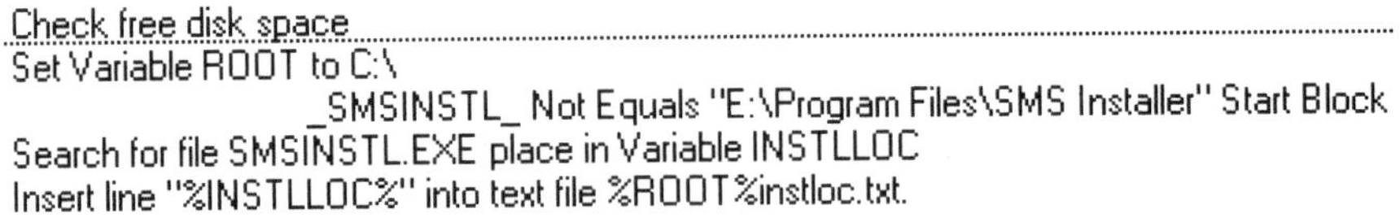

```
Check free disk space
Set Variable ROOT to C:\
          _SMSINSTL_ Not Equals "E:\Program Files\SMS Installer" Start Block
Search for file SMSINSTL.EXE place in Variable INSTLLOC
Insert line "%INSTLLOC%" into text file %ROOT%instloc.txt.
```

Figure 5-38 *Compiler variables script action window.*

The Value   The Value field holds the value the Compiler Variable If script action runs against the script logic to start the compiler block. This field accepts a string of text, a predefined variable (can be a script variable), or both. The field can be up to 255 characters in length.

Compiler Variables Example
   The following example pulls the compiler variable for SMS Installer's location from the Installation Properties and then verifies that it is in the correct directory by searching the local file system. If SMS Installer is located in the place already defined by the compiler variable, then the compiler block exits. If SMS Installer's location does not match the compiler variable, the new information is written to a text file in the root of the C: drive.

Other Script Actions Used:

1. Check Disk Space

2. Set Variable

3. Search for File

4. Insert Line into Text File

SMS Installer Window:
See Figure 5-38.

Script:

```
────Begin Script
item: Check Disk Space
end
item: Set Variable
  Variable=ROOT
  Value=C:\
end
item: Compiler Variable If
```

```
  Variable=_SMSINSTL_
  Value=E:\Program Files\SMS Installer
  Flags=00000001
end
item: Search for File
  Variable=INSTLLOC
  Pathname List=SMSINSTL.EXE
  Description English=Searching for SMS Installer Location
end
item: Insert Line into Text File
  Pathname=%ROOT%instloc.txt
  New Text=%INSTLLOC%
  Line Number=0
end
item: Compiler Variable Else
end
item: Compiler Variable End
end
———-End Script
```

Config ODBC Data Source

The Config ODBC Data Source dialog box, shown in Figure 5-39, is similar to the dialog box produced by the Options tab in

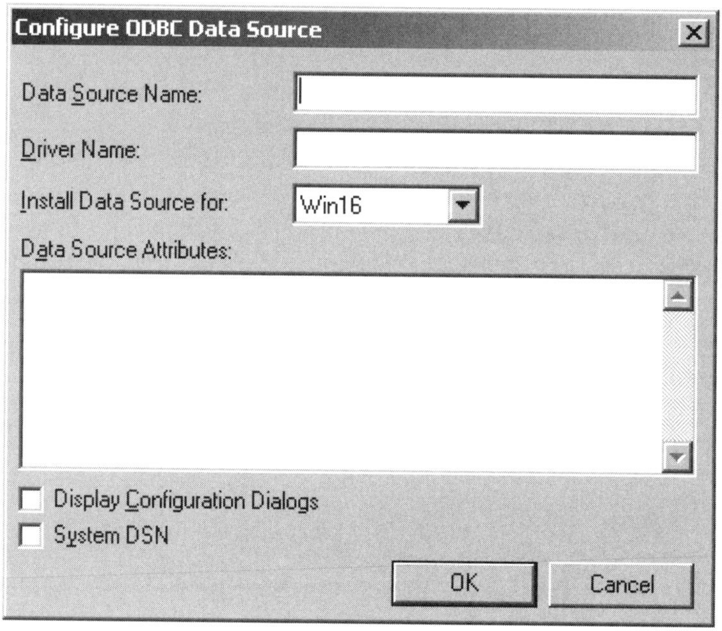

Figure 5-39 *Config ODBC Data Source dialog box.*

the Runtime group in the Installation Expert. The difference is that the script action requires all the information to be entered versus the Installation Expert providing the different selections for you.

When ODBC drivers are included with the SMS Installer script, the ODBC.INI on all operating systems is modified with the information; and, on Windows 9x and Windows NT systems, the registry is also updated with the information (see "Example of an ODBC.INI File" in Chapter 10 for an example). The actual ODBC driver must be installed on the target computer. A list of the installed drivers is kept in the ODBCINST.INI file on the target computer (see "Example of an ODBCINST.INI File" in Chapter 10). To install drivers using the SMS Installer Script Editor, use the Install ODBC Driver script action shown later in this chapter.

For a complete list of the SMS Installer default ODBC Data Sources, see "Data Source Attributes" in Chapter 04.

Config ODBC Data Source Options

Data Source Name   The data source name must be entered. The text, variables, or both entered here will be written to the [ODBC Data Sources] section in the ODBC.INI file on the local computer. The field can accept up to 255 characters.

Driver Name   The driver name entered here must already exist on the target computer. Driver names are listed in the ODBCINST.INI of the target computer. This field can accept up to 255 characters of text, variables, or both. SMS Installer will automatically determine the driver type (16-bit or 32-bit), so do not designate that information in this field. Enter only the driver name.

Install Data Source For   This option must be selected (Win16 or Win32) depending on the operating system that is targeted for installation.

Note   For Win16 clients, the ODBCINST.DLL file must be installed in the \WINDOWS\SYSTEM directory. For Win32 clients, the ODBCCP32.DLL file must be installed in the \WINDOWS\SYS-TEM32 directory.

```
Set Variable DBDIR to C:\DATABASE
Configure ODBC Data Source MyDataSource
```

Figure 5-40 *Config ODBC Data Source script action window.*

Data Source Attributes   The data source attributes are the
ODBC driver information specific to the instance of installation.
It the installation gives the user access to a particular database
and path, the data source attribute information must be entered.

Display Configuration Dialogs   This checkbox allows the user at
the target computer to customize the data source. Users will be
prompted to configure the ODBC data source themselves, which,
in most cases, may not be the best method of installation.
Enabling this option causes SMS Installer to check the
ODBCINST.INI file for the location of the driver's setup DLL file
so users can modify all attributes.

System DSN   This checkbox enables SMS Installer to install the
ODBC driver and attribute for all accounts on the computer to
access. This means that anyone logging on to the computer would
have access to the data source.

Config ODBC Data Source Example
    The following example configures the MS Access 32-bit data
source.

Other Script Actions Used:

    Set Variable
SMS Installer Window:
See Figure 5-40.

Script:

```
———-Begin Script
item: Set Variable
  Variable=DBDIR
  Value=C:\DATABASE
end
item: Configure ODBC Data Source
  Manager Variable=MyDataSource
  Driver Variable=Microsoft Access Driver (*.mdb)
  Attributes=DBQ=%DBDIR%\MYDB.mdb
```

```
Attributes=Description=This is My Database
Attributes=Driver=odbcjt32.dll
Attributes=DriverId=25
Attributes=FIL=MS Access
Attributes=ReadOnly=00
Attributes=SafeTransactions=0
Attributes=SystemDB=SYSTEM_DB_PATH
Attributes=ImplicitCommitSync=Yes
Attributes=MaxBufferSize=512
Attributes=PageTimeout=5
Attributes=Threads=3
Attributes=UserCommitSync=Yes
Attributes=
Flags=00000110
end
————End Script
```

Copy Local File(s)

The Copy Local File(s) dialog box, shown in Figure 5-41, allows you to copy files from one location to another on the local computer. This script action differs from the Install File(s) script action in that Copy Local File(s) does not pull files from the compiled executable. Rather, it is used for installing files that are not part of the compressed package. This is useful for separating non-program files from the script, such as temporary DLLs used by the Call DLL Function script item. The files used with this method must be available to the user performing the installation. Examples of this include when installing from a floppy diskette set, a CD-ROM, or a directory on a network drive.

Note   For files copied outside the SMS Installer compile executable, you will need to copy these files to their source yourself.

Copy Local File(s) Options

File Information   The File Information section sets the file copy parameters for the script.

- *Source*   The Source field is a required field that contains the source directory of the file that is to be copied. This field *must* start with a variable that has been previously defined. The drop-down box provides quick selection of variables already

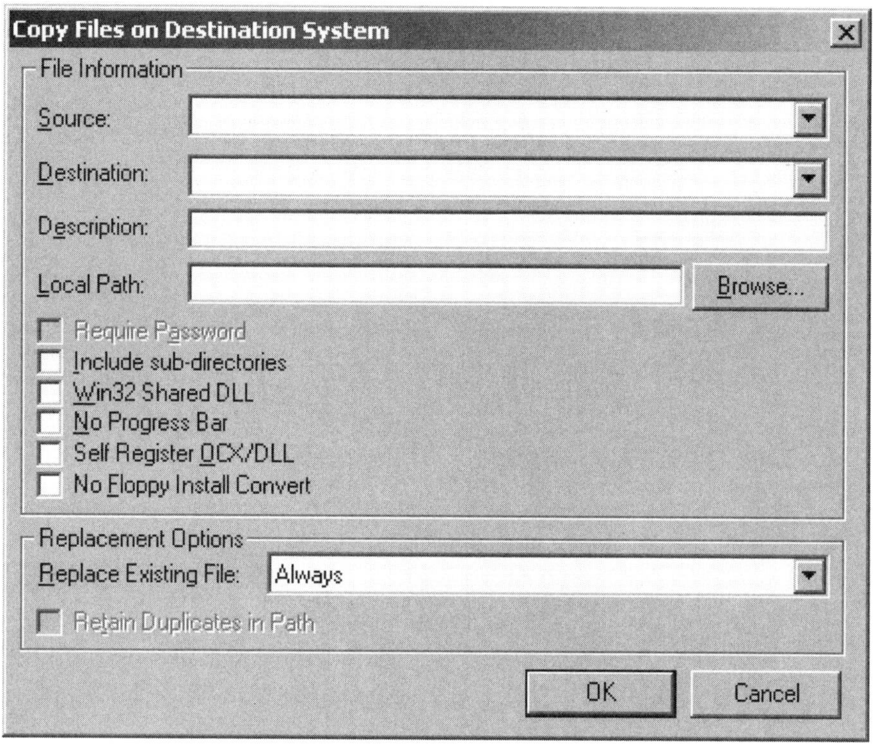

Figure 5-41 *Copy Local File(s) dialog box.*

defined in the script. The actual filename is not required if one
is listed in the Local Path field. This field will also accept the *
wildcard character for copying multiple files at once. For
example, if you want to copy all the help files from a source
directory, you can use the *.HLP parameter. If you want to
copy *all* files from a source directory, you can use the *.*
parameter. The field accepts up to 255 characters.

- *Destination*   The Destination field contains the location
  where the file(s) will be copied. The Destination information
  must start with a predefined variable. The drop-down list
  allows you to quickly select the available variables. The field
  will accept any string of text after the variable. If a single file
  has been entered into the Source or Local File fields, you must
  include the filename in this entry. If not, just the variable name
  will work. If wildcard characters are used in either the Source

or Local Files field, then you cannot enter an actual filename. The Destination field can also be used to rename the source file as it is copied. For example, if the source filename is SMSINSTL.HLP, you can rename the file INSTALLR.HLP when it is copied to the destination. You do not need to create the destination directory if it does not exist. SMS Installer automatically creates the destination directory when it copies the file. The field accepts up to 255 characters.

Note   When changing the name of the source file using the Destination field, be careful not to change the file's extension. Changing the file's extension will cause the file not to be associated with the application that runs it.

- *Description*   The Description field contains the text that is displayed on the progress bar dialog box as the file is copied. This helps the user understand what the installation is doing. The word "Copying" precedes whatever description you enter, so input the text with this in mind. For example, if you want the user to see "Copying Help Files...," just enter "Help Files...," This field accepts text, variables, or both up to 255 characters, but the description will be truncated if it goes beyond the window width.

- *Local Path*   The Local Path field specifies the pathname from where the source files are copied. It includes a Browse button to select the directory from the local computer's directory structure. The field accepts up to 255 characters of text, variables, or both. The information in this field is available only if wildcard characters are not used in the Source field.

- *Require Password*   The Require Password checkbox allows you to set a password for the file copy procedure. This checkbox is only enabled after setting an installation password through the Installation Properties on the General tab (Ctrl-Z). One password can be set per compiled script. The user's password entry should be one of the first items the script runs. Use this feature for the Copy Local File(s) if this script action is the first instance where the script makes changes to the target computer.

- *Include Subdirectories* If this checkbox is selected, all the files and directories underneath the source directory will be copied. If wildcards are used in either the source or local path, the subdirectories are searched for the same criteria and the files that match are copied.

- *Win32 Shared DLL* This selection tells the SMS Installer script that you are copying files that are shared by multiple applications (usually OCX/DLL/VBX/EXE files). Programs that share system files add to the registry increment counter. The registry stores an increment counter in the HKEY_LOCAL_MACHINE\SOFTWARE\Microsoft\Windows\CurrentVersion\SharedDLLs registry key. Each time a program tries to install a file, it first checks this key to determine if any other program uses the file. If it is being used, the installation increments the registry value by 1. Uninstall programs will decrement this value by 1 when the program is removed from the computer. This feature only works with Windows 9x and Windows NT computers. Selecting this checkbox will increment the counter by 1.

- *No Progress Bar* Selecting this checkbox causes the file copy progress bar to be hidden during the file copy.

- *Self Register OCX/DLL* On Windows 9x and Windows NT computers, this option queues DLL and OCX files for registering in the operating system when the script completes. The Self-Register OCX/DLL script action (shown later in this chapter) can also be used to register the files immediately.

- *No Floppy Install Convert* If you are using the Convert CD-ROM to Floppy selection in the Installation Properties (Ctrl-Z), this checkbox stops the compilation from including the files to copy in the compressed executable. If this is not selected, the copied files will be included in the compiled file anyway.

Replacement Options The Replacement Options tells the script what to do when it finds duplicate files in the destination.

- *Replace Existing File* This drop-down list is similar throughout SMS Installer when files are found in the local file system

that will be overwritten. It includes seven different options
which are defined in Table 5-4.

Table 5-4 *Replace existing file options.*

File Copy Option	Description
Always	When the same filename is found at the destination, it is always overwritten with the one included with the script.
If version number same or older	When the same filename is found at the destination, SMS Installer compares the version number between its copy and the current file. If the version number is the same or older, the current file is overwritten.
If date/time same or older	When the same filename is found at the destination, SMS Installer compares the date and time between its copy and the current file. If the date and time are the same or older, the current file is overwritten.
If date/time older	When the same filename is found at the destination, SMS Installer compares the date and time between its copy and the current file. If the date and time are older, the current file is overwritten.
If date/time and version number are same or older	When the same filename is found at the destination, SMS Installer compares the date, time, and version number between its copy and the current file. If the date, time, and version number are the same or older, the current file is overwritten.
If date/time and version number are older	When the same filename is found at the destination, SMS Installer compares the date, time, and version number between its copy and the current file. If the date, time, and version number are older, the current file is overwritten.
Never	When the same filename is found at the destination, SMS Installer skips the file copy.

- *Retain Duplicates in Path* This option is only available if using the Replace Existing File is set to Version Checking or Version and Date/Time Checking. This only works on Windows 9x and Windows NT computers.

Copy Local File(s) Example

The following example copies the SMS Installer help file from its current location to a Help directory at the root of the C: drive. It displays a message to the user while the copy is taking place.

Other Script Actions Used:

1. Check Disk Space

2. Set Variable

SMS Installer Window:
See Figure 5-42.

Script:

```
————-Begin Script
item: Check Disk Space
end
item: Set Variable
  Variable=ROOT
  Value=C:\
end
item: Set Variable
  Variable=INSTLLOC
  Value=E:\PROGRAM FILES\MICROSOFT SMS INSTALLER
end
item: Copy Local File
  Source=%INSTLLOC%\SMSINSTL.HLP
  Destination=%ROOT%HELP\SMSINSTL.HLP
  Description English=Copying Help Files...
  Flags=0000000001000011
end
————-End Script
```

```
Check free disk space
Set Variable ROOT to C:\
Set Variable INSTLLOC to E:\PROGRAM FILES\MICROSOFT SMS INSTALLER
Copy local file from %INSTLLOC%\SMSINSTL.HLP to %ROOT%HELP\SMSINSTL.HLP (Version)
```

Figure 5-42 *Copy Local File(s) script action window.*

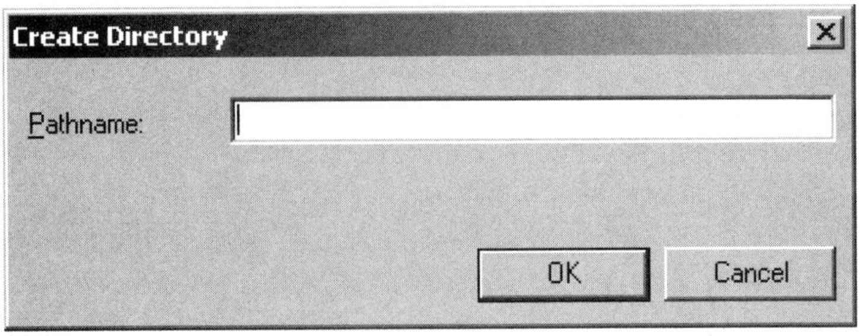

Figure 5-43 *Create Directory dialog box.*

```
Check free disk space
Set Variable ROOT to C:\
Create Directory %ROOT%MyDir
```

Figure 5-44 *Create Directory script action window.*

Create Directory

The Create Directory dialog box, shown in Figure 5-43, allows you to create empty directories in the file system. This script action is not necessary when the Copy Local File(s) or Install File(s) script actions are used. When these script items are used, the directory is created automatically.

The only option with this script action is entering the path information of the directory you want created. The entry *must* start with a variable defined earlier in the script. If the directory already exists in the file system, the creation will be skipped.

Create Directory Example

The following example creates an empty directory called MyDir at the root of the C: drive.

Other Script Actions Used:

1. Check Disk Space

2. Set Variable

SMS Installer Window:
See Figure 5-44.

Script:

```
————-Begin Script
item: Check Disk Space
```

```
end
item: Set Variable
  Variable=ROOT
  Value=C:\
end
item: Create Directory
  Pathname=%ROOT%MyDir
end
————-End Script
```

Create Service

The Create Service dialog box, shown in Figure 5-45, enables you to quickly add Windows NT services to the target computer through the script. Windows NT services run as a background process on the computer, and they run with a system security context. Running under the system security context allows the service to run even if the user is not logged onto the computer. A service generally runs under all user profiles on the computer.

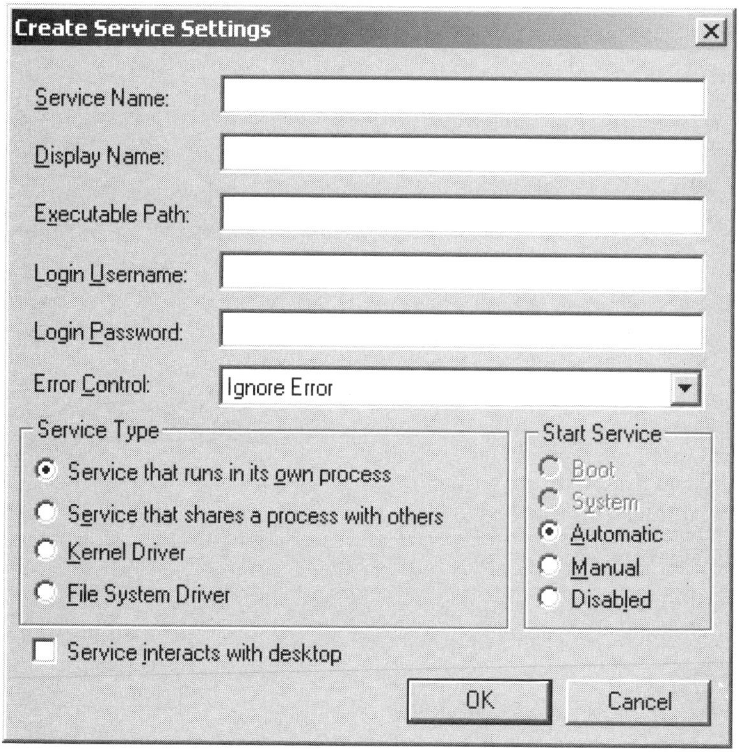

Figure 5-45 *Create Service dialog box.*

Create Service Options

Service Name   This is the name that will be displayed in the computer's service registry key. While this field can accept up to 255 characters, keep the name short for readability. The registry key that will be updated is HKEY_LOCAL_MACHINE\SYSTEM\CurrentControlSet\Services. The field accepts string of text, predefined variables, or both.

Display Name   The information entered into this field will be the name that is displayed in the Services list in the Control Panel applet on Windows NT and the Component Services Management Console in Windows 2000. Keep the display name under 30 characters. Even though this field accepts up to 255 characters, the Services display window is only 30 characters wide and any character number beyond 30 will not be shown. The field accepts string of text, predefined variables, or both. The Services applet reads the display name data from the service's registry key in a DisplayName value.

Executable Path   The Executable Path entry tells SMS Installer where the service executable resides on the local computer. This information is recorded in the computer's registry. The registry value is called ImagePath. The service can be distributed with the compiled executable, or it can already exist on the target computer. The service file can be a file with an .EXE or .DLL extension. The path information should already be included in a predefined variable. Use this variable with the actual service filename.

Login Username   The Login Username specifies the security account that runs the installed service. This enables you to provide more-granular security for each installed service. Though this feature is included with this script action, it is a smart practice to use the built-in LocalSystem account. Leaving the Login Username and Login Password fields blank causes SMS Installer to default to the LocalSystem account. This is the recommended method of installing the service. Services that use shared resources *must* run under the LocalSystem account. The account information is set in the Services registry key in the ObjectName value. If installing the service to run under a different account, the account must already have been created on the local computer or Windows NT domain. If using a domain account, you must use the \\DOMAIN\Account format. Alternatively, you can use the Get Registry Key Value script action (covered later in this chapter) to place the domain information into a variable for use throughout the script. This field will accept up to 255 characters, but the Windows NT system only allows a username length of 20 characters.

> The Login Username field can contain a variable that is defined earlier in the script. One method to obtain the variable is to prompt the user for the username and password values earlier in the script using the Prompt for Text or Custom Dialog script actions. This is not the best-case scenario. If users knows the username and password of a service, they can change the information. **Note**

Login Password The Login Password field contains the password that will be used with the Login Username field. If allowing the service to be installed under the LocalSystem account, leave this field blank. Keep in mind that Windows NT uses case-sensitive passwords, and that format should be followed when entering the password into this field. Even though this field accepts up to 255 characters (string of text, predefined variable, or both) the Windows NT system only allows passwords to be up to 14 characters.

Error Control The Error Control section has four options that control how the Windows NT Session Manager reports errors when it tries to start the service during the computer bootup. Session Manager runs the bootup services and processes. These are defined in the HKEY_LOCAL_MACHINE\SYSTEM\Current-ControlSet\Control\Session Manager registry key and run by the Session Manager service (SMSS.EXE). The following options are also set in the registry under the Service registry key, and then under the specific service name. The registry value is defined by the name ErrorControl. Setting the proper error control on the service is critical if installing a system driver that could affect the overall boot process.

- *Ignore Error*   If this option is selected, Session Manager records the error in the Windows NT Event Log, but continues to boot. The ErrorControl value is set to 0x0.

- *Normal Error*   If this option is selected, Session Manager records the error in the Windows NT Event Log, displays an error message, but continues to boot. The ErrorControl value is set to 0x1.

- *Severe Error*   If this option is selected, Session Manager records the error in the Windows NT Event Log and no message is displayed. The computer is rebooted using the Last Known Good startup configuration. The ErrorControl value is set to 0x2.

- *Critical Error*   If this option is selected, Session Manager tries to record the error in the Windows NT Event Log and no message is displayed. The computer is rebooted, and the Last Known Good configuration is attempted. The ErrorControl value is set to 0x3.

Service Type   The Service Type defines under which type of system context the service will run. The following options are presented:

- *Service that Runs in its Own Process*   Specifies that the installed application service runs completely on its own without any dependencies on other services.

- *Service that Shares a Process With Others*   Specifies that the installed application service runs with dependencies on other services. An example of a dependent service is a 16-bit executable that must start the WOW (Win16 on Win32) subsystem to run. The WOW subsystem provides limited backward-compatibility with 16-bit applications running on a 32-bit operating system.

- *Kernel Driver*   Specifies a service that is installed as a system driver.

- *File System Driver*   Specifies that a service that is installed as a driver for file system functions.

Start Service   The Start Service selection tells SMS Installer to set the boot options for the service. The Start value in the Services registry key is updated with the information. The following boot options are presented.

- *Boot*   If this option is selected, the operating system loader (NTLDR) starts the service. A service assigned this option generally means that the computer is dependent upon it to boot properly. An example of this would be a driver for a specific manufacturer's hard disk. The Start value in the Services registry key is set to 0.

- *System*   If this option is selected, the IoInitSystem function starts the service. A service assigned this option generally means that the operating system is dependent upon it to load properly. An example of this would be a driver for an installed network or video card. The Start value in the Services registry key is set to 0x1.

- *Automatic*   If this option is selected, the service is started every time the computer boots. The Start value in the Services registry key is set to 0x2.

- *Manual*   If this option is selected, the service must be started manually, either through user intervention or by another system process or application. The Start value in the Services registry key is set to 0x3. Some examples of manual services are the SMS Site System components. When an SMS process starts on a schedule, it "wakes up" the dependent service to complete its processing.

- *Disabled*   If this option is selected, the service is installed but cannot be started until its service Start value has been changed. The Start value in the Services registry key is set to 0x4. This is a helpful feature if you want to install a service before rolling out an application that is not ready for distribution.

Tip   The services installed will be available when the computer is rebooted. If you would like the services to be immediately avail-

> able, use this script action in conjunction with the Start/Stop
> Service script action.

Service Interacts with Desktop   If the service has an application
component and interface with which the user can interact, select
this option.

Create Service Example

The following example creates a service that is represented by
the MyServ.exe file in the \WINNT\SYSTEM32 directory.

SMS Installer Window:
See Figure 5-46.

Script:

```
———-Begin Script
item: Create Service
  Service Name=MyService
  Executable Path=%SYS32%\MyServ.exe
  Login User=administrator
  Login Password=password
  Service Type=16
  Boot Type=2
  Error Type=0
  Display Name English=This is My Service
end
———-End Script
```

Create Shortcut

The Create Shortcut dialog, shown in Figure 5-47, allows creation of shortcuts to files installed by the compiled executable or
programs that are already installed on the computer. Applications
usually have their own shortcuts installed in their predefined
program groups, but you may want to place the shortcut to the
program on the user's Windows desktop or the Windows 9x/Win-
dows NT Start menu for easier access. Using this method also
helps standardize the location of program shortcuts. This is useful

Create Service This is My Service

Figure 5-46 *Create Service script action window.*

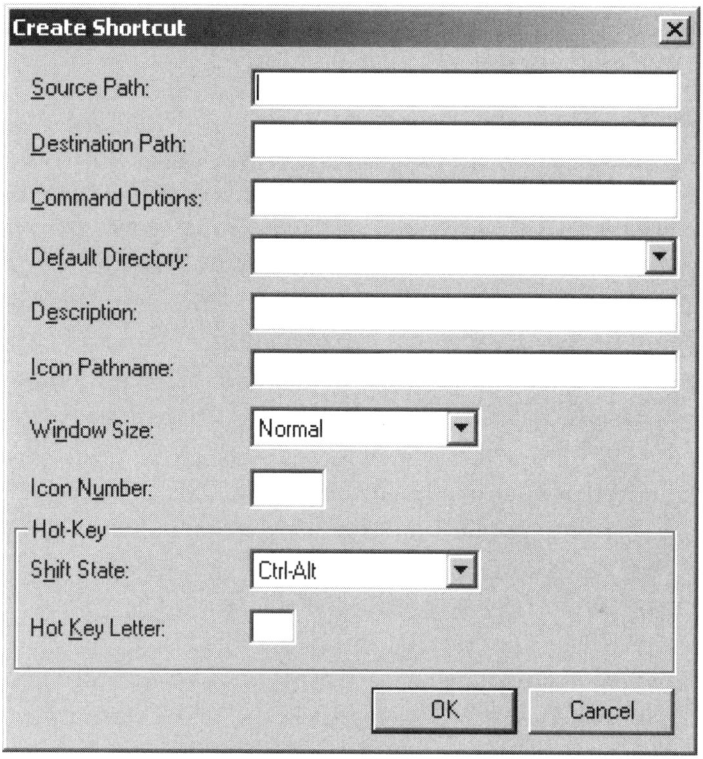

Figure 5-47 *Create Shortcut dialog box.*

in lowering the amount of support time needed to solve user support issues.

When you are creating shortcuts using the SMS Installer Script Editor, the Create Shortcut script action is the preferred method. The Add ProgMan Icons script action (shown earlier in this chapter) is another method but provides less functionality and is better for working with 16-bit Windows programs.

Note

Create Shortcut Options

Source Path The Source Path is the location of the program executable in the local file system to which the shortcut will be assigned. This should include full pathname and filename with extension. The field can accept predefined variables and will hold up to 255 characters.

Destination Path   The destination path is the location where the new shortcut will be created. The destination path *must* start with a variable for the full pathname. Then, you should enter the shortcut description and the shortcut extension of .LNK. All shortcut files on Windows 9x and Windows NT computers use the .LNK extension. If you enter the new Start Menu group name after the directory variable and before the shortcut description, it will be created automatically. You do not have to create the Start Menu group first. Use the standard directory structure format when setting the destination path (i.e., %STARTMENUDIR%\ Programs\My New Group\My New Shortcut.LNK). The field can accept text, predefined variables, or both, up to 255 characters.

Before the directory variable can be used, it must be defined. The following scripts define the directory variables by pulling the information from the computer's registry. They are separated into currently logged-on user (HKEY_CURRENT_USER registry key) and common user (HKEY_LOCAL_MACHINE registry key).

Logged-on User Startup Directory:

```
———-Begin Script
item: Get Registry Key Value
  Variable=STARTUPDIR
Key=Software\Microsoft\Windows\CurrentVersion\Explorer\\
Shell Folders
  Default=%WIN%\Start Menu\Programs\StartUp
  Value Name=StartUp
  Flags=00000010
end
———-End Script
```

Logged-on User Desktop Directory:

```
———-Begin Script
item: Get Registry Key Value
  Variable=DESKTOPDIR
  Key=Software\Microsoft\Windows\CurrentVersion\Explorer\
Shell Folders
```

```
    Default=%WIN%\Desktop
    Value Name=Desktop
    Flags=00000010
end
———-End Script
```

Logged-on User Start Menu Directory:

```
———-Begin Script
item: Get Registry Key Value
  Variable=STARTMENUDIR
Key=Software\Microsoft\Windows\CurrentVersion\Explorer\
Shell Folders
  Default=%WIN%\Start Menu
  Value Name=Start Menu
  Flags=00000010
end
———-End Script
```

Logged-on User Group Directory:

```
———-Begin Script
item: Get Registry Key Value
  Variable=GROUPDIR
Key=Software\Microsoft\Windows\CurrentVersion\Explorer\
Shell Folders
  Default=%WIN%\Start Menu\Programs
  Value Name=Programs
  Flags=00000010
end
———-End Script
```

Common User Startup Directory:

```
———-Begin Script
item: Get Registry Key Value
  Variable=CSTARTUPDIR
Key=Software\Microsoft\Windows\CurrentVersion\Explorer\
Shell Folders
  Default=%STARTUPDIR%
  Value Name=Common Startup
  Flags=00000100
end
———-End Script
```

Common User Desktop Directory:

```
————-Begin Script
item: Get Registry Key Value
  Variable=CDESKTOPDIR
Key=Software\Microsoft\Windows\CurrentVersion\Explorer\
Shell Folders
  Default=%DESKTOPDIR%
  Value Name=Common Desktop
  Flags=00000100
end
————-End Script
```

Common User Start Menu Directory:

```
————-Begin Script
item: Get Registry Key Value
  Variable=CSTARTMENUDIR
Key=Software\Microsoft\Windows\CurrentVersion\Explorer\
Shell Folders
  Default=%STARTMENUDIR%
  Value Name=Common Start Menu
  Flags=00000100
end
————-End Script
```

Common User Group Directory:

```
————-Begin Script
item: Get Registry Key Value
  Variable=CGROUPDIR
Key=Software\Microsoft\Windows\CurrentVersion\Explorer\
Shell Folders
  Default=%GROUPDIR%
  Value Name=Common Programs
  Flags=00000100
end
————-End Script
```

Command Options   This field allows the entering of any command-line switches, parameters, or options that should be assigned to the shortcut. For example, with this option, you can enter the location of a database file that the main program should open when it starts.

Default Directory   This optional field configures the new shortcut to point to another location when running the executable.

This is useful when the program is reliant on files in other directories that are not part of the PATH environment variable. The drop-down list allows selecting a predefined directory variable.

Description   The Description field adds comment information to the shortcut. If you open up the properties of a shortcut, you will see a Comment line. When using the Active Desktop, this comment information displays in a "pop-up" balloon as you temporarily hold the mouse cursor over the shortcut.

Icon Pathname   The Icon Pathname field allows you to choose another icon to associate with the shortcut instead of the program's default icon. This is helpful for assigning icons to programs that do not include icons, such as DOS applications. The file can be any file that contains icons such as EXE, DLL, ICO, and so on. If an icon is not assigned to the shortcut and the related program does not contain an icon, the system's default icon will be used. The full pathname and icon filename (with extension) must be entered. The field will accept predefined variables.

Window Size   The Window Size selection configures the shortcut's starting window state. It has three options:

- *Normal*   When this option is selected, the shortcut will run the program using the application vendor's default settings.

- *Minimized*   When this option is selected, the shortcut will run the program and the program will be minimized on the computer's taskbar.

- *Maximized*   When this option is selected, the shortcut will run the program and the program window will fill the entire screen area.

Icon Number   The icon number relates to icons contained in DLL or executable files. Icons are assigned numbers based on an internal index by the software vendor. This index is based on positive integers from 0-9999. If no number is entered in this field, the program's default icon will be used.

Hot-Key Section   The Hot-Key section allows you to assign a hot-key combination (a series of combined keystrokes pressed simultaneously) to the installed shortcut. If you look at the properties of an available shortcut, the Shortcut tab has a Shortcut Key field. When a hot key is assigned with this script action, it is this field that is updated. The Hot-Key section contains two options for setting the hot key. If the Hot-Key Letter field does not contain an entry, the Shift State selection is ignored and a key combination is not assigned to the shortcut.

- *Shift State*   The available options are Ctrl-Alt, Shift-Ctrl, Shift-Alt, Shift-Ctrl-Alt.

- *Hot Key-Letter*   Entering a letter or number in this field completes the hot-key information and enables the combination for the shortcut.

Create Shortcut Example

The following example creates a shortcut to the Microsoft calculator included with the operating system. It installs the shortcut directly on the Windows Start menu. For the Start menu variable to be available, the Get Registry Key Value script action is used to pull the STARTMENUDIR information from the registry key HKEY_CURRENT_USER\Software\Microsoft\Windows\CurrentVersion\Explorer\Shell Folders\Start Menu. The example assigns the Ctrl-Alt-C hot-key combination to the program. *Other Script Actions Used*:

1. Check Disk Space

2. Get Registry Key Value

SMS Installer Window:
See Figure 5-48.

Check free disk space
Get Registry Key Software\Microsoft\Windows\CurrentVersion\Explorer\Shell Folders place in Variable STARTMENUDIR
Create Shortcut from %SYS32%\CALC.exe to %STARTMENUDIR%\Microsoft Calculator.lnk

Figure 5-48 *Create Shortcut script action window.*

Script:

```
————-Begin Script
item: Check Disk Space
end
item: Get Registry Key Value
  Variable=STARTMENUDIR

Key=Software\Microsoft\Windows\CurrentVersion\Explorer\Shell
Folders
  Default=%WIN%\Start Menu
  Value Name=Start Menu
  Flags=00000010
end
item: Create Shortcut
  Source English=%SYS32%\CALC.exe
  Destination English=%STARTMENUDIR%\Microsoft
Calculator.lnk
  Key Type English=1603
  Flags=00000001
end
————-End Script
```

Custom Dialog

The Dialog Box Settings dialog box, shown in Figure 5-49, allows you to quickly create your own dialog boxes. SMS Installer has the Wizard Block that can be used in conjunction with this script action for creating one dialog box and having the rest uniform with the first. Or, you can create your own set of

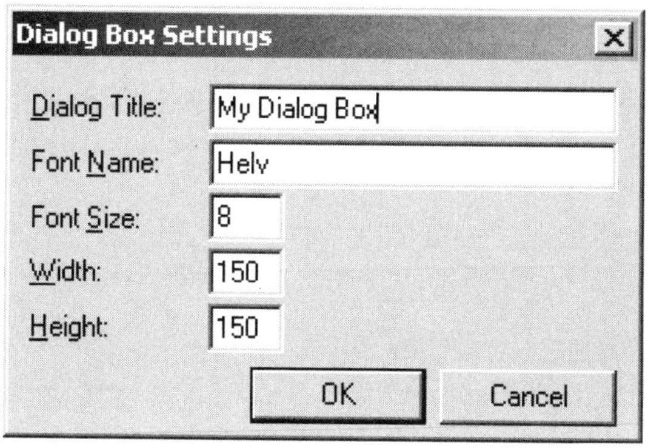

Figure 5-49 *Dialog Box Settings dialog box.*

dialog boxes that call each other and walk the user through an installation or a utility interface.

The dialog box is fully customizable. You can incorporate graphics, text, drop-down list boxes, radio dialog boxes, and so on. SMS Installer installs some already-created dialog boxes that you can use in your script or that you can use to customize into your own creation. The SMS Installer dialogs are located in the \Microsoft SMS Installer\Dialogs\Template directory. These are useful for learning the concepts of the Custom Dialog script action.

The first dialog box that is displayed when you double-click on the script action is the Dialog Box Settings window. This allows you to name the dialog box you will create, as well as change font and window size properties.

Dialog Box Settings Options

Dialog Title   The Dialog Title field allows you to name the new dialog box. The field will accept up to 255 characters of text, variables, or both. This title will be displayed in the dialog box's window title. Keep in mind that if the title is longer than the width of the window, it will be displayed in ellipses. Use this field to give the dialog box a brief description.

Font Name   The Font Name field allows you to change the display font that will be used when entering text on the dialog box. The default font is Helvetica (Helv). If SMS Installer cannot find the font you specify, it will revert to the default.

Font Size   The Font Size allows you to change the size of the display font. The default is 8-point.

Width   This is the default width for the dialog box window. The default is 150. This field accepts values from 53 to 9999.

Height   This is the default height for the dialog box window. The default is 150. This field accepts values from 53 to 9999.

Note   Once you have entered the Custom Dialog Editor (covered next), dialog box properties can be changed from within the interface.

Since the information entered here can be changed later, do not worry that the information entered will be permanent.

Once you have accepted the information entered into the Dialog Box Properties, the Custom Dialog Editor program, shown in Figure 5-50, will display with a blank dialog box that is based on the information entered into the properties. The dialog box title is automatically placed at the top of the window.

The Custom Dialog Editor is a full-featured program that allows the creation of powerful dialog boxes. The dialog boxes created with the editor can be used to walk the user through an installation, obtain information through user input that is placed into variables, and give more information about the program.

When using the Custom Dialog Editor, keep in mind that the interface you create will be seen by anyone who uses it. Plan your dialog boxes with this in mind. Make them intuitive, easy to read, and pleasant to the user's eyes.

While in the editor program, you can create multiple dialog boxes and place them into a set by clicking on File|New Dialog.

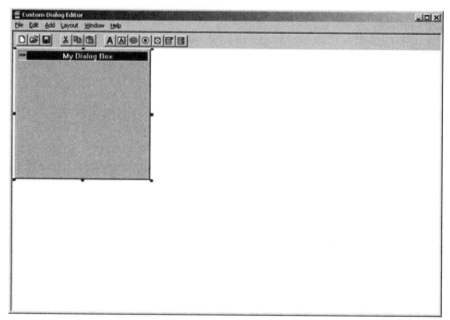

Figure 5-50 *Custom Dialog Editor.*

The first, or primary, dialog box that is created will be the first one the user sees. If you do not create a set of dialog boxes, each dialog box will need its own script action line.

The Custom Dialog Editor interface includes some quick toolbar buttons at the top, underneath the File menu. All of these buttons are also available on the File menu. For this reference, the toolbar buttons will be described, and then the File menu options that are not part of the toolbar will be covered.

 This is the toolbar button that creates a New dialog box. Clicking this button brings up the same Dialog Box Properties box as displayed when double-clicking the script action. Once the dialog properties have been entered and accepted, the new dialog box will display in the Custom Dialog Box interface for editing.

 The Open toolbar button opens a dialog box for searching the local file system for saved dialog box files. Dialog box files have a .DLG extension. You can create an entire library of dialog box files that you create, or you can modify the ones that are included with SMS Installer.

 The Save toolbar button saves the current dialog box if only one has been created, or it saves the entire set if more than one dialog box is available. There is no option for saving one file out of a set. If you need to only save one dialog box, you must select Window from the File menu and choose the unneeded dialog box(es). Then select Edit|Delete to remove the dialog box(es) you do not wish to save. Clicking this button displays a file system dialog box for navigating the local file system to save the dialog box or dialog box set.

This group of toolbar buttons is the standard Edit set. It uses the standard Windows Cut, Copy, and Paste functions. You can cut, copy, or paste any item from one dialog box to another.

 This toolbar button inserts a Static control onto the dialog box. The Static control places text and graphics on the dialog box that cannot be edited by the user. This is useful for giving the user information about the installation or utility, or communicating a

software license agreement. You can also use this control to calculate disk drive requirements for you.

When you click this toolbar button, the dialog box shown in
Figure 5-51 is displayed.

Static Control Properties Options

Text   The Text box allows entering of any text string, variables,
or both, up to 511 characters. If you want to create a new line of
text in the box, press Ctrl-Enter. Otherwise, the text entered will
be considered one line.

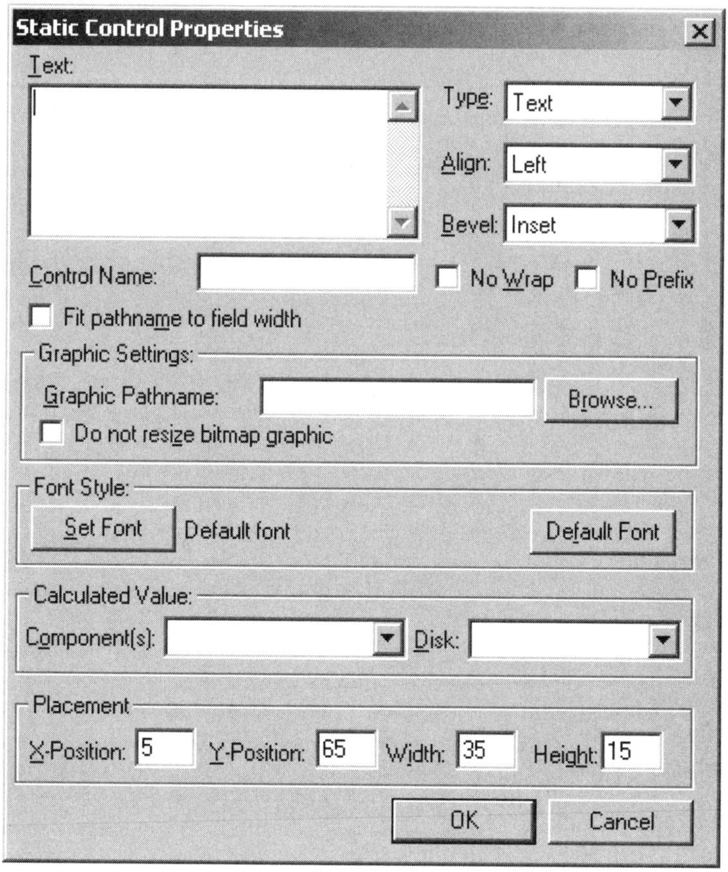

Figure 5-51 *Static Control Properties dialog box.*

- *Type* The Type drop-down list has five options to choose what type of Static control you want to create on the dialog box.

  1. *Text* If this option is selected, the text entered into the Text box will be displayed on the dialog box.

  2. *Group Box* If this option is selected, the information entered into the Text box will be displayed as a title at the top left of the Group box. This is useful for separating items on a dialog box such as navigation buttons or manual entry fields, and for giving the section a title.

  3. *Graphic* If this option is selected, any information in the Text box is ignored. Instead, a picture file will be placed on the dialog box. The picture must be a Windows bitmap format in either 16 or 256 colors. The graphic information, such as location in the file system and filename, must be defined in the Graphic Pathname field in the Graphic Settings section.

  4. *Frame/Rectangle* These two options provide the same function. If either is selected, a framed box will display on the dialog box. As with the Group box, this is useful for separating different sections. Any information entered into the Text box is ignored. The Frame and Rectangle options do not display a title.

- *Align* The Align options only apply to the text type. The drop-down list contains three options for aligning the text:

  1. *Left* The text will be displayed left-justified.
  2. *Center* The text will be displayed center-justified.
  3. *Right* The text will be displayed right-justified.

- *Bevel* This option applies only to the frame and rectangle types. It gives the selected type a three-dimensional effect. There are three options:

  1. *Inset* The frame or rectangle will appear to be recessed into the dialog box.
  2. *Flush* The frame or rectangle will appear to be level with the dialog box.
  3. *Outset* The frame or rectangle will appear to protrude out of the dialog box.

- *Control Name* Though available on the Static Control Properties dialog box, this feature is not yet supported.

- *No Wrap* Selecting this checkbox keeps the static text type from wrapping if it is longer than one line.

- *No Prefix* In scripting, Windows uses the ampersand (&) character to make letters or numbers available for quick access using the Alt key on the keyboard. For example, if &Next is entered into a field, the "N" will display with an underscore, and pressing *Alt-N* on the keyboard will execute the command. Selecting this checkbox disables this function and allows the ampersand to be displayed in the text.

- *Fit Pathname to Field Width* If a pathname is included in the Text box, selecting this checkbox will force the pathname to sit on one line. If this is not selected and the pathname is longer than the text box width, it will split across lines. Splitting the path across lines can be confusing to the user if trying to communicate the location of a file or directory in the local file system.

Graphic Settings The Graphic Settings section specifies the information about the picture file if the Type has been set to Graphic. If this Type has been selected, the Graphic Pathname field must be completed. Following are the options presented:

- *Graphic Pathname* This field holds the location information for the graphic file. It must contain the full path and filename. This field can accept 255 characters of text, predefined variables, or both. Graphic files for use with the Static control must be either 16 or 256 colors. A Browse button is included to search the local file system for graphic files if you do not know the pathname and filename.

- *Do Not Resize Bitmap Graphic* When your dialog box is displayed on the target computer, SMS Installer tries to match the computer's resolution. Selecting this checkbox keeps the graphic from matching the different resolution for each computer. The graphic can become pixilated and may not display correctly if this option is not enabled.

Font Style   The Font Style section sets the font properties for the Static control if you want it to be different than the default (Helvetica). This section only works with the Text and Group Box types. The following options are presented:

- *Set Font*   The Set Font button displays the Font dialog box and allows changing the Static control font. When the new Font is selected, the Static Control Properties is updated with the new information and the font properties are displayed next to the Set Font button.

- *Default Font*   Clicking the Default Font button resets the font to the setting on the Font tab of the Installation Properties dialog box (Ctrl-Z).

Note   The Installation Properties (Ctrl-Z) dialog box can only be accessed from the Script Editor window. Inputting Ctrl-Z in the Custom Dialog Editor will produce no effect.

Calculated Value   The Calculated Value section is a quick way to compute available hard disk space and display the information on the dialog box. This can only be used if Type is set to Text. If using this section, anything typed into the Text box will not be displayed.

- *Component(s)*   Any components added to the installation through the Select Components script action or on the Components tab of the Application Files group in the Installation Expert will be displayed in the drop-down box. When the disk parameter is calculated, the component sizes are subtracted from the total disk space before it is shown on the dialog box.

- *Disk*   The drop-down list allows selecting of the disk variables. These variables should have already been defined by using the Set Variable and the Check Disk Space script actions. The example in this section demonstrates this procedure.

Placement   The Placement section allows you to enter screen-positioning values for the Static control. While this feature is included on the Static Control Properties dialog box, it is much easier to change the size and position of the Static control by clicking and dragging with the mouse button. The following options are presented:

- *X-Position*   The X-Position is the horizontal location on the dialog box for the Static control. Measured in pixels, this coordinate starts from the upper left corner of a 640 × 480 screen.

- *Y-Position*   The Y-Position is the vertical location on the dialog box for the Static control. Also measured in pixels, this coordinate starts from the upper left corner of a 640 × 480 screen.

- *Width*   The Width relates to the horizontal size of the Static control.

- *Height*   The Height relates to the vertical size of the Static control.

This toolbar button inserts an Edit Text Control field onto the dialog box. The Edit Text control can be used to place read-only text onto the dialog box, as well as also single- or multiple-line fields for user entry. The entered information is placed into a variable that can be used with the rest of the script or the dialog box set. For instance, this is a useful feature for prompting the user for a password and placing the password into the variable. Then, the variable can be compared to the installation password previously defined using the Set Variable script action. If the password matches, the installation continues; if the entered password is not correct, the installation stops.

When the Edit Text toolbar button is clicked, the dialog box in Figure 5-52 is displayed.

Edit Text Control Properties Options

Default   The Default text box allows you to display text in the Edit Text Control field on the dialog box. The text will be editable unless you click the Read Only checkbox. Leaving this field blank will place a blank field for the user to enter informa-

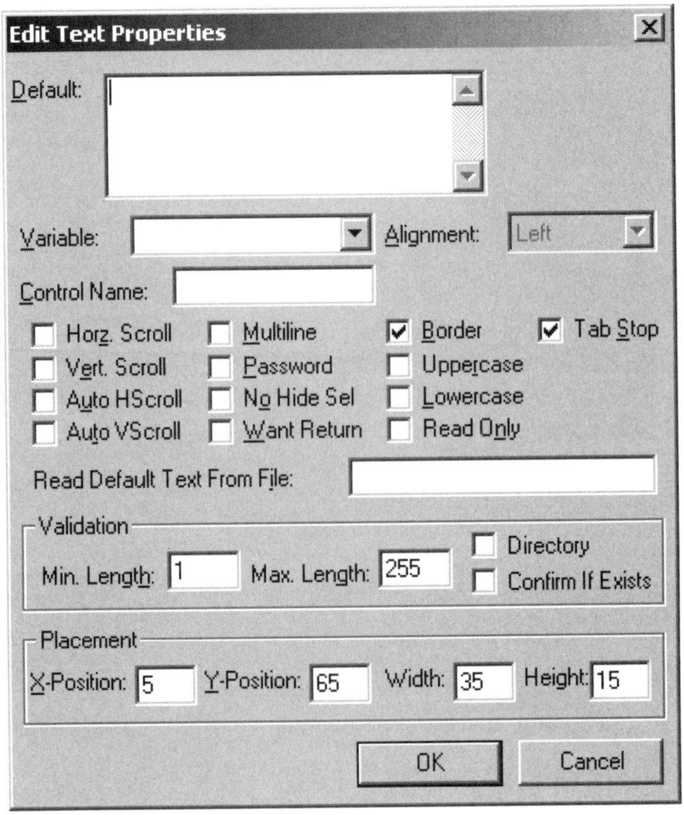

Figure 5-52 *Edit Text Properties dialog box.*

tion. A good use for the Default field is to prompt users for information and give them an example of the format they should use. For example, if asking the user to input his or her IP address, you could enter the standard IP octet format (XXX.XXX.XXX.XXX) in the Default field so the user can quickly identify with the information. The default setting for this field is single line. You can set it to be multiline by selecting the checkbox described later in this section. This field can accept strings of text, variables, or both and can hold up to 30 KB of text.

Note   The purpose of the Edit Text field is to allow the user to place information into a variable to be used with the rest of the script or the dialog box set. If you want to place read-only fields on the dialog box, the Static control would be the better option.

Variable   Choose a variable name that you want the entered information to be placed into. This does not have to be a predefined variable. The variable will be created on the fly and will be available to the rest of the script and also the dialog box set. The text is placed into the variable when the dialog box is closed, either by ending the dialog box routine or by clicking through to the next dialog boxes in succession.

Alignment   The Alignment drop-down box tells SMS Installer how to format the text entered into the Default box. This is only available if the Multiline checkbox is selected. This field contains three options:

- *Left*   The text will be displayed left-justified.

- *Center*   The text will be displayed center-justified.

- *Right*   The text will be displayed right-justified.

Control Name   Though available on the Edit Text Control Properties dialog box, this feature is not yet supported.

Horz. Scroll   When the Multiline checkbox is selected, this option places a horizontal scrollbar in the Edit Text control for the ability to scroll to read text if it is beyond the width of the field. It also allows the user to enter text beyond the width of the window. If not enabled, text beyond the size of the window will wrap to the next line.

Vert. Scroll   When the Multiline checkbox is selected, this option places a vertical scroll bar in the Edit Text control for the ability to scroll to read text if it is beyond the height of the field. This option *must* be enabled if you want the user to have the ability to enter more lines than is available based on the height of the text box.

Auto HScroll   This option adds the same functionality as the Horz. Scroll, but no scroll bar is added. If this is for a single line of text (versus multiline), this option *must* be enabled for the user to be able to enter text wider than the width of the field.

Auto VScroll   This option adds the same functionality as the Vert. Scroll, but no scroll bar is added.

Multiline   The Multiline checkbox enables multiline support for the Default text box. This allows the user to enter more text (if needed) than the size of the field. All information entered will be transferred to the variable. The default setting for the Edit Text control is single-line.

Password   If using this control to verify the installation password, enabling this checkbox echoes the user's keystrokes with asterisks. This helps the user count the correct characters to ensure the proper password is entered, and it also helps retain the security of the installation password. If this is not selected for a password field, the password will be displayed as it is typed. Anyone standing near the computer during the installation will be able to read the password and allow a possible unauthorized installation.

No Hide Sel   Enabling this option allows the selected field to retain its highlight when the control loses focus.

Want Return   This checkbox allows the user to hit the Enter key for a carriage return instead of the SMS Installer standard of Ctrl-Enter. This is a recommended selection because most users are not familiar with the Ctrl-Enter method. If you do not wish to enable this option, be sure to place some instruction on the dialog box for starting a new line of text.

Border   This selection thickens the border around the control, giving it a three-dimensional effect. This is selected by default. If this option is unselected, the Edit Text control will be displayed to the user as a white text box with no border. The borderless box does not display during design time, only during runtime.

Uppercase   This option converts all user input to capital letters. This option is useful if using the variable data to update other files on the computer such as the Autoexec.bat or Config.sys. It also aids in using text search functions in the script to locate case-sensitive information.

Lowercase   This option converts all user input to lowercase letters. This option is useful if using the variable data to update other files on the computer such as the Win.ini or System.ini. It also aids in using text search functions in the script to locate case-sensitive information.

Read Only   Selecting this option forces the Edit Text control to be read-only. The user will not be able to modify a field. This is a useful solution if providing the user with set information and using the Radio Button Control to prompt for a "Yes" or "No" answer.

Tab Stop   This option is checked by default. This causes the control to be included as a Tab function on the dialog box. Tab stops are a standard function of most dialog boxes. The Tab stop allows the user to use the keyboard's tab key to quickly navigate fields without using the mouse to select them.

> All controls placed on the dialog box can be part of the tab order. **Note**
> This procedure is discussed later in this section.

Read Default Text from File   This field allows you to pull information from a local file and have it display in the Default text box. The field can accept strings of text, predefined variables, or both. It can accept up to 255 characters. Any information entered into this field will overwrite the information in the Default text box.

Validation   The Validation section sets the amount of information that can be entered into the Edit Text control. The following options are presented:

- *Min. Length*   This field sets the minimum amount of characters that must be entered in the field. If the minimum is not met, the dialog box set will not continue.

- *Max. Length*   This field sets the maximum amount of characters that can be entered in the field. The maximum length of the Edit Text Control field is 255 characters.

- *Directory*   If using the Edit Text control to prompt the user for a directory location, this checkbox strips the trailing backslash off the entry before it is placed in the variable. This keeps the directory entry uniform. Some users may enter the backslash and it could cause the script not to complete, because the variable is not formatted properly. Use this selection to confirm that any directory information entered will be usable later in the script.

- *Confirm If Exists*   If using the Edit Text control to prompt the user for a directory location, this selection causes the script to verify that the directory exists before continuing. This is useful if using the Edit Text Control variable to create a directory in the local file system and you need users to verify that they want the directory created. A dialog box prompts the user.

Placement   The Placement section allows you to enter screen-positioning values for the Edit Text. While this feature is included on the Edit Text Properties dialog box, it is much easier to change the size and position by clicking and dragging with the mouse button. The following options are presented:

- *X-Position*   The X-Position is the horizontal location on the dialog box for the Edit Text. Measured in pixels, this coordinate starts from the upper left corner of a 640 × 480 screen.

- *Y-Position*   The Y-Position is the vertical location on the dialog box for the Edit Text. Also measured in pixels, this coordinate starts from the upper left corner of a 640 × 480 screen.

- *Width*   The Width relates to the horizontal size of the Edit Text.

- *Height*   The Height relates to the vertical size of the Edit Text.

 This toolbar button inserts a Push Button control on the dialog box. The push button is the tool that allows the user to navigate the dialog box set. The push button performs an action when it is clicked.

Note   Every dialog box that is created *must* include a push button. This is an SMS Installer requirement. Also, every push button created is automatically inserted into the tab order.

When this toolbar button is clicked, the dialog box in Figure 5-53 is displayed.

Push Button Properties Options

Label   The Label field is the actual text that will display on the push button. You can use the ampersand (&) with the label to make an Alt-Key combination for quick access to the button. For example, to give quick keyboard access to the Next button, enter &Next. The N will be underscored, and when the user types Alt-N, the Push Button action will be performed.

Variable   When the push button is activated, and there is an entry in the Value field, the value is assigned to the variable name

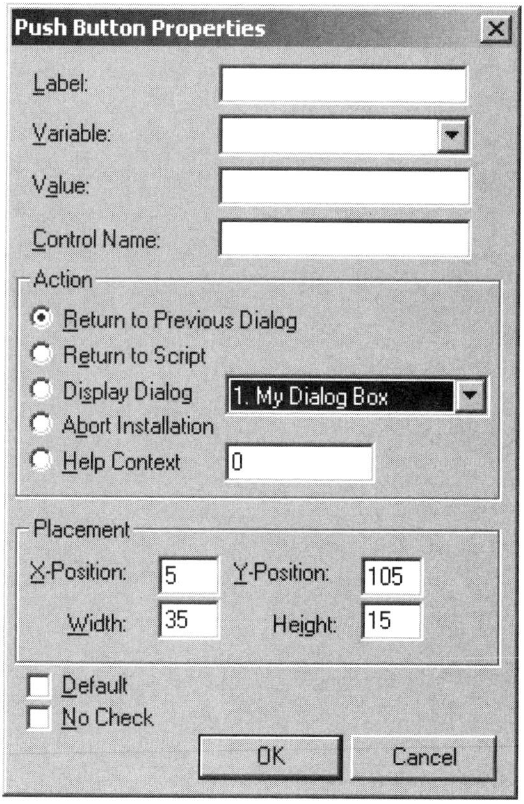

Figure 5-53 *Push Button Properties dialog box.*

that is entered in this field. The variable can be used to perform script logic within the dialog box set or to assign a variable value for use later in the script. The variable must have been defined earlier in the script. The drop-down list provides a list of the pre-defined variables for easy selection.

Tip   You can use the DISABLED variable to disable the Push Button. If you look at the default script that SMS Installer creates, it uses the Set Variable script action to set the DISABLED variable to equal the exclamation point (!), as in the following script example:

```
————-Begin Script
item: Set Variable
  Variable=DISABLED
  Value=!
end
————-End Script
```

Then, during the Wizard Dialog Box set, the exclamation point is used to disable the Push Button control. You can use this same type of logic to assign values to your Push Button variables.

Value   The Value field holds the data that will be placed into the variable when the push button is clicked.

Note   The Push Button control is the epitome of the SMS Installer script logic. Understanding this concept helps you understand the overall scheme. The plan, in this instance, is to place several different Push Button controls on one dialog box, each with its own value. When one push button is clicked, the new variable value will be used to branch the script into one direction. If the user decides to use a different push button, that value will send the script into another, entirely separate direction.

Control Name   Though available on the Push Button Control Properties dialog box, this feature is not yet supported.

Action   The Action section directs the dialog box set after the push button is clicked and the value has been assigned to the variable. The following options are available:

- *Return to Previous Dialog*   Selecting this option causes the previous dialog box to display. This is the same function as seen in the Back push button in standard installations. It allows users to go backwards in the installation to verify their input or to fix mistakes before the installation is initiated. If this is the first dialog box in the dialog box set, using this option will return the user to the previous script item. It is prudent to use the DISABLED variable for the Back button on the first dialog box.

- *Return to Script*   Selecting this option causes SMS Installer to skip the rest of the dialog box set and return to the script.

- *Display Dialog*   This selection includes a drop-down list for choosing other dialog boxes in the dialog set. This is a way to swiftly navigate through the dialog box set. This field must use a dialog box from the set that has already been created. All of the currently created dialog boxes will be available in the list. The dialog box title names are listed along with their numeric placement value (i.e., 1, 2, 3, etc.).

- *Abort Installation*   Selecting this option causes the push button to ask the user if he or she wants to exit the installation. If the user answers "Yes," the installation aborts. If "No" is selected, the user is returned to the dialog box and the script is resumed. This serves to create a Cancel or Exit Installation push button.

- *Help Context*   When adding Help features to the installation, this selection can display help information on the position in the installation. SMS Installer will open standard HLP files. A Set Variable script action must be used to point to a valid path for the HLP file. Set the variable name to WINHELP.

Placement   The Placement section allows you to enter screen-positioning values for the push button. While this feature is included on the Push Button Properties dialog box, it is much easier to change the size and position by clicking and dragging with the mouse button. The following options are presented:

- *X-Position*   The X-Position is the horizontal location on the dialog box for the push button. Measured in pixels, this coor-

dinate starts from the upper left corner of a 640 × 480
screen.

- *Y-Position*   The Y-Position is the vertical location on the dialog box for the push button. Also measured in pixels, this
  coordinate starts from the upper left corner of a 640 × 480
  screen.
- *Width*   The Width relates to the horizontal size of the push
  button.
- *Height*   The Height relates to the vertical size of the push
  button.

Default   Selecting this option causes this Push Button control to
be the default selected push button in the set. If the user hits the
Enter key while on the dialog box, this push button will be activated and perform its function. If you are using the push button
to navigate the dialog box set, it is a standard practice to configure the Next button as the default.

No Check   If this option is selected, the directory verification
function will not be performed. The user will not be prompted to
confirm a directory exists when exiting the dialog box.

 This toolbar button inserts a Radio Button control onto the
dialog box. The Radio Button provides users with a list of items
from which they can make one selection. This is useful when you
have predefined data that will be used with the rest of the script.
It is also helpful to users, since they do not have to enter the
information manually. Manual entry can produce incorrect data.

When this toolbar button is clicked, the dialog box in Figure
5-54 is displayed.

Radio Button Control Options

Radio Button Text   Text or variables entered into this field will
be displayed to the right of the radio button on the dialog box.
Using Ctrl-Enter to start new lines will cause a new radio button
to be created. Each line in the text box will be assigned to a separate radio button.

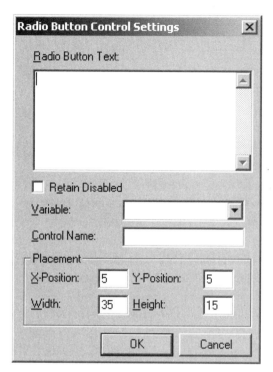

Figure 5-54 *Radio Button Control dialog box.*

Retain Disabled   Keeps the disabled letters (lowercase) specified in the Variable field. See the Variable field for more information.

Variable   The variable name entered here receives the value of the user's radio button selection. The variable must have been defined earlier in the script. This is a required field. You can use the Set Variable script action to create a variable name without a value. For example:

The RADIO variable is set to Null:

```
————-Begin Script
item: Set Variable
  Variable=RADIO
end
————-End Script
```

The RADIO variable is set to MyValue:

```
————-Begin Script
item: Set Variable
  Variable=RADIO
  Value=MyValue
end
       ————-End Script
```

When the user selects the radio button, the variable will be updated with a new value. Each radio button is automatically assigned a consecutive letter depending on its position in the Radio Button Text box (i.e., the first line is assigned "A," the second line is assigned "B," the third line is assigned "C," and so on). Alternatively, you can use the Set Variable script action to set which radio button is the default selection on the dialog box and also to disable specific buttons. The radio button uses upper- and lowercase letters to determine these functions.

For example, create three radio buttons. Each button will automatically be assigned the letters A, B, and C. The examples in Table 5-5 describe how the radio buttons will display with the variable value previously set.

Table 5-5 *Radio button examples.*

Variable Set To:	Display:
A	All radio buttons are enabled and the first button is the default.
B	All radio buttons are enabled and the second button is the default.
C	All radio buttons are enabled and the third button is the default.
Ac	The first two radio buttons are enabled, the first radio button is the default, and the third radio button is disabled.
aB	The first radio button is disabled, the last two radio buttons are enabled, and the second radio button is the default.
abC	The first two radio buttons are disabled, the last radio button is enabled, and it is the default selection.

The radio button set only reads this value to know how you want the buttons to display. Once the user selects their choice of options, the variable value is replaced with the user's selection.

Control Name Though available on the Radio Button Control Properties dialog box, this feature is not yet supported.

Placement The Placement section allows you to enter screen-positioning values for the radio button. While this feature is included on the Radio Button Control Properties dialog box, it is much easier to change the size and position by clicking and dragging with the mouse button. The following options are presented:

- *X-Position* The X-Position is the horizontal location on the dialog box for the Radio Button. Measured in pixels, this coordinate starts from the upper left corner of a 640 × 480 screen.

- *Y-Position* The Y-Position is the vertical location on the dialog box for the Radio Button. Also measured in pixels, this coordinate starts from the upper left corner of a 640 × 480 screen.

- *Width* The Width relates to the horizontal size of the radio button.

- *Height* The Height relates to the vertical size of the radio button.

This toolbar button inserts a Checkbox control onto the dialog box. The Checkbox control provides the user with a list of items from which they can make multiple selections. This is useful when you have predefined data that will be used with the rest of the script. It is also helpful for the user in that they do not have to enter the information manually. Manual entry can produce invalid data.

Clicking the Checkbox Control button displays the dialog box in Figure 5-55.

Checkbox Control Settings Options

Checkbox Text Text or variables entered into this field will be displayed to the right of the Checkbox control on the dialog box.

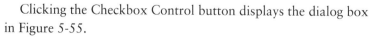

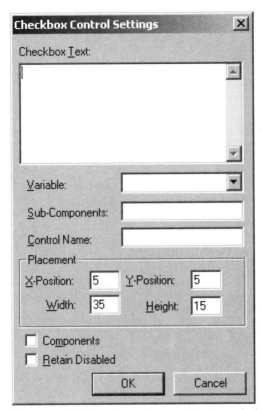

Figure 5-55 *Checkbox Control Settings dialog box.*

Using Ctrl-Enter to start new lines will cause a new checkbox to be created. Each line in the text box will be assigned to a separate checkbox.

Variable   The variable name entered here receives the value of the user's checkbox selection. The variable must have been defined earlier in the script. This is a required field. You can use the Set Variable script action to create a variable name without a value. For example:

The RADIO variable is set to Null:

```
———-Begin Script
item: Set Variable
  Variable=CHECKBOX
end
———-End Script
```

The RADIO variable is set to MyValue:

```
─────-Begin Script
item: Set Variable
  Variable=CHECKBOX
  Value=MyValue
end
─────-End Script
```

When the user selects the checkbox, the variable will be updated with a new value. Each checkbox is automatically assigned a consecutive letter depending on the position in the Checkbox text box (i.e., the first line is assigned A, the second line is assigned B, the third line is assigned C, and so on). Alternatively, you can use the Set Variable script action to set which checkbox is the default selection on the dialog box and also to disable specific checkboxes. The Checkbox control uses upper- and lowercase letters to determine these functions.

For example, create three checkboxes. Each checkbox will automatically be assigned the letters A, B, and C. The examples in Table 5-6 describe how the checkboxes will display with the variable value previously set.

Table 5-6   *Variable settings.*

Variable Set To:	Display:
A	All checkboxes are enabled, and the first checkbox is the default.
B	All checkboxes are enabled, and the second checkbox is the default.
C	All checkboxes are enabled, and the third checkbox is the default.
Ac	The first two checkboxes are enabled, the first checkbox is the default, and the third checkbox is disabled.
aB	The first checkbox is disabled, the last two checkboxes are enabled, and the second checkbox is the default.
abC	The first two checkboxes are disabled, the last checkbox is enabled, and it is the default selection.

The Checkbox control set only reads this value to know how you want the buttons to display. Once the user selects his or her choice of options, the variable value is replaced with the user's selection.

Because the Checkbox control allows the user to select multiple options, the output is different than the Radio Button control. The Radio Button control only outputs one letter to the variable. The Checkbox control outputs multiple letters to the variable depending on the user's selections. For example, if the user selects the first and third checkboxes, the variable will receive a value of AC. If the user selects the second and third checkboxes, the variable value will be BC. If the user selects only the third checkbox, the variable value will be C, and so on.

Depending on how many checkboxes you have created on the dialog box, the Checkbox control can create a multitude of scenarios for branching the script logic down many different paths. For example, an output of "AC" defines one path, an output of "AB" defines another, an output of "ABC" defines another, and so forth.

Subcomponents   This field accepts the predefined subcomponent names (separated by commas). The subcomponents are defined using the Select Components script action.

Control Name   Though available on the Checkbox Control Settings dialog box, this feature is not yet supported.

Placement   The Placement section allows you to enter screen-positioning values for the Checkbox control. While this feature is included on the Checkbox Control Settings dialog box, it is much easier to change the size and position by clicking and dragging with the mouse button. The following options are presented:

- *X-Position*   The X-Position is the horizontal location on the dialog box for the Checkbox control. Measured in pixels, this coordinate starts from the upper left corner of a 640 × 480 screen.

- *Y-Position*   The Y-Position is the vertical location on the dialog box for the Checkbox control. Also measured in pixels, this coordinate starts from the upper left corner of a 640 × 480 screen.

- *Width*   The Width relates to the horizontal size of the Checkbox control.

- Height   The Height relates to the vertical size of the Checkbox control.

Components   If using the Checkbox control to allow the user to select components, select this checkbox. The components can be defined by using the Select Components script action or by defining them in the Installation Expert on the Components tab of the Application Files group.

Retain Disabled   Keeps the disabled letters (lowercase) specified in the Variable field. See the Variable field for more information.

This toolbar button inserts a Combo Box control onto the dialog box. The combo box presents the user with a list of predefined items to make a choice. It also allows the user to enter a choice that is not in the list.

Clicking this toolbar button displays the dialog box shown in Figure 5-56.

Combo Box Control Settings Options

Combo Box Text   The Combo Box Text contains the list of items that will be displayed in the Combo Box control on the dialog box. Each new line you enter (Ctrl-Enter for a new line) will be displayed as a separate item in the list. This field will accept strings of text, predefined variables, or both.

> *Do not* enter text into this field if using the ProgMan Groups or Drive List options.   **Note**

Sort   Selecting this option causes the list entered into the Combo Box Text entry to be sorted (alphabetically) in ascending order. If this is not selected, the list will be displayed as it is entered.

Vert. Scroll   This option places a vertical scroll bar in the Combo Box control for the ability to scroll to read text if it is beyond the height of the field. This option *must* be enabled if you want the

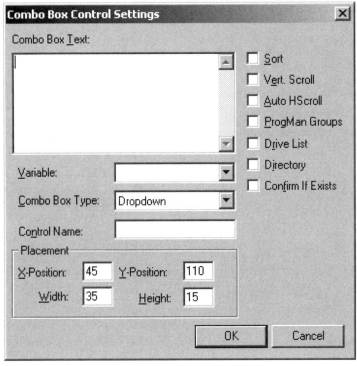

Figure 5-56 *Combo Box control settings.*

user to have the ability to enter more lines than available based
on the height of the text box.

Auto HScroll   This option *must* be enabled for the user to be
able to enter text wider than the width of the field. This allows
the Combo Box control to automatically scroll horizontally as the
user types.

ProgMan Groups   If this option is selected, the Combo Box control will display the current Program Manager groups (application groups) installed on the computer. The field is also editable,
allowing the user to enter another choice. This selection is used
when utilizing the Combo Box control to prompt the user for
what folder the application's icon and shortcut should be placed
in. When the user selects an item from the list, the actual application group name is placed into the variable.

Drive List   Select this option if using the Combo Box control to display a drive list on the local computer. Since this is a noneditable selection, Drop List Combo Box Type must be selected for this to work. This option allows the user to navigate the local computer's drive letters to choose a location for the installation of files.

Directory   If using the Combo Box control to prompt the user for a directory location, this checkbox strips the trailing backslash off the entry before it is placed in the variable. This keeps the directory entry uniform. Some users may enter the backslash, and it could cause the script not to complete because the variable is not formatted properly. Use this selection to confirm that any directory information entered will be usable later in the script.

Confirm If Exists   If using the Combo Box control to list directory locations, this selection causes the script to verify that the directory exists before continuing. This is useful if using the Combo Box Control variable to create a directory in the local file system and you need the user to verify that he or she wants the directory created. A dialog box prompts the user.

Variable   The variable name entered here receives the value of the user's selection. The variable must have been defined earlier in the script. This is a required field.

Combo Box Type   The Combo Box Type configures the type of combo box that will be placed onto the dialog box. The following options are available:

- *Simple*   This selection shows the entire list entered into the Combo Box Text field. The list does not drop down but is instead available to scroll through vertically if Vert. Scroll is enabled.

- *Dropdown*   This is a standard drop-down list. Clicking on the arrow displays the list entered into the Combo Box Text field. This combo box type is editable, allowing the user to enter additional values.

- *Drop List*   This is a standard drop-down list, but it is a noneditable field. Select this option if you do not want the user to be able to input additional information. This option *must* be selected if the Drive List option is being used.

Note You must resize the combo box to fit the list of text, or the drop-down list will not display.

Control Name Though available on the Combo Box Control Settings dialog box, this feature is not yet supported.

Placement The Placement section allows you to enter screen-positioning values for the Combo Box control. While this feature is included on the Combo Box Control Settings dialog box, it is much easier to change the size and position by clicking and dragging with the mouse button. The following fields are presented:

- *X-Position* The X-Position is the horizontal location on the dialog box for the Combo Box control. Measured in pixels, this coordinate starts from the upper left corner of a 640 × 480 screen.

- *Y-Position* The Y-Position is the vertical location on the dialog box for the Combo Box control. Also measured in pixels, this coordinate starts from the upper left corner of a 640 × 480 screen.

- *Width* The Width relates to the horizontal size of the Combo Box control.

- *Height* The Height relates to the vertical size of the Combo Box control.

 This toolbar button inserts a List Box control onto the dialog box. The List Box control is very similar to the Combo Box control and can be used in conjunction with it. The difference between the Combo Box control and the List Box control is that the List Box can be used to allow the user to select multiple items in the list. There is also a full-featured drive/directory list component built into the options of the List Box control.

Clicking this toolbar button displays the dialog box in Figure 5-57.

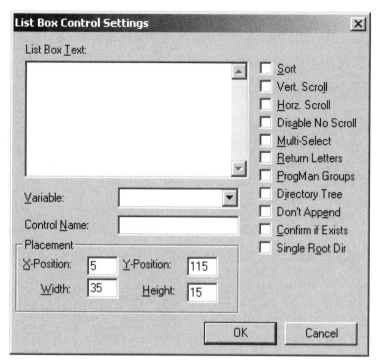

Figure 5-57 *List Box control settings.*

List Box Control Settings Options

List Box Text The List Box Text field contains the list of items that will be displayed in the List Box control on the dialog box. Each new line you enter (Ctrl-Enter for a new line) will be displayed as a separate item in the list. This field will accept strings of text, predefined variables, or both.

> *Do not* enter text into this field if using the ProgMan Groups option. **Note**

Sort Selecting this option causes the list entered into the List Box Text field to be sorted (alphabetically) in ascending order. If this is not selected, the list will be displayed as it is entered.

Vert. Scroll This option places a vertical scroll bar in the List Box control for the ability to scroll to read text if it is beyond the height of the field.

Horz. Scroll   This option places a horizontal scroll bar in the List Box control for the ability to scroll to read text if it is beyond the width of the field. It also allows the user to enter text beyond the width of the window. If not enabled, text beyond the size of the window will wrap to the next line.

Disable No Scroll   This selection places permanent horizontal and vertical scroll bars in the list window, even if the list items do not extend beyond the window size. Either Vert. Scroll or Horz. Scroll or both must be selected for this function to succeed.

Multiselect   This selection enables multiselect in the List Box Control. If this is enabled, the user can select multiple items in the list by clicking with the mouse. This does not use the normal Windows multiselect convention of using the Ctrl-Click (for selecting multiple items, one item at a time) or the Shift-Click (for selecting a range of multiple items). To select an item, the user clicks on it. To deselect an item, the user clicks on it again. When multiple list items are selected (highlighted), the variable receives all the values separated by spaces (unless the Return Letters option is checked).

Return Letters   This option turns the List Box control items into consecutive letters that are placed into the variable. For example, list item 1 would be A, list item 2 would be B, list item 3 would be C, and so on. The normal function of the List Box control is to return the exact text of the list item. Using the Return Letters option is useful if you know the list box items will not change. It is not useful for dynamic data such as the ProgMan Groups or Directory Tree options. If you need this functionality, the Check Box control might be the better option.

Note   Using the Return Letters option limits the list to 26 items because of the number of characters in the alphabet.

ProgMan Groups   If this option is selected, the List Box control will display the current Program Manager groups (application groups) installed on the computer. The field is also editable, allowing the user to enter another choice. This selection is employed when utilizing the List Box control to query the user as to what folder the application's icon and shortcut should be placed in. When the user selects an item from the list, the actual application group name is placed into the variable.

Directory Tree   Selecting this option creates a directory browse list on the dialog box. This is a full-featured interactive directory selection component. It includes an Edit field, a Directory Tree list, and a Disk Drive drop-down list. The example in this section displays a Directory Tree List Box control. When the user selects a drive and directory, the Edit field is updated. This updated information is transferred to the List Box variable. The full path information, with drive letter, is stored for use with the script. This is handy for allowing the user to choose the directory for the file installation. The user can also enter optional directory information. If you enter a directory path in the List Box Text field, it will be displayed in the Edit field when the dialog box is displayed. When the directory selection is changed, the default directory information is appended to the new directory information. This is helpful for ensuring the user does not overwrite an existing directory.

> Use the Confirm If Exists checkbox when using the List Box control to display the directory tree. If this method is not followed, when the user tries to manually enter a directory location and it already exists, the directory will be overwritten without warning.
>
> **Tip**

Don't Append   Used with the Directory Tree option, this option does not append the default directory information when the list selection changes.

Confirm If Exists   This checkbox, if selected, warns users that their selection already exists (if they select a directory that is already present in the file system). If they choose to continue, the directory will be overwritten with the new files. If they choose not to continue, the script will return to the directory selection dialog box to try again.

Single Root Dir   Even though this checkbox is available in SMS Installer, Microsoft has no future plans to enable it.

Variable   The variable name entered here receives the value of the user's selection. The variable must have been defined earlier in the script. This is a required field.

Control Name   Though available on the List Box Control Settings dialog box, this feature is not yet supported.

Placement   The Placement section allows you to enter screen-positioning values for the List Box control. While this feature is included on the List Box Control Settings dialog box, it is much easier to change the size and position by clicking and dragging with the mouse button. The following fields are presented:

- *X-Position*   The X-Position is the horizontal location on the dialog box for the List Box control. Measured in pixels, this coordinate starts from the upper left corner of a 640 × 480 screen.

- *Y-Position*   The Y-Position is the vertical location on the dialog box for the List Box control. Also measured in pixels, this coordinate starts from the upper left corner of a 640 × 480 screen.

- *Width*   The Width relates to the horizontal size of the List Box control.

- *Height*   The Height relates to the vertical size of the List Box control.

There are a few other actions in the Custom Dialog Editor that are not part of the toolbar button set. They are available on the File menu.

There are two options under the Edit selection on the File menu that should be noted.

Edit Menu

- *Dialog Box Properties*   The Dialog Box Properties selection opens the initial Custom Dialog Properties dialog box that is displayed when the script action is clicked. This can be used to change the dialog box properties within the Custom Dialog Editor.

- *Dialog Set Properties*   This box allows you to change the properties of the dialog box set. Clicking on this action displays the dialog box in Figure 5-58. The following three options are presented:

  1. *Dialog Set Name*   This field allows you to change the dialog box set name. Each dialog box set you create has a group name. When the first dialog box is created, its title becomes the default name for the entire set.

  2. *Display Variable*   This field is used with the Wizard Block. When the dialog box set is part of a Wizard Block, a DISPLAY variable must be defined. The DISPLAY variable is assigned to all the dialog boxes in the set.

  3. *Popup Called Dialogs*   Enabling this option causes the next dialog box to display on top of the previous dialog. The default is set to close each dialog box before the next dialog box displays.

There are seven options under the Layout selection on the File menu that should be clarified.

Layout Menu   You can select multiple controls on the dialog box by holding the Shift key and clicking the mouse button. With these selected, the following controls are available:

- *Align Controls Left*   This option shifts the controls to the left side of the dialog box.

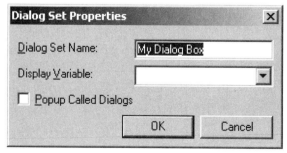

Figure 5-58 *Dialog Set Properties dialog box.*

- *Align Controls Right*   This option shifts the controls to the right side of the dialog box.

- *Align Controls Top*   This option shifts the controls to the top of the dialog box.

- *Align Controls Bottom*   This option shifts the controls to the bottom of the dialog box.

- *Space Evenly Down*   With multiple controls selected, this option spaces the controls evenly down (vertical) the dialog box.

- *Space Evenly Across*   With multiple controls selected, this option spaces the controls evenly across (horizontal) the dialog box.

- *Set Tab Order*   Included on the Edit menu is the option for quickly setting the tab order of the controls. When the user hits the Tab key on the keyboard, the focus changes from the current control to the next one. The order in which you create the controls on the dialog box will be the order numbers that the Custom dialog box automatically assigns to the controls. You should change this order to make the dialog box easier to use.

  When you click on the Set Tab Order selection, the tab stop numbers are displayed next to each control on the dialog box as shown in Figure 5-59.

  To change the Tab Order, just start clicking on the controls in the order that you want them to be available through the Tab key function.

The other item of note on the Custom Dialog Editor File menu is under the Window selection. The Delete Dialog command deletes the entire dialog box in the set.

Note   You cannot use the Delete Dialog command to delete the first dialog box in the set. To delete the first dialog box, you have to delete the entire Custom Dialog script action from the script.

Custom Dialog Box Example

The following example creates a simple two-box dialog set. The primary dialog box is displayed. When the Next button is

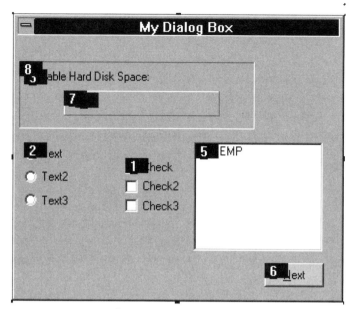

Figure 5-59 *Set Tab Order menu option.*

clicked, the second dialog box is displayed with a Finish button. It uses a Static control to display the amount of disk space on the C: drive. The first dialog box also includes a Radio Button and Checkbox control set. When the Finish button on the second dialog box is clicked, a line is placed into both a RADIO and a CHECK text file in the root of the C: drive containing the Radio Button Checkbox control variable selections, respectively. The Checkbox control set has the third option as the default selection, and the second option is disabled. For example purposes, the List Box control is used to show how it can be used to select a drive and directory. The output of the List Box control is placed in a MYDIR.TXT file in the root of the C: drive.

Other Script Actions Used:

1. Set Variable

2. Check Disk Space

SMS Installer Window:
See Figure 5-60.

```
Set Variable ROOT to C:\
Set Variable CDRIVE to C:
Set Variable CHECK to bC
Set Variable RADIO to B
Set Variable MYDIR to
Check free disk space
Custom Dialog "My Dialog Box 2"
Insert line "%RADIO%" into text file %ROOT%RADIO.TXT.
Insert line "%CHECK%" into text file %ROOT%CHECK.TXT.
Insert line "%MYDIR%" into text file %ROOT%MYDIR.TXT.
```

Figure 5-60 *Custom Dialog script action window.*

Script:

```
--------Begin Script
item: Set Variable
  Variable=ROOT
  Value=C:\
end
item: Set Variable
  Variable=CDRIVE
  Value=C:
end
item: Set Variable
  Variable=CHECK
  Value=bC
end
item: Set Variable
  Variable=RADIO
  Value=B
end
item: Set Variable
  Variable=MYDIR
end
item: Check Disk Space
end
item: Custom Dialog Set
  Name=My Dialog Box 2
  item: Dialog
    Title English=My Dialog Box
    Width=196
    Height=177
    Font Name=Helv
    Font Size=8
    item: Push Button
      Rectangle=147 138 182 153
      Destination Dialog=1
      Action=2
```

```
    Create Flags=01010000000000010000000000000000
    Text English=&Next
  end
  item: Static
    Rectangle=35 34 129 52
    Variable=CDRIVE
    Value=CDRIVE
    Create Flags=01010000000000000000000000000000
  end
  item: Static
  Rectangle=5 20 93 35
  Create Flags=01010000000000000000000000000000
  Text English=Available Hard Disk Space:
  end
  item: Static
    Rectangle=2 15 141 56
    Action=3
    Create Flags=01010000000000000000000000000111
  end
  item: Static
    Rectangle=28 33 120 48
    Action=4
    Create Flags=01010000000000000000000000000110
  end
  item: Radio Button
    Rectangle=5 65 40 108
    Variable=RADIO
    Create Flags=01010000000000010000000000001001
    Text English=Text
    Text English=Text2
    Text English=Text3
    Text English=
  end
  item: Checkbox
    Rectangle=49 69 84 105
    Variable=CHECK
    Create Flags=01010000000000010000000000000011
    Text English=Check
    Text English=Check2
    Text English=Check3
    Text English=
  end
  item: Listbox
    Rectangle=106 65 180 130
    Variable=MYDIR
    Create Flags=01010000100000010000000101000000
    Flags=0000110000001010
    Text English=C:\TEMP
```

```
       Text English=
      end
     end
     item: Dialog
       Title English=My Dialog Box 2
       Width=150
       Height=150
       Font Name=Helv
       Font Size=8
       item: Push Button
         Rectangle=98 103 133 118
         Action=1
         Create Flags=01010000000000010000000000000000
         Text English=E&xit
        end
       end
      end
     item: Insert Line into Text File
    Pathname=%ROOT%RADIO.TXT
    New Text=%RADIO%
    Line Number=0
  end
  item: Insert Line into Text File
    Pathname=%ROOT%CHECK.TXT
    New Text=%CHECK%
    Line Number=0
  end
  item: Insert Line into Text File
    Pathname=%ROOT%MYDIR.TXT
    New Text=%MYDIR%
    Line Number=0
  end
  ———-End Script
```

Custom Graphic

Clicking the Custom Graphic script action opens the Custom Graphic Editor, shown in Figure 5-61. The Custom Graphic Editor allows you to create custom graphics to display on the background of the installation screen. This component is a full-featured graphic editor, though not as powerful as some other third-party programs. It provides the convenience of being able to create graphics within the SMS Installer interface.

The File and Layout functions are the same as those in the Custom Dialog Editor. For this reference, the toolbar buttons will be described. They provide all the actions available for creating a

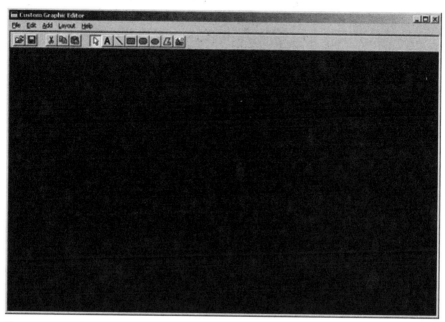

Figure 5-61 *Custom Graphic Editor.*

custom graphic. To work with the toolbar buttons, simply click on the button to select the item, and then select an area on the graphic workspace where it will be placed.

This toolbar function inserts a text element into the custom graphic. Clicking on this toolbar button brings up the dialog box in Figure 5-62.

Text Settings Options

Text   Enter the text that you wish to display in the graphic. This field does not support variables.

Extra Bold   This thickens and darkens the text entered into the Text field, making it more prominent.

Shadow   This selection displays the text with a light shadow underneath, giving it a three-dimensional effect.

Alignment   This drop-down selection sets the text to left-justified, center-justified, or right-justified.

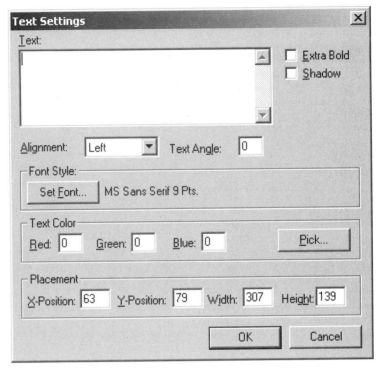

Figure 5-62 *Text Settings dialog box.*

Text Angle   This input field allows you to change the angle of the text. Enter a numeric value in degrees.

Font Style   The Font Style allows you to select the type of display font for the text. Click the Set Font button to pick from the font list on the computer.

Text Color   The Text Color changes the color of the text font. It allows manual entry of the RED, GREEN, and BLUE variables. It is easier to use the Pick button to select the color you want to use.

Placement   The Placement section allows you to enter screen-positioning values for the text element. The following fields are presented:

- *X-Position*   The X-Position is the horizontal location on the dialog box for the text element. Measured in pixels, this coordinate starts from the upper left corner of a 640 × 480 screen.

- *Y-Position*   The Y-Position is the vertical location on the dialog box for the text element. Also measured in pixels, this coordinate starts from the upper left corner of a 640 × 480 screen.

- *Width*   The Width relates to the horizontal size of the text element.

- *Height*   The Height relates to the vertical size of the text element.

> The placement and size of the graphic can be changed on the Custom Graphic Editor screen.

Note

This toolbar button places a line element into the custom graphic. Selecting this toolbar button displays the dialog box in Figure 5-63.

Line Settings Options

Line Style   The Line Style field predetermines the type of line that is placed into the custom graphic. The options are Solid, Dashed, Dotted, Dashed and Dotted, and Double Dots.

Line Arrows   The Line Arrows option places arrows at the ends of the line element. The options are None, Left, Right, and Both.

Line Direction   This is used in conjunction with the Line Arrows selection. The Line Direction option determines whether the arrow points toward the line body or away from it. The options are Descending and Ascending.

Line Width   This thickens the size of the line element. This value can be from 0 to 255.

Line Color   This changes the color of the line element. It allows manual entry of the `RED`, `GREEN`, and `BLUE` variables. It is easier to use the Pick button to select the color you want to use.

Placement   This section allows you to enter screen-positioning values for the Line Element. The following fields are presented:

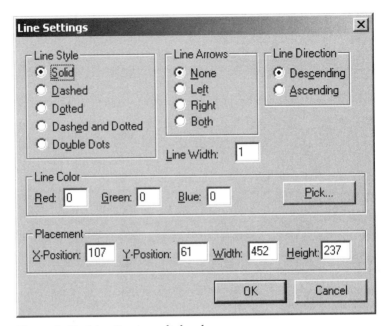

Figure 5-63 *Line Settings dialog box.*

- *X-Position*   The X-Position is the horizontal location on the dialog box for the line element. Measured in pixels, this coordinate starts from the upper left corner of a 640 × 480 screen.

- *Y-Position*   The Y-Position is the vertical location on the dialog box for the line element. Also measured in pixels, this coordinate starts from the upper left corner of a 640 × 480 screen.

- *Width*   The Width relates to the horizontal size of the line element.

- *Height*   The Height relates to the vertical size of the line element.

Note   The placement and size of the graphic can be changed on the Custom Graphic Editor screen.

This toolbar button inserts a rectangle element into the custom graphic. Selecting this toolbar button displays the dialog box in Figure 5-64.

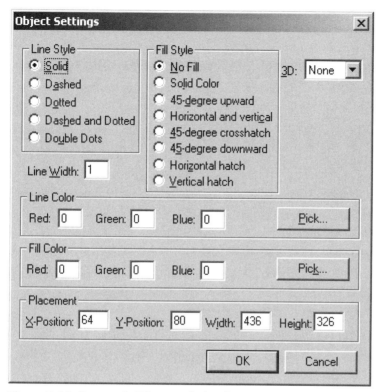

Figure 5-64 *Rectangle Element dialog box.*

Rectangle Element Settings Options

Line Style The Line Style field controls the type of line that is placed around the rectangle in the custom graphic. The options are Solid, Dashed, Dotted, Dashed and Dotted, and Double Dots.

Fill Style The Fill Style field provides different options for applying patterns to the colors inside the rectangle element. The options are No Fill, Solid Color, 45-degree Upward, Horizontal and Vertical, 45-degree Crosshatch, 45-degree Downward, Horizontal Hatch, and Vertical Hatch.

3D This list allows you to create a three-dimensional effect for the rectangle element. The options are None, Inset, Flush, Outset, and Border.

Line Width   The Line Width field thickens the size of the border around the rectangle element. This value can be from 0 to 255.

Line Color   The Line Color field changes the color of the border around the rectangle element. It allows manual entry of the RED, GREEN, and BLUE variables. It is easier to use the Pick button to select the color you want to use.

Fill Color   The Fill Color changes the color of the inside of the rectangle element. It allows manual entry of the RED, GREEN, and BLUE variables. It is easier to use the Pick button to select the color you want to use.

Placement   The Placement section allows you to enter screen-positioning values for the rectangle element. The following fields are presented:

- *X-Position*   The X-Position is the horizontal location on the dialog box for the rectangle element. Measured in pixels, this coordinate starts from the upper left corner of a 640×480 screen.

- *Y-Position*   The Y-Position is the vertical location on the dialog box for the rectangle element. Also measured in pixels, this coordinate starts from the upper left corner of a 640×480 screen.

- *Width*   The Width relates to the horizontal size of the rectangle element.

- *Height*   The Height relates to the vertical size of the rectangle element.

Note   The placement and size of the graphic can be changed on the Custom Graphic Editor screen.

This toolbar button inserts a rounded rectangle element into the custom graphic. Selecting this toolbar button displays the dialog box in Figure 5-65.

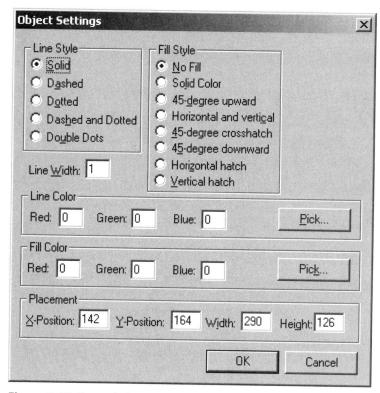

Figure 5-65 *Rounded Rectangle Element dialog box.*

Rounded Rectangle Settings Options

Line Style   The Line Style field dictates the type of line that is placed around the rounded rectangle in the custom graphic. The options are Solid, Dashed, Dotted, Dashed and Dotted, and Double Dots.

Fill Style   The Fill Style field provides different options for applying patterns to the colors inside the rounded rectangle element. The options are No Fill, Solid Color, 45-degree Upward, Horizontal and Vertical, 45-degree Crosshatch, 45-degree Downward, Horizontal Hatch, and Vertical Hatch.

Line Width   The Line Width field thickens the size of the border around the rounded rectangle element. This value can be from 0 to 255.

Line Color   The Line Color field changes the color of the border around the rounded rectangle element. It allows manual entry of the RED, GREEN, and BLUE variables. It is easier to use the Pick button to select the color you want to use.

Fill Color   The Fill Color field changes the color of the inside of the rounded rectangle element. It allows manual entry of the RED, GREEN, and BLUE variables. It is easier to use the Pick button to select the color you want to use.

Placement   The Placement section allows you to enter screen-positioning values for the Rounded Rectangle Element. The following fields are presented:

- *X-Position*   The X-Position is the horizontal location on the dialog box for the rounded rectangle element. Measured in pixels, this coordinate starts from the upper left corner of a 640×480 screen.

- *Y-Position*   The Y-Position is the vertical location on the dialog box for the rounded rectangle element. Also measured in pixels, this coordinate starts from the upper left corner of a 640×480 screen.

- *Width*   The Width relates to the horizontal size of the rounded rectangle element.

- *Height*   The Height relates to the vertical size of the rounded rectangle element.

Note   The placement and size of the graphic can be changed on the Custom Graphic Editor screen.

This toolbar button inserts an ellipse element into the custom graphic. Selecting this toolbar button displays the dialog box in Figure 5-66.

Ellipse Element Settings Options

Line Style   The Line Style field governs the type of line that is placed around the ellipse in the custom graphic. The options are Solid, Dashed, Dotted, Dashed and Dotted, and Double Dots.

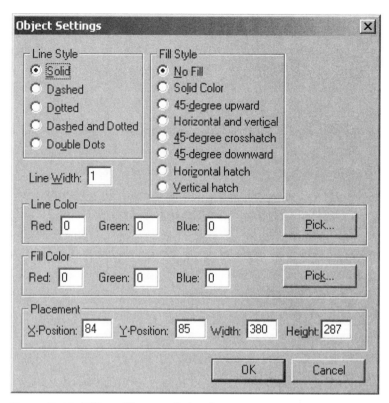

Figure 5-66 *Ellipse Element dialog box.*

Fill Style   The Fill Style field provides different options for applying patterns to the colors inside the Ellipse Element. The options are: No Fill, Solid Color, 45-degree Upward, Horizontal and Vertical, 45-degree Crosshatch, 45-degree Downward, Horizontal Hatch, and Vertical Hatch.

Line Width   The Line Width field thickens the size of the border around the ellipse element. This value can be from 0 to 255.

Line Color   The Line Color field changes the color of the border around the ellipse element. It allows manual entry of the RED, GREEN, and BLUE variables. It is easier to use the Pick button to select the color you want to use.

Fill Color   The Fill Color field changes the color of the inside of the ellipse element. It allows manual entry of the RED, GREEN, and BLUE variables. It is easier to use the Pick button to select the color you want to use.

Placement   The Placement section allows you to enter screen-positioning values for the ellipse element. The following options are presented:

- *X-Position*   The X-Position is the horizontal location on the dialog box for the ellipse element. Measured in pixels, this coordinate starts from the upper left corner of a 640 × 480 screen.

- *Y-Position*   The Y-Position is the vertical location on the dialog box for the ellipse element. Also measured in pixels, this coordinate starts from the upper left corner of a 640 × 480 screen.

- *Width*   The Width relates to the horizontal size of the ellipse element.

- *Height*   The Height relates to the vertical size of the ellipse element.

Note   The placement and size of the graphic can be changed on the Custom Graphic Editor screen.

 This toolbar button inserts a polygon element into the custom graphic. Selecting this toolbar button allows you to click points on the graphic screen until your desired shape has been created. When the shape is formed, hitting the Escape key on the keyboard displays the dialog box in Figure 5-67.

Polygon Element Settings Options

Line Style   The Line Style field determines the type of line that is placed around the polygon in the Custom Graphic. The options are Solid, Dashed, Dotted, Dashed and Dotted, and Double Dots.

Fill Style   The Fill Style field provides different options for applying patterns to the colors inside the polygon element. The options are No Fill, Solid Color, 45-degree Upward, Horizontal and Vertical, 45-degree Crosshatch, 45-degree Downward, Horizontal Hatch, and Vertical Hatch.

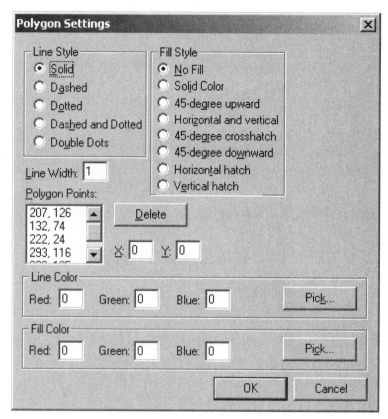

Figure 5-67 *Polygon Element dialog box.*

Line Width   The Line Width field thickens the size of the border around the polygon element. This value can be from 0 to 255.

Polygon Points   The Polygon Points section allows you to manually edit the polygon's shape using the X and Y screen variables. To change the points, select it in the list and modify the X or Y values. If you want to delete a point, highlight it in the list and click on the Delete button.

Line Color   The Line Color field changes the color of the border around the polygon element. It allows manual entry of the RED, GREEN, and BLUE variables. It is easier to use the Pick button to select the color you want to use.

Fill Color   The Fill Color field changes the color of the inside of the ellipse element. It allows manual entry of the RED, GREEN, and BLUE variables. It is easier to use the Pick button to select the color you want to use.

Placement The Placement section allows you to enter screen-positioning values for the ellipse element. The following fields are presented:

- *X-Position* The X-Position is the horizontal location on the dialog box for the ellipse element. Measured in pixels, this coordinate starts from the the upper left corner of a 640 × 480 screen.

- *Y-Position* The Y-Position is the vertical location on the dialog box for the ellipse element. Also measured in pixels, this coordinate starts from the upper left corner of a 640 × 480 screen.

- *Width* The Width relates to the horizontal size of the ellipse element.

- *Height* The Height relates to the vertical size of the ellipse element.

Note The placement and size of the graphic can be changed on the Custom Graphic Editor screen.

This toolbar button inserts a bitmap element into the custom graphic. The bitmap element allows you to incorporate existing graphic files in the custom graphic from the file system.

When this toolbar button is selected, the Bitmap Settings dialog box is displayed, as shown in Figure 5-68.

Bitmap Element Settings Options

Pathname The Pathname field points to a bitmap graphic in the local file system. This field cannot accept variable names defined in the script. The Browse button allows you to search the local file system for the file.

Transparent Selecting this option causes a specific color in your bitmap file to be transparent. The specific color is set by the Transparent Color settings. When a color is set as transparent,

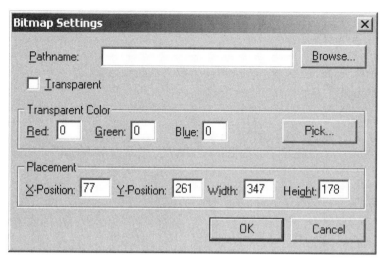

Figure 5-68 *Bitmap Settings dialog box.*

the installation's background color shows through the transparent areas.

Transparent Color This option controls the color in the bitmap that will be transparent. Though you can use the Red, Green, and Blue fields to enter the color value, the Pick button allows you to pick the color from the palette.

Placement The Placement section allows you to enter screen-positioning values for the bitmap element. The following fields are presented:

- *X-Position* The X-Position is the horizontal location on the dialog box for the bitmap element. Measured in pixels, this coordinate starts from the upper left corner of a 640 × 480 screen.

- *Y-Position* The Y-Position is the vertical location on the dialog box for the bitmap element. Also measured in pixels, this coordinate starts from the upper left corner of a 640 × 480 screen.

- *Width* The Width relates to the horizontal size of the bitmap element.

- *Height*   The Height relates to the vertical size of the bitmap element.

Note   The placement and size of the graphic can be changed on the Custom Graphic Editor screen.

There are a few other items of note on the File and Edit menus of the Custom Graphic Editor. These items are not part of the toolbar set.

File Menu

File Save As...   The File Save As allows you to save your graphic file in the file system as a GRF file. This saved file can be retrieved later for other SMS Installer scripts.

Edit Menu

Bring to Front   With a graphic element highlighted, choosing this option moves the object to the front of all the other graphic elements.

Send to Back   With a graphic element highlighted, choosing this option moves the object behind the other graphic elements.

Graphic Properties   The Graphic Properties option sets the default display for all graphic elements. When this option is selected, the dialog box in Figure 5-69 appears.

The following graphic settings options are presented:

- *X-Position*   The X-Position is the horizontal location on the dialog box for all graphic elements. Measured in pixels, this coordinate starts from the upper left corner of a 640 × 480 screen.

- *Y-Position*   The Y-Position is the vertical location on the dialog box for all graphic elements. Also measured in pixels, this coordinate starts from the upper left corner of a 640 × 480 screen.

- *Erase Num*   Whenever you add custom graphics to your installation, the graphic is assigned a number and recorded in

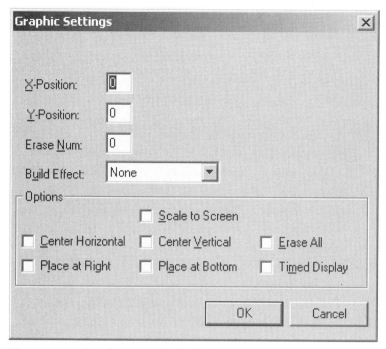

Figure 5-69 *Graphic Settings dialog box.*

an internal index. This parameter removes the graphic from that index.

- *Build Effect*   The Build Effect adds motion to the selected graphic. There are six options:
    1. *None*   The graphic appears with the installation screens.
    2. *Fade in*   The graphic appears faint at first, then slowly intensifies until it reaches full resolution in the installation screen at coordinates specified by the X and Y parameters.
    3. *From Top*   The graphic slides into view from the top of the installation screen and comes to rest at the coordinates specified by the X and Y parameters.
    4. *From Bottom*   The graphic slides into view from the bottom of the installation screen and comes to rest at the coordinates specified by the X and Y parameters.
    5. *From Left*   The graphic slides into view from the left of the installation screen and comes to rest at the coordinates specified by the X and Y parameters.

6. *From Right* The graphic slides into view from the right of the installation screen and comes to rest at the coordinates specified by the X and Y parameters.

- *Options Section* The Options section has seven fields:
  1. *Scale to Screen* This selection directs the custom graphic to cover the entire installation screen. The graphic is stretched to fit the entire background.
  2. *Center Horizontal* The graphic is centered across the screen at the Y coordinate. When selected, this disables the X-Position entry.
  3. *Center Vertical* The graphic is centered vertically on the screen at the X coordinate. When selected, this disables the Y-Position entry.
  4. *Erase All* All graphic files are removed from the internal index and the SMS Installer background.
  5. *Place at Right* The graphic is pushed all the way to the right of the installation screen at the Y coordinate. When selected, this disables the X-Position entry.
  6. *Place at Bottom* The graphic is arranged at the bottom of the installation screen. When selected, this disables the Y-Position entry.
  7. *Timed Display* The Timed Display option calculates the number of custom graphic files selected, with the overall installation time, and then spaces the graphic files to display accordingly throughout the installation.

Custom Graphic Example

The following example creates a custom graphic that includes the text element, the line element, the ellipse element, and the rectangle element.

SMS Installer Window:

See Figure 5-70

Figure 5-70 *Custom Graphic script action window.*

Script:

```
———-Begin Script
item: Custom Graphic
  Width=465
  Height=295
  item: Rectangle
    Rectangle=23 29 465 295
    Flags=00000001
    Pen Width=1
    Brush Color=12632256
    Brush Style=1001
    Extra Flags=00000011
  end
  item: Text
    Text English=This is a custom graphic!
    Rectangle=54 61 435 101
    Pen Color=8388608
    Pen Style=6
    Pen Width=1
    Extra Flags=00000010
    Name=MS Sans Serif
    Font Style=-24 0 0 0 400 0 0 0 1 2 1 34
  end
  item: Ellipse
    Rectangle=146 111 310 266
    Pen Width=1
    Brush Color=65535
    Brush Style=1001
  end
  item: Ellipse
    Rectangle=187 148 207 174
    Pen Width=1
    Brush Style=1001
  end
  item: Ellipse
    Rectangle=241 146 261 172
    Pen Width=1
    Brush Style=1001
  end
  item: Line
    Rectangle=188 204 269 205
    Pen Width=2
    Brush Style=1000
  end
end
———-End Script
```

Delete File(s)

The Delete File(s) dialog allows you to use SMS Installer to delete files and directories from the local file system of the target computer (see Figure 5-71). If you are using this script action to delete installed files that are used during the installation, see the Get Temporary Filename script action. This allows you to place a filename in a variable that SMS Installer automatically deletes when the script has completed.

Delete File(s) Options

Pathname   The Pathname field is the full path and filename that is to be deleted. The entry *must* start with a predefined variable. The asterisk (*.*) characters are supported. The field can accept text and variables up to 255 characters.

Note   SMS Installer has a built-in feature that protects the wildcard character deletion in any Windows system directory such as the \Windows, \Windows\System, \Temp, and \Windows\Temp.

Include Subdirectories   Selecting this option will automatically delete any directories beneath the directory specified for deletion. This saves time from having to create separate script lines for each directory.

Remove Directory Containing Files   This option deletes the directory containing the files marked for deletion.

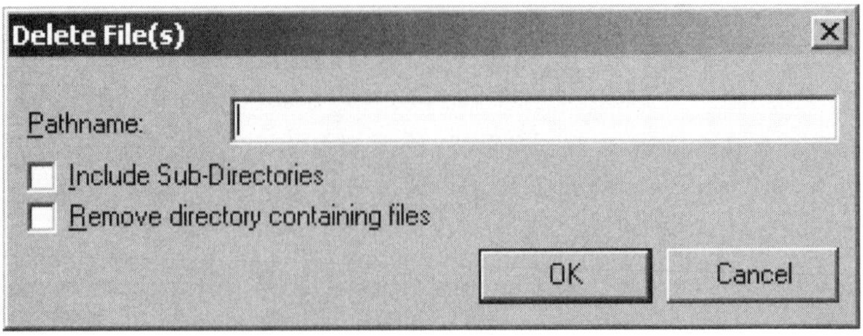

Figure 5-71 *Delete File(s) dialog box.*

```
Check free disk space
Set Variable ROOT to C:\
Create Directory %ROOT%MYDIR
Insert line "This File is Marked for Deletion. Please close this file before continuing." into text file %ROOT%MYDIR\DEL.TXT.
Display Message "Before Continuing..."
Delete File(s) %ROOT%MYDIR\*.*
```

Figure 5-72 *Delete File(s) script action window.*

> SMS Installer will *only* delete directories that are empty.   **Note**

Delete File(s) Example

The following example creates a directory on the root of the C: drive called MYDIR and places a text file in the directory. Then, the script prompts you to verify that the file and directory exist. After confirmation, the file and directory are deleted.

Other Script Actions Used:

1. Check Disk Space

2. Set Variable

3. Create Directory

4. Insert Line into Text File

5. Display Message

SMS Installer Window:
See Figure 5-72.

Script:

```
————-Begin Script
item: Check Disk Space
end
item: Set Variable
  Variable=ROOT
  Value=C:\
end
item: Create Directory
  Pathname=%ROOT%MYDIR
end
```

```
item: Insert Line into Text File
  Pathname=%ROOT%MYDIR\DEL.TXT
  New Text=This File is Marked for Deletion. Please close
this file before continuing.
  Line Number=0
end
item: Display Message
  Title English=Before Continuing...
  Text English=Before continuing, check for the existence
of the DEL.TXT file in the C:\MYDIR directory. This file
and directory will be deleted when you click OK.
  Flags=00100100
end
item: Delete File
  Pathname=%ROOT%MYDIR\*.*
  Flags=00001100
end
————-End Script
```

Display Graphic

The Display Graphic dialog box, shown in Figure 5-73, allows you to select Windows bitmap files from the local computer to be

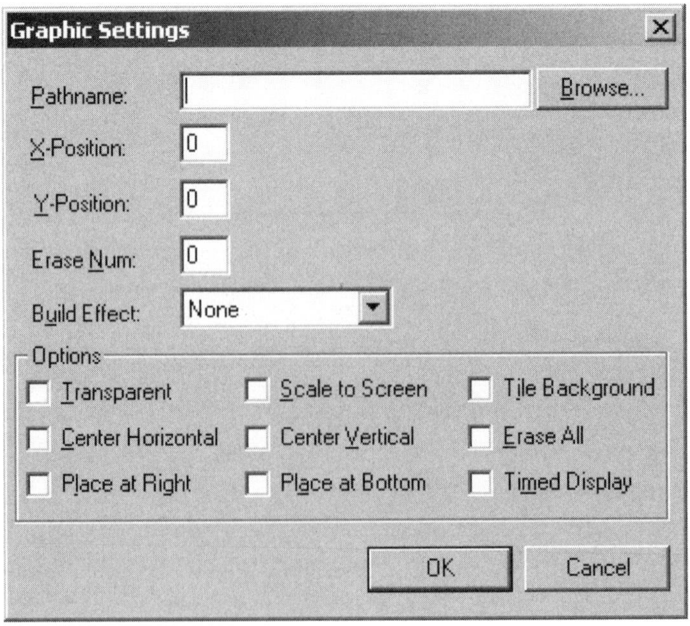

Figure 5-73 *Display Graphic dialog box.*

displayed on the background of the installation screen. These graphic files can help you customize the installation for your company with logos, pictures, and so on. Up to 15 graphic files can be displayed at one time. But keep in mind that the more graphics SMS Installer has to process, the slower the installation performance will be. When SMS Installer compiles the script, the graphic files are compressed into the executable.

Display Graphic Settings Options

Pathname The Pathname field accepts any standard Windows bitmap graphic file. The field can accept strings of text, variables, or both to point to the file.

X-Position The X-Position is the horizontal location on the dialog box for all graphic elements. Measured in pixels, this coordinate starts from the upper left corner of a 640×480 screen.

Y-Position The Y-Position is the vertical location on the dialog box for all graphic elements. Also measured in pixels, this coordinate starts from the upper left corner of a 640×480 screen.

Erase Num Whenever you add custom graphics to your installation, the graphic is assigned a number and recorded in an internal index. This parameter removes the graphic from the index.

Build Effect The Build Effect adds motion to the selected graphic. The following options are presented:

- *None* The graphic appears with the installation screens.

- *Fade in* The graphic appears faint at first, and then slowly intensifies until it reaches full resolution in the installation screen at the coordinates specified by the X and Y parameters.

- *From Top* The graphic slides into view from the top of the installation screen and comes to rest at the coordinates specified by the X and Y parameters.

- *From Bottom* The graphic slides into view from the bottom of the installation screen and comes to rest at the coordinates specified by the X and Y parameters.

- *From Left* The graphic slides into view from the left of the installation screen and comes to rest at the coordinates specified by the X and Y parameters.

- *From Right* The graphic slides into view from the right of the installation screen and comes to rest at the coordinates specified by the X and Y parameters.

Options Section The following options are presented in this section:

- *Transparent* The custom graphic remains faint during the installation, blending with the background colors.

- *Scale to Screen* This selection advises the custom graphic to cover the entire installation screen. The graphic is stretched to fit the entire background.

- *Tile Background* Duplicate copies of the graphic are placed end-to-end, horizontal and vertical, until it fills the entire background like a tiled floor.

- *Center Horizontal* The graphic is centered horizontally on the screen at the Y coordinate. When selected, this disables the X-Position entry.

- *Center Vertical* The graphic is centered vertically on the screen at the X coordinate. When selected, this disables the Y-Position entry.

- *Erase All* All graphic files are removed from the internal index and the SMS Installer background.

- *Place at Right* The graphic is pushed all the way to the right of the installation screen at the Y coordinate. When selected, this disables the X-Position entry.

- *Place at Bottom* The graphic is arranged at the bottom of the installation screen. When selected, this disables the Y-Position entry.

- *Timed Display* The Timed Display option calculates the number of custom graphic files selected, with the overall installation time, and then spaces the graphic files to display accordingly throughout the installation.

```
Check free disk space
Display Graphic E:\Folders\McGraw Hill\Scripts\Chapter Five\SMSTrentbn.bmp (Tile)
Sleep for 5000 Milliseconds
```

Figure 5-74 *Display Graphic script action window.*

Display Graphic Example

The following example displays a tiled bitmap file on the background of the installation screen. The Sleep function has been added to let the graphic display for 5 seconds.

Other Script Actions Used:

1. Check Disk Space

2. Sleep

SMS Installer Window:
See Figure 5-74.

Script:

```
————-Begin Script
item: Check Disk Space
end
item: Display Graphic
  Pathname English=E:\Folders\McGraw Hill\Scripts\Chapter
Five\SMSTrentbn.bmp
  X Position=32768
  Flags=0000000001011000
end
item: Sleep
  Sleep=5000
end
————-End Script
```

Display Message

The Display Message script action allows you to present informative text to the user on a dialog box as shown in Figure 5-75. It can be used to describe what steps are next in the installation, give instructions, or start a logic block based on the user's Yes or No answer.

Display Message Settings Options

Message Title   The Message Title is a required field. The entry will be displayed as the title of the dialog box that is presented to the user. This field can accept strings of text, variables, or both, up to 80 characters. If the entered information is longer than the width of the dialog box, the text will be displayed in ellipses, so try to keep the title under 40 characters.

Message Text   The Message Text field contains the information you want the user to read. This field accepts strings of text, variables, or both, up to 511 characters. You can use the Ctrl-Enter key combination to enter blank lines into the field.

Tip   Because SMS Installer uses the percent sign (%) to signify a variable, if you ever want to display the percent sign, you need to enter two percent signs for every one. For example, if you want to display "25%" in the message text, you would enter 25%%.

Message Icon   You can assign a specific icon to the message dialog box. The icon represents the type of information that is being

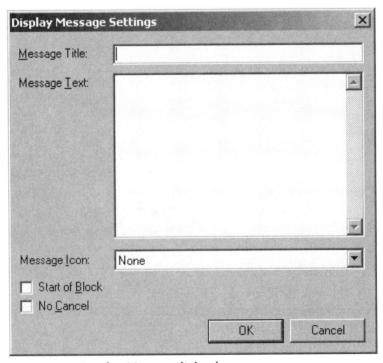

Figure 5-75 *Display Message dialog box.*

displayed. For instance, if the information being presented is critical in nature, you may want to use the Exclamation icon or the Stop icon. The graphic representation helps the user understand the situation. There are four icon options available in the drop-down list, as shown in Figures 5-76 through 5-79.

Start of Block   If this option is selected, the message box will be used to start an If/Else block statement. The OK button is automatically changed to a Yes button, and a No button is added.

> If the Start of Block option is used, you must complete the If/Else   **Note**
> block in the script. Add an Else Statement script action if there are
> conditions that must be met, or an End Block if answering "No" to
> the message box stops the block logic.

No Cancel   Selecting this option causes the Cancel button to not display on the dialog box. The Cancel button used with this script action causes users to be prompted as to whether they

Figure 5-76 *Informational icon.*

Figure 5-77 *Exclamation icon.*

Figure 5-78 *Question icon.*

Figure 5-79 *Stop icon.*

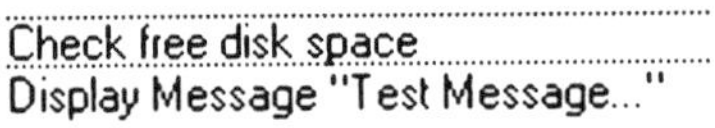

```
Check free disk space
Display Message "Test Message..."
```

Figure 5-80 *Display Message script action window.*

would like to exit the installation. If the message is informational only, the Cancel button could end the script.

Display Message Example

The following example displays a simple message box.

Other Script Actions Used:

Check Disk Space

SMS Installer Window:

See Figure 5-80.

Script:

```
———-Begin Script
item: Check Disk Space
end
item: Display Message
 Title English=Test Message...
 Text English=This is a test message.
 Flags=00100100
end
———-End Script
```

Display ReadMe File

The Display ReadMe File dialog box, shown in Figure 5-81, allows you to display any text file to the user. The text file must already exist on the target computer, and you must know its location. The best method to accomplish this is to include the text file in the compressed executable, install it to the target computer (using the Install File(s) script action), and then to use the Display ReadMe File script action to present the installed file.

Note   The text file must be under 30 KB in size.

ReadMe Settings Options

File Pathname   This field holds the path information to the location of the text file. The file must be on the target computer. This

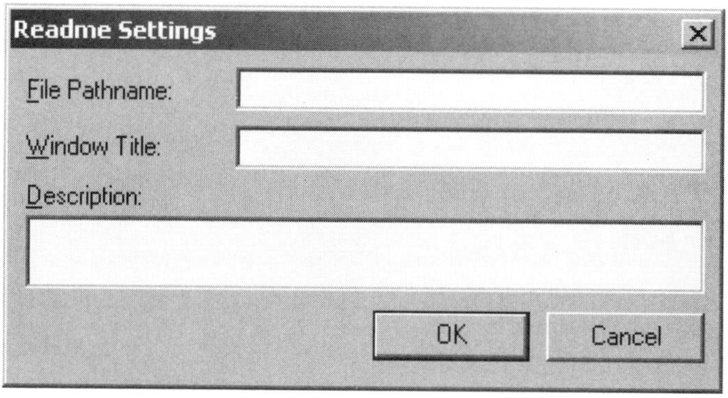

Figure 5-81 *Display ReadMe File dialog box.*

field will accept strings of text, variables, or both, up to 255 characters.

Window Title   The Window Title is a required field. The entry will be displayed as the title of the dialog box that is presented to the user. This field can accept strings of text, variables, or both, up to 255 characters. If the entered information is longer than the width of the dialog box, the text will be displayed in ellipses, so try to keep the title under 40 characters.

Description   The Description information is centered between the box that displays the text file and the OK and Cancel buttons. Though this field will accept up to four lines of text, only two lines will display. The Description field is used to provide more information about the text file. This field uses the standard Ctrl-Enter command to create a new line.

> The OK button on the dialog box returns the user to the script.   **Note**
> The Cancel button displays the Abort Installation dialog prompt.

Display ReadMe File Example
    The following example installs a Readme.txt file to the root of the C: drive and then displays the information to the user in a dialog box. After the information in the dialog box has been read, and the OK button has been clicked, the Readme.txt file is deleted.

Other Script Actions Used:

1. Check Disk Space

2. Set Variable

3. Install File(s)

4. Delete File(s)

SMS Installer Window:
See Figure 5-82.

Script:

```
————-Begin Script
item: Check Disk Space
end
item: Set Variable
  Variable=SCRIPTLOC
  Value=E:\FOLDERS
end
item: Set Variable
  Variable=ROOT
  Value=C:\
end
item: Install File
  Source=E:\Folders\McGraw Hill\Scripts\Chapter
Five\Readme.txt
  Destination=%ROOT%Readme.txt
  Flags=0000000000000010
end
item: Display ReadMe File
  Pathname=%ROOT%README.TXT
  Title English=ReadMe...
  Description English=This is information you should be
aware of...
end
item: Delete File
  Pathname=%ROOT%README.TXT
end
————-End Script
```

```
Check free disk space
Set Variable SCRIPTLOC to E:\FOLDERS
Set Variable ROOT to C:\
Install File E:\Folders\McGraw Hill\Scripts\Chapter Five\Readme.txt to %ROOT%Readme.txt
Display ReadMe File %ROOT%README.TXT
Delete File(s) %ROOT%README.TXT
```

Figure 5-82 *Display ReadMe File script action window.*

Output:
See Figure 5-83.

Edit INI File

The Edit INI File dialog box, shown in Figure 5-84, allows you
to modify INI files. You can add, delete, and modify existing INI
sections, or create a brand-new INI file. When the script action is
run, SMS Installer looks for the INI file specified in the File field.
If the file is not found, a new INI file is automatically created
with the filename provided.

> This script action does not cause a reboot of the computer. If
> modifying the SYSTEM.INI file, use the RESTART variable to cause
> the computer to recycle the operating system. Or, use the Add to
> SYSTEM.INI script action.

Note

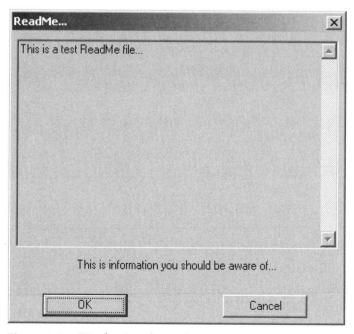

Figure 5-83 *Display Readme File script output.*

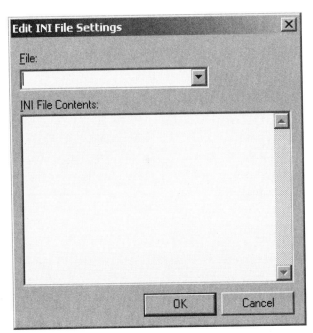

Figure 5-84 *Edit INI File dialog box.*

Edit INI File Settings Options

File   This field *must* start with a predefined variable name. It points to the location of the INI file that should be modified or created. The field can accept text strings, variables, or both, up to 255 characters.

INI File Contents   The INI File Contents box allows you to enter information that should be added, deleted, or modified in the INI file. This field *must* start with an INI section name. Section names are formatted with brackets (e.g., [INI_SECTION]). For examples of INI files, see Chapter 10 (Win.ini and System.ini). If the INI section is a new section, it will be placed at the bottom of the INI file. This field accepts strings of text, variables, or both. The text box is limited to 30 KB of information.

Note   A lot of INI value strings use case-sensitive entries. If you are modifying existing INI file contents, the value and section names must match exactly.

More Information

Deleting INI Information To delete an entire INI section, type the section title into the INI File Contents box ([INI_SECTION]), and leave the rest of the information blank. To delete one value, type the section title and variable name, and leave the value blank.

Example—Deleting one value:

```
[INI_SECTION]
INIVariable=
```

Modifying Existing INI Information To modify an existing entry, type the section title in the INI File Contents box, the INI variable, and the new INI value.

Example—Modifying the value:

```
***Information already present in INI file:
[INI_SECTION]
INIVariable=OLDVALUE

***Information entered into the INI File Contents text box:
[INI_SECTION]
INIVariable=NEWVALUE
```

Edit INI File Example

The next example prompts the user for his/her Social Security number and then creates a MYINI.INI file in the root of the C: drive that contains the information in a User Information section.

Other Script Actions Used:

1. Check Disk Space

2. Prompt for Text

3. Set Variable

SMS Installer Window:
See Figure 5-85.

```
Check free disk space
Prompt "Social Security Number" Variable SSN
Set Variable ROOT to C:\
Edit INI File %ROOT%MYINI.INI
```

Figure 5-85 *Edit INI File script action window.*

Script:

```
---------Begin Script
item: Check Disk Space
end
item: Prompt for Text
  Window Title English=Enter Value...
  Text English=Please enter your social security number...
  Prompt Title English=Social Security Number
  Default English=XXX-XX-XXXX
  Variable=SSN
end
item: Set Variable
  Variable=ROOT
  Value=C:\
end
item: Edit INI File
  Pathname=%ROOT%MYINI.INI
  Settings=[User Information]
  Settings=
  Settings=SSN=%SSN%
  Settings=
end
---------End Script
```

Edit Registry

The Edit Registry dialog box, shown in Figure 5-86, provides manual entry of registry key modifications, additions, and deletions. As mentioned, if you are not familiar with the structure and the criticality, working with the registry can lead to serious computer problems. Be very careful that you understand the implications of making the wrong modifications and be sure to test the registry modifications, on a test PC before trying them on a production computer. Deleting or modifying the wrong registry keys and values can cause the computer not to boot. For more information on the Windows Registry, see "Registry Overview" in Chapter 07.

Edit Registry Settings Options

Registry Keys   The standard Windows 9x and Windows NT Registry root keys are available for modification:

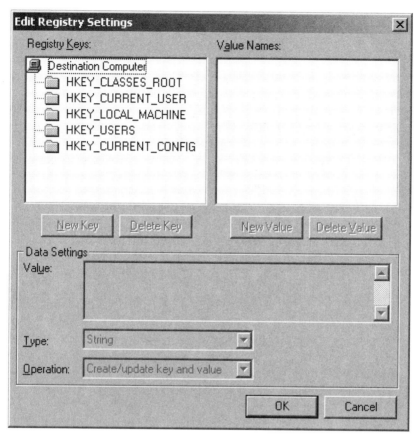

Figure 5-86 *Edit Registry dialog box.*

HKEY_CLASSES_ROOT, HKEY_CURRENT_USER,
HKEY_LOCAL_MACHINE, HKEY_USERS, HKEY_CUR-
RENT_CONFIG.

> If the user does not have administrator privileges on the com-   **Note**
> puter, only the HKEY_CURRENT_USER and HKEY_CLASSES_ROOT
> can be modified through the SMS Installer script. You may need to
> use a utility to temporarily give the user administrator context
> (see "Building the SMS Installer Toolkit" in Chapter 10 for more
> information).

Two buttons are presented:

- *New Key button*   The New Key button allows you to enter new registry key information. You can complete the information presented on the dialog box or make further modifications after you have accepted the input on the Edit Registry Settings window.

- *Delete Key button*   The Delete Key button relates to the Edit Registry dialog box only. It is for deleting any keys that either exist in this window or have been created with this interface. It does not mark registry keys for deletion unless you compile the blank key in the script and the key already exists in the registry. You must highlight the key in the Registry Keys window for the button to become active.

Value Names   The Value Names box contains the current value names, which represent the information in the Value box in the Data Settings section. The value name is merely a brief title to describe what data it contains (displayed in the Value box).

Two buttons are presented:

- *New Value button*   The New Value button allows you to enter new registry value information. You can complete the information presented on the dialog box or make further modifications after you have accepted the input on the Edit Registry Settings window.

- *Delete Value button*   The Delete Value button relates to the Edit Registry dialog box only. It is for deleting any values that either exist in this window or have been created with this interface. It does not mark registry values for deletion unless you compile blank values into the script and the value already exists in the registry. You must highlight the value in the Value Names window for the button to become active.

Data Settings   The Data Settings section accepts the actual registry data input and allows you to configure the type of information the data represents. The following fields are presented:

- *Value*   The Value field holds the information associated with the highlighted value name.

- *Type* The Type drop-down box specifies the format the value will have in the registry key. Six options are available:

  1. *String* Data stored in strings of information. This data type is usually Standard English entries, indicating information stored in an easily readable format. Hence, this data type is easy to understand and the easiest to modify. If script variables are used for this type, the variables are converted to their literal data when the script is compiled.

  2. *Unexpanded String* Like the String data type, this type stores alphanumeric data. But unlike the String data type, it does not convert script values to their literal data when the script is compiled. Instead, the variable names are stored in the registry. Use this type to store environment variables into the registry.

  3. *Multiple Strings* Data stored in multiple string values. Most values are stored in a readable format, instead of hex or binary. This is similar to the String data, but it can contain multiple lines of data.

  4. *Double Word* Double word, or DWORD, is data stored in 4 bytes. This data type can be viewed in hexadecimal, binary, or decimal and usually indicates things such as memory addresses, interrupt settings, device factors, and so on. The value can be from 0 to 0xFFFFFFFF.

  5. *Binary/Hex* Data is stored in binary or hex format. This usually indicates hardware component information. Since it is binary or hex, having vendor-specific information about the binary or hex variables is a must before making any modifications. Any values entered into this field that are not in binary or hex are converted to zero.

  6. *None* The None option is used when deleting registry keys and registry key values.

- *Operation* The Operation drop-down list contains the following options, which tell the SMS Installer what operation the script action should perform:

  1. *Create/update key and value* Creates a new key and value or modifies or replaces a current key and value.

  2. *Create empty key* Creates an empty registry key with no data and no values.

3. *Remove key and all subkeys*   Removes an entire key, its subkeys, and its values.

4. *Remove value only*   Removes the data and values but leaves the registry key alone.

Edit Registry Example

The following example modifies the default save paths for Microsoft Word 2000 and Microsoft Excel 2000. The Values display C:\MYDATA as the new path. The script can be modified and then compiled to contain any path value you want. For more information on this example, see "Default File Save Location in MS Word and MS Excel 2000" in Chapter 06.

SMS Installer Window:
See Figure 5-87.

Script:

```
————-Begin Script
item: Edit Registry
  Total Keys=3
  item: Key
    Key=Software\Microsoft\Office\9.0\Excel\Options
    New Value=C:\MyData
    Value Name=DefaultPath
    Root=1
  end
  item: Key
    Key=Software\Microsoft\Office\9.0\Word\Options
    New Value=C:\MyData
    Value Name=DOC-PATH
    Root=1
  end
  item: Key
    Key=Software\Microsoft\Office\9.0\Word\Options
    New Value=C:\MyData\AutoSave
  Value Name=AUTOSAVE-PATH
  Root=1
 end
end
————-End Script
```

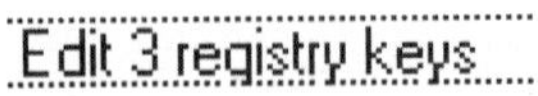

Edit 3 registry keys

Figure 5-87 *Edit Registry script action window.*

Else Statement

The Else Statement script action has no associated dialog box. Double-clicking on the script action places it into the highlighted area of the script. The Else Statement action allows you to create branching script logic to perform TRUE/FALSE functions. This script action must be used in conjunction with a script action that starts a logic block and the End Block script action. For a list of the SMS Installer script actions that start a logic block, see "Script Actions That Start a Logic Block" in Chapter 10.

Else Statement Example

The following example uses the Get System Information script action to pull the registered owner name from the computer and place it in a variable. If the variable data matches the information placed into the variable of the If/While statement, the user is presented with a message indicating the installation can continue. Otherwise (i.e., Else), if the owner information does not match the variable, the user is prompted with a message stating the installation will not continue.

Other Script Actions Used:

1. Check Disk Space

2. Get System Information

3. If/While Statement

4. Display Message

5. End Block

SMS Installer Window:
See Figure 5-88.

```
Check free disk space
Get System Information into CONAME
If CONAME Equals "MyCompany" then
   Display Message "Registered Company..."
Else
   Display Message "Registered Company..."
End Block
```

Figure 5-88 *Else Statement script action window.*

Script:

```
———-Begin Script
item: Check Disk Space
end
item: Get System Information
  Variable=CONAME
  Flags=00000111
end
item: If/While Statement
  Variable=CONAME
  Value=MyCompany
end
item: Display Message
  Title English=Registered Company...
  Text English=The installation has checked the registered
owner of this software and the approval has succeeded. The
installation will continue normally...
  Flags=00100100
end
item: Else Statement
end
item: Display Message
  Title English=Registered Company...
  Text English=The installation has checked the registered
owner of this software and approval has FAILED. The instal-
lation will stop...
  Flags=00110000
end
item: End Block
end
———-End Script
```

End Block

The End Block script action completes a logic block. There must be one End Block statement for every If/Then/While statement that exists in the script.

Note

Logic blocks can be contained within other logic blocks. When this scenario exists in the script, it is easy to forget to include additional End Block script actions. The SMS Installer script will not compile if it exists in this condition. When you try to compile the

Figure 5-89 *End Block warning.*

script, the End Block Warning dialog box (Figure 5-89) will be displayed, and the script line that contains the error will be highlighted once the error box is cleared.

End Block Example

The following example pulls the computer's time zone information from the registry. It then verifies the information against what the time zone should be. If the information is correct, the user is presented with a message indicating the setting is correct and the installation can continue normally. If the information is incorrect, a message is displayed asking the user to modify the time zone information, and the user is notified that the installation will exit. This is a good script to use when software, such as the SMS client software, is dependent on the correct time zone settings.

Other Script Actions Used

1. Set Variable

2. Check Free Disk Space

3. Get Registry Key Value

4. If/While Statement

5. Else Statement

6. Display Message

7. Exit Installation

SMS Installer Window:
See Figure 5-90.

```
Set Variable PST to Pacific Standard Time
Set Variable CST to Central Standard Time
Set Variable MST to Mountain Standard Time
Set Variable EST to Eastern Standard Time
Check free disk space
Get Registry Key SYSTEM\CurrentControlSet\Control\TimeZoneInformation place in Variable TZONE
If TZONE Equals "%EST%" then
  Display Message "Time Zone Settings..."
Else
  Display Message "Incorrect Time Zone Settings..."
  Exit Installation
End Block
```

Figure 5-90 *End Block script action window.*

Script:

```
--------Begin Script
item: Set Variable
  Variable=PST
  Value=Pacific Standard Time
end
item: Set Variable
  Variable=CST
  Value=Central Standard Time
end
item: Set Variable
  Variable=MST
  Value=Mountain Standard Time
end
item: Set Variable
  Variable=EST
  Value=Eastern Standard Time
end
item: Check Disk Space
end
item: Get Registry Key Value
  Variable=TZONE
    Key=SYSTEM\CurrentControlSet\Control\TimeZoneInformation
  Value Name=StandardName
  Flags=00000100
end
item: If/While Statement
  Variable=TZONE
  Value=%EST%
end
item: Display Message
  Title English=Time Zone Settings...
  Text English=Your computer's time zone is to %TZONE%.
This is the correct setting.
  Text English=
```

```
  Text English=No modification needs to be made.
  Text English=
  Text English=The installation will now continue...
  Flags=00100100
end
item: Else Statement
end
item: Display Message
  Title English=Incorrect Time Zone Settings...
  Text English=Your computer's time zone is set incor-
rectly. It is currently set to %TZONE%. It should be set to
%EST%.
  Text English=
  Text English=Please make the appropriate changes before
continuing.
  Text English=
  Text English=The installation will now exit.
  Flags=00101000
end
item: Exit Installation
end
item: End Block
end
───────End Script
```

Execute Program

The Execute Program dialog box, shown in Figure 5-91, allows you to run additional programs external to SMS Installer. The program must already exist on the computer. The program

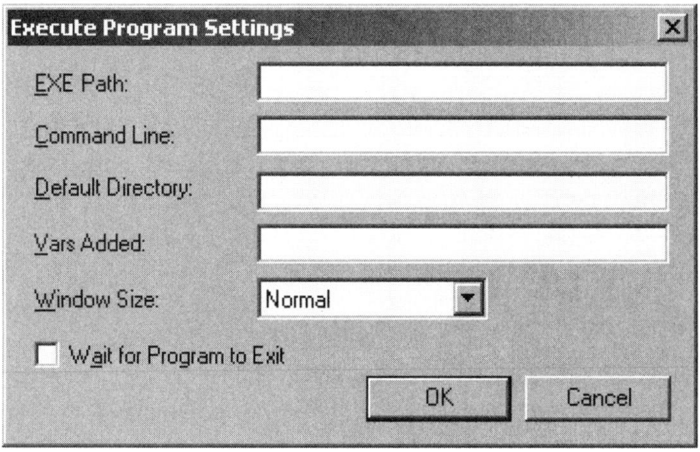

Figure 5-91 *Execute Program dialog box.*

can be installed by the script or can have been installed previously. The ability to run external programs gives SMS Installer more functionality. It provides the ability to compensate for options that SMS Installer does not provide, such as giving temporary local administrator rights to the computer when an installation requires it. For a listing of programs useful to SMS Installer, see "Building the SMS Installer Toolkit" in Chapter 10.

Note   Executing external programs with the same name as the one currently running is not supported in Windows installations. If you want to call another SMS Installer–generated executable from within a script, make sure the file has a different name.

This script action is useful for running programs at the end of SMS Installer script (e.g., most installations give users the choice to run the actual program after the application is installed).

Note   If both the program and installation will be running from a floppy diskette set, you must use the Allow Floppy Disk Change script action before this one.

Execute Program Settings Options

EXE Path   The EXE Path field contains the full path and executable name of the external program that will run. This field accepts text strings, variables, or both, up to 255 characters.

Command Line   This field allows entering any command-line switches, parameters, or options that should be used when the program is run. This field accepts text strings, variables, or both, up to 127 characters.

Default Directory   This optional field configures the external program to point to another location when run. If the external program relies on other files to run, they must be in the same directory from where it is run. If the program is reliant on files located in a different directory, this field is mandatory. This field accepts text strings, variables, or both, up to 255 characters.

Vars Added This field accepts a list of predefined variable names separated by commas. If variables are placed in this field, they will be available to the external program, to modify or query.

Window Size The Window Size selection configures the program's starting window state. It has the following options:

- *Normal* When this is selected, the program will run using the application vendor's default settings.

- *Minimized* When this is selected, the program will start minimized on the computer's taskbar.

- *Maximized* When this is selected, the program window will fill the entire display area.

Wait for Program to Exit Selecting this option will cause the SMS Installer script to be suspended until the external program has finished. If this option is not chosen, the script will continue to run while the external program finishes. If the script will use information created or gathered by the external program, this option is required for the script to complete successfully.

Execute Program Example

The following example checks the local operating system. If the operating system is Windows NT, the external program IPCONFIG is called. The IPCONFIG information is passed to a text file in the root of the C: drive. The user is presented with a dialog box containing the computer's current TCP/IP information. If the operating system is not Windows NT, an error message is displayed stating that the utility only runs on Windows NT and that the utility will exit.

Other Script Actions Used:

1. Check Disk Space

2. Set Variable

3. Check Configuration

4. Display Readme File

5. Else Statement

6. Display Message

7. End Block

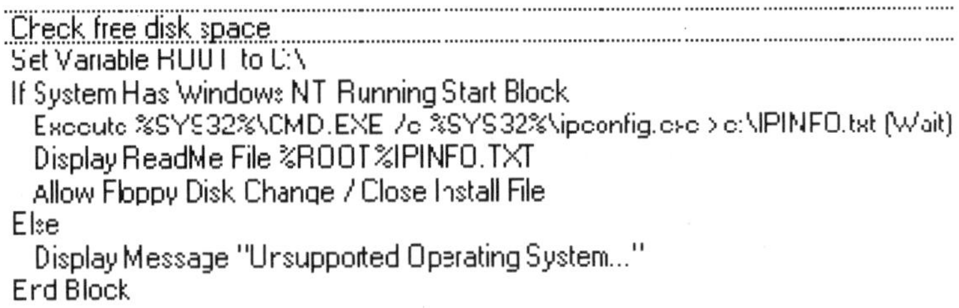

```
Check free disk space
Set Variable ROOT to C:\
If System Has Windows NT Running Start Block
    Execute %SYS32%\CMD.EXE /c %SYS32%\ipconfig.exe > c:\IPINFO.txt (Wait)
    Display ReadMe File %ROOT%IPINFO.TXT
    Allow Floppy Disk Change / Close Install File
Else
    Display Message "Unsupported Operating System..."
End Block
```

Figure 5-92 *Execute Program script action window.*

SMS Installer Window:

See Figure 5-92.

Script:

```
————Begin Script
item: Check Disk Space
end
item: Set Variable
  Variable=ROOT
  Value=C:\
end
item: Check Configuration
  Flags=10100000
end
item: Execute Program
  Pathname=%SYS32%\CMD.EXE
  Command Line=/c %SYS32%\ipconfig.exe >c:\IPINFO.txt
  Flags=00000110
end
item: Display ReadMe File
  Pathname=%ROOT%IPINFO.TXT
  Title English=Windows NT TCP/IP Configuration
  Description English=The information listed is the most
current TCP/IP settings for this computer.
end
item: Allow Floppy Disk Change
end
item: Else Statement
end
item: Display Message
  Title English=Unsupported Operating System...
  Text English=This utility only runs with Windows NT. The
program will now exit...
  Flags=00110000
end
item: End Block
end
————End Script
```

Exit Installation

The Exit Installation script action has no associated dialog box. Double-clicking on the script item places it in the highlighted area of the script. This script action causes the script to terminate completely and exit without warning to the user. You should not use this at the end of the script unless you are using it for testing small blocks of the script. In this case, placing it at the end of a block allows you to test up to that point in the script. This operation is similar to using the debugging features described at the beginning of this chapter.

Exit Installation Example

The following example displays a simple message indicating that the installation has been successful and will now exit.

Other Script Actions Used:

1. Check Disk Space

2. Display Message

SMS Installer Window:
See Figure 5-93.

Script:

```
————Begin Script
item: Check Disk Space
end
item: Display Message
  Title English=Exiting...
  Text English=The installation was successful! The instal-
lation will now exit.
  Flags=00100100
end
item: Exit Installation
end
————End Script
```

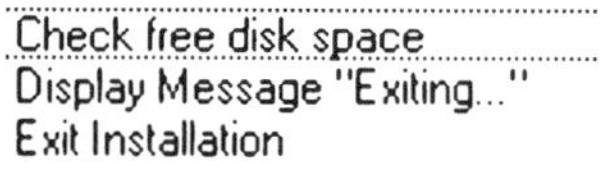

Check free disk space
Display Message "Exiting..."
Exit Installation

Figure 5-93 *Exit Installation script action window.*

Find File in Path

The Find File in Path dialog box, shown in Figure 5-94, allows you to search for the existence of a file in the local file system. The script action searches for the first occurrence of the specified file and places the location information into a variable that can be used with the remainder of the script.

Find File in Path Options

File Name   This field contains the actual filename for which the script will search. The field will accept up to 255 characters and wildcard characters (*).

Note   If using the wildcard character to find files in the file system, only use this with the Remove Filename option selected. Otherwise, the variable will receive a NULL (blank) value.

Variable Name   This creates the variable that will receive the location information of the file when it is found. If the file is not found, the variable receives a blank value. The blank value is useful for logic blocks that perform a function if the file is not on the local file system of the target computer. If the file is not present, you can choose a logic branch to proceed with its installation. This is helpful for verifying the existence of an external program,

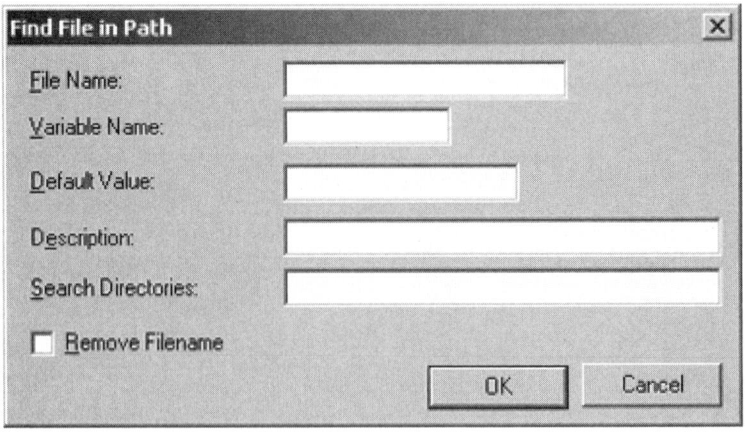

Figure 5-94 *Find File in Path dialog box.*

installing it if is not found, and for using the Execute Program script action to run it.

Default Value This optional field holds the default value that is entered into the variable if the specified file cannot be found during the search.

Description The Description field contains the information the user sees as the script searches for the specified file. If this field is left blank, the user will not see a message. This field accepts text strings, variables, or both, up to 255 characters. Only 75 characters will be visible to the user.

Search Directories If you know where the file is generally located, this field allows you to target specific directories when using this script action. Otherwise, the entire file system will be searched for the specified filename. A semicolon separates the directory names. This field can accept text strings, variables, or both, but it is a better practice to define the directory information earlier in the script with the Set Variable script action. This allows entries in this field to be shorter and more manageable.

Remove Filename Selecting this checkbox causes SMS Installer to strip the filename from the directory path information. This is beneficial for performing software upgrades. The script action finds the path based on the old filename and then overwrites the new file.

Find File in Path Example

The following example sets a variable that contains the common path to the SMS Software Inventory Agent. It then searches for the SINV32.EXE file. If it is not found (variable equals NULL), a warning is displayed to the user. If the search was successful, the user is presented with an informational screen displaying the path to the file.

Other Script Actions Used:

1. Check Disk Space
2. Set Variable

```
Check free disk space
Set Variable OSDIR to C:\WINNT
Set Variable SMSCLIENT to %OSDIR%\MS\SMS\CLICOMP\SINV
Find file SINV32.EXE in %SMSCLIENT% and place into Variable SOFTINV
If SOFTINV Equals "" then
  Display Message "File not found..."
Else
  Display Message "Software Inventory Agent..."
End Block
```

Figure 5-95 *Find File in Path script action window.*

3. If/While Statement

4. Display Message

5. Else Statement

6. End Block

SMS Installer Window:

See Figure 5-95.

Script:

```
————-Begin Script
item: Check Disk Space
end
item: Set Variable
  Variable=OSDIR
  Value=C:\WINNT
end
item: Set Variable
  Variable=SMSCLIENT
  Value=%OSDIR%\MS\SMS\CLICOMP\SINV
end
item: Find File in Path
  Variable=SOFTINV
  Pathname List=SINV32.EXE
  Search Directories=%SMSCLIENT%
  Description English=Searching for the old Software
Inventory Agent...
  Flags=00000001
end
item: If/While Statement
  Variable=SOFTINV
end
item: Display Message
  Title English=File not found...
  Text English=The SMS Software Inventory Agent was not
```

```
found on this computer!
  Text English=
  Text English=Please contact your local technical support
for assistance.
  Flags=00101000
end
item: Else Statement
end
item: Display Message
  Title English=Software Inventory Agent...
  Text English=The SMS Software Inventory Agent was found
in the %SOFTINV% directory.
  Text English=
  Text English=The upgrade will now continue...
  Flags=00100100
end
item: End Block
end
————-End Script
```

Get Environment Variable

The Get Environment Variable dialog box, shown in Figure 5-96, allows you to retrieve environment information from the computer and place it into a variable. The variable value can be used with the remainder of the script.

Environment variables are common to the operating system. If you open an MS-DOS prompt on the computer, type in the SET command, and hit the Enter key, a list of local environment vari-

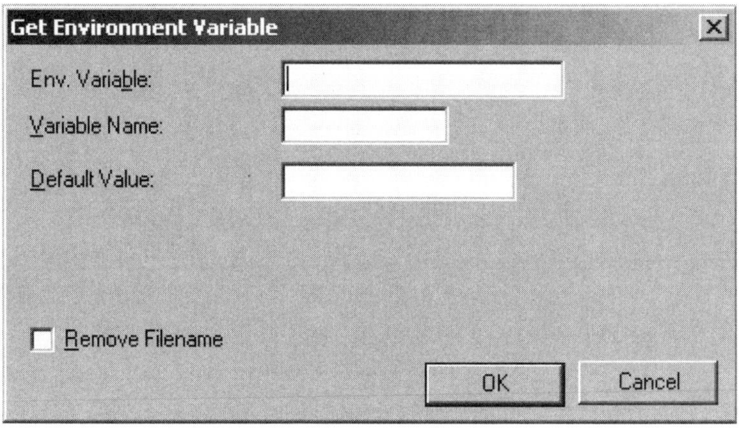

Figure 5-96 *Get Environment Variable dialog box.*

ables will display. The second example in this section does this for you and displays the environment variable contents in a dialog box window. There are a number of components that set the computer's environment variables. Environment variables are set through the Autoexec.bat file, the Config.sys file, the Command Interpreter, network login scripts, and so on. Environment variables are memory-resident values the computer needs to perform certain functions. For example, when an application begins an installation, it must know where the Windows directory is located. The application queries the `SystemRoot` environment variable to find that the Windows directory is C:\WINDOWS. This environment variable is important because the Windows program files can be installed in any directory. Adding the `SystemRoot` value to the operating system means any application will be able to find the Windows directory no matter where it is located.

A common use of this script action is to retrieve the computer's `PATH` information from the environment variable.

Get Environment Variable Options

Env. Variable   This field contains the operating system environment variable name that you want to retrieve and place into the script variable. This cannot be a script variable name. This field can accept up to 255 characters.

Variable Name   The Variable Name field creates a new variable in which the environment variable value will be stored for use with the script. If the environment variable is not found, the variable name will receive a blank value, unless the Default Value field has been filled out.

Default Value   This optional field contains the value that will be placed into the script variable should the environment value not be found. The field accepts text strings, variables, or both, up to 255 characters.

Tip   A good rule of thumb for the Default Value field in *all* script actions that retrieve values instead of pathnames is to place the word NOTFOUND in the field. When using logic blocks, it is simple to remember this value. For example, you can use an If/While statement to warn the user if the SystemRoot environment variable is not found in the computer's configuration:

```
———-Begin Script
item: Check Disk Space
end
item: Get Environment Variable
  Variable=OSDIR
  Environment=SystemRoot
  Default=NOTFOUND
end
item: If/While Statement
  Variable=OSDIR
  Value=NOTFOUND
end
item: Display Message
  Title English=Operating System Directory...
  Text English=The Operating System is not configured on
this computer. Please contact local technical support
immediately to have this issue resolved.
  Flags=00010000
end
item: Exit Installation
end
item: End Block
end
———-End Script
```

Remove Filename   If using this script action to retrieve PATH information from the environment variable, any filenames will be stripped from the information. If this script action is used and only directory information is retrieved from the PATH environment value, the last path statement will be stripped from the output.

Get Environment Variable Example 1
   The following example retrieves the SystemRoot environment variable and displays the output in a dialog box.

Other Script Actions Used:

1. Check Disk Space

2. Display Message

SMS Installer Window:
See Figure 5-97.

Script:

```
————-Begin Script
item: Check Disk Space
end
item: Get Environment Variable
  Variable=OSDIR
  Environment=SystemRoot
end
item: Display Message
  Title English=Windows directory...
  Text English=The operating system files for this computer
are installed in the %OSDIR% directory.
  Flags=00100100
end
————-End Script
```

Get Environment Variable Example 2

The following is not necessarily an example of the Get Environment Variable script action but a utility to retrieve the computer's environment variable information. It sends the output of the SET command to a text file, which is displayed in a dialog box window using the Display ReadMe File script action. The information can be used to determine a local environment variable to place into an SMS Installer script variable. This runs on Windows NT only.

Other Script Actions Used:

1. Check Disk Space

2. Set Variable

3. Execute Program

4. Display Readme File

SMS Installer Window:
See Figure 5-98.

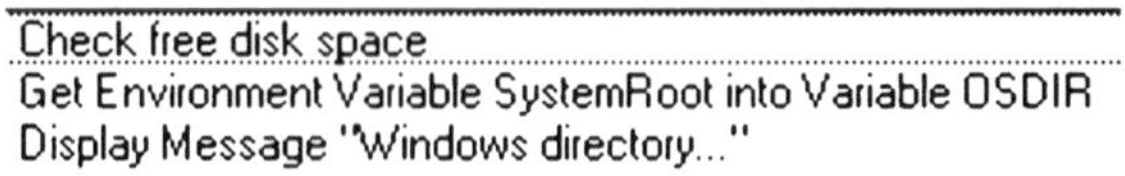

```
Check free disk space
Get Environment Variable SystemRoot into Variable OSDIR
Display Message "Windows directory..."
```

Figure 5-97 *Get Environment Variable script action window.*

```
Check free disk space
Set Variable ROOT to C:\
Execute %SYS32%\CMD.EXE /c SET >%ROOT%ENVVAR.TXT (Wait)
Display ReadMe File %ROOT%ENVVAR.TXT
```

Figure 5-98 *Retrieve Local Computer Environment Variables.*

Script:

```
————-Begin Script
item: Check Disk Space
end
item: Set Variable
  Variable=ROOT
  Value=C:\
end
item: Execute Program
  Pathname=%SYS32%\CMD.EXE
  Command Line=/c SET >%ROOT%ENVVAR.TXT
  Flags=00000010
end
item: Display ReadMe File
  Pathname=%ROOT%ENVVAR.TXT
  Title English=Environment Variables...
  Description English=The list shows the environment vari-
ables that are currently defined on the computer.
end
————-End Script
```

Get Name/Serial Number

The Get Name/Serial Number script action prompts the user for three fields of information. While the script action's name indicates the gathering of name and serial number information, these three fields can be configured for any type of information. This is a way of readily collecting information from the user without having to create a dialog box set using the Custom Dialog script action. Each piece of information is placed into its own variable, which can be used with the remainder of the script.

The dialog box presented to the user will only contain the fields in which you have entered information (see Figure 5-99). If you fill out the Name Prompt and the Company fields, these two fields will be the only ones to display. Any field left blank will be ignored and will automatically be left off the dialog box.

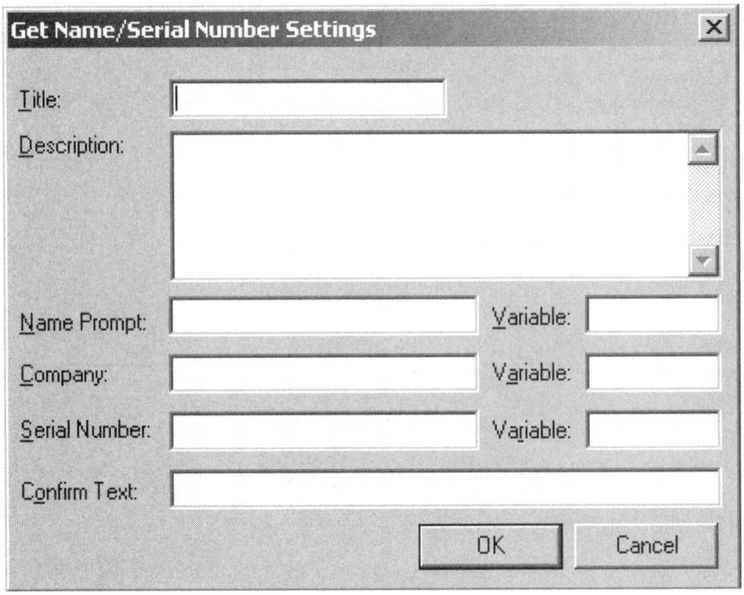

Figure 5-99 *Get Name/Serial Number dialog box.*

Note   If the user does not enter information into all the fields on the presented dialog box, the script will not progress. The user *must* enter information into all fields you configure to display.

Get Name/Serial Number Settings Options

Title   The Title is a required field. The entry will be displayed as the title of the dialog box that is presented to the user. This field can accept strings of text, variables, or both, up to 255 characters. If the entered information is longer than the width of the dialog box, the text will be displayed in ellipses, so try to keep the title under 60 characters.

Description   The Description field allows you to display more information to the user. This can be used to describe the data being gathered and why it is being retrieved. This field can accept text strings, variables, or both, up to 511 characters. The lines in this box will be truncated if they exceed 45 characters, so use Ctrl-Enter to create new lines as needed. This field will only display up to five lines on the dialog box.

Name Prompt   Name Prompt allows you to enter descriptive text about the first user input field. Though displayed as "Name Prompt" on the Get Name/Serial Number Settings dialog box, the user dialog box will display whatever text name you enter here.

- *Variable*   Entering a variable name in this field creates a new variable that receives the value of the user's entry into the Name Prompt field.

Company   Company allows you to enter descriptive text about the second user input field. Though displayed as "Company" on the Get Name/Serial Number Settings dialog box, the user dialog box will display the text name that you enter here.

- *Variable*   Entering a variable name in this field creates a new variable that receives the value of the user's entry into the Company field.

Serial Number   Serial Number allows you to enter descriptive text about the third user-input field. Though displayed as "Serial Number" on the Get Name/Serial Number Settings dialog box, the user dialog box will display the text name that you enter here.

- *Variable*   Entering a variable name in this field creates a new variable that receives the value of the user's entry into the Serial Number field.

Confirm Text   If text is entered into this field, the user will be prompted to verify their typed information. If the user answers "Yes," the script continues. If the user answers "No," the user will be returned to the input screen to correct the information. Since the verification dialog box (shown in Figure 5-100) displays Yes and No buttons, make sure to include a question in the Confirm Text field.

Get Name/Serial Number Example

The following example uses this script action to retrieve the username, Social Security number, and telephone number.

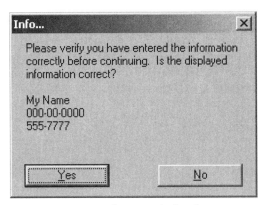

Figure 5-100 *Verification dialog box.*

Other Script Actions Used:

Check Disk Space

SMS Installer Window:

See Figure 5-101.

Script:

```
————-Begin Script
item: Check Disk Space
end
item: Get Name/Serial Number
   Name Variable=UNAME
   Company Variable=SSN
   Serial Variable=TPHONE
   Title English=Info...
   Name Prompt English=Your Name:
   Company Prompt English=Social Security number:
   Serial Prompt English=Telephone:
   Description English=In the fields below, please enter
your name, Social Security number, and telephone before
continuing.
   Confirmation Text English=Please verify you have entered
the information correctly before continuing. Is the dis-
played information correct?
   end
————-End Script
```

```
Check free disk space
Get Serial Number
```

Figure 5-101 *Get Name/Serial Number script action window.*

Get ProgMan Group

The Get ProgMan Group dialog box, shown in Figure 5-102, prompts the user to either select or enter an application group in which the new installation's shortcut will be installed. The script action uses the DDE Link to Program Manager to read all the currently installed group names and display them in a list for selection. When the user makes a selection from the list, the input field is automatically updated.

Get ProgMan Group Options

Window Name   The Window Name is a required field. This entry will be displayed as the title of the dialog box that is presented to the user. This field can accept strings of text, variables, or both, up to 255 characters. If the entered information is longer than the width of the dialog box, the text will be displayed in ellipses, so try to keep the title under 40 characters.

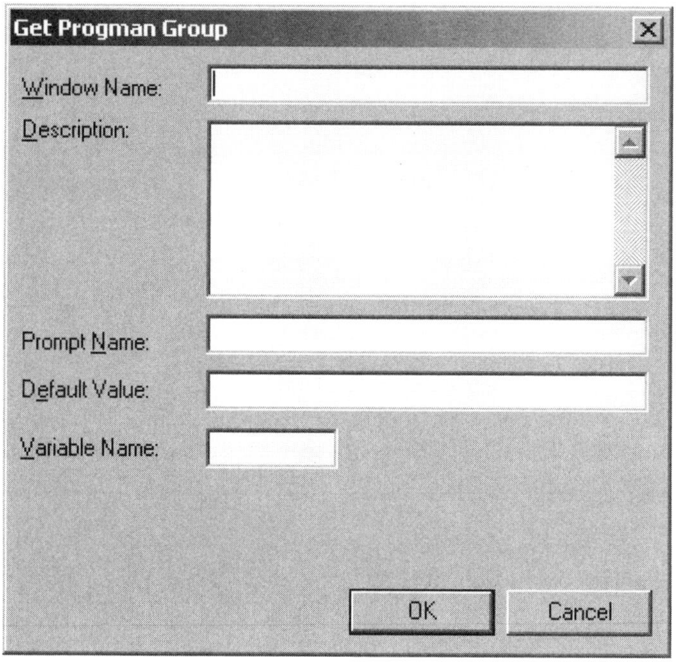

Figure 5-102 *Get ProgMan Group dialog box.*

```
Check free disk space
Prompt for Program Manager Group into Variable USERPROG
```

Figure 5-103 *Get ProgMan Group script action window.*

Description   The Description field allows you to display more information to the user. This field can accept text strings, variables, or both, up to 511 characters. The lines in this box will be truncated if they exceed 45 characters, so use Ctrl-Enter to create new lines as needed. This field will only display up to five lines on the dialog box.

Prompt Name   This field allows you to enter descriptive text about the group input field.

Default Value   Entering a value in this field will display a default application group name in the user input field on the dialog box. The user can accept the listed default, select from the list, or type in a new preference.

Variable Name   The variable name entered in this field will accept the user's group selection, and a new variable will be created containing the value. This variable can be used with the remainder of the script.

Get ProgMan Group Example
The following example prompts the user to select a local application group to install the installation's shortcut.

Other Script Actions Used:

   Check Disk Space
SMS Installer Window:
See Figure 5-103.

Script:

```
---------Begin Script
item: Check Disk Space
end
item: Get ProgMan Group
  Variable=USERPROG
  Window English=Application Group...
```

```
   Description English=Please select the application group
you would like the application to be installed into...
   Description English=
   Description English=You may also enter your own applica-
tion group in the available field.
   Title English=Application Group
end
—————-End Script
```

Output:

See Figure 5-104.

Get Registry Key Value

The Get Registry Key Value dialog box, shown in Figure 5-105, allows you to retrieve data stored in the computer's registry and place it in a variable. The variable can be used with the remainder of the script. Since the registry records all computer settings, this script action is useful for retrieving information that may be different from computer to computer, such as hardware settings or user-specific customizations. For more information on

Figure 5-104 *Get ProgMan Group output dialog box.*

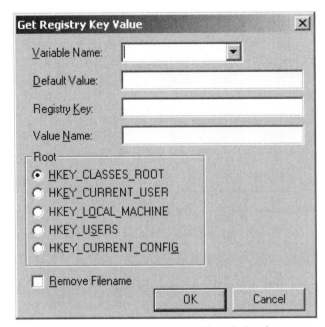

Figure 5-105 *Get Registry Key Value dialog box.*

the registry and the information contained there, see "Registry Overview" in Chapter 07.

Get Registry Key Value Options

Variable Name   The Variable Name drop-down list allows the selection of any predefined variables that should receive the data value retrieved from the registry key. The field also accepts new variables that should be created to contain the retrieved value.

Default Value   The Default Value field is used to provide a default data value if the registry information is not found. This ensures that the variable receives a value so the script can continue. For instance, if the data value is not found, the default value can be set to NULL. You can then use script logic (If/While statement) to terminate the script or to look for the necessary information elsewhere on the computer. This field accepts text strings, variables, or both, up to 255 characters.

Registry Key   This field contains the registry key path information. The format of this information should start after the Root key information. The Root key information is selected in the Root section of the dialog box. For example, if the data value you are retrieving exists in \HKEY_LOCAL_MACHINE\SOFT-WARE\Microsoft\Windows NT\CurrentVersion\Winlogon, just enter `\SOFTWARE\Microsoft\Windows NT\CurrentVersion\Winlogon`. This field accepts text strings, variables, or both, up to 255 characters.

Value Name   The Value Name field contains the registry data value name from which you want to retrieve the information (data value) to insert into the variable. An example of a data value would be the `DefaultUserName` in the \HKEY_LOCAL_MACHINE\SOFTWARE\Microsoft\Windows NT\CurrentVersion\Winlogon registry key.

Root   The Root key section allows you to quickly select the registry Root key from which to retrieve the information. The options are HKEY_CLASSES_ROOT, HKEY_CURRENT_USER, HKEY_LOCAL_MACHINE, HKEY_USERS, HKEY_CUR-RENT_CONFIG. For more information on the type of data contained in each key, see "Registry Overview" in Chapter 07.

Remove Filename   If retrieving path information from the registry to place in the variable, selecting the Remove Filename option will automatically strip the filename (if present) from the end of the path. This is useful for retrieving the path to install an upgraded version of a software package. If the filename remains in the path information, the variable information would have to be parsed (Parse String script action) to remove the filename.

Get Registry Key Value Example

The following example retrieves the current logon name of the computer and places the information into a LogName.txt file in the root of the C: drive.

Other Script Actions Used:

1. Check Disk Space

2. Set Variable

3. Insert Line into Text File

SMS Installer Window:

See Figure 5-106.

Script:

```
--------Begin Script
item: Check Disk Space
end
item: Set Variable
  Variable=ROOT
  Value=C:\
end
item: Get Registry Key Value
  Variable=REGVAR
  Key=SOFTWARE\Microsoft\Windows NT\CurrentVersion\Winlogon
  Value Name=DefaultUserName
  Flags=00000100
end
item: Insert Line into Text File
  Pathname=%ROOT%LogName.TXT
  New Text=Logon Name = %REGVAR%
  Line Number=0
end
--------End Script
```

Get System Information

The Get System Information script action, the dialog box for which is shown in Figure 5-107, is a shortcut for obtaining system information on the target PC. This powerful feature can acquire several key items from the configuration of the computer and place the information in a variable. SMS Installer does the legwork of retrieving the information. This variable can be used with the remainder of the script.

Get System Information Options

Variable The Variable field creates a new script variable that receives the retrieved information. The drop-down list allows selecting a predefined variable.

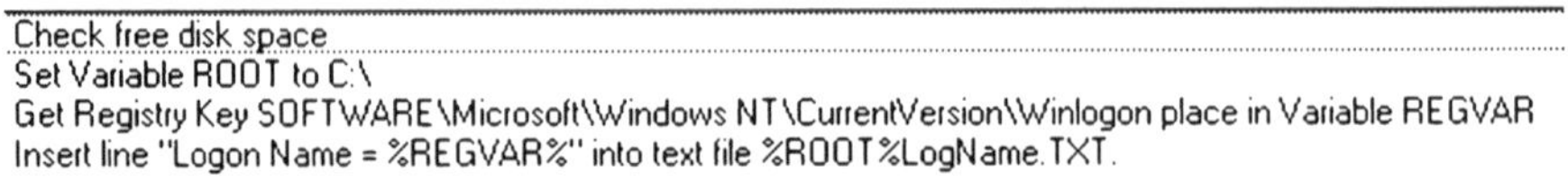

Check free disk space
Set Variable ROOT to C:\
Get Registry Key SOFTWARE\Microsoft\Windows NT\CurrentVersion\Winlogon place in Variable REGVAR
Insert line "Logon Name = %REGVAR%" into text file %ROOT%LogName.TXT.

Figure 5-106 *Get Registry Key Value script action window.*

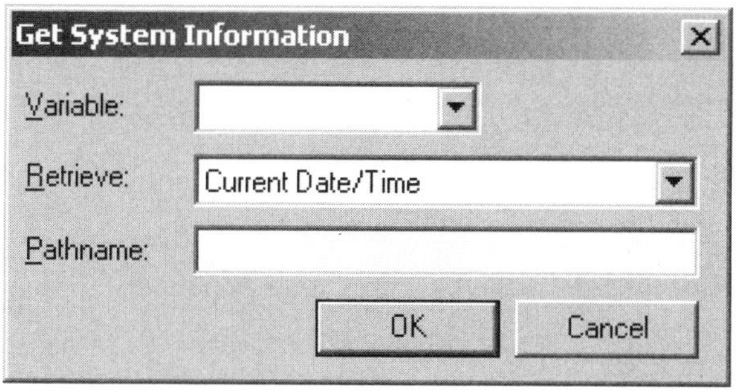

Figure 5-107 *Get System Information dialog box.*

Retrieve   The Retrieve drop-down box allows you to select one of the items in the list for retrieval. There are 19 items available, as shown in Table 5-7.

Pathname   If selecting an item that requires a pathname, this field allows you to enter the path information (see the Requires Pathname Field column on the table for a list of items that use the Pathname Field). This field accepts text strings, variables, or both, up to 255 characters.

Get System Information Example

   The following example obtains the size of the Windows NT command interpreter and inserts the information into a text file in the root of the C: drive.

Other Script Actions Used:

1. Set Variable

2. Check Disk Space

3. Insert Line into Text File

SMS Installer Window:
See Figure 5-108

Script:

```
————-Begin Script
item: Set Variable
  Variable=ROOT
  Value=C:\
end
item: Set Variable
  Variable=SYSTEM32
```

```
   Value=%ROOT%WINNT\SYSTEM32
end
item: Check Disk Space
end
item: Get System Information
   Variable=FILESIZE
   Pathname=%SYSTEM32%\CMD.EXE
   Flags=00001110
end
item: Insert Line into Text File
   Pathname=%ROOT%CMD.TXT
   New Text=The Command Interpreter on this computer is %FILESIZE%
bytes.
   Line Number=0
end
———-End Script
```

Table 5-7   *Retrieve options.*

Item	Description	Requires Pathname Field
Current Date/Time	Retrieves the current data and time of the target computer.	No
Windows Version	Retrieves the Windows version of the computer in "Major.Minor.BuildNumber" format. Example: 5.00.2128	No
DOS Version	Retrieves the DOS version of the computer in "Major.Minor" format. Example: 6.22	No
K Bytes Available Memory	Retrieves the currently available resource memory.	No
File Date/Time Modified	Retrieves the date and time a file (indicated in the Pathname field) was last modified.	Yes
File Version Number	Retrieves the version number of a file specified in the Pathname field. The file must have a version resource header for this item to work. It returns the data in the standard x.x.x.x. format.	Yes

Table 5-7 *Retrieve options. (Continued)*

Item	Description	Requires Pathname Field
Registered Owner Name	Retrieves the installed user name that was used during the Windows operating system installation.	No
Registered Company Name	Retrieves the installed company name that was used during the Windows operating system installation.	No
Drive Type for Pathname	Retrieves the drive type of the path listed in the Pathname field. Each drive type is represented by a letter, which is placed into the variable: C = CD-ROM F = Floppy Drive (removable) H = Hard Drive N = Network R = RAM Drive	Yes
First Network Drive	Retrieves the drive letter of the computer's first network drive (configured in the Network Properties) in the letter/colon format. Example: F:	No
First CD-ROM Drive	Retrieves the drive letter of the first configured CD-ROM drive in the computer in the letter/colon format (Example: D:). If no CD-ROM is found on the computer, the returned variable is blank.	No
Win32s Version	Retrieves the Win32 version number running on the computer. If none is found, the variable receives a blank value.	No
Full UNC Pathname	Converts the information in the Pathname field to UNC (Universal Naming Convention) format. Example: \\ServerName\Share\Directory.	Yes

Table 5-7 *Retrieve Options.. (Continued)*

Item	Description	Requires Pathname Field
Installation EXE Pathname	Retrieves the full pathname and executable name of the SMS compiled installation file.	No
File Size	Retrieves the size of the file specified in the Pathname field.	Yes
Volume Serial Number	Retrieves the serial number of the drive specified in the Pathname field.	Yes
Volume Label	Retrieves the volume label name of the drive specified in the Pathname field.	Yes
Windows Logon Name	Retrieves the current Windows Networking logon name from the target computer.	No
Service Pack Number	Retrieves the computer's installed service pack number.	No

Get Temporary Filename

The Get Temporary Filename dialog box, shown in Figure 5-109, allows you to put installed files into a variable name. When the script is completed, the file will automatically be deleted. This is advantageous for including other toolkit utilities (see "Building the SMS Installer Toolkit" in Chapter 10), employing the utilities during the installation, and having SMS Installer delete them for you without using the Delete File(s) script action.

```
Set Variable ROOT to C:\
Set Variable SYSTEM32 to %ROOT%WINNT\SYSTEM32
Check free disk space
Get System Information into FILESIZE
Insert line "The Command Interpreter on this computer is %FILESIZE% bytes." into text file %ROOT%CMD.TXT.
```

Figure 5-108 *Get System Information script action window.*

Another use of this script action is placing a DLL file into the temporary variable that will be used with the Call DLL Function script action.

Get Temporary Filename Options

Variable This script action only has one item to configure. The Variable field allows you to create a new variable or choose a pre-defined variable from the drop-down box.

> The Get Temporary Filename script action should be used in conjunction with the Install File(s) script action (shown in the example in this section).

Note

Get Temporary Filename Example

The following example retrieves the TEMP environment variable and places the value into the TMPFILE script variable. The LANGUAGE.INI file is installed into the TMPFILE location and is then deleted when the script completes.

Other Script Actions Used:

1. Check Disk Space

2. Get Environment Variable

3. Install File(s)

4. Display Message

SMS Installer Window:
See Figure 5-110.

Figure 5-109 *Get Temporary Filename dialog box.*

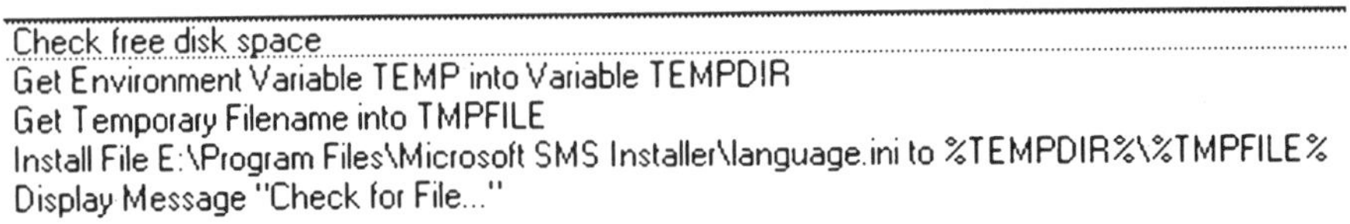

Check free disk space
Get Environment Variable TEMP into Variable TEMPDIR
Get Temporary Filename into TMPFILE
Install File E:\Program Files\Microsoft SMS Installer\language.ini to %TEMPDIR%\%TMPFILE%
Display Message "Check for File..."

Figure 5-110 *Get Temporary Filename script action window.*

Script:

```
--------Begin Script
item: Check Disk Space
end
item: Get Environment Variable
  Variable=TEMPDIR
  Environment=TEMP
end
item: Get Temporary Filename
  Variable=TMPFILE
end
item: Install File
  Source=E:\Program Files\Microsoft SMS Installer\lan-
guage.ini
  Destination=%TEMPDIR%\%TMPFILE%
  Flags=0000000000000010
end
item: Display Message
  Title English=Check for File...
  Text English=Check for the existence of the installed
file before continuing. It is located in the %TEMPDIR%
directory.
  Text English=
  Text English=After the installation the file will auto-
matically be deleted.
  Flags=00100100
end
--------End Script
```

Tip   The computer's temporary directory should be used when installing the file that will be placed into the temporary variable. Use the Get Environment Variable script action for retrieving the computer's Temp directory information (shown in the example). Each computer's Temp directory may be in different locations. Retrieving the specific directory will ensure the file in the temporary variable is deleted. If a valid Temp directory is not specified, SMS Installer will be unable to automatically delete the file when the script has completed.

If/While Statement

The If/While Statement script action allows you to create an SMS Installer logic block in the script. It compares one variable value to another variable value or constant value and branches into different actions depending on the result you set in the Conditions field (see Figure 5-111). This is the definition of a Boolean expression.

> The If/While Statement script action must be used in conjunction with the Else Statement and End Block script actions to complete the logic block.
>
> **Note**

If/While Block Settings Options

If Variable   The If Variable drop-down box allows you to select a predefined variable from the list. This field *must* be a predefined variable.

Conditions   The Conditions drop-down box allows you to select the operator that will be applied between the variable and the item listed in the Value field. The following options are presented:

- *Equals*   This condition compares the Value data against the variable. This is a case-sensitive comparison that returns a TRUE value if the data and variable match. The compared data can be numeric or alphanumeric.

Figure 5-111   *If/While Statement dialog box.*

- *Not Equal*   This condition performs a case-sensitive comparison between the variable and the value and returns a TRUE value if the data is not equal. The compared data can be numeric or alphanumeric.

- *Contains*   This condition compares the Value data against the variable. This is a case-sensitive comparison that checks for the existence of the *entire* string between the data and variable. The compared data can be numeric or alphanumeric.

- *Does Not Contain*   This condition compares the Value data against the variable. This is a case-sensitive comparison that ensures the *entire* string between the data and variable *does not* exist. It returns a TRUE value if the condition is met. The compared data can be numeric or alphanumeric.

- *Equals (Ignore Case)*   This condition compares the Value data against the variable. This is a comparison that returns a TRUE value if the data and variable match. The condition is not case-sensitive. The compared data can be numeric or alphanumeric.

- *Not Equal (Ignore Case)*   This condition performs a comparison between the variable and the value that is not case-sensitive and returns a TRUE value if the data is not equal. The compared data can be numeric or alphanumeric.

- *Greater Than*   This condition performs a comparison between the variable and the value to determine if the variable is greater than the value. It returns a value of 1 (TRUE) if the condition is met and a value of 0 (FALSE) if it is not.

- *Greater Than or Equal*   This condition performs a comparison between the variable and the value to determine if the variable is equal to or greater than the Value. It returns a value of 1 (TRUE) if the condition is met and a value of 0 (FALSE) if it is not.

- *Less Than*   This condition performs a comparison between the variable and the value to determine if the variable is less than the value. It returns a value of 1 (TRUE) if the condition is met and a value of 0 (FALSE) if it is not.

- *Less Than or Equal*   This condition performs a comparison between the variable and the value to determine if the variable is less than or equal to the value. It returns a value of 1 (TRUE) if the condition is met and a value of 0 (FALSE) if it is not.

- *Contains Any Letters In*   This condition compares the Value data against the variable. This is a case-sensitive comparison that checks *any* similar alphanumeric characters between the data and variable. The compared data can be numeric or alphanumeric. It returns a value of 1 (TRUE) if the condition is met and a value of 0 (FALSE) if it is not.

- *Contains Letters Not In*   This condition compares the Value data against the variable. This is a case-sensitive comparison that ensures that *any* similar alphanumeric characters *do not* exist between the data and variable. The compared data can be numeric or alphanumeric.

- *Length Equal To*   This condition compares the length of the variable string to a numeric value entered into the Value field. It returns a value of 1 (TRUE) if the condition is met and a value of 0 (FALSE) if it is not.

- *Expression True*   This condition allows you to check complex expressions for a TRUE value. For example, you can use the Set Variable script action to perform calculations and then use the Expression True option to verify the calculation. (For an example of a complex expression, see the Set Variable script action example. For a QuickList of the valid Complex Expressions, see "Complex Expressions QuickList" in Chapter 10.)

The Value   The Value field contains the value to which the variable data will be compared. This is a mandatory field to complete the Boolean expression. If this field is empty, the logic block will compare the NULL value to the variable contents (see the example in this section). This field accepts text strings, variables, or both, up to 255 characters.

Action   The Action section defines what type of logic block should be created. The following options are presented:

- *Start If Block*   Selecting this option starts an If logic block. The If block is used for values you want to act upon once. The values generally do not change.

- *Start While Block*   Selecting this option starts a While logic block. A While block is used with values that change during the script action. For example, you could create a script that prompts the user before overwriting existing files or include a No to All button on the dialog box. If the user continues to click Yes to overwrite the file(s), the value remains TRUE and the user is continually prompted for each file. When the user clicks the No to All button, the value becomes FALSE, the script does not overwrite any files, and the user is not prompted again. The script will continue to cycle through the loop until the FALSE value is placed into the variable.

Perform Loop at Least Once   If you selected the Start While Block action to start a While logic block, this option forces the script to perform the loop once even if the Boolean value returns FALSE the first time. This is useful for forcing the block actions to perform at least once.

If/While Statement Example

The following example retrieves the computer's TEMP directory variable. If one is available, a success dialog box displays to the user and the installation continues normally. If the TEMP directory environment variable has not been defined on the computer, an error dialog box is presented to the user and the installation exits. *Other Script Actions Used*:

1. Check Disk Space

2. Get Environment Variable

3. Display Message

4. Else Statement

5. End Block

SMS Installer Window:
See Figure 5-112.

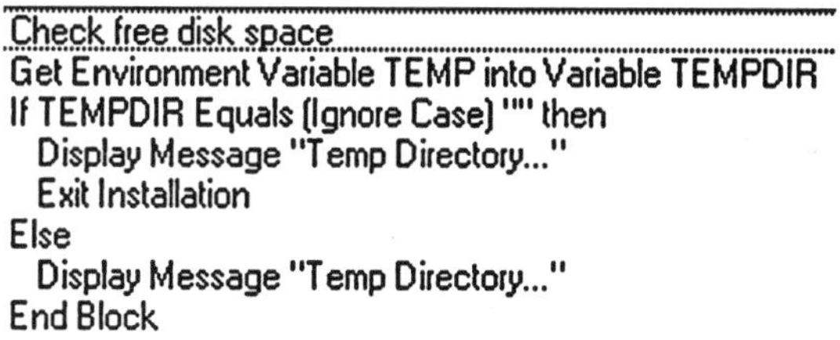

```
Check free disk space
Get Environment Variable TEMP into Variable TEMPDIR
If TEMPDIR Equals (Ignore Case) "" then
  Display Message "Temp Directory..."
  Exit Installation
Else
  Display Message "Temp Directory..."
End Block
```

Figure 5-112 *If/While Statement script action window.*

Script:

```
--------Begin Script
item: Check Disk Space
end
item: Get Environment Variable
  Variable=TEMPDIR
  Environment=TEMP
end
item: If/While Statement
  Variable=TEMPDIR
  Flags=00000100
end
item: Display Message
  Title English=Temp Directory...
  Text English=A Temporary directory has not been set up on
your computer. Please contact your local technical support.
  Text English=
  Text English=The installation will now exit.
  Flags=00101000
end
item: Exit Installation
end
item: Else Statement
end
item: Display Message
  Title English=Temp Directory...
  Text English=Your computer is successfully configured with
a proper Temporary directory. It is located at %TEMPDIR%.
  Text English=
  Text English=The installation will now continue...
  Flags=00100100
end
item: End Block
end
--------End Script
```

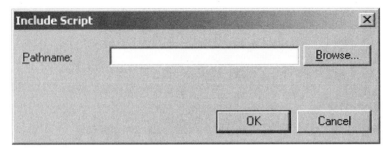

Figure 5-113 *Include Script dialog box.*

Include Script

The Include Script script action, the dialog box for which is shown in Figure 5-113, allows you to include other SMS Installer scripts within the current script. This allows you to create a library of "scriplets" that contain commonly used functions and reuse them with other scripts without having to recode the information. For example, if you consistently use the same variables for your scripts, create a script containing only your common variables, and include it at the beginning of every script.

Include Script Options

Pathname   The only option for the Include Script action is to enter the script location. A Browse button is included to locate the script (.IPF) in the local file system. This field will accept variables as the path, but it *must* be a compiler variable. Script variables will not work. Pressing Ctrl-Z on the keyboard brings up the Installation Properties dialog box. Create your variables on the Compiler Variables Tab. For more information see "Compiler Variables Tab" in Chapter 04.

Note   When including other scripts, watch for conflicting variable names. If you generally use the same variable names, make sure you modify any duplicates. This can put the wrong values into the variables and cause the script to produce the wrong results.

Include Script Example

The following example includes a script from the file system.

```
Check free disk space
Include Script: E:\Folders\McGraw Hill\Scripts\Chapter Five\Display Graphic.ipf
```

Figure 5-114 *Include Script script action window.*

Other Script Actions Used:

Check Disk Space

SMS Installer Window:

See Figure 5-114.

Script:

```
———-Begin Script
item: Check Disk Space
end
item: Include Script
 Pathname=E:\Folders\McGraw Hill\Scripts\Chapter Five\Dis-
play Graphic.ipf
end
———-End Script
```

Insert Line into Text File

The Insert Line into Text File dialog box, shown in Figure 5-115, allows you to insert information into any text file. As long as the file is ASCII text-based, this script action will work. Because INI files are also text-based, this script action can be used to modify these files. The Add Device to SYSTEM.INI script action causes the user to be prompted to restart the computer. If the modification to the SYSTEM.INI is not critical and can wait until the user restarts the computer, this script action can make the INI modification without causing a reboot message.

> **Tip** The Insert Line into Text File script action is a great tool for testing the script variables. In the File to Edit field, input the path and a new filename. In the Text to Insert field, input the variable name of the value you want to test. When the script action runs, the value is placed into the text file. The text file can then be opened and the values viewed to verify that the correct data is being used with the script functions.

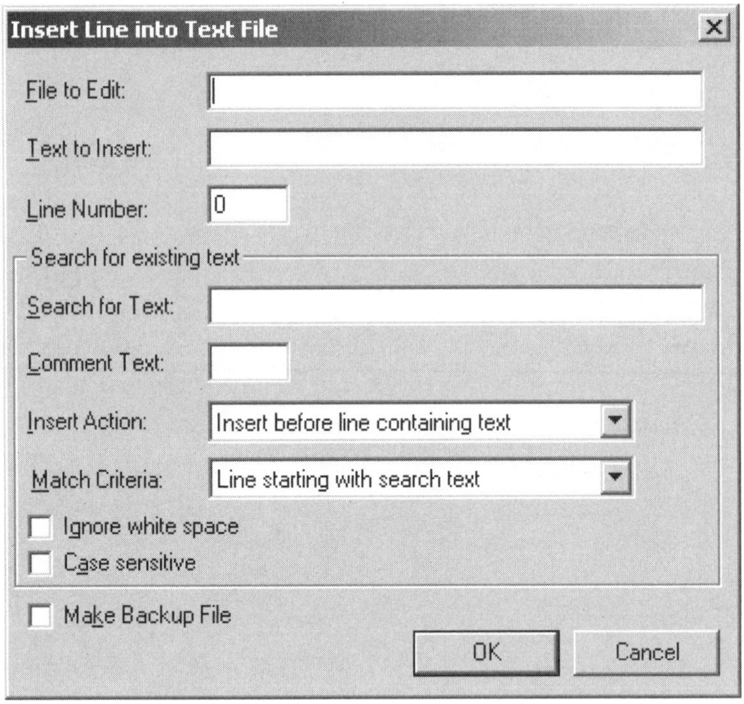

Figure 5-115 *Insert Line into Text File dialog box.*

Insert Line into Text File Options

File to Edit   This field contains the path and filename of the text file you wish to modify. You can also create new text files by inputting a path and a new filename. The field accepts text strings, predefined variables, or both, up to 255 characters.

Text to Insert   The Text to Insert field contains the actual text string that will be inserted into the text file. This field accepts text strings, predefined variables, or both, up to 255 characters.

Note   This script action only inserts one line of text. Use a separate Insert Line into Text File script action for each line you need to add.

Line Number   The Line Number field gives you the ability to select your preference of line number for the new command line. This value can be any number from 0 to 32,000. A value of 0 instructs SMS Installer to place the line of text at the last line of the file.

Search for Existing Text   The following options are presented:

- *Search for Text*   Included with the Insert Line into Text File Details dialog box is the ability to perform context searches of the current information in the text file. This search can help locate data for deleting, modifying, replacing, or marking. The Search for Text line allows you to input text to search for in the file. Once the text is found, there are several things that can be done with the information using the Insert Action list.

- *Comment Text*   The Comment Text option takes the input from here and comments-out the line identified in the search string. This is useful for replacing lines in the text file without deleting them. Commenting-out the line serves as a backup in the event the original line is needed later. Restoring from the backup file, if the Make Backup File option is selected, can quickly restore the text file to its original state by removing the comment information from the beginning of the com- mented line. Use the standard comment text (i.e., REM, /*, ;, etc.).

- *Insert Action*   Once the search line has been identified, there are three actions you can choose from:
  1. Insert before line containing text
  2. Replace line containing text
  3. Insert after line containing text

- *Match Criteria*   For the search, you can also define the way SMS Installer matches information in the text file with the fol- lowing criteria settings:
  1. Line starting with search text
  2. Line containing search text
  3. Line ending with search text

- *Ignore White Space*   The Ignore White Space option tells SMS Installer to ignore additional white spaces or blank lines in the text file.

- *Case Sensitive*   The Case Sensitive checkbox maximizes the search functionality by making the search case-sensitive. If you

```
Set Variable ROOT to C:\
Check free disk space
Get Environment Variable TEMP into Variable TEMPDIR
Insert line "The TEMP directory for this computer is:  %TEMPDIR%" into text file %ROOT%NEWTEXT.TXT.
```

Figure 5-116 *Insert Line into Text File script action window.*

know that the string you are looking for has a specific letter case, choosing this option will narrow the search.

Make Backup File   The Make Backup File checkbox tells SMS Installer to make a backup copy of the text file before the line(s) of text are added. The backup file keeps the same name as the original file but changes the extension to .001. Each time the file is updated and a backup is created, the extension will increment by 1. For example, if you see a file extension of .012, you know the text file has been modified 12 times.

Insert Line into Text File Example

The following example retrieves the TEMP directory environment variable and inserts the information in a NEWTEXT.TXT text file in the root of the C: drive.

Other Script Actions Used:

1. Set Variable

2. Check Disk Space

3. Get Environment Variable

SMS Installer Window:
See Figure 5-116.

Script:

```
————-Begin Script
item: Set Variable
 Variable=ROOT
 Value=C:\
end
item: Check Disk Space
end
item: Get Environment Variable
  Variable=TEMPDIR
  Environment=TEMP
end
```

```
item: Insert Line into Text File
  Pathname=%ROOT%NEWTEXT.TXT
  New Text=The TEMP directory for this computer is: %TEM-
PDIR%
  Line Number=0
end
———-End Script
```

Install DirectX

The Install DirectX dialog box, shown in Figure 5-117, allows you to quickly include the DirectX files in the SMS Installer script. The files needed for the setup must be in a directory path on the local computer during the compilation. DirectX works with Windows 9x and Windows NT. DirectX is a software driver system for computer multimedia hardware that enhances elements such as full-color graphics, video, 3D animation, and surround sound.

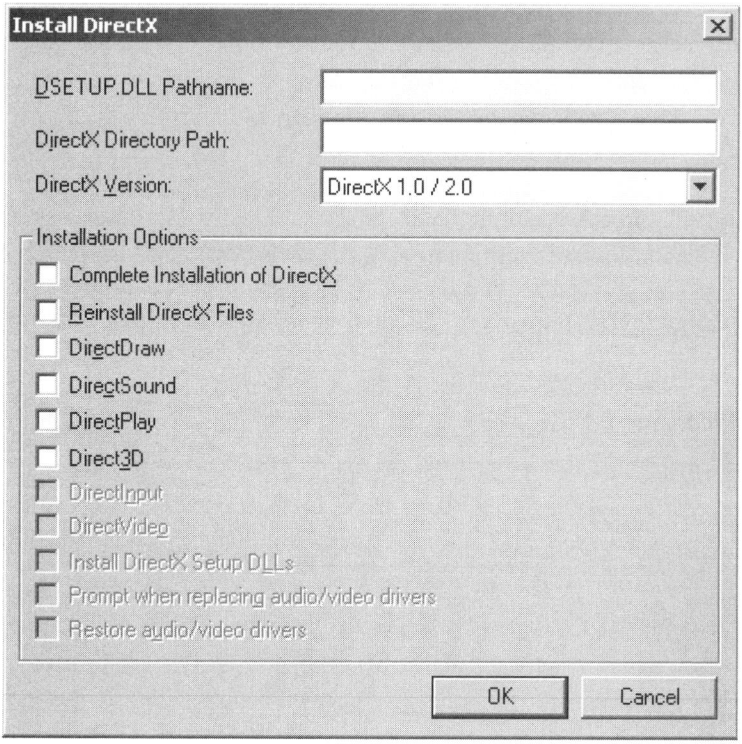

Figure 5-117 *Install DirectX dialog box.*

Install DirectX Options

DSETUP.DLL Pathname   This field contains the full pathname
to the DirectX setup DSETUP.DLL file (the filename is not
required). The field accepts text strings, predefined variables, or
both, up to 255 characters.

DirectX Directory Path   This field contains the directory path
information that points to the DirectX setup files. The field accepts
text strings, predefined variables, or both, up to 255 characters.

DirectX Version   The drop-down list allows you to select the
version of DirectX for installation. Because of the differences in
the first two versions of DirectX, they are separated from 3.0 or
higher. The installation options change based on the version
selected for installation (see Table 5-8).

Installation Options   The Installation Options section provides
several different ways of installing the DirectX components. You
can select a complete installation or a sub-select of the different
components. Some of the items may not be available based on the
version selected. See the Version Support column in the table for
more information.

Install DirectX Example

The following example installs the DirectDraw and Direct3D
components of DirectX. It prompts the user when overwriting the
audio and video drivers.

SMS Installer Window:
See Figure 5-118.

Script:

```
————-Begin Script
item: Set Variable
  Variable=DIRXLOC
  Value=E:\DIRECTX
end
item: Set Variable
  Variable=SYS32
  Value=C:\WINNT\SYSTEM32
end
item: Install DirectX
```

```
DirectX Pathname=%DIRXLOC%
Setup Pathname=%SYS32%
Extra Flags=268435969
end
————End Script
```

Table 5-8 *Installation options.*

Installation Option	Description	Version Support
Complete Installation of DirectX	Performs a component complete installation of the DirectX version selected. Selecting this option disables the individual component selection, except Reinstall DirectX Files.	1.0, 2.0, 3.0+
Reinstall DirectX Files	Completely reinstalls the DirectX components.	1.0, 2.0
DirectDraw	DirectDraw provides world-class game graphics on computers running Windows 9x Windows NT version 4.0 or Windows 2000.	1.0, 2.0, 3.0+
DirectSound	DirectSound is the audio component of DirectX. It uses features such as low-latency mixing play-back, accelerated hardware, and 3D positioning to achieve professional-quality audio performance.	1.0, 2.0, 3.0+
DirectPlay	DirectPlay makes it easy to connect games over the Internet, a modem link, or a network.	1.0, 2.0, 3.0+
Direct3D	Direct3D is designed to enable world-class game and interactive three-dimensional (3D) graphics on a computer running Microsoft Windows operating systems.	1.0, 2.0, 3.0+

Table 5-8 *Installation Options. (Continued)*

Installation Option	Description	Version Support
DirectInput	DirectInput provides a state-of-the-art interface for a variety of input devices (joysticks, headgear, multi-button mice, etc.), as well as force-feedback.	3.0+
DirectVideo	DirectVideo is designed to provide transparent video playback speed improvements with video cards offering DirectDraw support. Direct Video is a draw handler that uses DirectDraw.	3.0+
Install DirectX Setup DLLs	This option compiles the DirectX Setup files in the SMS Installer script. This is useful for distri-buting the files for another indivi-dual to use in creating distribution packages.	3.0+
Prompt When Re-placing Audio/Video Drivers	This option warns the user that the audio or video drivers are being overwritten during the installation and provides a choice to continue.	3.0+
Restore Audio/Video Drivers	This option restores the original audio and video drivers.	3.0+

Install File(s)

The Install File(s) script action is the script function that actually installs the files on the target computer (see Figure 5-119). The Install File(s) script action provides two basic functions:

1. It marks the files from the local file system that will be compressed into the compiled executable.

```
Set Variable DIRXLOC to E:\DIRECTX
Set Variable SYS32 to C:\WINNT\SYSTEM32
Install DirectX from directory %DIRXLOC%
```

Figure 5-118 *Install DirectX script action window.*

2. It decompresses the files and copies them to the proper directory during the installation.

> Using drag-and-drop, you can instantly add files to the SMS   **Tip**
> Installer script that are automatically placed into an Install File(s)
> script action. To do so:
>
> 1. Open SMS Installer.
> 2. Open an instance of Windows Explorer.
> 3. Find the file(s) you want to install with the script.
> 4. Highlight the file(s) and drag-and-drop them to the SMS
>   Installer program window.
>
> SMS Installer then displays the Install File(s) script action dialog
> box, but both the heading of the dialog box and the Source Path-
> name field indicate the drag-and-drop procedure has been suc-
> cessful.

Install Files From Installation Executable Options

Source Pathname The Source Pathname field is a required field
that contains the source directory of the file that is to be installed.
This field must start with a variable that has been previously
defined, unless the Browse button is used to select the file from
the local file system. This field will also accept the * wildcard
character for copying multiple files at once. For example, if you
want to copy all the help files from a source directory, you can
use the *.HLP parameter. If you want to copy *all* files from a
source directory, you can use the *.* parameter. The field accepts
up to 255 characters.

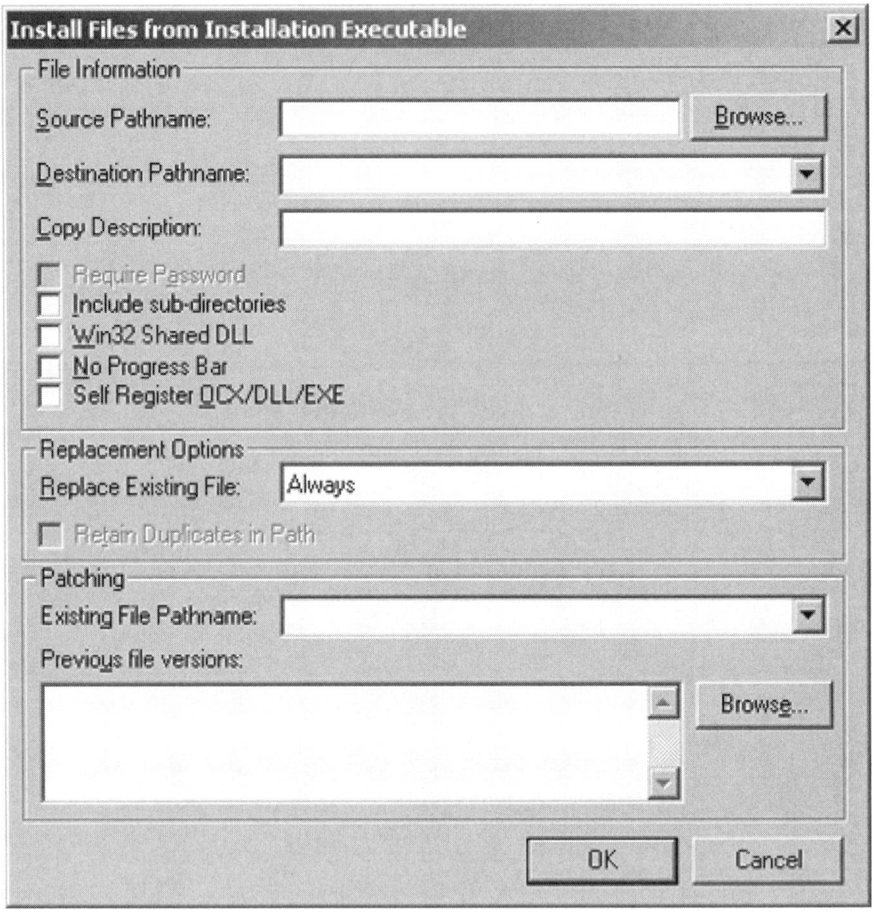

Figure 5-119 *Install File(s) dialog box.*

Note The files for the Source Pathname can be selected three ways:

1. Enter a directory name, and all the files underneath the directory will be compressed into the compiled executable.
2. Enter a directory path and filename, and the specific file will be compressed into the compiled executable.
3. Use wildcard characters with the filename, and all the files that match the criteria will be compressed into the compiled executable.

Destination Pathname   The Destination Pathname field contains the location where the file(s) will be installed. The destination pathname information *must* start with a predefined variable. The drop-down list allows you to quickly select the available variables. The field will accept any string of text after the variable. If a single file has been entered into the Source or Local File fields, you must include the filename in this entry. If not, just the variable name will work. If wildcard characters are used in either the Source or Local Files field, then you cannot enter an actual filename. The Destination field can also be used to rename the source file as it is copied. For example, if the source filename is SMSINSTL.HLP, you can rename the file INSTALLR.HLP when it is copied to the destination. You do not need to create the destination directory if it does not exist. SMS Installer automatically creates the destination directory when it installs the file. The field accepts up to 255 characters.

Copy Description The Copy Description field contains the text that is displayed on the progress bar dialog box as the file is installed. This helps the user understand what the installation is doing. The word "Copying" precedes whatever description you enter, so input the text with this in mind. For example, if you want the user to see "Copying Help Files...," just enter Help Files.... This field accepts text, variables, or both, up to 255 characters, but the description will be truncated if it goes beyond the window width.

Require Password The Require Password checkbox allows you to set a password for the file installation procedure. This checkbox is only enabled after setting an installation password through the Installation Properties on the General tab (Ctrl-Z). One password can be set per compiled script. The user's password entry should be one of the first items the script runs. Use this feature if this script action is the first instance where the script makes changes to the target computer.

Include Subdirectories If this checkbox is selected, all the files and directories underneath the source directory will be installed. If wildcards are used in either the source or local path, the subdirectories are searched for the same criteria and the files that match are installed.

Win32 Shared DLL   This selection tells the SMS Installer script that you are installing files that are shared by multiple applications (usually OCX/DLL/VBX/EXE files). Programs that share system files add to the registry increment counter. The registry stores an increment counter in the HKEY_LOCAL_MACHINE\ SOFTWARE\Microsoft\Windows\CurrentVersion\SharedDLLs registry key. Each time a program tries to install a file, it first checks this key to determine if any other program uses the file. If it is being used, the installation increments the registry value by 1. Uninstall programs will decrement this value by 1 when the program is removed from the computer. This feature only works with Windows 9x and Windows NT computers. Selecting this checkbox will increment the counter by 1.

No Progress Bar   Selecting this checkbox causes the file copy progress bar to be hidden during the file copy.

Self Register OCX/DLL/EXE   On Windows 9x and Windows NT computers, this option queues DLL and OCX files for registering in the operating system when the script completes. The Self-Register OCX/DLL script action (shown later in this chapter) can also be used to register the files immediately.

Replacement Options   The Replacement Options tell the script what to do when it finds duplicate files in the destination. The following fields are presented:

- *Replace Existing File*   This drop-down list is similar throughout SMS Installer when files are found in the local file system that will be overwritten. It includes seven different options, defined in Table 5-9.

- *Retain Duplicates in Path*   This option is only available if the Replace Existing File is set to Version Checking or Version and Date/Time Checking. This only works on Windows 9x and Windows NT computers.

Patching   SMS Installer provides the feature of being able to patch an application. Patching an application involves replacing only the files that have been updated instead of having to reinstall

Table 5-9 *Replace Existing File Options.*

File Copy Option	Description
Always	When the same filename is found at the destination, it is always overwritten with the one included with the script.
If version number same or older	When the same filename is found at the destination, SMS Installer compares the version number between its copy and the current file. If the version number is the same or older, the current file is overwritten.
If date/time same or older	When the same filename is found at the destination, SMS Installer compares the date and time between its copy and the current file. If the date and time is the same or older, the current file is overwritten.
If date/time older	When the same filename is found at the destination, SMS Installer compares the date and time between its copy and the current file. If the date and time is older, the current file is overwritten.
If date/time and version number are same or older	When the same filename is found at the destination, SMS Installer compares the date, time, and version number between its copy and the current file. If the date, time, and version number is the same or older, the current file is overwritten.
If date/time and version number are older	When the same filename is found at the destination, SMS Installer compares the date, time, and version number between its copy and the current file. If the date, time, and version number is older, the current file is overwritten.
Never	When the same filename is found at the destination, SMS Installer skips the file copy.

the entire application. SMS Installer compares each file in the original installed version with the upgrade version and creates a new, smaller version with only the changes. The smaller file is much easier to distribute for updates to applications than distributing a full application installation.

The following fields are presented:

- *Existing File Pathname*   This field contains the location on the target computer where the files to be patched are located. If wildcards are used in the Source Pathname field, the entry must be a path. If the Source Pathname field contains a single filename, the pathname must point to a file listed in the Previous File Versions box.

- *Previous File Versions*   The Previous File Versions field will list the older versions of files you want to install, to patch or to update. If wildcards are used in the Source Pathname field, this box should only contain directory names. The list can contain up to 255 entries.

Install File(s) Example

The following example creates a MYAPP directory on the C: drive and installs the compressed AT.EXE Windows NT command.

Other Script Actions Used:

1. Check Disk Space

2. Set Variable

3. Create Directory

SMS Installer Window:
See Figure 5-120.

```
Check free disk space
Set Variable MYAPPDIR to C:\MYAPP
Create Directory %MYAPPDIR%
Install File C:\WINNT\system32\at.exe to %MyAppDir%\at.exe
```

Figure 5-120 *Install File(s) script action window.*

Script:

```
———-Begin Script
item: Check Disk Space
end
item: Set Variable
  Variable=MYAPPDIR
  Value=C:\MYAPP
end
item: Create Directory
  Pathname=%MYAPPDIR%
end
item: Install File
  Source=C:\WINNT\system32\at.exe
  Destination=%MyAppDir%\at.exe
  Flags=0000000000000010
end
———-End Script
```

Install MMC Snap-in

The Install MMC Snap-in dialog box, shown in Figure 5-121, allows you to compress MMC (Microsoft Management Console) DLL files into the compiled executable. When the snap-in is installed on the target computer, it is automatically installed to the System32 directory and registered with the operating system. When you open the MMC in administrative mode, by running the MMC /A command, along with Add/Remove Snap-in (Ctrl+M), the newly installed snap-in will be available for selection in the list.

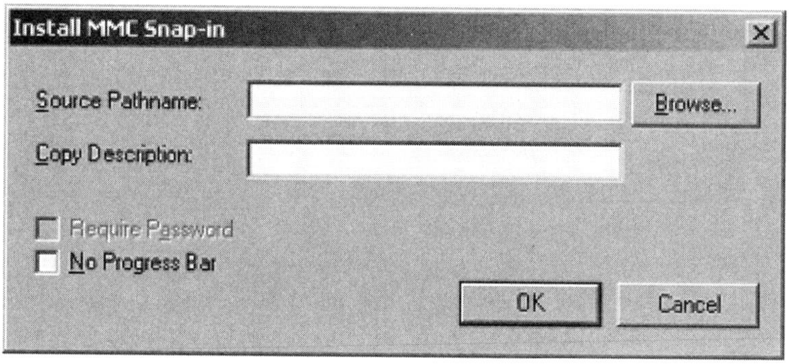

Figure 5-121 *Install MMC Snap-in dialog box.*

Install MMC Snap-in Options

Source Pathname   The Source Pathname field is a required field that contains the source directory of the snap-in file that is to be installed. This field must start with a variable that has been previously defined, unless the Browse button is used to select the file from the local file system. This field will also accept the * wildcard character for copying multiple files at once. For example, if you want to copy all the help files from a source directory, you can use the *.HLP parameter. If you want to copy *all* files from a source directory, you can use the *.* parameter. The field accepts up to 255 characters.

Note   The files for the source pathname can be selected in one of three ways:

1. Enter a directory name, and all the files underneath the directory will be compressed into the compiled executable.
2. Enter a directory path and filename, and the specific file will be compressed into the compiled executable.
3. Use wildcard characters with the filename, and all the files that match the criteria will be compressed into the compiled executable.

Copy Description   The Copy Description field contains the text that is displayed on the progress bar dialog box as the file is installed. This helps the user understand what the installation is doing. The word "Copying" precedes whatever description you enter, so input the text with this in mind. For example, if you want the user to see "Copying MMC Snap-in...," just enter MMC Snap-in. ... This field accepts text, variables, or both, up to 255 characters, but the description will be truncated if it goes beyond the window width.

Require Password   The Require Password checkbox allows you to establish a password for the snap-in installation procedure. This checkbox is only enabled after setting an installation password through the Installation Properties on the General tab (Ctrl-Z). One password is possible per compiled script. The user's password entry should be one of the first items the script runs. Use this feature if this script action is the first instance where the script makes changes to the target computer.

No Progress Bar Selecting this checkbox causes the file copy progress bar to be hidden during the file copy.

Install MMC Snap-in Example

The following example installs the IIS (Internet Information Server) Administrator MMC Snap-in. It also requires a password for the installation. The password has been set to PASSWORD via the Installation Properties-Global Tab (Ctrl-Z).

Other Script Actions Used:

Check Disk Space

SMS Installer Window:
See Figure 5-122.

Script:

```
————-Begin Script
item: Check Disk Space
end
item: Install MMC Snap-in
  Source=C:\WINNT\system32\inetsrv\iisadmin.dll
  Destination=%SYS32%\iisadmin.dll
  Description English=IIS Administrator MMC Snap-in
  Flags=0011000010000011
end
————-End Script
```

Install ODBC Driver

Before a user can access a specific database, the driver must be installed and configured on the computer. The Install ODBC Driver dialog box, shown in Figure 5-123, allows installation of the Open DataBase Connector files for the specified driver and configuration of the computer's ODBCINST.INI file (located in the C:\WINDOWS\SYSTEM or C:\WINNT\SYSTEM32 directory)

```
Check free disk space
Install MMC Snap-in C:\WINNT\system32\inetsrv\iisadmin.dll
```

Figure 5-122 *Install MMC Snap-in script action window.*

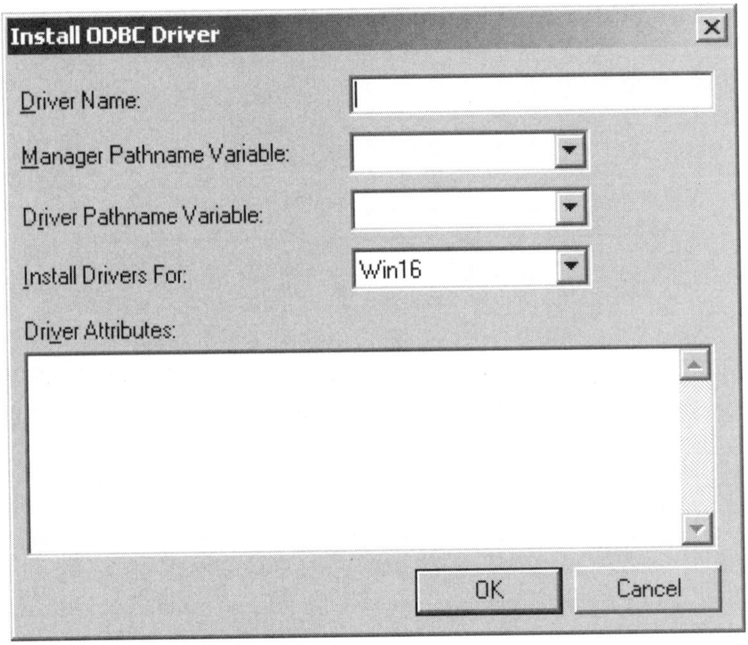

Figure 5-123 *Install ODBC Driver dialog box.*

with the driver information. When an application uses the driver, it checks the ODBCINST.INI file for specific driver information. On Windows 9x and Windows NT computers, the ODBC information is also contained in the registry. For an example of an ODBINST.INI file, see Chapter 10.

The software components of the ODBC driver are configured using the Config ODBC Data Source script action. This should be used in conjunction with the Install ODBC Driver script action if you are installing a driver specifically to access a database.

Install ODBC Driver Options

Driver Name   The Driver Name field contains the description of the driver that will be installed. While this field will accept any description, it is a good practice to use the driver name, version, and type (16-bit, 32-bit). The field accepts text strings, variables, or both, up to 255 characters.

Manager Pathname Variable   This is a required field that points to the directory that is used to install the ODBC DLL manager

file. The ODBC Manager is the transport that loads the ODBC
driver file when a database is accessed. The drop-down list allows
you to choose a predefined variable. Entering a new variable
name in this field will create a new variable. If this field is left
blank, the compiler will return an error.

Driver Pathname Variable This is a required field that points to
the directory that is used to install the ODBC DLL driver file. The
drop-down list allows you to choose a predefined variable. Entering a new variable name in this field will create a new variable. If
this field is left blank, the compiler will return an error.

Install Drivers For The Install Drivers For drop-down list allows
you to choose either the 16-bit or 32-bit driver. Base your selection on the target computer's operating system and database
requirement.

Driver Attributes The Driver Attributes box allows you to
include the specific ODBC driver information that should be
inserted into its own section of the ODBCINST.INI file. The
ODBINST.INI example in Chapter 10 includes several driver section references. These are the specific driver attributes. The driver
and setup attributes *must* be entered into the box for this script
action to work.

Example of the MS FoxPro Driver and Setup attributes:

```
Driver=C:\WINNT\System32\odbcjt32.dll
Setup=C:\WINNT\System32\odfox32.dll
```

Install ODBC Driver Example

The following example installs the MS FoxPro 3.0 ODBC dri-
ver and modifies the ODBCINST.INI file with the driver details.
SMS Installer Window:
See Figure 5-124.

```
Check free disk space
Install ODBC Driver Microsoft FoxPro Driver (*.dbf) (32 bit)
```

Figure 5-124 *Install ODBC Driver script action window.*

Script:

```
────-Begin Script
item: Check Disk Space
end
item: Install ODBC Driver
  Manager Variable=MANAGER
  Driver Variable=DRIVER
  Attributes=Microsoft FoxPro Driver (*.dbf) (32 bit)
  Attributes=Driver=C:\WINNT\System32\odbcjt32.dll
  Attributes=Setup=C:\WINNT\System32\odfox32.dll
  Attributes=DriverODBCVer=C:\WINNT\System32\03.0
  Attributes=32 bit=1
  Attributes=
  Flags=00000001
end
────-End Script
```

Modify Component Size

The Modify Component Size dialog box, shown in Figure 5-125, allows you to change the amount of hard disk space SMS Installer calculates for a specified installation component. Software components are defined through the Components tab in the Application Files group of the Installation Expert. The components are a combined set of files available for installation that the user can choose to install. This script action allows you to increase the component's disk space requirement. This is helpful if you want to ensure the computer always has a set amount of hard disk space available. For example, Windows 9x does not function properly if the hard disk does not have at least 50 MB free. Problems will present themselves, such as the inability to print or run a number of applications simultaneously without errors. Increasing the component size increases the chance that the SMS Installer installation will not be able to install if the adequate amount of hard disk space is not available after the installation.

Note   The Check Disk Space script action can automatically retrieve the component(s) installation size.

The Modify Component Size script action is generally used with an If/While block using the Contains Any Letters In

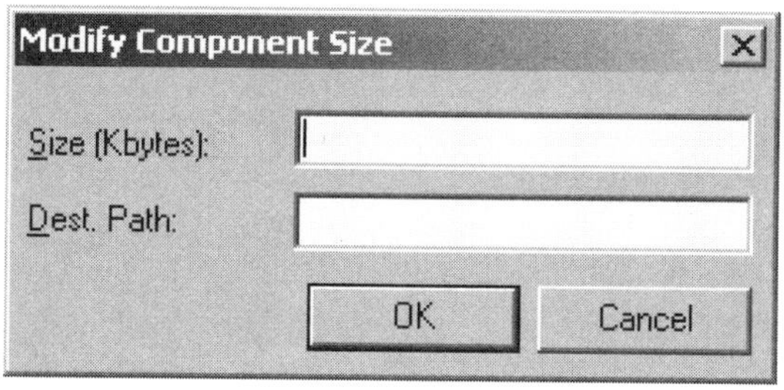

Modify Component Size

Size (Kbytes):

Dest. Path:

OK   Cancel

Figure 5-125 *Modify Component Size dialog box.*

conditional statement. This logic block is run to determine the user's component selections.

> If the SMS Installer script calls an external installation program, you should include this component information in the script and use the Modify Component Size script action to place the hard disk space requirements in the script. If you do not use this method, the hard disk requirement will not calculate correctly and the installation could fill up the hard drive without warning.

Note

Modify Component Size Options

Size (Kbytes)   The Size field allows you to enter a numeric value (in kilobytes) to represent how large the component requirement size should be increased by.

Dest. Path   The Dest. Path (Destination Path) contains the component that should be modified. The path *must* start with a predefined variable. This field can accept text strings, variables, or both, up to 255 characters.

Modify Component Size Example

The following example modifies the COMPONENT1 variable and increases the component by 300 KB. It first uses the If/While statement to verify the user's component selections. The Check Disk Space script action automatically calculates the initial component size requirement and the Modify Component Size script action increases the requirement.

Other Script Actions Used:

1. Check Disk Space

2. If/While Statement

3. Install File(s)

4. End Block

SMS Installer Window:
See Figure 5-126.
Script:

```
————-Begin Script
item: Check Disk Space
  Component=COMPONENTS
end
item: If/While Statement
  Variable=COMPONENTS
  Value=A
  Flags=00001010
end
item: Install File
  Source=c:\MYAPP\at.exe
  Destination=%MAINDIR%\at.exe
  Flags=0000000000000010
end
item: End Block
end
item: Modify Component Size
  Pathname=300
  Size=COMPONENT1
end
————-End Script
```

Open/Close INSTALL.LOG

When SMS Installer makes physical changes to the computer, it is recorded into an installation log file. This file is used with the uninstall process to perform a full removal of the application. A full removal puts the computer back to its original condition before

```
Check free disk space
If COMPONENTS Contains Any Letters In "A" then
  Install File c:\MYAPP\at.exe to %MAINDIR%\at.exe
End Block
Modify Component Size: 300
```

Figure 5-126 *Modify Component Size script action window.*

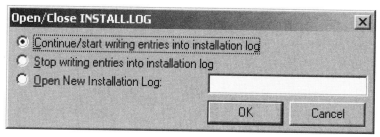

Figure 5-127 *Open/Close INSTALL.LOG dialog box.*

the application was installed. The Open/Close INSTALL.LOG dialog box, shown in Figure 5-127, allow you to control the information that is written to the installation log. When the script is created using the Repackage facility, the installation log creation and updating is handled automatically. The script action is used primarily to further customize the information that is placed into the log file. It is also used as a manual script item if creating the installation script entirely in the Script Editor.

This same script action is used to open, close, and create installation log files. Each function must receive its own script line item.

Open/Close INSTALL.LOG Options

Continue/Start Writing Entries into Installation Log   Selecting this option continues writing to an installation that was closed due to the Stop Writing Entries into Installation Log option. Before this selection will work, a log file must have been created and opened using the Open New Installation Log selection.

Stop Writing Entries into Installation Log   Selecting this option stops the writing process and closes the current installation log.

Open New Installation Log   The Open New Installation Log option creates a new installation log in the location specified in the Log File Pathname field, as follows. It is also used to open existing log files.

Log File Pathname   Though this field is not labeled, it contains the location information for the log file. Both the path and filename must be entered into this field if the Open New Installation Log option is selected. This field accepts text strings, variables, or both up to 255 characters.

Note When the SMS Installer uninstall process runs, it looks for a log file named INSTALL.LOG in the application's installation directory. If the log file will be used for the uninstall process, keep it with the SMS Installer convention; otherwise, the uninstall process could fail.

Open/Close INSTALL.LOG Example

The following example opens an installation log in the application directory and names it MyInstall.log. The example then starts the log-write process before installing the program file. The log file is then closed when the computer changes are complete.

Other Script Actions Used:

1. Check Disk Space

2. Set Variable

3. Install File(s)

SMS Installer Window:
See Figure 5-128.

Script:

```
————-Begin Script
item: Check Disk Space
end
item: Set Variable
  Variable=APPDIR
  Value=C:\MyApp
end
item: Open/Close INSTALL.LOG
  Pathname=%APPDIR%\MyInstall.log
  Flags=00000010
end
```

```
Check free disk space
Set Variable APPDIR to C:\MyApp
Open new installation log file %APPDIR%\MyInstall.log
Continue/Start writing to installation log
Install File C:\MYAPP\at.exe to %APPDIR%\at.exe
Stop writing to installation log
```

Figure 5-128 *Open/Close INSTALL.LOG script action window.*

```
item: Open/Close INSTALL.LOG
end
item: Install File
  Source=C:\MYAPP\at.exe
  Destination=%APPDIR%\at.exe
  Flags=0000000000000010
end
item: Open/Close INSTALL.LOG
  Flags=00000001
end
————-End Script
```

Parse String

The Parse String script action, the dialog box for which is shown in Figure 5-129, allows you to take long strings of text and split them into two new strings. This is useful for retrieving a portion of the string to place into a variable. Once the portion of the string is placed into the variable, the new variable data can be used with the rest of the script.

Parse String Options

Source Value   The Source Value is the actual text string that will be split. Any text (up to 255 characters) can be typed into this

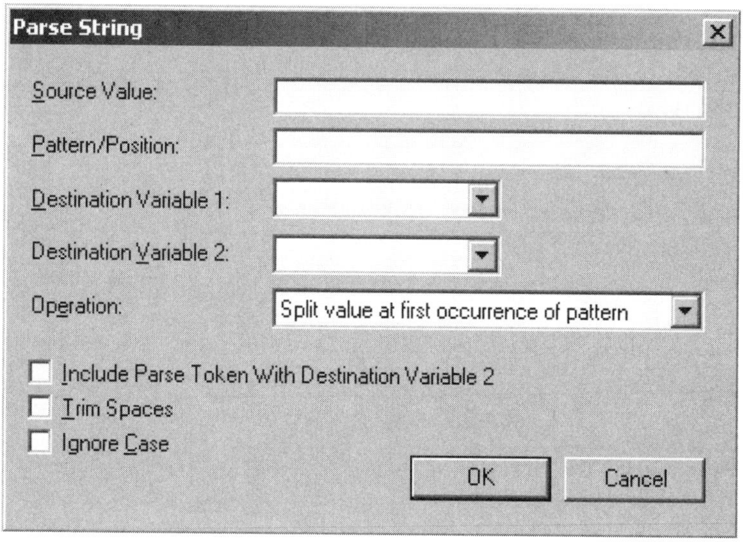

Figure 5-129 *Parse String dialog box.*

field, or a variable that has been defined earlier in the script can be used.

Pattern/Position   The location of the split is defined in the Pattern/Position field. This field can contain a number location (beginning with 1, based on total number of characters) or a location based on a text pattern (up to 255 characters). This field can also use a predefined variable for splitting the text occurrence.

Destination Variable 1   This variable field will contain the first string of text after the split and will be available to the rest of the script. This drop-down list allows selecting of a preexisting variable, but a new variable name can be entered.

Destination Variable 2   This variable field will contain the second string of text after the split and will be available to the rest of the script. This drop-down list allows selecting of a preexisting variable, but a new variable name can be entered.

Note   When entering a new variable name into the Destination Variable fields, make sure the variable name is not already being used by another script function.

Operation   The Operation selection tells the Parse String action where to split the text string. It contains four options, as shown in Table 5-10.

Include Parse Token With Destination Variable 2   When the Parse String action splits the text string, it removes the pattern identified in the Pattern/Position field. Selecting this checkbox forces the Parse String action to include the given pattern with the output of Destination Variable 2, as seen in the following example:

UNCHECKED—The output with this option unchecked:

```
String: C:\Program Files
Parse Token: \
Destination Variable 1 value: C:
Destination Variable 2 value: Program Files
```

CHECKED—The output with this option selected:

Table 5-10 *Operation selection options.*

Operation	Description
Split Value at First Occurrence of Pattern	Splits the string at the first occurrence (left to right) of the defined pattern. If the value is not found in the text string, the entire data string is placed into Destination 1, and Destination 2 is left blank.
Split Value at Last Occurrence of Pattern	Splits the string at the last occurrence (left to right) of the defined pattern. If the value is not found in the text string, the entire data string is placed into Destination 2, and Destination 1 is left blank.
Split Value at Position From Left	Splits the string from the left based on the supplied position number. If the value is not found at the position in the text string, the entire data string is placed into Destination 1, and Destination 2 is left blank.
Split Value at Position From Right	Splits the string based on the right based on the supplied position number. If the value is not found in the text string, the entire data string is placed into Destination 2, and Destination 1 is left blank.

```
String: C:\Program Files
Parse Token: \
Destination Variable 1 value: C:
Destination Variable 2 value: \Program Files
```

Including the parsing token allows you to use the values of both variables with the script, instead of losing the parse pattern during the parsing procedure. When the variable is parsed, the data of the specified pattern is lost unless this option is enabled.

Trim Spaces   With this checkbox selected, the Parse action automatically removes and ignores all spaces at the beginning and end of the text string.

Ignore Case   With this checkbox selected, the Parse action ignores the character case as it is typed in the Pattern/Position field.

Note   Some strings may need to be parsed more than once to produce the desired result. The following parse string example presents this procedure.

Parse String Example

The following example retrieves the video driver information from the computer's registry. It places the registry information from HKEY_LOCAL_MACHINE\Hardware\Devicemap\Video into a variable, and then uses the Parse script action twice. It parses the information the first time to split the hive information from the data value. It parses the second time to split the video driver name from the rest of the data value. Then the script uses the video driver name to query the HKEY_LOCAL_MACHINE\ System\CurrentControlSet\Services\<videodrivername>\Device0 to get the actual manufacturer's driver name.

For example purposes, the script writes the information to a Video.txt file in the root of the C: drive. The output for the reference computer looks like this:

VIDEO.TXT Contents:

```
Video Hardware Key:
\REGISTRY\Machine\System\ControlSet001\Services\neo20xx\
Device0
First Parse Variable: \REGISTRY\Machine\System\
ControlSet001
2nd Parse Variable: neo20xx\Device0
Final Output/Video Driver Name: neo20xx
Video Driver Manufacturer Name: NeoMagic MagicGraph256AV
driver
```

Other Script Actions Used:

1. Check Disk Space

2. Set Variable

3. Get Registry Key Value

4. Insert Line into Text File

SMS Installer Window:
See Figure 5-130.

Script:

```
————-Begin Script
item: Check Disk Space
end
item: Set Variable
  Variable=ROOT
  Value=C:\
end
item: Get Registry Key Value
  Variable=VIDDRIVER
  Key=Hardware\Devicemap\Video
  Value Name=\Device\Video0
  Flags=00000100
end
item: Insert Line into Text File
  Pathname=%ROOT%Video.txt
  New Text=Video Hardware Key: %VIDDRIVER%
  Line Number=0
end
item: Parse String
  Source=%VIDDRIVER%
  Pattern=\Services\
  Variable1=BEFORE
  Variable2=AFTER
  Flags=00000001
end
item: Insert Line into Text File
  Pathname=%ROOT%video.txt
  New Text=First Parse Variable: %BEFORE%
  Line Number=0
end
```

```
Check free disk space
Set Variable ROOT to C:\
Get Registry Key Hardware\Devicemap\Video place in Variable VIDDRIVER
Insert line "Video Hardware Key:  %VIDDRIVER%" into text file %ROOT%Video.txt.
Parse String "%VIDDRIVER%" into BEFORE and AFTER
Insert line "First Parse Variable:  %BEFORE%" into text file %ROOT%video.txt.
Insert line "2nd Parse Variable:  %AFTER%" into text file %ROOT%video.txt.
Parse String "%AFTER%" into VIDBEFORE and VIDAFTER
Insert line "Final Output/Video Driver Name:  %VIDBEFORE%" into text file %ROOT%video.txt.
Get Registry Key System\CurrentControlSet\Services\%VIDBEFORE%\Device0 place in Variable CHIPSETNAME
Insert line "Video Driver Manufacturer Name:  %CHIPSETNAME%" into text file %ROOT%Video.txt.
```

Figure 5-130 *Parse String script action window.*

```
item: Insert Line into Text File
  Pathname=%ROOT%video.txt
  New Text=2nd Parse Variable: %AFTER%
  Line Number=0
end
item: Parse String
  Source=%AFTER%
  Pattern=\Device0
  Variable1=VIDBEFORE
  Variable2=VIDAFTER
end
item: Insert Line into Text File
  Pathname=%ROOT%video.txt
  New Text=Final Output/Video Driver Name: %VIDBEFORE%
  Line Number=0
end
item: Get Registry Key Value
  Variable=CHIPSETNAME

Key=System\CurrentControlSet\Services\%VIDBEFORE%\Device0
  Value Name=Device Description
  Flags=00000100
end
item: Insert Line into Text File
  Pathname=%ROOT%Video.txt
  New Text=Video Driver Manufacturer Name: %CHIPSETNAME%
  Line Number=0
end
————-End Script
```

Play Multimedia File

The Play Multimedia File script action allows you to play
video and sound files during the installation script. This feature
provides a richer experience for the user. You can use this script
action to alert the user with sounds for errors. You can play a
song during the entire installation or how a movie that walks
the user through the steps to complete the installation (see Figure
5-131).

Tip   Playing multimedia files on the computer will increase the
resources needed to perform the installation. Make sure the target computer has adequate sound and video hardware and
enough memory for the included files. You can use the Check System Configuration script action before playing the multimedia
files to verify the computer meets the minimum requirements.

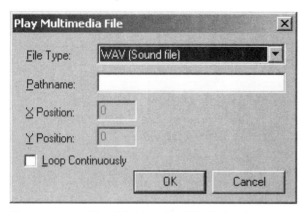

Figure 5-131 *Play Multimedia File dialog box.*

Use a logic block (If/While Statement script action) to skip playing
the files if the computer system does not adequately support the
file types.

Play Multimedia File Options

File Type   The File Type drop-down box allows you to select
what type of file will be used for the script action. SMS Installer
supports two types:

- *WAV (Sound File)*   The WAV file is a Windows standard format for computer sounds such as sound effects, voice, and
  music. It has a .wav file extension.

- *AVI (Video File)*   The AVI file is a Windows standard format
  for computer full-motion video. It has an .avi file extension.

Pathname   The Pathname field is a mandatory field that *must*
start with a predefined variable. This field contains the location, in
the local file system, of the multimedia file. The multimedia file
must exist on the target computer. To ensure the file exists, include
it with the script and install it before the script action plays it. This
field accepts text strings, variables, or both, up to 255 characters.

X Position   The X-Position is the horizontal location on the
computer screen. Measured in pixels, this coordinate starts from
the upper left corner of a 640 × 480 screen. Because this option

is display-related, it is only available when the AVI file type has been selected.

Y Position   The Y-Position is the vertical location on the computer screen. Also measured in pixels, this coordinate starts from the upper left corner of a 640 × 480 screen. Because this option is display-related, it is only available when the AVI file type has been selected.

Loop Continuously   Selecting this option causes the specified multimedia file to play continuously during the entire script.

Play Multimedia File Example

The following example verifies that the computer hardware can play WAV files. If the computer meets the requirement, a WAV file is installed and then played. The SLEEP script action is used to allow the WAV file to play for 10 seconds. If the hardware does not meet the requirement to play the WAV file, the script exits.

Other Script Actions Used:

1. Check Disk Space

2. Check Configuration

3. Install File

4. Sleep

5. Else Statement

6. Exit Installation

7. End Block

SMS Installer Window:
See Figure 5-132.

```
Check free disk space
If System Has WAV File Playback Support Start Block
  Install File C:\WINNT\Media\ir_begin.wav to %WIN%\Media\ir_begin.wav
  Play Multimedia File %WIN%\Media\ir_begin.wav
  Sleep for 10000 Milliseconds
Else
  Exit Installation
End Block
```

Figure 5-132 *Play Multimedia File script action window.*

Script:

```
————Begin Script
item: Check Disk Space
end
item: Check Configuration
  Flags=10111100
end
item: Install File
  Source=C:\WINNT\Media\ir_begin.wav
  Destination=%WIN%\Media\ir_begin.wav
  Flags=0000000000010010
end
item: Play Wave File
 .Pathname=%WIN%\Media\ir_begin.wav
  Flags=00000001
end
item: Sleep
  Sleep=10000
end
item: Else Statement
end
item: Exit Installation
end
item: End Block
end
————End Script
```

Prompt for Text

The Prompt for Text dialog box, shown in Figure 5-133, allows you to ask the user for a single line of text that is inserted into a variable. The variable value can be used with the remainder of the script. This script action is beneficial for retrieving user-specific information and preferences.

Prompt Settings Options

Window Name   The Window Name is a required field. The entry will be displayed as the title of the dialog box that is presented to the user. This field can accept strings of text, variables, or both, up to 64 characters. If the entered information is longer than the width of the dialog box, the text will be displayed in ellipses, so try to keep the title under 40 characters.

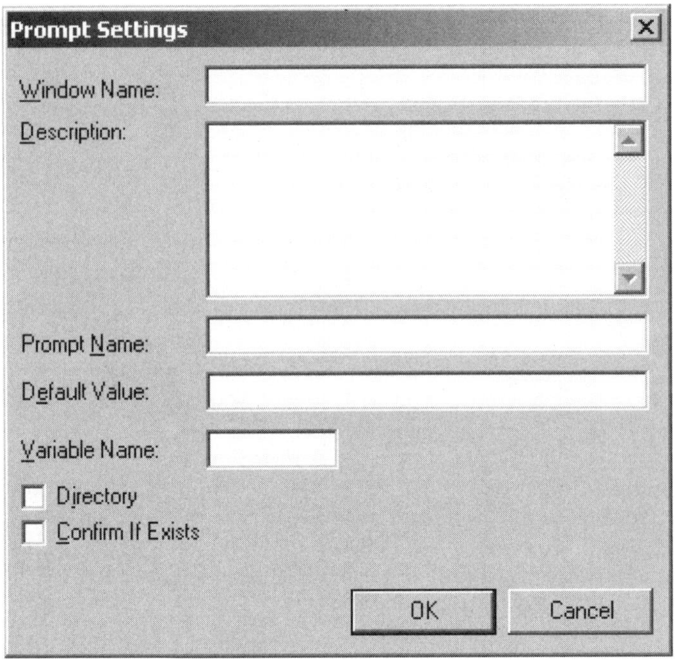

Figure 5-133 *Prompt for Text dialog box.*

Description   The Description is the text you want the user to read. Use this field to specify the information for which you are prompting the user. This field accepts strings of text, variables, or both, up to nine lines of text. You can use the Ctrl-Enter key combination to enter blank lines or to separate paragraphs.

Prompt Name   This required field allows you to enter identifying text about the user input field. It places a field title at the left of the input box. Though this field accepts text strings, variables, or both up to 255 characters, any prompt over 35 characters will wrap underneath the input and list boxes.

Default Value   When information is entered into the Default Value field, the information will be displayed in the user's input box. This helps the user by displaying a default format string in the user entry field. For example, if the user is not knowledgeable of the IP Address format, place XXX.XXX.XXX.XXX in this field. Or, you can input the common information into this field, such as a server name, drive letter, directory name, and so on. This field accepts text strings, variables, or both, up to 255 characters.

Variable Name The variable name entered in this field will be created and the user's input will be placed into the new variable. This field can contain a new name or one previously defined in the script.

Directory If prompting the user for directory information, selecting this option strips the last backslash off the user's input before it is placed in the variable. This keeps the directory entry uniform. Some users may enter the backslash, and it could cause the script not to complete because the variable is not formatted properly. Use this selection to confirm that any directory information entered will be usable later in the script.

Confirm If Exists This checkbox, if selected, warns users that their directory selection already exists (if they have chosen a directory that is already present in the file system). It also informs them that if they choose to continue, the directory will be overwritten with the new files. If they choose not to continue, the script will return to the Prompt for Text dialog box to try again. Use this option only if prompting the user for directory information.

Prompt for Text Example

The following example retrieves the user's login name through the USERNAME environment variable and compares it to the user's input. If the values match, a message is displayed, indicating the installation will continue. If the values do not match, a message indicating the installation will not continue displays. When the user hits the OK button, the error information, time, and date is written to an error log file in the %SYS32% directory.

Other Script Actions Used:

1. Check Disk Space

2. Get Environment Variable

3. If/While Statement

4. Display Message

```
 Check free disk space
Get Environment Variable USERNAME into Variable NETNAME1
Prompt "Network Login Name:" Variable NETNAME2
If NETNAME1 Equals (Ignore Case) "%NETNAME2%" then
  Display Message "Success..."
Else
  Display Message "Failure..."
  Get System Information into DATE
  Insert line "**** ERROR ****" into text file %SYS32%\NETNAME.LOG.
  Insert line "%DATE%" into text file %SYS32%\NETNAME.LOG.
  Insert line "Name User Entered:  %NETNAME2%" into text file %SYS32%\NETNAME.LOG.
  Insert line "Name Configured on System:  %NETNAME1%" into text file %SYS32%\NETNAME.LOG.
  Insert line "****************************" into text file %SYS32%\NETNAME.LOG.
End Block
```

Figure 5-134 *Prompt for Text script action window.*

5. Else Statement

6. Insert Line into Text File

7. End Block

SMS Installer Window:
See Figure 5-134.

Script:

```
————-Begin Script
item: Check Disk Space
end
item: Get Environment Variable
  Variable=NETNAME1
  Environment=USERNAME
end
item: Prompt for Text
  Window Title English=Login Name...
  Text English=Please enter your network login name below.
This will be verified with the system.
  Prompt Title English=Network Login Name:
  Variable=NETNAME2
end
item: If/While Statement
  Variable=NETNAME1
  Value=%NETNAME2%
  Flags=00000100
end
item: Display Message
```

```
   Title English=Success...
   Text English=The network login name you entered, matches
the name configured on this computer. The installation will
continue...
   Flags=00000100
end
item: Else Statement
end
item: Display Message
   Title English=Failure...
   Text English=The network login name you entered, does not
match the name configured on this computer. Please check to
make sure you entered the correct information. If the
information is correct, contact your local technical sup-
port.
   Flags=00110000
end
item: Get System Information
   Variable=DATE
end
item: Insert Line into Text File
   Pathname=%SYS32%\NETNAME.LOG
   New Text=**** ERROR ****
   Line Number=0
end
item: Insert Line into Text File
   Pathname=%SYS32%\NETNAME.LOG
   New Text=%DATE%
   Line Number=0
end
item: Insert Line into Text File
   Pathname=%SYS32%\NETNAME.LOG
   New Text=Name User Entered: %NETNAME2%
   Line Number=0
end
item: Insert Line into Text File
   Pathname=%SYS32%\NETNAME.LOG
   New Text=Name Configured on System: %NETNAME1%
   Line Number=0
end
item: Insert Line into Text File
   Pathname=%SYS32%\NETNAME.LOG
   New Text=************************
   Line Number=0
end
item: End Block
end
————-End Script
```

Radio Button Dialog

The Radio Button Dialog script action allows you to present the user with predefined selections. The user's choice is placed into a variable to be used with an If/While Statement script action to branch the script logic based on the variable value. This script action can display up to 10 different components, allowing only 1 to be selected by the user (see Figure 5-135).

Any type of information can be obtained from the user by using this method. A good example of this script action is to ask the user for a customized installation, a minimal installation, or a complete/full installation. Based on the user's selection, you can insert a logic block to branch to the correct script procedure to install the correct file set.

Radio Button Settings Options

Title   The Title is a required field. The entry will be displayed as the title of the dialog box that is presented to the user. This field

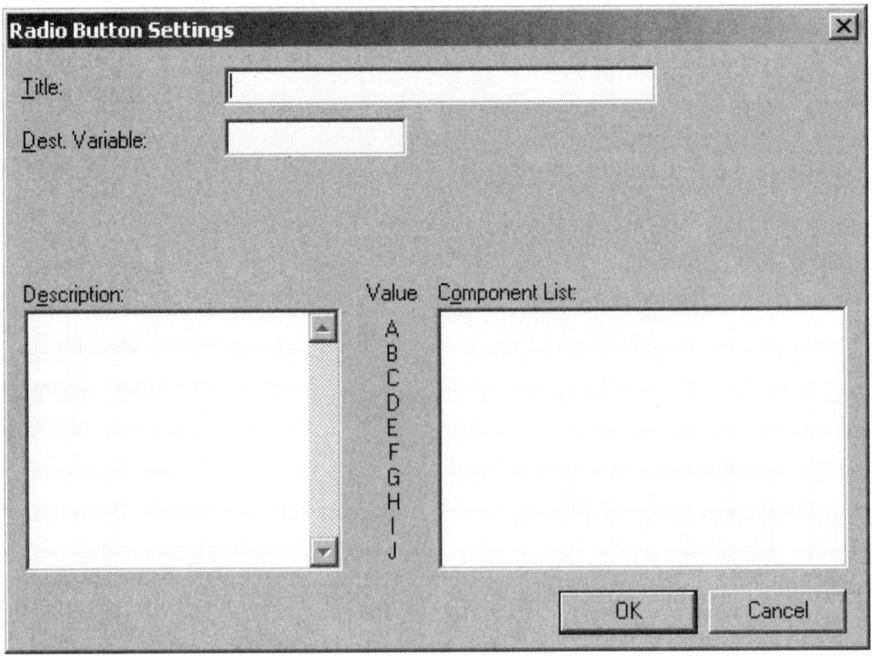

Figure 5-135 *Radio Button dialog box.*

can accept strings of text, variables, or both, up to 255 characters. If the entered information is longer than the width of the dialog box, the text will be displayed in ellipses, so try to keep the title under 60 characters.

Dest. Variable (Destination Variable)   The variable name entered here receives the value of the user's radio button selection. The variable must have been defined earlier in the script. This is a required field.

When the user selects the radio button, the variable will be updated with a new value. You can use the Set Variable script action to establish which radio button is the default selection on the dialog box and also to disable specific buttons. The radio button uses upper- and lowercase letters to determine these functions. In the example in this section, the SERVNAME variable receives the user's value. Earlier in the script, the Set Variable script action would be used to direct SERVNAME to one of the options shown in Table 5-9.

For example, create three radio buttons by inputting three items in the Component List. Each button will automatically be assigned the letters A, B, and C based on the Value column. The examples in Table 5-11 describe how the radio buttons will display with the variable value previously set.

The Radio Button set only reads this value to know how you want the buttons to display. Once the user selects his or her choice of options, the variable value is replaced with the user's selection.

Description   The Description is the information you want the user to read. Use this field to specify the data for which you are prompting the user. This field accepts strings of text, variables, or both, up to five lines of text. You can use the Ctrl-Enter key combination to enter blank lines or to separate paragraphs.

Value   The Value column indicates the alphanumeric character that will be assigned to the Dest. Variable based on the user's selection. The letter associated with the variable is the value that is inserted. Use an If/While statement to insert a logic block based on the letter value.

Table 5-11 *Radio Button examples.*

Variable Set To:	Display:
A	All radio buttons are enabled, and the first button is the default.
B	All radio buttons are enabled, and the second button is the default.
C	All radio buttons are enabled, and the third button is the default.
Ac	The first two radio buttons are enabled, the first radio button is the default, and the third radio button is disabled.
aB	The first radio button is disabled, the last two radio buttons are enabled, and the second radio button is the default.
abC	The first two radio buttons are disabled, the last radio button is enabled, and it is the default selection.

Component List   The Component List allows up to 10 different entries. The names entered into each line will be displayed next to their own dialog button on the dialog box. When the radio button next to the component is selected, the Dest. Variable receives the corresponding letter from the Value List. Each option is limited to 45 characters.

Radio Button Dialog Example
The following example prompts for a server name to be selected. The value selection is then displayed in a message box.

Other Script Actions Used:

1. Check Disk Space

2. Display Message

SMS Installer Window:
See Figure 5-136.

```
Check free disk space
Display Radio Button Dialog into Variable SERVNAME
Display Message "Variable Output..."
```

Figure 5-136 *Radio Button Dialog script action window.*

Script:

```
------Begin Script
item: Check Disk Space
end
item: Radio Button Dialog
  Variable=SERVNAME
  Title English=Select Server...
  Description English=Please select your default login
server name.
  Radio Button English=SERVER1
  Radio Button English=SERVER2
  Radio Button English=SERVER3
  Radio Button English=SERVER4
end
item: Display Message
  Title English=Variable Output...
  Text English=Based on the selection, the SERVNAME vari-
able received a value of "%SERVNAME%".
  Flags=00100100
end
------End Script
```

Read INI Value

The Read INI Value dialog box, shown in Figure 5-137, allows you to read values from application configuration files. The values retrieved from the INI file are placed into a variable to be

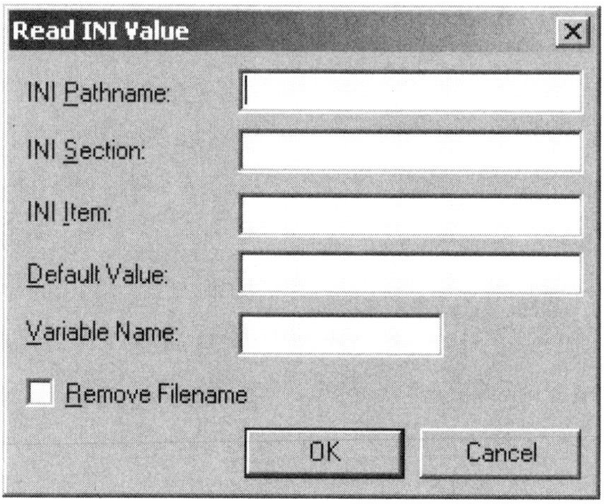

Figure 5-137 *Read INI Value dialog box.*

used with the remainder of the script. One use for this script action is discovering application-specific paths and using the information for software upgrades.

INI files are used by applications to obtain user- or computer-specific information that is not automatically included in the application itself. In 16-bit computer systems, this allowed the software vendor to provide rich customization features to the user. Currently, 32-bit applications use the Windows Registry to store the customization information. INI files are still incorporated into applications for general backward-compatibility. See Chapter 10 for examples of INI files.

Read INI Value Options

INI Pathname   The INI Pathname field contains the location of the INI file in the local file system. This field must include the path and INI filename with extension (.INI). INI files are generally installed to the application's main directory, but some can exist in the C:\WINDOWS or C:\WINNT directories. This field accepts text strings, predefined variables, or both, up to 255 characters.

INI Section   Information in INI files is broken into sections. The section headings are enclosed in brackets (example: [INI_HEADING]). The INI section field contains the section name (without brackets) where the INI Item that is being retrieved is located. This field accepts text strings, predefined variables, or both, up to 255 characters.

INI Item   The INI item is the actual value that will be placed into the variable. Under each INI section heading exists INI items with values. INI items use a standard item=value format (e.g., AppPath=C:\MyApp). From the previous example, the C:\MyApp is the value that is inserted into the variable. This field accepts text strings, predefined variables, or both, up to 255 characters.

Default Value   If the INI item is not found, the information in the Default Value field will be placed into the variable. This field accepts text strings, predefined variables, or both, up to 255 characters.

```
Check free disk space
Set Variable ROOT to C:\
Create Directory %ROOT%MyApp
Edit INI File %ROOT%MyApp\MyINI.INI
Read INI Value from %ROOT%MyApp\MyINI.INI into Variable INSTPATH
Display Message "Install Path..."
```

Figure 5-138 *Read INI Value script action window.*

Variable Name   The Variable Name receives the value that is retrieved from the INI file. This value can be used with the remainder of the script. This field can accept predefined variables, or a new one will be created if a new name is entered.

Remove Filename   When you are using the Read INI Value script action to retrieve path information from an INI file, the Remove Filename selection causes SMS Installer to strip the filename (if it exists) from the pathname. This is useful for placing just the path information into the variable.

Read INI Value Example

The following example creates a MyApp directory in the root of the C: drive. Then a new INI file is created, and the information is inserted. The Read INI Value script action is used to obtain the installation path value from the INI file and then to display the information in a dialog box.

Other Script Actions Used:

1. Check Disk Space

2. Set Variable

3. Create Directory

4. Edit INI File

5. Display Message

SMS Installer Window:
See Figure 5-138.

Script:

```
———-Begin Script
item: Check Disk Space
end
```

```
item: Set Variable
  Variable=ROOT
  Value=C:\
end
item: Create Directory
  Pathname=%ROOT%MyApp
end
item: Edit INI File
  Pathname=%ROOT%MyApp\MyINI.INI
  Settings=[MyINI_Section]
  Settings=
  Settings=InstallPath = C:\MyApp
  Settings=
end
item: Read INI Value
  Variable=INSTPATH
  Pathname=%ROOT%MyApp\MyINI.INI
  Section=MyINI_Section
  Item=InstallPath
  Default=NOTFOUND
end
item: Display Message
  Title English=Install Path...
  Text English=Your application is installed in %INSTPATH%.
  Flags=00100100
end
————-End Script
```

Read/Update Text File

The Read/Update Text File dialog box, shown in Figure 5-139, allows the SMS Installer script to interact with information con-

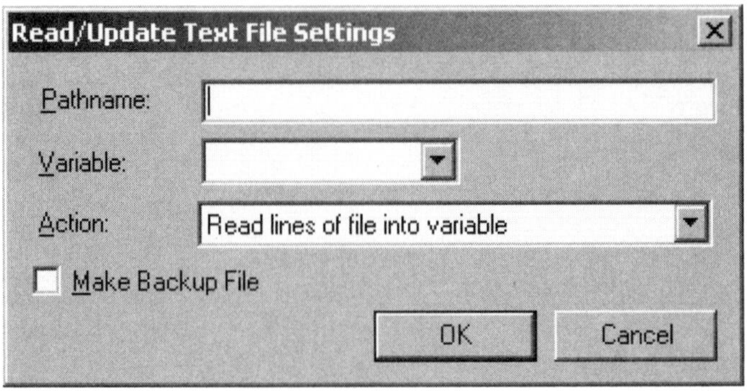

Figure 5-139 *Read/Update Text File dialog box.*

tained in text files. The script action both inserts new lines into the text file and reads lines from the text file.

> Using this script action to read lines of a text file starts a While block. This causes SMS Installer to read every line of text in the file, one at a time, until the variable contains the file's entire contents. Once the While block starts, you cannot break out of the loop. Because of this, you should be careful using this script action with large text files.

Note

Read/Update Text File Settings Options

Pathname   The Pathname field describes the location of the text file in the local file system. The entire pathname and filename with extension must be entered into this field. This field accepts text strings, predefined variables, or both, up to 255 characters.

Variable   This mandatory field is the name of the variable that will either receive text lines during a read or contain text lines that are inserted into the text file. If using this script action to update a text file, the variable must be defined earlier in the script. If using the script action to read lines into the variable, the variable can be a new variable name.

Action   The Action drop-down box allows you to select whether this script action should read or update the text file. The options are as follows:

- *Read Lines of File into Variable*   Reads the entire contents of the text file line-by-line. This option starts a While block. The While block returns a TRUE value as long as unread lines exist in the text file. When a FALSE value is returned, all lines of text have been read into the variable and the While block ends.

- *Update File with New Contents of Variable*   Inserts the variable value in the specified text file and starts a While block. Updating the text file with the variable value replaces the text file's entire contents. Each line in the text file will be replaced by the contents of the variable. For example, if the text file

```
Check free disk space
Set Variable ROOT to C:\
Insert line "This file is a test file for the Read/Update Text File Script Action." into text file %ROOT%MYTEXT.TXT.
Read lines of file %ROOT%MYTEXT.TXT into variable MYTEXT Start Block
   Display Message "Text File Contents..."
End Block
```

Figure 5-140 *Read/Update Text File script action window.*

contains 20 lines of text and the variable contains the value. This is Text, each of the 20 lines will be modified to read "This is Text."

Make Backup File   The Make Backup File checkbox is used if the script action is updating text in the file. This selection causes SMS Installer to create a backup of the text file before it is updated. The backup file keeps the same name as the original file, but it changes the extension to .001. Each time the file is updated and a backup is created, the extension will increment by 1. For example, if you see a file extension of .012, you know the text file has been modified 12 times.

Read/Update Text File Example

The following example creates a new text file the root of the C: drive and inserts text into the file. The Read/Update Text File script action reads the text and displays it in a dialog box.

Other Script Actions Used:

1. Check Disk Space

2. Set Variable

3. Insert Line into Text File

4. Display Message

5. End Block

SMS Installer Window:
See Figure 5-140.

Script:

```
───────-Begin Script
item: Check Disk Space
end
```

```
item: Set Variable
  Variable=ROOT
  Value=C:\
end
item: Insert Line into Text File
  Pathname=%ROOT%MYTEXT.TXT
  New Text=This file is a test file for the Read/Update
Text File Script Action.
  Line Number=0
end
item: Read/Update Text File
  Variable=MYTEXT
  Pathname=%ROOT%MYTEXT.TXT
end
item: Display Message
  Title English=Text File Contents...
  Text English=The following information is contained in
your text file:
  Text English=
  Text English="%MYTEXT%"
  Flags=00100100
end
item: End Block
end
————-End Script
```

Read/Write Binary File

The Read/Write Binary File dialog box, shown in Figure 5-141, allows you to read values from and write values to any binary

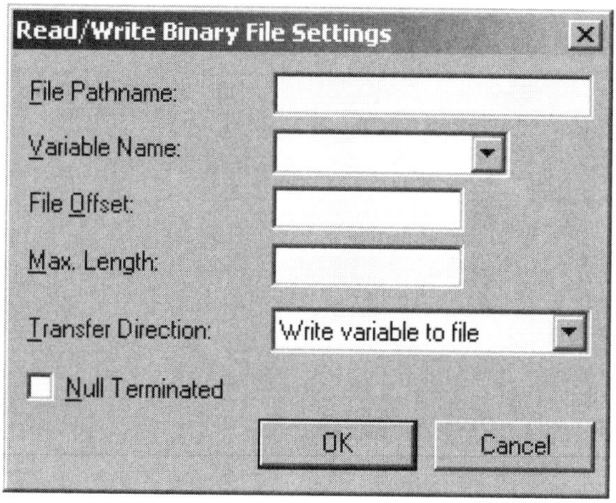

Figure 5-141 *Read/Write Binary File dialog box.*

format file. Binary files are files that have been written with a programming language and compiled by the associated compiler. Examples of binary files are files with extensions of .EXE, .COM, .DLL, and so on. You must have an understanding of binary files before using this script action. Inserting data into a binary file can corrupt the file, keeping it from performing its original functions. Binary files include both text and hexadecimal information in the file format. This script action is used to retrieve those values.

One way to view information about the binary file is to use a program like QuickView, which reads the binary file's header information (seen in the example below). This information can also be viewed using any text file program, such as Notepad.

CMD.EXE Binary Header Information:
WINDOWS EXECUTABLE
32bit for Windows 95 and Windows NT

Technical File Information:
Image File Header

```
            _Signature: 00004550
              Machine: Intel 386
   Number of Sections: 0003
      Time Date Stamp: 37b2156c
      Symbols Pointer: 00000000
    Number of Symbols: 00000000
Size of Optional Header: 00e0
      Characteristics: Relocation info stripped from
                       file.
                       File is executable (i.e. no unre-
                       solved external references).
                       Line numbers stripped from file.
                       Local symbols stripped from file.
                       32 bit word machine.
                       Debugging info stripped from file
                       in .DBG file
```

```
Image Optional Header
                       _Magic: Magic: 010b
               Linker Version: 5.12
                 Size of Code: 0001ac00
   Size of Initialized Data: 0002ac00
 Size of Uninitialized Data: 00000000
     Address of Entry Point: 0001a4c0
```

```
            Base of Code: 00001000
            Base of Data: 0001c000
              Image Base: 4ad00000
        Section Alignment: 00001000
          File Alignment: 00000200
Operating System Version: 5.00
           Image Version: 5.00
       Subsystem Version: 4.00
               Reserved1: 00000000
           Size of Image: 00048000
         Size of Headers: 00000600
                Checksum: 0003a227
               Subsystem: Image runs in the
                          Windows character
                          subsystem.
       DLL Characteristics: 32768
     Size of Stack Reserve: 00100000
      Size of Stack Commit: 00001000
      Size of Heap Reserve: 00100000
       Size of Heap Commit: 00001000
             Loader Flags: 00000000
    Size of Data Directory: 00000010
Import Directory Virtual Address: abbc
    Import Directory Size: 0064
       Resource Directory
          Virtual Address: a000
   Resource Directory Size: d7b0
Debug Directory Virtual Address: 1300
      Debug Directory Size: 001c
```

Header Information

```
_____Signature: 5a4d
           Last Page Size: 0090
       Total Pages in File: 0003
          Relocation Items: 0000
      Paragraphs in Header: 0004
  Minimum Extra Paragraphs: 0000
  Maximum Extra Paragraphs: ffff
     Initial Stack Segment: 0000
     Initial Stack Pointer: 00b8
    Complemented Checksum: 0000
Initial Instruction Pointer: 0000
       Initial Code Segment: 0000
   Relocation Table Offset: 0040
           Overlay Number: 0000
                 Reserved: 0000 0000 0000 0000
                          0000 0000 0000 0000
                          0000 0000 0000 0000
```

```
                                        0000 0000 0000 0000
                    Offset to New Header: 000000d8
                    Memory Needed:        2K
```

Read/Write Binary File Settings Options

File Pathname   The File Pathname contains the full path and file-name of the binary file that this script action will be modifying. The field accepts text strings, variables, or both, up to 255 characters.

Variable Name   If reading the binary file, this field contains the variable that will receive the binary data. If writing to a binary file, this predefined variable name will contain the value that will be written to the file. The drop-down box allows you to select a predefined value for writing to the binary file. If a new variable name is entered, SMS Installer will create it.

File Offset   The File Offset field accepts a numeric value. This numeric value sets the position in the binary file for reading and writing the data. If the field is left blank, it will default to zero. This field accepts any predefined variables as long as the variable data contains a numeric value.

Max. Length   This field contains a numeric value to indicate the maximum number of characters (in bytes) to read from the binary file. If this field is left blank, the entire file length will be read. The field can accept a predefined variable as long as the variable data contains a numeric value.

Transfer Direction   This drop-down box allows you to select which action this script action will perform. There are two options:

1. *Write Variable to File*   This option writes the variable data to the binary file.
2. *Read Variable From File*   This option reads the binary data and inserts it into the specified variable.

Null Terminated   This selection is used when you are writing to a binary file. It adds a NULL value to the end of the variable data when it is written to the file.

Read/Write Binary File Example

The following example reads the Windows NT command interpreter file (CMD.EXE) and displays the retrieved data in a message box.

Other Script Actions Used:

1. Check Disk Space

2. Display Message

SMS Installer Window:
See Figure 5-142.

Script:

```
————-Begin Script
item: Check Disk Space
end
item: Read/Write File Data
  Pathname=%SYS32%\CMD.EXE
  Variable=CMDVAR
  Offset=0
  Max Length=25
  Flags=00000001
end
item: Display Message
  Title English=Binary Data...
  Text English=The retrieved binary data:
  Text English=
  Text English=%CMDVAR%
  Flags=00100100
end
————-End Script
```

Register Font

The Register Font script action causes SMS Installer to automatically register fonts with the operating system. When using the Install File(s) script action, you can install the fonts and make them available immediately after the installation. On Windows 9x and Windows NT computers, fonts are registered in the sys-

```
Check free disk space
Read Variable CMDVAR from file %SYS32%\CMD.EXE
Display Message "Binary Data..."
```

Figure 5-142 *Read/Write Binary File script action window.*

tem registry in the HKEY_LOCAL_MACHINE\SOFTWARE\ Microsoft\\CurrentVersion\Fonts registry key. On Windows 3.x computers the fonts are registered in the WIN.INI in the [FONTS] section. Both methods retrieve the font name and the font filename in the values (see Figure 5-143).

When a font is registered with the operating system, it is available to all applications that support extended fonts. This script action is also useful when you are using a font on the script dialog boxes that is not installed on the target computer. A logic block can be used to determine if the font exists on the computer before it is installed and registered (see the example in this section).

To register a font, SMS Installer needs two items: the font filename and the font name. The font filename is the font name with the .TTF extension. The font name is the display name of the font. Using the previous registry key, the following is an example of the data registered to the standard Arial font:

```
Font Name: Arial (TrueType)
Font Filename: ARIAL.TTF
```

Register Font Settings Options

Font Filename   This field accepts just the font filename with the extension that should be registered with the operating system. The pathname is not used. When the font is installed, it should be installed in the C:\Windows\System or C:\Winnt\System32 directory. This script action looks for the font in these directories when it tries to register it with the system. This field accepts text strings, predefined variables, or both, up to 255 characters.

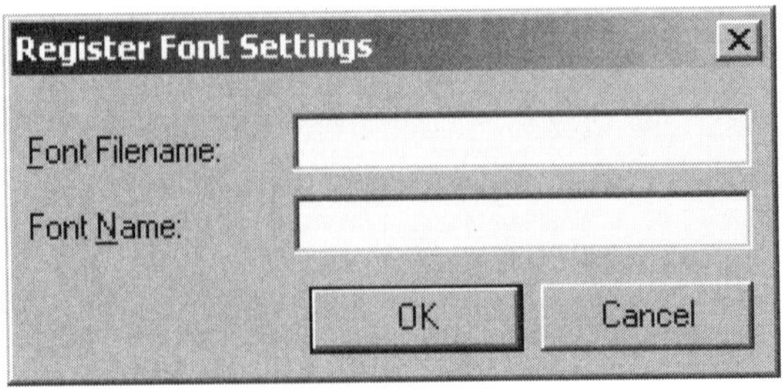

Figure 5-143 *Register Font dialog box.*

```
Check free disk space
Get Registry Key SOFTWARE\Microsoft\Windows NT\CurrentVersion\Fonts place in Variable ARIALEX
If ARIALEX Equals "NOTFOUND" then
    Display Message "Arial Font Installation..."
    Install File C:\WINNT\Fonts\Arial.ttf to %WIN%\Fonts\Arial.ttf
    Register font Arial (TrueType)
Else
    Display Message "Arial Font..."
End Block
```

Figure 5-144 *Register Font script action window.*

Font Name   This is the font's display name that will be registered with the system. If the font is a Windows TrueType font, the
font name must be followed by (TrueType). An example for the
Arial font would be "Arial (TrueType)." Placing the (TrueType)
text after the font name ensures that the TrueType icon will be
used for the registered font file. This field accepts text strings,
predefined variables, or both, up to 255 characters.

Register Font Example

The following example checks the computer's registry to find
the existence of the Arial font. If it is found, the installation continues normally. If it is not found, the user is prompted to install
and register the font on the system.

Other Script Actions Used:

1.   Check Disk Space

2.   Get Registry Key Value

3.   If/While Statement

4.   Display Message

5.   Else Statement

6.   End Block

SMS Installer Window:
See Figure 5-144.

Script

```
————-Begin Script
item: Check Disk Space
end
item: Get Registry Key Value
```

```
        Variable=ARIALEX
        Key=SOFTWARE\Microsoft\Windows NT\CurrentVersion\Fonts
        Default=NOTFOUND
        Value Name=Arial (TrueType)
        Flags=00000100
      end
      item: If/While Statement
        Variable=ARIALEX
        Value=NOTFOUND
      end
      item: Display Message
        Title English=Arial Font Installation...
        Text English=The standard Arial Font was not found on
this computer. It must be installed before the installation
will continue.
        Text English=
        Text English=Click OK to install the font.
        Flags=00001000
      end
      item: Install File
        Source=C:\WINNT\Fonts\Arial.ttf
        Destination=%WIN%\Fonts\Arial.ttf
        Flags=0000000000000010
      end
      item: Register Font
        Filename=Arial (TrueType)
        Font name English=Arial.ttf
      end
      item: Else Statement
      end
      item: Display Message
        Title English=Arial Font...
        Text English=The Arial Font has been found and is
installed correctly on this computer.
        Text English=
        Text English=The installation will now continue.
        Flags=00000100
      end
      item: End Block
      end
      ————-End Script
```

Remark

The Remark script action, the dialog box for which is shown in Figure 5-145, allows you to place blank lines or strings of text in the SMS Installer script. This script action is useful for docu-

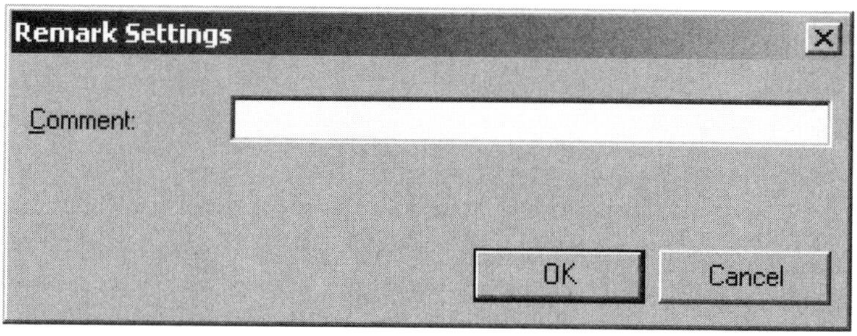

Figure 5-145 *Remark dialog box.*

menting the script within the script itself and for spacing the different script processes for better readability.

Good documentation with a script is a must. This gives you the ability to go back at a later time and understand exactly what the script does. It also aids others, should the script be shared with multiple locations.

Remark Settings Options

Comment   Enter the comment text you want placed into the script line. If the line is left blank, a blank line will be inserted into the script. This field accepts text strings up to 255 characters. Though this script action accepts 255 characters, you may want to use multiple lines for readability if entering a large amount of text. If the text goes beyond the program's screen width, the information will be harder to read.

Remark Example

The following example uses the Remark script action to document the portion of the script. According to the documentation included in the script, the script retrieves the Common Files directory information from the computer and displays it in a dialog box if it is found. If it is not found, the script exits.
Other Script Actions Used:

1. Check Disk Space

2. Get Environment Variable

3. If/While Statement

```
Rem The following script portion, gets the environment variable for the
Rem Common shared files on the computer. If the value is not found, the
Rem installation exits. If the value is found, the variable is displayed in
Rem a dialog box.

Check free disk space
Get Environment Variable CommonProgramFiles into Variable COMMONLOC
If COMMONLOC Equals "NOTFOUND" then
   Exit Installation
Else
   Display Message "Common Files Location..."
End Block
```

Figure 5-146 *Remark script action window.*

4. Exit Installation

5. Else Statement

6. Display Message

7. End Block

SMS Installer Window:

See Figure 5-146.

Script:

```
————-Begin Script
item: Remark
  Text=The following script portion, gets the environment
variable for the
end
item: Remark
  Text=Common shared files on the computer. If the value is
not found, the
end
item: Remark
  Text=installation exits. If the value is found, the vari-
able is displayed in
end
item: Remark
  Text=a dialog box.
end
item: Remark
end
item: Check Disk Space
end
item: Get Environment Variable
  Variable=COMMONLOC
```

```
    Environment=CommonProgramFiles
    Default=NOTFOUND
end
item: If/While Statement
    Variable=COMMONLOC
    Value=NOTFOUND
end
item: Exit Installation
end
item: Else Statement
end
item: Display Message
    Title English=Common Files Location...
    Text English=The Common Files directory was found at
%COMMONLOC%.
    Flags=00100100
end
item: End Block
end
———-End Script
```

Remove from SYSTEM.INI

The Remove from SYSTEM.INI dialog box, shown in Figure 5-147, allows a quick way of removing devices from the SYSTEM.INI file. The resulting script action removes items from the 386 Enhanced ([386Enh]) section of the SYSTEM.INI. While the script action name states the device is removed from the file, the device is only commented-out using the semicolon (;). A backup of the original file is created using the SMS Installer numbering scheme. The backup file keeps the same name as the original file but changes the extension to .001. Each time the file is updated and a backup is created, the extension will increment by 1. For example, if you see a file extension of .012, you know the Autoexec.bat has been modified 12 times.

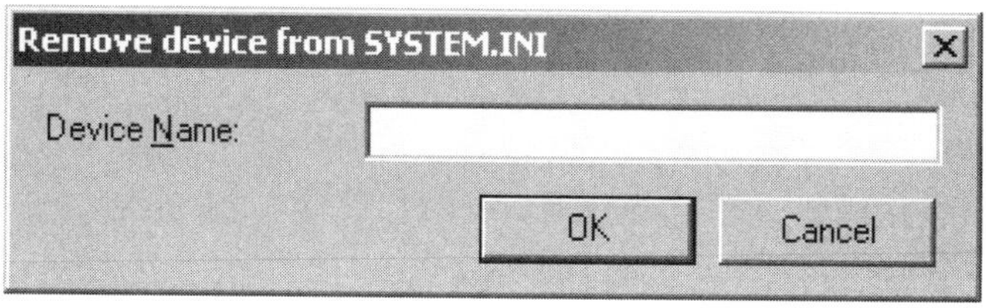

Figure 5-147 *Remove device from SYSTEM.INI dialog box.*

Tip   Because this script action interacts with the SYSTEM.INI file, the user is always prompted to restart the computer. Device additions/deletions/modifications in the 386 Enhanced section are not made available to the system until the computer is restarted. If you want to suppress the restart message, you can use one of two methods:

1. Use the Set Variable script action at the end of the script. Type RESTART in the Variable field. Leave the New Value field blank. For more information on this procedure, see "Suppressing the Restart" in Chapter 08.
2. Use the Edit INI File script action, described in this chapter, to edit the SYSTEM.INI file.

Remove from SYSTEM.INI Options

Device Name   The only option on the Remove from SYSTEM.INI dialog box is the entry field for the device that should be removed. This entry *must* include both the device name and the value. For the example in this section, this entry is "RESTART=S." If the entered device name is not found in the SYSTEM.INI, the script action produces no result and the user is not prompted to restart the computer. This field will accept text strings, predefined variables, or both, up to 255 characters.

Remove from SYSTEM.INI Example

The following example removes the RESTART=S from the 386 Enhanced section of the SYSTEM.INI file. For more information on using the RESTART variable, see Chapter 08.

Other Script Actions Used:

Check Disk Space

SMS Installer Window:

See Figure 5-148.

```
Check free disk space
Remove device RESTART=S from SYSTEM.INI
```

Figure 5-148 *Remove from SYSTEM.INI script action window.*

Script:

```
————-Begin Script
item: Check Disk Space
end
item: Remove from SYSTEM.INI
  Device=RESTART=S
end
————-End Script
```

Rename File/Directory

The Rename File/Directory dialog box, shown in Figure 5-149, allows a convenient way of renaming a file or directory in the local file system.

Rename File/Directory Options

Old Pathname   This field must start with a variable and include the full pathname and/or file name with extension. This field sets the initial reference to the location that will be modified by the information in the New Filename field. This field accepts text strings, predefined variables, or both, up to 255 characters.

New Filename   This field contains the new name of the directory or file. Even though the title of this field references "Filename," it is also used to rename a directory name. Only enter a name; do not enter a full path, as that information is already contained in the Old Pathname field. When renaming a file, you must enter the filename and file extension; otherwise, the file will be renamed without an extension, and the file's application association will be lost.

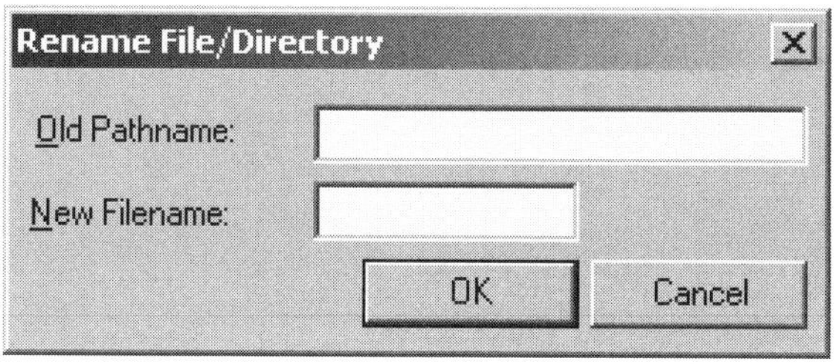

Figure 5-149 *Rename File/Directory dialog box.*

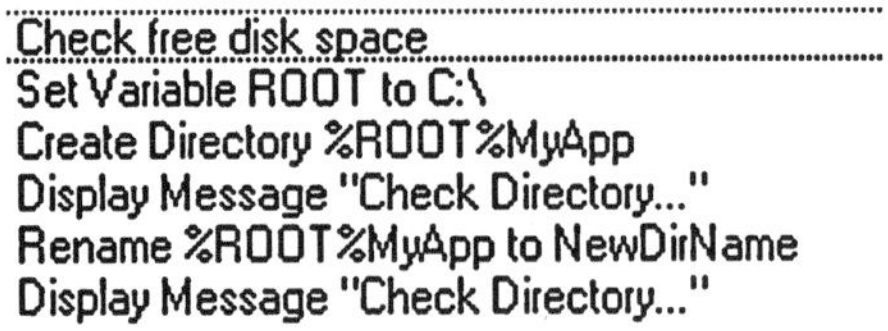

```
Check free disk space
Set Variable ROOT to C:\
Create Directory %ROOT%MyApp
Display Message "Check Directory..."
Rename %ROOT%MyApp to NewDirName
Display Message "Check Directory..."
```

Figure 5-150 *Rename File/Directory script action window.*

Rename File/Directory Example

The following example creates a MyApp directory in the root of the C: drive. It then renames the directory as NewDirName.

Other Script Actions Used:

1. Check Disk Space

2. Set Variable

3. Create Directory

4. Display Message

SMS Installer Window:
See Figure 5-150.

Script:

```
————Begin Script
item: Check Disk Space
end
item: Set Variable
  Variable=ROOT
  Value=C:\
end
item: Create Directory
  Pathname=%ROOT%MyApp
end
item: Display Message
  Title English=Check Directory...
  Text English=Before continuing, check the current name of
the MyApp directory located in the root of the C: drive.
  Flags=00100100
end
item: Rename File/Directory
  Old Pathname=%ROOT%MyApp
  New Filename=NewDirName
end
item: Display Message
  Title English=Check Directory...
```

```
Text English=The MyApp directory name has been changed.
Verify the directory name has changed to NewDirName
  Flags=00100100
end
────-End Script
```

Search for File

The Search for File dialog box, shown in Figure 5-151, allows you to search for a specific file in the local or network file system and places the location in a variable. The variable can be used with the remainder of the script. This script action is useful for locating directories for software upgrades or verifying the existence of the application. If used to search network drives, it can verify the user has the proper directory rights on the network.

Search for File Options

File Name   The File Name field contains the filename with file extension for which the script action will search. This field accepts text strings, predefined variables, or both, up to 255 characters.

Variable Name   The Variable Name entered in this field will receive the path information from the search function. This field

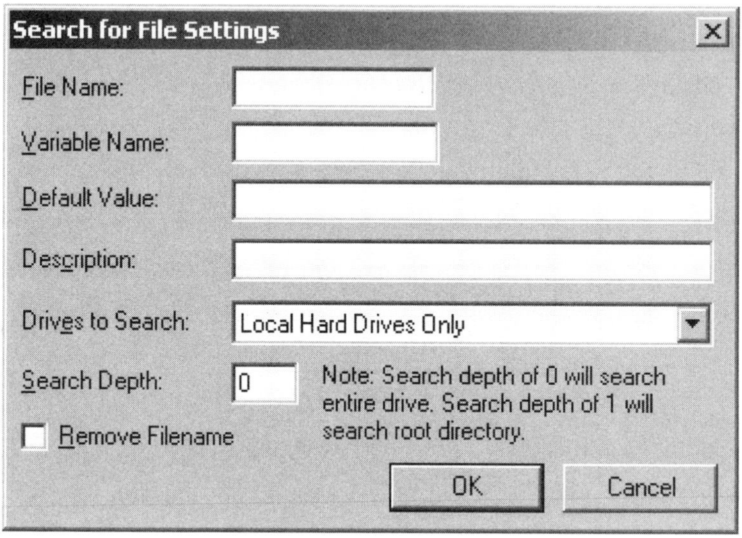

Figure 5-151 *Search for File dialog box.*

can accept a predefined variable, but entering a new name will create a variable.

Default Value   This optional field holds the default value that is entered into the variable if the specified file cannot be found during the search. This field accepts text strings, predefined variables, or both, up to 255 characters.

Description   The Description field contains the text that is displayed on the progress bar dialog box as the script searches for the specified file. This helps the user understand what the search function is doing. Some searches can take an extended amount of time, depending on the size of the drives being searched and the number of files. Using a description message reassures the user that the process has not stalled. This field accepts text strings, predefined variables, or both. Though this field will accept up to 255 characters, any character number beyond 65 will not be displayed.

Drives to Search   This drop-down box allows you to select what type of search will be performed. It offers the following options.

- *Local Hard Drives Only*   All local hard drive letters are identified and searched.

- *Network Drives Only*   The first network drive letter is identified, and drives from that reference on are searched.

- *Both Local and Network Drives*   All drive letters (except CD-ROM and floppy drives) are searched for the specified file.

Search Depth   The Search Depth value tells the script how thorough the search function should be. This is a numeric field, where:

0=Entire drive(s) specified in the Drives to Search drop-down list. 1=Only the root directory of the drive(s) specified in the Drives to Search drop-down list.

Remove Filename   Selecting this checkbox causes SMS Installer to strip the filename from the directory path information. It causes just the directory information to be placed into the variable.

Search for File Example

The following example searches for the Windows NT Command Interpreter (CMD.EXE) on all local computer drives. The script prompts with the location information if the file is found. If it is not found, an error message is displayed and the script exits.

Other Script Actions Used:

1. Check Disk Space

2. If/While Statement

3. Display Message

4. Exit Installation

5. Else Statement

6. End Block

SMS Installer Window:
See Figure 5-152.

Script:

```
————-Begin Script
item: Check Disk Space
end
item: Search for File
  Variable=CMDLOC
  Pathname List=CMD.EXE
  Default=NOTFOUND
  Description English=Searching for the Windows NT Command
Interpreter
  Flags=00000001
end
item: If/While Statement
  Variable=CMDLOC
  Value=NOTFOUND
end
```

```
Check free disk space
Search for file CMD.EXE place in Variable CMDLOC
If CMDLOC Equals "NOTFOUND" then
    Display Message "Command Intrepeter..."
    Exit Installation
Else
    Display Message "Command Intrepeter..."
End Block
```

Figure 5-152 *Search for File script action window.*

```
item: Display Message
  Title English=Command Interpreter...
  Text English=The Windows NT Command Interpreter was not
found on this computer. The installation will now exit.
  Flags=00010000
end
item: Exit Installation
end
item: Else Statement
end
item: Display Message
  Title English=Command Interpreter...
  Text English=The Windows NT Command Interpreter was found
in the %CMDLOC% directory.
  Flags=00000100
end
item: End Block
end
————-End Script
```

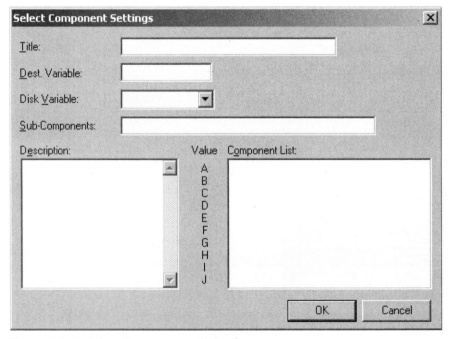

Figure 5-153 *Select Components dialog box.*

Select Components

The Select Components dialog box, shown in Figure 5-153, allows you to prompt the user with a list of installation components. Software components are defined through the Components tab in the Application Files group of the Installation Expert. The components are a combined set of files available for installation that the user can choose to install.

Select Components Options

Title The Title is a required field. The entry will be displayed as the title of the dialog box that is presented to the user. This field can accept strings of text, variables, or both up, to 255 characters. If the entered information is longer than the width of the dialog box, the text will be displayed in ellipses, so try to keep the title under 60 characters.

Dest. Variable The variable name entered here receives the value of the user's checkbox selection. The variable must have been defined earlier in the script. This is a required field.

When the user selects the checkboxes, the variable(s) will be updated with a new value. You can use the Set Variable script action to set which checkbox is the default selection on the dialog box and also to disable checkboxes. The default selection is the one that will automatically perform its function when the user hits the Enter key. The checkbox uses upper and lowercase letters to determine these functions.

For example, create three checkboxes by inputting three items in the Component List. Each checkbox will automatically be assigned the letters A, B, and C based on the Value column. The examples in Table 5-12 describe how the checkboxes will display with the variable value previously set.

The Component checkbox set only reads this value to know how you want the checkboxes to display. Once the user selects his or her choice of options, the variable value is replaced with the user's selection.

Disk Variable The Disk Variable option references the drive where the components will be installed. This variable must be

Table 5-12 *Variable examples.*

Variable Set To:	Display:
A	All checkboxes are enabled, and the first checkbox is the default.
B	All checkboxes are enabled, and the second checkbox is the default.
C	All checkboxes are enabled, and the third checkbox is the default.
Ac	The first two checkboxes are enabled, the first checkbox is the default, and the third checkbox is disabled.
aB	The first checkbox is disabled, the last two checkboxes are enabled, and the second checkbox is the default.
abC	The first checkboxes are disabled, the last checkbox is enabled, and it is the default selection.

predefined in the script. It causes SMS Installer to automatically calculate the component space requirements and displays the total hard disk space available after the installation is complete.

Subcomponents   This field accepts any subcomponent's variable names defined in the script. The subcomponents must be defined previously and separated by commas.

Description   The Description is the information you want the user to read. Use this field to specify the data for which you are prompting the user. This field accepts strings of text, variables, or both, up to six lines of text. You can use the Ctrl-Enter key combination to enter blank lines or to separate paragraphs.

Value   The Value column indicates the alphanumeric character that will be assigned to the Dest. Variable based on the user's selection. The letter associated with the variable is the value that is inserted. Use an If/While statement to insert a logic block based on the letter value.

Component List The Component List allows up to 10 different entries. The names entered into each line will be displayed next to their own checkbox on the dialog box. When the checkbox next to the component is selected, the Dest. Variable receives the corresponding letter from the Value List. Each option is limited to 45 characters.

Select Components Example

The following example displays a component selection box that displays four components.

Other Script Actions Used:

Check Disk Space

SMS Installer Window:

See Figure 5-154.

Script:

```
───────-Begin Script
item: Check Disk Space
end
item: Set Variable
  Variable=CDRIVE
  Value=C:
end
item: Select Components
  Dest. Variable=COMPONENT
  Disk Variable=CDRIVE
  Title English=Select Components...
  Description English=Select the components for installa-
tion...
  Components English=COMPONENT1
  Components English=COMPONENT2
  Components English=COMPONENT3
  Components English=COMPONENT4
  Components English=
end
───────-End Script
```

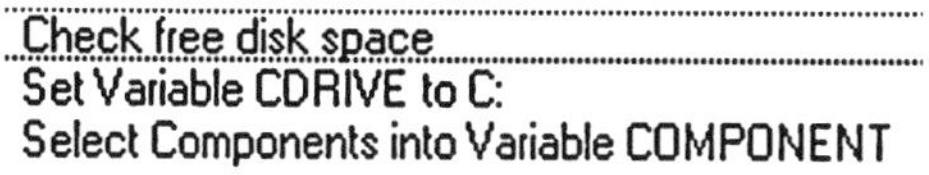

```
Check free disk space
Set Variable CDRIVE to C:
Select Components into Variable COMPONENT
```

Figure 5-154 *Select Components script action window.*

Self-Register OCXs/DLLs

OCX and DLL files must be registered with the operating system before they are recognized for use. Any OCX or DLL files that are installed during the installation are queued to register automatically at the end of the script. See Figure 5-155.

Self-Register OCXs/DLLs Settings Options

Description/Pathname   This field serves two purposes and depends on the action selection:

> *Description*   If the Register All Pending OCXs/DLLs action is selected, this field should contain information to be displayed to the user on a dialog box. The message displays until all files have been registered with the system. This field accepts text strings, predefined variables, or both. Though the field accepts up to 255 characters, only 65 will be displayed.

> *Pathname*   If the Queue Existing File for Registration action is selected, this field must contain a full path and filename (with extension) to the file that is to be registered. The file must be installed on the computer before using this option in the script action. This field accepts text strings, predefined variables, or both, up to 255 characters.

Action Selections   There are two Action Selections for this script action. The selection changes the function of the Description/Pathname field.

- *Register All Pending OCXs/DLLs*   This option immediately starts registering all OCX and DLL files included with the

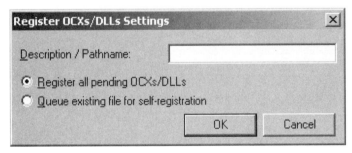

Figure 5-155 *Self-Register OCXs/DLLs dialog box.*

installation. The message from the Description/Pathname field is displayed in a dialog box to the user during the process.

- *Queue Existing File for Self-Registration* This selection queues the file specified in the Description/Pathname field for registration. The file must be installed on the computer before using this option in the script action. This option is similar to the Self-Register OCX/DLL/EXE option on the Install File(s) script action dialog box.

Self-Register OCXs/DLLs Example

The following example shows the standard way of using the Self-Register OCXs/DLLs script action.

Other Script Actions Used:

Check Disk Space

SMS Installer Window:

See Figure 5-156.

Script:

```
————Begin Script
item: Check Disk Space
end
item: Self-Register OCXs/DLLs
  Description English=Updating System Configuration, Please
Wait...
end
————End Script
```

Set File Attributes

The Set File Attributes dialog box, shown in Figure 5-157, allows you to set the file attributes for one or many files. The script action operates like the DOS Attrib command, but it allows you to supply this function within the SMS Installer script. This script action is helpful for setting specific file attributes to stop the user from deleting them or even locating them in the file system.

Check free disk space
Self-Register OCXs/DLLs/EXEs

Figure 5-156 *Self-Register OCXs/DLLs script action window.*

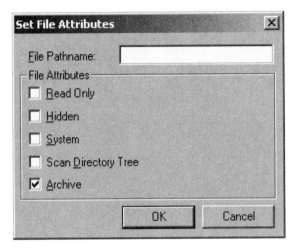

Figure 5-157 *Set File Attributes dialog box.*

Set File Attributes Options

File Pathname   This field contains the full path and filename with extension whose file attribute will be changed. Wildcard characters (*.*) can be used in this field to change multiple files in the directory at once. This field accepts text strings, predefined variables, or both, up to 255 characters.

File Attributes   The File Attributes section allows you to select the file attribute options for the specified file(s). You can select multiple options at once. The options are as follows:

- *Read Only*   This marks the file(s) as Read Only (R). This means the file cannot be overwritten or information cannot be written to it.

- *Hidden*   This marks the file(s) as Hidden (H). This option hides the file from view within the operating system.

- *System*   This marks the file(s) as System (S). This option tells the operating system that the file is part of the system.

- *Scan Directory Tree*   If this option is selected, the same criteria listed by wildcard characters in the File Pathname field are applied to all subdirectories underneath the specified location.

```
Check free disk space
Get Environment Variable COMSPEC into Variable CMDINTR
Set File Attributes
Display Message "Check File Attribute..."
Set File Attributes
Display Message "Check File Attribute..."
```

Figure 5-158 *Set File Attributes script action window.*

- *Archive* Selecting this option marks the file as Archive (A).
  The Archive attribute marks the archive bit of the file and is
  used by incremental backups.

Set File Attributes Example

The following example retrieves the COMSPEC (command
interpreter location) variable from the operating system to insert
the location into a value. The file's attribute is set to Read Only
and a message displays to verify the attribute change. Then, the
script removes the Read Only attribute.

You can check the file attribute by right-clicking on it through
Windows Explorer and choosing properties. Another method is
to use the ATTRIB <filename> MS-DOS command line.

Other Script Actions Used:

1. Check Disk Space

2. Get Environment Variable

3. Display Message

SMS Installer Window:
See Figure 5-158.

Script:

```
———-Begin Script
item: Check Disk Space
end
item: Get Environment Variable
  Variable=CMDINTR
  Environment=COMSPEC
  Default=NOTFOUND
end
item: Set File Attributes
  Pathname=%CMDINTR%
```

```
  Flags=00000001
end
item: Display Message
  Title English=Check File Attribute...
  Text English=Before continuing, check the %CMDINTR% file
attributes. It is now set to Read Only.
  Flags=00100100
end
item: Set File Attributes
  Pathname=%CMDINTR%
end
item: Display Message
  Title English=Check File Attribute...
  Text English=Before continuing, check the %CMDINTR% file
attributes. The Read Only attribute has been removed.
  Flags=00100100
end
————-End Script
```

Set Variable

SMS Installer is all about variables. A majority of the options
in all script actions require information to start with predefined
variables. Variables allow you to place large amounts of information into a neatly packed name that is read by SMS Installer. It is
a sensible practice to use variables extensively throughout the
script. Whenever a script calls for information, use a variable
with the script action instead of entering a string of text. (See Figure 5-159.) This allows the information to be available to all

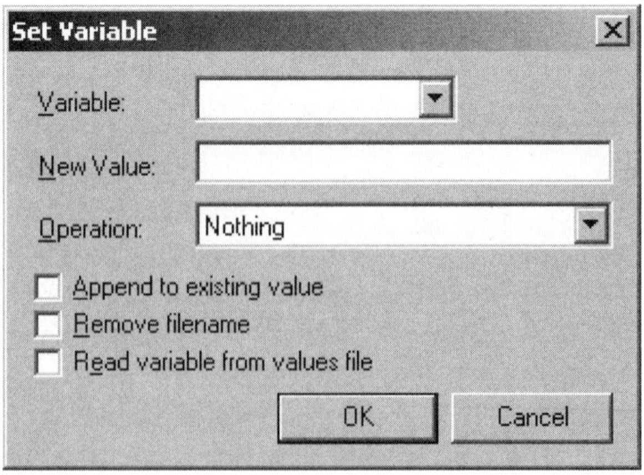

Figure 5-159 *Set Variable dialog box.*

script sections instead of just the one instance. Variables can be used to branch script logic based on the equality or inequality of its compared value.

For the most part, variable values are used as a data constant. The value never changes and it is used to provide items such as pathnames, filenames, registry values, environment values, and so on. In some instances, the value within the variable must be changed to accommodate other script actions, such as when creating complex expressions or calculations.

Variable Rules—SMS Installer variables should adhere to the following rules: **Tip**

1. Variables should always begin with a letter.
2. Variables should only include letters, numbers, and underscore characters.
3. Variables should be no longer than 14 characters.

Set Variable Options

Variable This field is used to either select a predefined variable from the drop-down list, or to create a brand-new variable name. If you select a predefined variable, this script action is used to change the current value of the variable. The variable name should not exceed 14 characters.

New Value The New Value field contains the value that will be inserted into the variable. This field accepts text strings, variables, or both, up to 255 characters.

Operation The Operation drop-down box allows you to specify what type of action will be performed on the variable. There are nine options:

- *Nothing* This option accepts the value as entered and places it into the variable name.

- *Increment* This option adds 1 to the total if the value contains numeric data. The Append to Existing Value must be selected for this option to work.

- *Decrement*   This option subtracts 1 from the total if the value contains numeric data. Append to Existing Value must be selected for this option to work.

- *Remove Trailing Backslashes*   If the value contains path or registry information, this option removes the last backslash.

- *Convert to Long Filename*   A file may sometimes be installed using the short 8.3 format. The tilde (~) character is used to represent the rest of the filename. If the value contains path and/or file information, this option converts the short filename data to the long filename format. The file must already exist on the target computer for this option to be successful. This option is only supported on Windows 9x and Windows NT computers.

- *Convert to Short Filename*   This option converts a long file-name format file to its short filename alias. The file must already exist on the target computer for this option to be successful. This option is only supported on Windows 9x and Windows NT computers.

Note   Some applications do not support long filenames. Converting the long filenames to the short filename format allows the applications to run properly. Even though the file is converted to its short alias, Windows Explorer will still read the file properly. Windows 9x and Windows NT read the tilde (~) character after the filename and then read the rest of the filename to display it correctly.

- *Convert to Uppercase*   This option converts the entire variable value to uppercase letters.

- *Convert to Lowercase*   This option converts the entire variable value to lowercase letters.

- *Evaluate Expression*   The Evaluate Expression must be selected when using complex operators or complex expressions. The example in this section shows a simple calculation that uses the Evaluate Expression. For a list of the complex operators and complex expressions, see Chapter 10.

```
Check free disk space
Set Variable ROOT to C:\
Set Variable NUM1 to 500
Set Variable NUM2 to 450
Set Variable SUM to NUM1 + NUM2
Insert line "The Sum of 500 + 450 is:  %SUM%" into text file %ROOT%ADD.TXT.
```

Figure 5-160 *Set Variable script action window.*

Append to Existing Value   The selection appends the existing variable value to the new one specified in the value field. This checkbox *must* be checked if using Increment and Decrement options. If text is contained in the Value field, the text is appended to the current text value.

Remove Filename   If path and file information are contained in the value, the filename is stripped from the value.

Read Variable from Values File   If running the script from a command line, this option allows you to read variable values from a file in the file system. This only runs in manual mode (for more information, see "Command Line QuickList" in Chapter 10).

Set Variable Example

The following example uses the Evaluate Expression option of the Set Variable script action to perform a simple calculation and output the result to a text file.

Other Script Actions Used:

1. Check Disk Space

2. Insert Line into Text File

SMS Installer Window:
See Figure 5-160.

Script:

```
————-Begin Script
item: Check Disk Space
end
item: Set Variable
  Variable=ROOT
  Value=C:\
end
```

```
item: Set Variable
  Variable=NUM1
  Value=500
  Flags=00100000
end
item: Set Variable
  Variable=NUM2
  Value=450
  Flags=00100000
end
item: Set Variable
  Variable=SUM
  Value=NUM1 + NUM2
  Flags=00100000
end
item: Insert Line into Text File
  Pathname=%ROOT%ADD.TXT
  New Text=The Sum of 500 + 450 is: %SUM%
  Line Number=0
end
————-End Script
```

Sleep

The Sleep script item, the dialog box for which shown in Figure 5-161, is used for halting the SMS Installer script for a specified period of time. This allows other items in the script to finish processing before the script continues. This is a good feature to use if calling other executables outside the script and waiting for them to finish. The Sleep function must be tested thoroughly for timing with the rest of the script and the other executables.

Sleep Options

Sleep for Milliseconds   Sleep is measured in milliseconds. For instance, 2000 milliseconds equal 2 seconds, 10,000 milliseconds

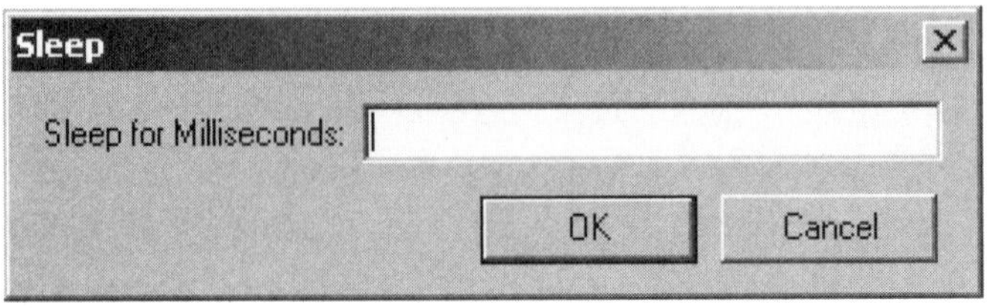

Figure 5-161 *Sleep dialog box.*

equal 10 seconds, 30,000 milliseconds equal 30 seconds, 60,000 milliseconds equal 1 minute, and so on. Do not use a comma to input the value.

Sleep Example

The following sample script (utilizing the Sleep function) is beneficial for backup of critical system files before installing an application. It backs up the DLLs from the \WINNT\SYSTEM32 directory to a specified Backup directory in E:\BACKUP. The Sleep function waits for 1 full minute before continuing.

Other Script Actions Used:

1. Check Disk Space

2. Set Variable

3. Execute Program

SMS Installer Window:
See Figure 5-162.

Script:

```
————-Begin Script
item: Check Disk Space
end
item: Set Variable
  Variable=DLLBACKUP
  Value=E:\BACKUP
end
item: Execute Program
  Pathname=%SYS32%\XCOPY.EXE
  Command Line=%SYS32%\*.DLL %DLLBACKUP% /S/E/C
  Flags=00000110
end
item: Sleep
  Sleep=60000
end
————-End Script
```

```
Check free disk space
Set Variable DLLBACKUP to E:\BACKUP
Execute %SYS32%\XCOPY.EXE %SYS32%\*.DLL %DLLBACKUP% /S/E/C (Wait)
Sleep for 60000 Milliseconds
```

Figure 5-162 *Sleep script action window.*

Start/Stop Service

The Start/Stop Service dialog box, shown in Figure 5-163, is used for stopping or starting a Windows NT service on the PC during the script. Of course, the user running the script must have rights to Start/Stop services. To elevate the user privileges, you can use the SU.EXE utility in conjunction with the SMS Installer script to start or stop a service without giving the local user additional rights (see "Building the SMS Installer Toolkit" in Chapter 10 for more information).

Note   There are no errors associated with the function if the service does not start or stop because of a rights issue.

Start/Stop Service Settings Options

Service Name   This field contains the display name of the service. The field accepts text strings, predefined variables, or both, up to 255 characters.

Start Service   Selecting this option starts the service specified in the Service Name field.

Stop Service   Selection of this option stops the service specified in the Service Name field.

Start/Stop Service Example

The following example stops the Norton AntiVirus service on the Windows NT computer.

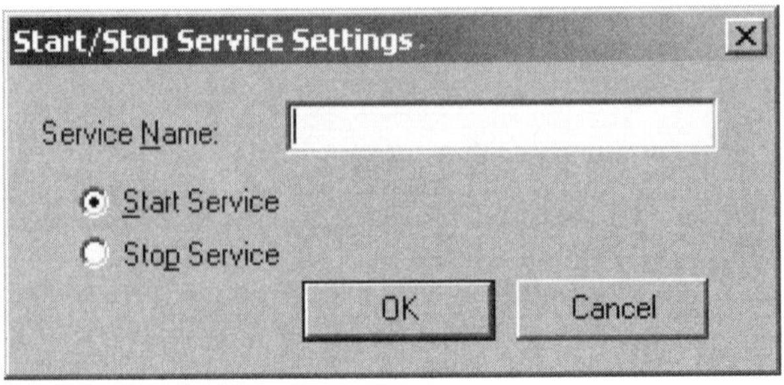

Figure 5-163 *Start/Stop Service dialog box.*

Other Script Actions Used:

Check Disk Space

SMS Installer Window:
See Figure 5-164.

Script:

```
───────-Begin Script
item: Check Disk Space
end
item: Start/Stop Service
  Service Name=NAV Alert
  Flags=00000001
end
───────-End Script
```

To find out the display name of a service, look in the Services-Control Panel applet, or check in the registry at HKEY_LOCAL_MACHINE\CurrentControlSet\Services. Directly under Services is the list of service display names.

Also, the following short script will pull the services information from the registry on a local or remote machine and create a text file to hold the information. It utilizes the REG.EXE utility described in "Building the SMS Installer Toolkit" in Chapter 10.

```
───────-Begin Script
item: Check Disk Space
end
item: Set Variable
  Variable=RESKITLOC
  Value=E:\NTRESKIT\
end
item: Execute Program
  Pathname=%RESKITLOC%SERVICES.CMD
  Flags=00000110
end
item: Sleep
  Sleep=10000
End
───────-End Script
```

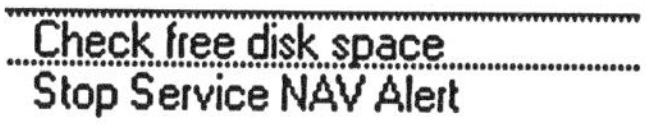

```
Check free disk space
Stop Service NAV Alert
```

Figure 5-164 *Start/Stop Service script action window.*

The script runs a SERVICES.CMD. CMD files are command files that run like batch files for Windows NT. The contents of the SERVICES.CMD file are as follows:

**E:\NTRESKIT\REG.EXE QUERY HKLM\System\
CurrentControlSet\Services >c:\service.txt**

The reason for creating a CMD file for this script is the "greater-than" sign or pipe command at the end of the REG.EXE command line. This pipe command sends the information gathered from the REG Query into a text file for viewing later. When running a pipe command from within the Windows environment or with the SMS Installer Execute script item, the pipe is not recognized as a valid command line option. The pipe command is only recognized if run from an MS-DOS prompt. Creating the CMD file allows the REG output to be sent to the text file.

As shown in the REG.EXE reference section in Chapter 10, REG.EXE can be used to query remote computers as well. This is particularly helpful if the service you want to start/stop does not exist on your computer.

Win32 System Directory

The Win32 System Directory, shown in Figure 5-165, obtains the target computer's System directory and places the path in a variable. For instance, if the computer runs Windows 3.x or Windows 9x, the normal return value is C:\WINDOWS\SYSTEM. If it is a Windows NT machine, the normal value is C:\WINNT\SYSTEM. Some computers may have had the operating system loaded into a different directory than the standard. This script item compensates for that possibility.

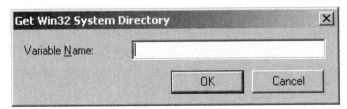

Figure 5-165 *Win32 System Directory dialog box.*

Win32 System Directory Options

Variable Name   The Variable Name field contains the variable that will receive the Win32 System Directory value.

Win32 System Directory Example

The following example retrieves the Win32 System directory and places it into the SYSTEMDIR variable.

Other Script Actions Used:

Check Disk Space

SMS Installer Window:
See Figure 5-166.

Script:

```
─────-Begin Script
item: Check Disk Space
end
item: Win32 System Directory
  Variable=SYSTEMDIR
end
─────-End Script
```

Wizard Block

The Wizard Block dialog box, shown in Figure 5-167, allows you to create customized dialog box set properties that are applied to all dialog boxes in the set. This is a quick way to format the size and look of one dialog box and have the rest of the set automatically configured in the same uniform manner.

For complete information on the creation of custom dialog boxes, see the Custom Dialog script action reference earlier in this chapter.

Wizard Block Settings Options

Dialog Boxes   The Dialog Boxes window automatically displays all the custom dialogs created that exist between the Wizard Block and the End Block script actions.

```
Check free disk space
Read Win32 System Directory into SYSTEMDIR
```

Figure 5-166 *Win32 System Directory script action window.*

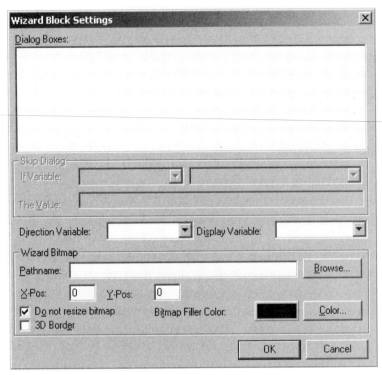

Figure 5-167 *Wizard Block dialog box.*

Skip Dialog Section   The Skip Dialog section allows you to skip the highlighted dialog box in the Dialog Boxes window by applying certain conditions:

- *If Variable*   The If Variable drop-down box allows you to select a predefined variable whose value will be compared to the information in the Value field based on the Conditions selection.

- *Conditions*   The Conditions drop-down list allows you to specify what condition will be used between the If Variable and the Value fields. This list includes the following 14 options:

  1. *Equals*   This condition compares the Value data against the variable. This is a case-sensitive comparison that returns a TRUE value if the data and variable match. The compared data can be numeric or alphanumeric.
  2. *Not Equal*   This condition performs a case-sensitive

comparison between the variable and the Value data and returns a TRUE value if the data is not equal. The compared data can be numeric or alphanumeric.

3. *Contains*   This condition compares the Value data against the variable. This is a case-sensitive comparison that checks for the existence of the *entire* string between the data and variable. The compared data can be numeric or alphanumeric.

4. *Does Not Contain*   This condition compares the Value data against the variable. This is a case-sensitive comparison that ensures the *entire* string between the data and variable *does not* exist. The compared data can be numeric or alphanumeric.

5. *Equals (Ignore Case)*   This condition compares the Value data against the variable. This is a comparison that returns a TRUE value if the data and variable match. The condition is not case-sensitive. The compared data can be numeric or alphanumeric.

6. *Not Equal (Ignore Case)*   This condition performs a comparison between the Variable and the Value data that is not case-sensitive and returns a TRUE value if the data is not equal. The compared data can be numeric or alphanumeric.

7. *Greater Than*   This condition performs a comparison between the variable and the Value data to determine if the variable is greater than the value. It returns a value of 1 (TRUE) if the condition is met and a value of 0 (FALSE) if it is not.

8. *Greater Than or Equal*   This condition performs a comparison between the variable and the value to determine if the variable is equal or greater than the value. It returns a value of 1 (TRUE) if the condition is met and a value of 0 (FALSE) if it is not.

9. *Less Than*   This condition performs a comparison between the variable and the value to determine if the variable is less than the value. It returns a value of 1 (TRUE) if the condition is met and a value of 0 (FALSE) if it is not.

10. *Less Than or Equal* This condition performs a comparison between the variable and the value to determine if the variable is less than or equal to the value. It returns a value of 1 (TRUE) if the condition is met and a value of 0 (FALSE) if it is not.

11. *Contains Any Letters In* This condition compares the Value data against the variable. This is a case-sensitive comparison in which checks *any* similar alphanumeric characters between the data and variable. The compared data can be numeric or alphanumeric. It returns a value of 1 (TRUE) if the condition is met and a value of 0 (FALSE) if it is not.

12. *Contains Letters Not In* This condition compares the Value data against the variable. This is a case-sensitive comparison in which it ensures that *any* similar alphanumeric characters *do not* exist between the data and variable. The compared data can be numeric or alphanumeric.

13. *Length Equal To* This condition compares the length of the variable string to a numeric value entered into the Value field. It returns a value of 1 (TRUE) if the condition is met and a value of 0 (FALSE) if it is not.

14. *Expression True* This condition allows you to check complex expressions for a TRUE value. For example, you can use the Set Variable script action to perform calculations and then use the Expression True option to verify the calculation. (For an example of a complex expression, see the Set Variable script action example earlier in the chapter. For a list of the valid complex expressions, see Chapter 10: "Complex Expression QuickList").

- *The Value* The Value field contains the value to which the variable data will be compared. This is a mandatory field to complete the Boolean expression. If this field is empty, the logic block will compare the NULL value to the variable contents (see the example in this section). This field accepts text strings, variables, or both, up to 255 characters.

Direction Variable   The Direction Variable name can be entered in this field. When a direction variable is used, SMS Installer automatically places values to be used with the Back and Next buttons on the dialog boxes. The automatic values are N for Next and B for Previous. Each dialog box should receive the same direction variable name set here. The example in this section includes establishing this variable on the Push Button controls. This field accepts predefined variables selected from the drop-down list or new variables.

Display Variable   The Display Variable is used by the dialog box set to create logic based on the display name of the box. Each dialog box in the set must have this variable applied to it. The Dialog Set Properties (described in detail in the Custom Dialog script action reference earlier in this chapter) predetermines the display name of the dialog box. When the dialog box is presented, the dialog box's display name is placed into the Display Variable field. The new value (dialog box display name) can be used for logic in the dialog box set. When the next dialog box in the set is displayed, the Display Variable is updated with the new value. This field accepts predefined variables selected from the drop-down list or new variables.

Wizard Bitmap Section   The Wizard Block allows you to add a custom bitmap to all dialog boxes in the set. The following fields are presented:

- *Pathname*   This field contains the path and filename with extension of the bitmap file that will be displayed on each dialog box. This field accepts text strings, predefined variables, or both. The Browse button allows you to select a file from the local file system.

- *X-Pos*   The X-Pos is the horizontal location on the dialog box for bitmap file. Measured in pixels, this coordinate starts from the upper left corner of a 640 × 480 screen.

- *Y-Pos*   The Y-Pos is the vertical location on the dialog box for the bitmap file. Also measured in pixels, this coordinate starts from the upper left corner of a 640 × 480 screen.

```
Check free disk space
Wizard Block
    Custom Dialog "DialogBox1"
    Custom Dialog "DialogBox2"
    Custom Dialog "DialogBox3"
End Block
```

Figure 5-168 *Wizard Block script action window.*

- *Do Not Resize Bitmap*   When the bitmap is shown on computers with different resolutions, SMS Installer will try to compensate for the display change. Selecting this option causes the bitmap to retain its original size on all configurations.

- *Bitmap Filler Color*   The Bitmap Filler Color option creates a color border around the graphic. The color can be set by clicking the Color button. The standard SMS Installer color dialog box is used to pick the color.

- *3D Border*   Selection of this option causes the bitmap image to be displayed as inlaid on the dialog box set.

Wizard Block Example

This example displays three custom dialogs in a Wizard Block.

Other Script Actions Used:

1. Check Disk Space

2. Custom Dialog

3. End Block

SMS Installer Window:
See Figure 5-168.

Script:

```
————-Begin Script
item: Check Disk Space
end
item: Wizard Block
  Direction Variable=DIRECTION
  Display Variable=DISPLAY
  Bitmap Pathname=E:\Folders\McGraw Hill\Scripts\Chapter
Five\SMSTrentbn.bmp
  X Position=0
```

```
   Y Position=0
   Filler Color=0
   Flags=00000010
end
item: Custom Dialog Set
  Name=DialogBox1
  Display Variable=DISPLAY
  item: Dialog
  Title English=Dialog1
  Width=277
  Height=150
  Font Name=Helv
  Font Size=8
  item: Push Button
    Rectangle=230 110 265 125
    Variable=DIRECTION
    Value=N
    Create Flags=01010000000000010000000000000000
    Text English=&Next_1
   end
  end
end
item: Custom Dialog Set
  Name=DialogBox2
  Display Variable=DISPLAY
  item: Dialog
    Title English=Dialog2
    Width=277
    Height=150
    Font Name=Helv
    Font Size=8
    item: Push Button
      Rectangle=229 110 264 125
      Variable=DIRECTION
      Value=N
      Action=1
      Create Flags=01010000000000010000000000000000
      Text English=&Next_2
    end
  end
end
item: Custom Dialog Set
  Name=DialogBox3
  Display Variable=DISPLAY
  item: Dialog
    Title English=Dialog3
    Width=277
    Height=150
```

```
Font Name=Helv
Font Size=8
item: Push Button
  Rectangle=230 109 265 124
  Variable=DIRECTION
  Value=N
  Create Flags=01010000000000010000000000000000
  Text English=&Next_3
end
  end
end
item: End Block
end
────-End Script
```

Other Menu Selections

There are a few other items of note that are not included on the
Script Editor toolbar but are available on the File menu.

Note These menu selections are also available in the Installation Expert
under the Edit menu.

Source Directories (Ctrl-D)

After the script is compiled and the installation files have been
compressed into the executable, you may need to move the source
files for one reason or another. With the script (.IPF) open, you
can change where the script references the source files by using
the Change Source Directories dialog box, shown in Figure 5-
169. It is accessed either by typing Ctrl-D or by selecting
Edit|Source Directories on the File menu. The list box on the
Change Source Directories dialog box shows all the unique directories in the installation script.

Change Source Directories Options

New Pathname With this option you highlight each unique
directory in the list box, and then enter the new path where the
source files have been relocated.

Change Subdirectories If this selection is chosen, the subdirectories underneath the new pathname are automatically incorporated
into the script properties.

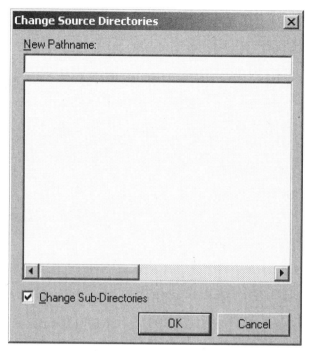

Figure 5-169 *Change Source Directories dialog box.*

Dialog Templates (Ctrl-B)

The Dialog Templates box, shown in Figure 5-170, allows you select the built-in SMS Installer dialog templates for editing. You can modify the current templates and save them with your own filename for use in future scripts. When the dialog template is selected, it is opened in the Custom Dialog Editor. For detailed information on the Custom Dialog Editor, see the Custom Dialog script action reference earlier in this chapter. The Dialog Templates list is accessed by typing Ctrl-B, or by selecting Edit|Dialog Templates on the File menu.

Installer Messages (Ctrl-E)

With the Installer Message dialog box, shown in Figure 5-171, you can customize the default SMS Installer messages. SMS Installer generates a standard message set for different procedures in the script. Typing Ctrl-E or selecting Edit|Installer Messages on the File menu can access the Installer Message dialog box. For a

Figure 5-170 *Dialog Templates dialog box.*

Figure 5-171 *Installer Messages dialog box.*

list of the default Installer Messages, see "Default SMS Installer Messages" in Chapter 10.

Installer Messages Options

Language Name   This drop-down box allows you to change the language of the Installer Messages. Clicking on a different language will change all the message text.

> SMS Installer supports up to 15 simultaneous languages per script.   **Note**

Translated Name   This field is automatically updated with the translated language name when the Language Name changes. You can also update this field.

Messages   The Messages box lists the default message subjects available to SMS Installer.

Message Text   The Message Text box allows you to change the display text of the subject highlighted in the Messages box.

Select Language Dialog Section   The Select Language Dialog section allows you to globally modify the way the Select Language dialog box displays. The following options are presented:

- *Dialog Title*   The Dialog Title field allows you to change the default title on the Select Language dialog box.

- *Dialog Text*   The Dialog Text field changes the default communication the user sees when prompted to select the preferred language.

Send Mail

Selecting File|Send Mail accesses the Send Mail option. The Send Mail option opens a new e-mail message and attaches the current script for distribution via a MAPI e-mail system.

Rollback Support

Rollback Support in SMS Installer allows the user to return the application to its previous state before the software installation.

There are two items that must be enabled before Rollback is available:

1. *Uninstall Support*   Uninstall support is enabled through the Installation Expert by clicking on Runtime Support, Runtime Options, and Uninstall Support.

2. *Backup Replaced Files Option*   Backup Replaced Files is enabled through the Installation Expert by clicking on Installation Interface, Wizard Dialogs, and Backup Replaced Files.

Enabling these options changes the backup information in the SMS Installer script:

```
————-Begin Script
item: Set Variable
  Variable=BACKUP
  Value=%MAINDIR%\BACKUP
  Flags=10000000
end
item: Set Variable
  Variable=DOBACKUP
  Value=A
end
————-End Script
```

As shown, the BACKUP variable receives the value %MAINDIR%\BACKUP and the DOBACKUP variable is changed to A (the value is B if the options are not enabled).

Then, later in the script, the DOBACKUP If/While block is started:

```
————-Begin Script
item: If/While Statement
  Variable=DOBACKUP
  Value=A
end
item: Set Variable
  Variable=BACKUPDIR
  Value=%BACKUP%
end
item: End Block
end
————-End Script
```

The BACKUPDIR variable receives the contents of the %BACKUP% variable.

When the Install File(s) script action section is started, any files that are overwritten or modified during the file install process are copied to the Backup directory. When the rollback is initiated, the files from this directory are used to restore the application to its previous state.

In addition to the Backup procedure being added to the script, the ROLLBACK.IPF script is included with the compiled executable. In the Script Editor, if you click the drop-down list for the Event and choose the Cancel Event, you will see the ROLLBACK.IPF inserted with an Include Script script action.

With the Rollback feature enabled, whenever a user chooses to uninstall an SMS Installer–generated application, a dialog box will prompt to either uninstall the application completely or to perform a rollback procedure.

Each time the same application is installed with Rollback support enabled, the overwritten and modified files are placed into the Backup directory. As the same files are copied to the Backup directory over and over, it receives an incremental file extension (i.e., .001, 002, 003, etc.). Because of this feature, rollback can be performed multiple times to restore an application to any previous state in the series not just the last installation. If a user selects to roll back an application but no previous backup exists, the rollback will automatically start the uninstall process and the application will be completely removed from the computer.

Rollbacks can be performed automatically. A rollback procedure uses the same Uninst32.exe file that the uninstall procedure uses, and the same install.log file is used for the rollback information. Using some method of distribution (i.e., SMS, e-mail, etc.), the rollback command line can be initiated on the target computer.

Using the Uninstall command-line options, you can perform an automatic, silent rollback procedure. The command line would be as follows:

```
Uninst32.exe /s /a /r c:\MyApp\install.log
/a = automatic uninstall
/s = silent uninstall
/r = rollback
```

For details on the command-line options for the Uninstall process, see "Command Line QuickList" in Chapter 10.

Advanced Techniques

Creating Utilities with SMS Installer

As seen in Chapter 05, the Script Editor can be a powerful tool
for modifying and customizing software installations. Because of
the rich features and functions of the Script Editor, it can also be
used to develop solutions to problems. You can easily create
small, standalone utilities to accommodate user requests, automate difficult tasks, and fix computer issues.

Although not necessary, it helps if you understand the theory
of developing solutions. Using critical thinking and logical steps
to create a solution will exhibit itself in the final result. The same
logical steps can be used in many facets of any solution.

There are three logical steps to developing a solution:

1. Conceptualize

2. Visualize

3. Utilize

Conceptualize

Conceptualizing relates directly to the actual concept. The concept is the birth of a solution. It could have come in the form of a
request from management, a user, or a coworker. It could have
been flagged as an issue from monitoring a help desk problem
that has escalated into a common problem plaguing the user population. Or it could have been identified by a recurring systemwide problem.

Visualize

Visualizing relates to the understanding of the issue, understanding that it is a problem, and creating a complete picture of
the path that needs to be taken to create the solution. By understanding all these things, you can achieve the goal. Visualizing
involves not only understanding the issue but also understanding
what it will take to fix the issue.

Utilize

Utilizing means to take the concept and the visualization and
create the solution. This is the actual, physical work involved during the creation of the solution.

These are a lot of fancy words just to say, "Someone asked me if it was possible to easily delete the entries from the Recent Files list, and I said, `Yeah, I can probably create a small utility for you.'" But, the idea is to learn to think logically. (We'll see the Recent Files list in the following example.)

The same logical thinking can help in other areas, not just in creating utilities. For instance, writing a book requires logical thinking and an understood path. In this case, the concept is the subject of the book, the visualization shows itself in the outline of the book, and the utilization is taking the subject and the outline and forming the complete book.

This logical thinking will help create full-featured utilities using SMS Installer that are complete and work in all instances. A utility could be created to satisfy one person, but creating an excellent utility requires that the utility work for anyone and for all computers.

SMS Installer's features allow the creation of standalone utilities. The functions of Setup Icon Pathname (seen in Chapter 04) and the ability to create custom dialog boxes (seen in Chapter 05) makes this possible. The next four examples will walk through the creation of four utilities: CleanDoc!, SysConfig, WinNWUser, and CCEXIMP. The examples provide a walkthrough for creating standalone utilities. They also help you to understand the importance of following basic script logic and fully documenting when creating your scripts.

CleanDoc! Utility

Windows 9x and Windows NT keep track of the documents that are accessed on the Start|Documents menu. This is convenient for quickly retrieving recent documents without having to navigate the file system to find them. Though this is a helpful feature, some users may require this menu to be cleaned out periodically. Removing sensitive documents from quick access adds an extra level of security. This is helpful to users who travel frequently and are afraid the computer could be stolen or accessed while they are away from it.

Navigating to Start|Settings|Taskbar and clicking on the Clear button clears the recent Documents folder. But very few users

Figure 6-1 *CleanDoc! Initial dialog box.*

know this technique, and the ones who do rarely take the time to use this feature. The CleanDoc! utility, shown in Figure 6-1, does this for the user and can be placed anywhere on the computer (Desktop, Start menu, etc.) for quick access.

The Recent Documents Start menu item is basically just a folder in a user-profile directory structure on the computer. Under the Windows and WINNT directories the following directory structure exists:

```
\%WIN%\Profiles\%LOGON_NAME%\Recent
```

On my computer, this would relate to:
```
C:\WINNT\Profiles\ rtrent\Recent
```

When a registered document is opened, a shortcut to the document is automatically created in this directory. The operating system displays these shortcuts on the Start|Documents menu. When the CleanDoc! utility runs, it finds the specific user's profile directory and deletes the shortcuts.

For this example, the script is broken down into functional sections:

Section 1   The first section is to set the variables that will be used later that are not set by other means. For example, later in the script, a variable value is set by using the Get System Information script action to place the user's profile name into a variable. The Set Variables section sets the APPTITLE (utility name) and the DISABLED (the value for disabling certain dialog button controls) variables.

Set Variables:

```
item: Set Variable
  Variable=APPTITLE
  Value=CleanDoc
  Flags=10000000
end
item: Set Variable
  Variable=DISABLED
  Value=!
end
```

Section 2   As mentioned, the second function retrieves the Windows Logon Name environment variable and places it into the WINNAME variable.

Get Windows Logon Name for user's profile directory:

```
item: Get System Information
  Variable=WINNAME
  Flags=00010001
end
```

Section 3   The third section takes the contents of the WINNAME variable and builds the directory structure to the user's RECENT folder on the computer. This directory structure is placed into the RECENTDIR variable. The WIN variable in the directory value is a SMS Installer constant variable. See "Predefined Variables" in Chapter 10 for a list of these default variables. Notice the percent signs (%) preceding and following the variable name. Remember the Tip from Chapter 05: When creating a new variable, do not use percent signs around the name; when using the variable, use a preceding and subsequent percent sign.

Place the Recent Documents folder into a variable:

```
item: Set Variable
  Variable=RECENTDIR
  Value=%WIN%\PROFILES\%WINNAME%\RECENT
end
```

Section 4   The fourth section displays a custom-created dialog box. This dialog box prompts the user to begin deleting the recent documents or to cancel the process. A custom graphic control has been added to the dialog box. For detailed information on using the Custom Dialog script action, refer to the Custom Dialog script action section in Chapter 05.

Display initial user dialog box:

```
item: Custom Dialog Set
  Name=CleanDoc!
  item: Dialog
    Title English=CleanDoc!
    Width=150
    Height=150
    Font Name=Helv
    Font Size=8
    item: Static
      Rectangle=5 5 23 25
      Action=2
      Create Flags=01010000000000000000000000001011
      Pathname English=E:\Folders\McGraw Hill\Scripts\
Chapter Six\CleanDOC\docs.bmp
    end
    item: Static
      Rectangle=11 31 141 46
      Create Flags=01010000000000000000000000000000
      Flags=0000000000000001
      Name=Arial
      Font Style=-19 0 0 0 700 0 0 0 0 3 2 1 34
      Text English=Welcome to CleanDoc!
    end
    item: Static
      Rectangle=14 50 126 66
      Create Flags=01010000000000000000000000000000
      Text English=This utility will clean out the
Documents folder on your START Menu.
    end
    item: Static
      Rectangle=6 86 131 102
```

```
        Create Flags=01010000000000000000000000000000
        Text English=Click CleanIT! to continue or Cancel to
stop...
     end
     item: Push Button
        Rectangle=45 114 90 129
        Variable=DIRECTION
        Value=N
        Create Flags=01010000000000010000000000000001
        Text Danish=&Nëste >
        Text Dutch=&Volgende >
        Text English=&CleanIT! >
        Text Finnish=&Seuraava >
        Text French=&Suivant >
        Text German=&Weiter >
        Text Italian=&Avanti >
        Text Norwegian=&Neste >
        Text Portuguese=&Seguinte >
        Text Spanish=&Siguiente >
        Text Swedish= &NÑsta >
     end
     item: Push Button
        Rectangle=95 114 140 129
        Action=3
        Create Flags=01010000000000010000000000000000
        Text Danish=Annuller
        Text Dutch=Annuleren
        Text English=Cancel
        Text Finnish=Peruuta
        Text French=Annuler
        Text German=Abbrechen
        Text Italian=Annulla
        Text Norwegian=Avbryt
        Text Portuguese=Cancelar
        Text Spanish=Cancelar
        Text Swedish= Avbryt
     end
   end
 end
end
```

Section 5   The fifth section contains the default SMS Installer
script requirement of including the Check Disk Space script
action with every script. If this is not included, the script will not
compile and an error message will display. The CleanDoc! utility
does not require a space requirement calculation. You can just
add a blank Check Disk Space script action to the script when
disk space requirements are not an issue. You can also suppress

the error message altogether and not include this script action. See the Check Disk Space script action reference in Chapter 05 for information on modifying the progress bar value.

Required Check Free Disk Space script action:

```
item: Check Disk Space
   Component=COMPONENTS
end
```

Section 6 The sixth section performs the deletion of the document shortcuts in the RECENT folder. It uses the Delete File(s) script action with wildcard characters. At this point the `RECENT-DIR` variable contains the entire directory structure information to the user's RECENT folder in the Profile directory.

Delete the files in the RECENT files folder:

```
item: Delete File
   Pathname=%RECENTDIR%\*.*
end
```

Section 7 The seventh (and last) section displays a Finished dialog box to the user indicating that the recent documents information has been deleted and the utility has completed. (See Figure 6-2.) Keep in mind, unless you are purposely creating a silent util-

Figure 6-2 *Finished dialog box.*

ity, any utility you create should include a Finished dialog box. This lets the user know when he or she can continue to work or when it is okay to shut down the computer. This is just a common courtesy.

Display the Finished dialog box to the user:

```
item: Custom Dialog Set
  Name=Finished!
  item: Dialog
    Title English=Finished!
    Width=150
    Height=150
    Font Name=Helv
    Font Size=8
    item: Static
      Rectangle=5 5 23 25
      Action=2
      Create Flags=01010000000000000000000000001011
      Pathname English=E:\Folders\McGraw Hill\Scripts\
Chapter Six\CleanDOC\docs.bmp
    end
    item: Static
      Rectangle=14 41 131 63
      Create Flags=01010000000000000000000000000000
      Text English=The recent Documents folder has been
successfully cleaned!
    end
    item: Push Button
      Rectangle=93 111 138 126
      Variable=DIRECTION
      Value=N
      Create Flags=01010000000000010000000000000001
      Text Danish=&Udfor
      Text Dutch=&Voltooien
      Text English=&Finish
      Text Finnish=&Valmis
      Text French=Ter&miner
      Text German=&Weiter
      Text Italian=&Fine
      Text Norwegian=&Fullfor
      Text Portuguese=&Concluir
      Text Spanish=&Finalizar
      Text Swedish=S&lutfîr
    end
    item: Static
      Rectangle=46 95 126 110
      Create Flags=01010000000000000000000000000000
```

```
        Text English=Click Finish to exit CleanDoc!
      end
      item: Static
        Rectangle=46 8 109 23
        Create Flags=01010000000000000000000000000000
        Flags=0000000000000001
        Name=Arial
        Font Style=-21 0 0 0 700 0 0 0 0 3 2 1 34
        Text English=CleanDoc!
      end
   end
end
```

When compiled, the CleanDoc! utility is around 150 KB. Because of the small size, the utility can be distributed via e-mail. Or, it can be compiled into a second SMS Installer script that installs the utility on the user's computer in the location you specify with the program's shortcut created for quick access (i.e., Desktop, Start menu, App folder, etc.). It can then be distributed via the preferred method and media (i.e., Microsoft Systems Management Server, floppy diskette set, CD, etc.). For more information on distribution methods, see "Distributing the Installation" in Chapter 03.

SysConfig Utility

On occasion, applications can overwrite settings in the Autoexec.bat and Config.sys files. This can keep software applications from running correctly when the path statement becomes too long or the buffers are resized. Or, God forbid, a user could actually delete the Autoexec.bat and Config.sys files. For some applications, these files are crucial to their operation.

The SysConfig utility helps the user re-create and personalize these files. Since the utility size is under 160 KB, it can easily be e-mailed to remote users. Or, it can be distributed via your preferred distribution method. For more information on distribution methods, see "Distributing the Installation" in Chapter 03.

For this example the script is broken down into functional sections:

Section 1   Section 1 sets the variables that cannot be set by another means. The section sets the application title, the ROOT

variable to C:\, and the DISABLED variable to ! for use with the
custom dialog box set.

Set variables:

```
item: Set Variable
  Variable=APPTITLE
  Value=Boot-up Re-Configuration Utility
  Flags=10000000
end
item: Set Variable
  Variable=ROOT
  Value=C:\
end
item: Set Variable
  Variable=DISABLED
  Value=!
end
```

Section 2   The second section uses the Edit INI File script action
to set the RESTART variable in the SYSTEM.INI. This, along with
the Add Device to SYSTEM.INI section near the end of the script,
ensures the user is prompted to restart the computer at the completion of the utility. For more information on using this method,
see "The RESTART Variable" in Chapter 08.

Add the RESTART *value to the* [386Enh] *section in the*
SYSTEM.INI:

```
item: Edit INI File
  Pathname=%WIN%\SYSTEM.INI
  Settings=[386Enh]
  Settings=RESTART=
  Settings=
end
```

Section 3   The third section of the script creates the user interface using a Wizard Block to create a dialog box set. The Wizard
Block contains five dialog boxes:

1. *Welcome dialog box*   The Welcome dialog box initiates the
   user interface and explains the steps that will be followed during the utility. The Welcome dialog box is not a required item
   but is more of a common courtesy billboard for the user. If

users accidentally execute the file, the initial screen will let
them know they are not running the program they intended.
The Welcome dialog box is shown in Figure 6-3.

2. *Network User Name dialog box*   The Network User Name
   dialog box presents the user with an Edit Text control to allow
   entering of the network username. This entered text is placed
   into the LNAME variable. The Network User Name dialog box
   is shown in Figure 6-4.

3. *Login Server Name dialog box*   The Login Server Name dialog box presents the user with a list of available server names
   in the form of a Combo Box control (drop-down box). The
   value is placed into the PREFSERV variable. The Login Server
   Name dialog box is shown in Figure 6-5.

4. *Network Group dialog box*   The Network Group dialog box
   presents another Combo Box control that allows the user to
   select a predefined network group name. Later in the script,
   this places a SET GROUP= line in the Autoexec.bat file. When
   the booting computer initiates the Autoexec.bat, the GROUP
   name is added as an environment variable. This is helpful for
   basing collections on the environment variable when using
   Systems Management Server. For example, if one option is
   FINANCIAL, you can create a computer collection called
   FINANCIAL. This allows you to target specific departments for
   software distribution. The user-selected value is placed into
   the NETGROUP variable. The Network Group dialog box is
   shown in Figure 6-6.

5. *Ready dialog box*   The Ready dialog box tells the user that
   all the information has been gathered and the system configuration process is ready to start. No changes are made to the
   computer until the user clicks the Next push button. The
   Ready dialog box is shown in Figure 6-7.

Each dialog box includes Next, Cancel, and Back push button
controls. The Next button moves to the next dialog box in the
set. The Cancel button allows the user to cancel the configuration
at any time. The Back button moves to the previous dialog box in
the set, allowing users to correct mistakes or verify their input
was correct.

Display the User Interface through the Wizard Block:

```
item: Wizard Block
  Direction Variable=DIRECTION
  Display Variable=DISPLAY
  X Position=0
  Y Position=0
  Filler Color=0
end

item: Custom Dialog Set
  Name=Welcome!
  Display Variable=DISPLAY
  item: Dialog
    Title English=Welcome!
    Width=150
    Height=150
    Font Name=Helv
    Font Size=8
    item: Static
      Rectangle=32 9 136 22
      Create Flags=01010000000000000000000000000001
      Flags=0000000000000001
      Name=Arial
      Font Style=-13 0 0 0 700 255 0 0 3 2 1 34
      Text English=System Configuration Utility
    end
    item: Static
```

Figure 6-3 *Welcome dialog box.*

```
      Rectangle=14 31 141 57
      Create Flags=01010000000000000000000000000000
      Text English=This utility will reset your PC startup
files. To continue, you will need to know the following
information:
      end
      item: Static
        Rectangle=10 5 28 25
        Action=2
        Create Flags=01010000000000000000000000001011
        Pathname English=E:\Folders\McGraw Hill\Scripts\
Chapter Six\SysCFG\syscfgf.bmp
      end
      item: Static
        Rectangle=15 63 85 96
        Create Flags=01010000000000000000000000000000
        Text English=1) Network User Name 2) Login Server Name
3) Network Group
      end
      item: Push Button
        Rectangle=96 111 141 126
        Action=3
        Create Flags=01010000000000010000000000000000
        Text Danish=Annuller
        Text Dutch=Annuleren
        Text English=Cancel
        Text Finnish=Peruuta
        Text French=Annuler
        Text German=Abbrechen
        Text Italian=Annulla
        Text Norwegian=Avbryt
        Text Portuguese=Cancelar
        Text Spanish=Cancelar
        Text Swedish= Avbryt
      end
      item: Push Button
        Rectangle=42 110 87 125
        Variable=DIRECTION
        Value=N
        Create Flags=01010000000000010000000000000001
        Text Danish=&Nëste >
        Text Dutch=&Volgende >
        Text English=&Next >
        Text Finnish=&Seuraava >
        Text French=&Suivant >
        Text German=&Weiter >
        Text Italian=&Avanti >
        Text Norwegian=&Neste >
```

```
        Text Portuguese=&Seguinte >
        Text Spanish=&Siguiente >
        Text Swedish= &NÑsta >
      end
      item: Static
        Rectangle=7 95 95 106
        Create Flags=01010000000000000000000000000000
        Flags=0000000000000001
        Name=Arial
        Font Style=-11 0 0 0 400 255 0 0 0 3 2 1 34
        Text English=Click Next to Continue...
      end
    end
  end

item: Custom Dialog Set
  Name=LNAME
  Display Variable=DISPLAY
  item: Dialog
    Title English=Network User Name
    Width=150
    Height=150
    Font Name=Helv
    Font Size=8
    item: Static
      Rectangle=32 9 136 22
      Create Flags=01010000000000000000000000000001
```

Figure 6-4 *Network User Name dialog box.*

```
        Flags=0000000000000001
        Name=Arial
        Font Style=-13 0 0 0 700 255 0 0 0 3 2 1 34
        Text English=System Configuration Utility
        end
        item: Static
        Rectangle=10 5 28 25
        Action=2
        Create Flags=01010000000000000000000000001011
        Pathname English=E:\Folders\McGraw Hill\Scripts\
Chapter Six\SysCFG\syscfgf.bmp
        end
        item: Push Button
        Rectangle=96 111 141 126
        Action=3
        Create Flags=01010000000000010000000000000000
        Text Danish=Annuller
        Text Dutch=Annuleren
        Text English=Cancel
        Text Finnish=Peruuta
        Text French=Annuler
        Text German=Abbrechen
        Text Italian=Annulla
        Text Norwegian=Avbryt
        Text Portuguese=Cancelar
        Text Spanish=Cancelar
        Text Swedish= Avbryt
        end
        item: Push Button
        Rectangle=47 111 92 126
        Variable=DIRECTION
        Value=N
        Create Flags=01010000000000010000000000000001
        Text Danish=&Nëste >
        Text Dutch=&Volgende >
        Text English=&Next >
        Text Finnish=&Seuraava >
        Text French=&Suivant >
        Text German=&Weiter >
        Text Italian=&Avanti >
        Text Norwegian=&Neste >
        Text Portuguese=&Seguinte >
        Text Spanish=&Siguiente >
        Text Swedish= &NÑsta >
        end
        item: Static
        Rectangle=7 95 95 106
        Create Flags=01010000000000000000000000000000
        Flags=0000000000000001
```

```
    Name=Arial
    Font Style=-11 0 0 0 400 255 0 0 0 3 2 1 34
    Text English=Click Next to Continue...
  end
  item: Static
    Rectangle=5 30 131 57
    Create Flags=01010000000000000000000000000000
    Text English=Enter your Network User Name. Your user
name will be the first initial of your first name, followed
by your last name up to 8 characters.
  end
  item: Static
    Rectangle=5 58 139 73
    Create Flags=01010000000000000000000000000000
    Text English=Example: Joe Smithsonian would be
JSMITHSO
  end
  item: Static
    Rectangle=3 76 62 89
    Create Flags=01010000000000000000000000000000
    Text English=Network User Name:
  end
  item: Editbox
    Control Name=NETNAME
    Rectangle=61 74 139 89
    Variable=LNAME
    Help Context=16711681
    Create Flags=01010000100000010000000000000000
```

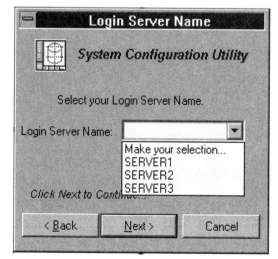

Figure 6-5 *Login Server Name dialog box.*

```
            end
         end
end

item: Custom Dialog Set
  Name=PREFSERV
  Display Variable=DISPLAY
  item: Dialog
    Title English=Login Server Name
    Width=150
    Height=150
    Font Name=Helv
    Font Size=8
    item: Static
      Rectangle=32 9 136 22
      Create Flags=01010000000000000000000000000001
      Flags=0000000000000001
      Name=Arial
      Font Style=-13 0 0 0 700 255 0 0 0 3 2 1 34
      Text English=System Configuration Utility
    end
    item: Static
      Rectangle=10 5 28 25
      Action=2
      Create Flags=01010000000000000000000000001011
      Pathname English=E:\Folders\McGraw Hill\Scripts\
Chapter Six\SysCFG\syscfgf.bmp
    end
    item: Push Button
      Rectangle=97 111 142 126
      Action=3
      Create Flags=01010000000000010000000000000000
      Text Danish=Annuller
      Text Dutch=Annuleren
      Text English=Cancel
      Text Finnish=Peruuta
      Text French=Annuler
      Text German=Abbrechen
      Text Italian=Annulla
      Text Norwegian=Avbryt
      Text Portuguese=Cancelar
      Text Spanish=Cancelar
      Text Swedish= Avbryt
    end
    item: Push Button
      Rectangle=49 111 94 126
      Variable=DIRECTION
      Value=N
```

```
      Create Flags=01010000000000010000000000000001
      Text Danish=&Nëste >
      Text Dutch=&Volgende >
      Text English=&Next >
      Text Finnish=&Seuraava >
      Text French=&Suivant >
      Text German=&Weiter >
      Text Italian=&Avanti >
      Text Norwegian=&Neste >
      Text Portuguese=&Seguinte >
      Text Spanish=&Siguiente >
      Text Swedish= &NÑsta >
   end
   item: Static
      Rectangle=7 95 95 106
      Create Flags=01010000000000000000000000000000
      Flags=0000000000000001
      Name=Arial
      Font Style=-11 0 0 0 400 255 0 0 0 3 2 1 34
      Text English=Click Next to Continue...
   end
   item: Static
      Rectangle=2 57 61 70
      Create Flags=01010000000000000000000000000000
      Text English=Login Server Name:
   end
   item: Static
      Rectangle=23 38 113 53
      Create Flags=01010000000000000000000000000000
      Text English=Select your Login Server Name.
   end
   item: Combobox
      Rectangle=61 54 133 106
      Variable=PREFSERV
      Create Flags=01010000000000010000001000000010
      Text English=Make your selection...
      Text English=SERVER1
      Text English=SERVER2
      Text English=SERVER3
      Text English=
   end
   item: Push Button
      Rectangle=3 111 48 126
      Variable=DIRECTION
      Value=B
      Create Flags=01010000000000010000000000000000
      Text Danish=< &Tilbage
      Text Dutch=< &Terug
```

```
          Text English=< &Back
          Text Finnish=< &Edellinen
          Text French=< &PrÇcÇdent
          Text German=< &ZurÅck
          Text Italian=< &Indietro
          Text Norwegian=< &Tilbake
          Text Portuguese=< &Anterior
          Text Spanish=< &Atrts
          Text Swedish=< &FîregÜende
       end
     end
end

item: Custom Dialog Set
  Name=NETGROUP
  Display Variable=DISPLAY
  item: Dialog
  Title English=Network Group
  Width=150
  Height=150
  Font Name=Helv
  Font Size=8
  item: Static
    Rectangle=32 9 136 22
    Create Flags=01010000000000000000000000000001
    Flags=0000000000000001
    Name=Arial
    Font Style=-13 0 0 0 700 255 0 0 0 3 2 1 34
```

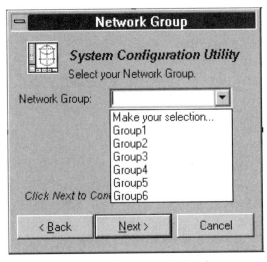

Figure 6-6 *Network Group dialog box.*

```
    Text English=System Configuration Utility
  end
  item: Static
    Rectangle=10 5 28 25
    Action=2
    Create Flags=01010000000000000000000000001011
    Pathname English=E:\Folders\McGraw Hill\Scripts\Chapter
Six\SysCFG\syscfgf.bmp
  end
  item: Push Button
    Rectangle=97 111 142 126
    Action=3
    Create Flags=01010000000000010000000000000000
    Text Danish=Annuller
    Text Dutch=Annuleren
    Text English=Cancel
    Text Finnish=Peruuta
    Text French=Annuler
    Text German=Abbrechen
    Text Italian=Annulla
    Text Norwegian=Avbryt
    Text Portuguese=Cancelar
    Text Spanish=Cancelar
    Text Swedish= Avbryt
  end
  item: Push Button
    Rectangle=49 111 94 126
    Variable=DIRECTION
    Value=N
    Create Flags=01010000000000010000000000000001
    Text Danish=&Nëste >
    Text Dutch=&Volgende >
    Text English=&Next >
    Text Finnish=&Seuraava >
    Text French=&Suivant >
    Text German=&Weiter >
    Text Italian=&Avanti >
    Text Norwegian=&Neste >
    Text Portuguese=&Seguinte >
    Text Spanish=&Siguiente >
    Text Swedish= &NÑsta >
  end
  item: Static
    Rectangle=7 95 95 106
    Create Flags=01010000000000000000000000000000
    Flags=0000000000000001
    Name=Arial
    Font Style=-11 0 0 0 400 255 0 0 0 3 2 1 34
```

```
        Text English=Click Next to Continue...
      end
      item: Static
        Rectangle=5 36 50 48
        Create Flags=01010000000000000000000000000000
        Text English=Network Group:
      end
      item: Static
        Rectangle=34 21 124 31
        Create Flags=01010000000000000000000000000000
        Text English=Select your Network Group.
      end
      item: Combobox
        Rectangle=58 34 130 133
        Variable=NETGROUP
        Create Flags=01010000000000010000001000000010
        Text English=Make your selection...
        Text English=Group1
        Text English=Group2
        Text English=Group3
        Text English=Group4
        Text English=Group5
        Text English=Group6
        Text English=
      end
      item: Push Button
        Rectangle=3 111 48 126
        Variable=DIRECTION
        Value=B
        Create Flags=01010000000000010000000000000000
        Text Danish=< &Tilbage
        Text Dutch=< &Terug
        Text English=< &Back
        Text Finnish=< &Edellinen
        Text French=< &PrÇcÇdent
        Text German=< &ZurÅck
        Text Italian=< &Indietro
        Text Norwegian=< &Tilbake
        Text Portuguese=< &Anterior
        Text Spanish=< &Atr†s
        Text Swedish=< &FîregÜende
      end
    end
  end

  item: Custom Dialog Set
    Name=START
    Display Variable=DISPLAY
```

Figure 6-7 *Ready dialog box.*

```
item: Dialog
   Title English=Ready!
   Width=150
   Height=150
   Font Name=Helv
   Font Size=8
   item: Static
     Rectangle=32 9 136 22
     Create Flags=01010000000000000000000000000001
     Flags=0000000000000001
     Name=Arial
     Font Style=-13 0 0 0 700 255 0 0 0 3 2 1 34
     Text English=System Configuration Utility
   end
   item: Static
     Rectangle=10 5 28 25
     Action=2
     Create Flags=01010000000000000000000000001011
     Pathname English=E:\Folders\McGraw Hill\Scripts\
Chapter Six\SysCFG\syscfgf.bmp
   end
   item: Push Button
     Rectangle=97 111 142 126
     Action=3
     Create Flags=01010000000000010000000000000000
     Text Danish=Annuller
     Text Dutch=Annuleren
```

```
                    Text English=Cancel
                    Text Finnish=Peruuta
                    Text French=Annuler
                    Text German=Abbrechen
                    Text Italian=Annulla
                    Text Norwegian=Avbryt
                    Text Portuguese=Cancelar
                    Text Spanish=Cancelar
                    Text Swedish= Avbryt
                 end
                 item: Push Button
                   Rectangle=49 111 94 126
                   Variable=DIRECTION
                   Value=N
                   Create Flags=01010000000000010000000000000001
                   Text Danish=&Nëste >
                   Text Dutch=&Volgende >
                   Text English=&Next >
                   Text Finnish=&Seuraava >
                   Text French=&Suivant >
                   Text German=&Weiter >
                   Text Italian=&Avanti >
                   Text Norwegian=&Neste >
                   Text Portuguese=&Seguinte >
                   Text Spanish=&Siguiente >
                   Text Swedish= &NÑsta >
                 end
                 item: Static
                   Rectangle=7 95 95 106
                   Create Flags=01010000000000000000000000000000
                   Flags=0000000000000001
                   Name=Arial
                   Font Style=-11 0 0 0 400 255 0 0 0 3 2 1 34
                   Text English=Click Next to Continue...
                 end
                 item: Static
                   Rectangle=9 44 133 63
                   Create Flags=01010000000000000000000000000000
                   Text English=The utility has acquired all the
information it needs. The configuration will now begin.
                 end
                 item: Push Button
                 Rectangle=3 111 48 126
                 Variable=DIRECTION
                 Value=B
                 Create Flags=01010000000000010000000000000000
                 Text Danish=< &Tilbage
```

```
      Text Dutch=< &Terug
      Text English=< &Back
      Text Finnish=< &Edellinen
      Text French=< &PrÇcÇdent
      Text German=< &ZurÅck
      Text Italian=< &Indietro
      Text Norwegian=< &Tilbake
      Text Portuguese=< &Anterior
      Text Spanish=< &Atrﬂs
      Text Swedish=< &FîregÜende
    end
  end
end
item: End Block
end
```

Section 4   The fourth section contains the default SMS Installer script requirement of including the Check Disk Space script action with every script. If this is not included, the script will not compile and an error message will display. The SysConfig utility does not require a space requirement calculation. You can just add a blank Check Disk Space script action to the script when disk space requirements are not an issue. You can also suppress the error message altogether and not include this script action. See the Check Disk Space script action reference in Chapter 05 for information on modifying the progress bar value.

Required Check Free Disk Space script action:

```
item: Check Disk Space
  Component=COMPONENTS
end
```

Section 5   The fifth section searches for the Autoexec.bat and Config.sys files in the local file system and places their locations into variables. These files are always located in the root directory of the computer's boot drive and could be placed into variables by using the Set Variable script action. Using the search method allows you to use the variables with the remainder of the script. After the files are placed into the variables CONFIGLOC and AUTOLOC, the files are renamed with a .bak extension to back them up.

Search for Autoexec.bat and Config.sys, place the locations in a variable, and then rename the files:

```
item: Search for File
  Variable=CONFIGLOC
  Pathname List=CONFIG.SYS
  Flags=00001000
end
item: Rename File/Directory
  Old Pathname=%CONFIGLOC%
  New Filename=config.bak
end
item: Search for File
  Variable=AUTOLOC
  Pathname List=AUTOEXEC.BAT
  Flags=00001000
end
item: Rename File/Directory
  Old Pathname=%AUTOLOC%
  New Filename=autoexec.bak
end
```

Section 6   The sixth section creates a brand-new Autoexec.bat file with specific commands, environment variables, and the values that were selected by the user during the Wizard Block.

Create new Autoexec.bat file and specific items:

```
item: Add to AUTOEXEC.BAT
  New Text=@ECHO OFF
end
item: Add to AUTOEXEC.BAT
  New Text=CLS
end
item: Add to AUTOEXEC.BAT
  New Text=PROMPT $P$G
end
item: Add to AUTOEXEC.BAT
  New Text=SET PATH=C:\WINDOWS;C:\WINDOWS\COMMAND;C:\
  Line Number=0
end
item: Add to AUTOEXEC.BAT
  New Text=SET COMSPEC=C:\COMMAND.COM
  Line Number=0
end
item: Add to AUTOEXEC.BAT
  New Text=SET TEMP=C:\TEMP
end
```

```
item: Add to AUTOEXEC.BAT
  New Text=SET GROUP=%NETGROUP%
  Line Number=0
end
item: Add to AUTOEXEC.BAT
  New Text=SET PREFSERV=%PREFSERV%
  Line Number=0
end
item: Add to AUTOEXEC.BAT
  New Text=SET LNAME=%LNAME%
  Line Number=0
end
item: Add to AUTOEXEC.BAT
  New Text=CLS
end
```

Section 7   The seventh section creates a brand-new Config.sys
file with directory pointers to device files and environment memory configurations.

Create new Config.sys file and specific items:

```
item: Add to CONFIG.SYS
  New Text=DEVICE=C:\WINDOWS\HIMEM.SYS
end
item: Add to CONFIG.SYS
  New Text=DEVICE=C:\WINDOWS\EMM386.EXE NOEMS
  Line Number=0
end
item: Add to CONFIG.SYS
  New Text=DOS=HIGH,UMB
end
item: Add to CONFIG.SYS
  New Text=FILES=120
end
item: Add to CONFIG.SYS
  New Text=SHELL=C:\COMMAND.COM C:\ /P /E:2048
end
```

Section 8   The eighth section completes the RESTART variable by
using the Add to SYSTEM.INI script action. It sets the value to S,
which restarts the computer. For more information on using this
method, see "The RESTART Variable" in Chapter 08.

Set computer to reboot to use the new files:

```
item: Add to SYSTEM.INI
```

```
        Device=RESTART=S
end
```

Section 9   The ninth section displays the Finished dialog box, shown in Figure 6-8, using the Wizard Block script action. When the user accepts the Finished dialog by clicking on the Finish push button, the script prompts to restart the computer.

Display the Finished dialog box to the user through a Wizard Block:

```
item: Wizard Block
  Direction Variable=DIRECTION
  Display Variable=DISPLAY
  X Position=0
  Y Position=0
  Filler Color=0
end
item: Custom Dialog Set
  Name=FINISHED
  Display Variable=DISPLAY
  item: Dialog
    Title English=Finished!
```

Figure 6-8 *Finished dialog box.*

```
     Width=150
     Height=150
     Font Name=Helv
     Font Size=8
     item: Static
       Rectangle=32 9 136 22
       Create Flags=01010000000000000000000000000001
       Flags=0000000000000001
       Name=Arial
       Font Style=-13 0 0 0 700 255 0 0 0 3 2 1 34
       Text English=System Configuration Utility
     end
     item: Static
       Rectangle=10 5 28 25
       Action=2
       Create Flags=01010000000000000000000000001011
       Pathname English=E:\Folders\McGraw Hill\Scripts\
Chapter Six\SysCFG\syscfgf.bmp
     end
     item: Static
       Rectangle=9 44 133 77
       Create Flags=01010000000000000000000000000000
       Text English=The configuration is finished. Your PC
will need to be restarted for the configuration to take
effect.
     end
     item: Push Button
       Rectangle=90 110 135 125
       Variable=DIRECTION
       Value=N
       Create Flags=01010000000000010000000000000001
       Text Danish=&Udfør
       Text Dutch=&Voltooien
       Text English=&Finish
       Text Finnish=&Valmis
       Text French=Ter&miner
       Text German=&Weiter
       Text Italian=&Fine
       Text Norwegian=&Fullfør
       Text Portuguese=&Concluir
       Text Spanish=&Finalizar
       Text Swedish=S&lutfîr
     end
   end
end
item: End Block
end
```

Figure 6-9 *WinNWUser Utility.*

WinNWUser Utility

The WinNWUser utility, shown in Figure 6-9, displays users currently logged in to a NetWare 3.1x server. Instead of using the NetWare Userlist.exe from the command line, this SMS Installer script includes the Userlist.exe in the compiled script, copies it to a temporary directory, runs the command line, and then displays the results in a dialog box window. This is a good example of using third-party utilities to extend SMS Installer functionality.

For this example, the script is broken down into functional sections.

Section 1   The first section contains the default SMS Installer script requirement of including the Check Disk Space script action with every script. If this is not included, the script will not compile and an error message will display. The WinNWUser utility does not require a space requirement calculation. You can just add a blank Check Disk Space script action to the script when disk space requirements are not an issue. You can also suppress the error message altogether and not include this script action. See the Check Disk Space script action reference in Chapter 05 for information on modifying the progress bar value.

Required Check Free Disk Space script action:

```
Check Disk Space
item: Check Disk Space
end
```

Section 2   The second section gets the operating system's environment variable for the location of the temporary directory. This is the directory the Userlist.exe will be installed to.

Get TEMP environment variable:

```
item: Get Environment Variable
  Variable=TEMPDIR
```

```
   Environment=TEMP
end
```

Section 3 The third section places a common NetWare directory, F:\PUBLIC, in the FDRIVE variable. This will be used to verify that the computer has a valid network connection.

Set variable FDRIVE *for checking network connection:*

```
item: Set Variable
  Variable=FDRIVE
  Value=F:\PUBLIC
end
```

Section 4 The command line for this utility is configured only
to run on a Windows NT computer. The fourth section verifies
that the computer is running Windows NT and exits the installation if it is not.

Check OS version and exit if not Windows NT:

```
item: Check Configuration
  Message English=This utility only runs on Windows NT. The
utility will now exit.
  Title English=Windows NT...
  Flags=01000000
end
```

Section 5 The fifth section verifies the F:\PUBLIC directory
exists on the computer. A logic block is started. If the network
connection exists, the Userlist.exe is run and the current
logged-on user list is displayed. If the network connection does
not exist, the Else statement is run, which exits the utility.

Check for proper network connection and start block if exists:

```
item: Check if File/Dir Exists
  Pathname=%FDRIVE%
  Flags=00000100
end
```

Section 6 The sixth section installs the Userlist.exe file into the
temporary directory on the computer. This is the location from
which the command line will be run.

Install USERLIST.EXE into the temporary directory:

```
item: Install File
 Source=E:\Folders\packages\NWUser\USERLIST.EXE
   Destination=%TEMPDIR%\USERLIST.EXE
   Flags=0000000000100010
end
```

Section 7   The seventh section displays a dialog box, shown in
Figure 6-10, for entering the server name. The server name that is
entered into the Edit Text control will be used as a command-line
variable. If the server names never change in your organization,
you can exchange the Edit Text control for a Combo Box control
(drop-down list) and input the predefined server names for quick
selection.

Display the server name entry dialog:

```
item: Custom Dialog Set
  Name=Server Name...
   item: Dialog
    Title English=Server Name...
    Width=203
    Height=169
    Font Name=Helv
```

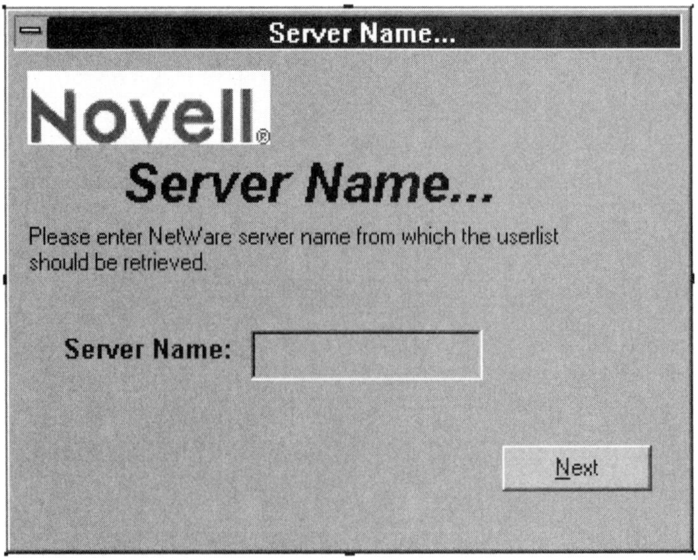

Figure 6-10 *Server Name dialog box.*

```
    Font Size=8
    item: Static
      Rectangle=5 52 164 78
      Create Flags=01010000000000000000000000000000
      Text English=Please enter NetWare server name from
which the userlist should be retrieved.
    end
    item: Static
      Rectangle=33 30 185 50
      Create Flags=01010000000000000000000000000000
      Flags=0000000000000001
      Name=Arial
      Font Style=-27 0 0 0 700 255 0 0 0 3 2 1 34
      Text English=Server Name...
    end
    item: Push Button
      Rectangle=144 121 188 135
      Variable=DIRECTION
      Value=N
      Create Flags=01010000000000010000000000000000
      Text English=&Next
    end
    item: Static
      Rectangle=5 5 76 28
      Action=2
      Create Flags=01010000000000000000000000001011
      Pathname English=E:\Folders\McGraw Hill\Scripts\
Chapter Six\WinNWUser\novlogo.bmp
    end
    item: Editbox .
      Rectangle=71 86 138 100
      Variable=SERVER
      Help Context=16711681
      Create Flags=01010000100000010000000000000000
    end
    item: Static
      Rectangle=15 86 68 101
      Create Flags=01010000000000000000000000000000
      Flags=0000000000000001
      Name=Arial
      Font Style=-13 0 0 0 700 0 0 0 0 3 2 1 34
      Text English=Server Name:
    end
  end
end
```

Section 8 The eighth section runs the USERLIST.EXE command, checks the logged-in user list on the server name entered,

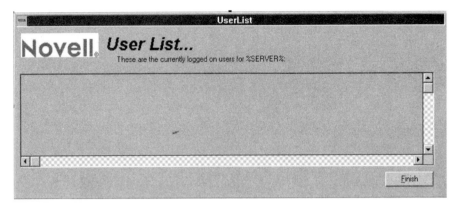

Figure 6-11 *User List dialog box.*

and inserts the output to the ULIST.LOG file in the temporary directory location. See Figure 6-11.

Command line syntax for USERLIST.EXE:
```
Usage: UserList [fileserver/][name] [/Address | /Object]
[/Continuous]
```

Run USERLIST.EXE with command line:
```
item: Execute Program
  Pathname=%TEMPDIR%\USERLIST.EXE
  Command Line=%SERVER%/ /Address>%TEMPDIR%\ULIST.LOG
  Default Directory=%TEMPDIR%
  Flags=00000110
end
```

Section 9 The ninth section displays a dialog box with a Read Only Edit Text control. The Edit Text control displays the contents of the Ulist.log file.

```
item: Custom Dialog Set
  Name=Server Name...
  item: Dialog
    Title English=UserList
    Width=396
    Height=178
    Font Name=Helv
    Font Size=8
  item: Static
    Rectangle=83 6 235 26
```

```
    Create Flags=01010000000000000000000000000000
    Flags=0000000000000001
    Name=Arial
    Font Style=-27 0 0 0 700 255 0 0 0 3 2 1 34
    Text English=User List...
  end
  item: Push Button
    Rectangle=336 138 380 152
    Variable=DIRECTION
    Value=N
    Create Flags=01010000000000010000000000000000
    Text English=&Finish
  end
  item: Editbox
    Rectangle=4 44 380 132
    Value=%TEMPDIR%\ULIST.LOG
    Help Context=16711681
    Create Flags=01010000101100010000100000000100
  end
  item: Static
    Rectangle=93 26 256 39
    Create Flags=01010000000000000000000000000000
    Text English=These are the currently logged on users
for   %SERVER%:
  end
  item: Static
    Rectangle=5 5 76 28
    Action=2
    Create Flags=01010000000000000000000000001011
    Pathname English=E:\Folders\packages\NWUser\novlogo.bmp
   end
  end
end
```

Section 10   The tenth section removes the USERLIST.EXE and ULIST.LOG file from the computer.

Delete USERLIST.EXE and created text file:

```
item: Delete File
  Pathname=%TEMPDIR%\USERLIST.EXE
end
item: Delete File
  Pathname=%TEMPDIR%\ULIST.LOG
end
```

Section 11   The eleventh section contains the Else statement that runs if the network connection, specified by the FDRIVE variable,

is not found. An error message is displayed, as shown in Figure
6-12, and the utility exits.

*Display network connection error message if network does not
exist:*

```
item: Else Statement
end
item: Display Message
  Title English=Network Connection...
  Text English=You are not logged into the network. Please
check your network connection before trying to rerun this
program.
  Text English=
  Text English=The program will now exit.
  Flags=00101000
end
item: End Block
end
```

CCEXIMP Utility

Organizations that use Lotus cc:Mail for an e-mail client must
use command-line utilities for exporting user messages, personal
e-mail lists, and so on. The command-line utilities are included
with the mobile client in the application's program directory.
Occasionally, the user's mobile post office will become corrupt,
and a new e-mail database will need to be created. The user, of
course, does not wish to lose messages or any personal settings.
The CCEXIMP utility allows you to perform an export of the
mail message and personal settings and also enables you to
import the data after a new post office has been created.

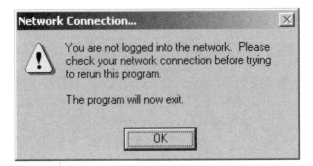

Figure 6-12 *Invalid Network Connection error.*

The CCEXIMP utility uses the included Lotus utilities for importing/exporting, but it provides a quick windows interface that is easier to use than just typing commands into a MS-DOS window.

The utility is based on the following DOS commands:

To Export all mail from a cc:Mobile account:

From the c:\ccmobile prompt, type:

```
Export localpo (password) c:\ccmobile\ccdatal
mailbox/"lastname, firstname" @(path and filename)
```

To Import the mail file created above:

From the c:\ccmobile prompt, type:

```
Import localpo (password) c:\ccmobile\ccdatal @(path and
filename)
```

To Export Public mailing lists from a cc:Mobile account:

From the c:\ccmobile prompt, type:

```
Export localpo (password) c:\ccmobile\ccdatal list @(path
and filename)
```

To Import the mailing list file created above:

From the c:\ccmobile prompt, type:

```
Import localpo (password) c:\ccmobile\ccdatal directory
@(path and filename)
```

For this example, the script is broken down into functional sections:

Section 1   The first section contains the default SMS Installer script requirement of including the Check Disk Space script action with every script. If this is not included, the script will not compile and an error message will display. The CCEXIMP utility does not require a space requirement calculation. You can just add a blank Check Disk Space script action to the script when disk space requirements are not an issue. You can also suppress the error message altogether and not include this script action.

See the Check Disk Space script action reference in Chapter 05 for information on modifying the progress bar value.

Check Disk Space Script Action:

```
item: Check Disk Space
end
```

Section 2   The second section sets the script variables that are not set by other means. Since this script uses radio buttons on the dialog boxes, the RADIO1 and RADIO2 variables must be determined before the dialog box set. RADIO2 is entered as a value of B. This causes the second radio button on the dialog box to be the default. For more information on this procedure, see the Custom Dialog script action reference in Chapter 05. Also in the Set Variable section, the directory location of the user settings and private e-mail list is placed into the MB1DIRLOC variable for use later.

Set Variables:

```
item: Set Variable
  Variable=ROOT
  Value=C:\
end
item: Set Variable
  Variable=RADIO1
end
item: Set Variable
  Variable=RADIO2
  Value=B
end
item: Set Variable
  Variable=MB1DIRLOC
  Value=%WIN%\CCMAIL\MB1DIR
end
```

Section 3   When cc:Mail is installed and the user's post office is configured, cc:Mail places its own INI section in the WIN.INI file. The third section retrieves information from this INI section and places it into variables for use with the script. It retrieves the cc:Mail program path, since each installation could result in a different location and drive of the application's program files. Then, the username is retrieved and placed into the USER variable. This username is the login name to the cc:Mail mobile post office. The default value for the variable is set to NOTFOUND in the event cc:Mail has not been set up correctly on the computer.

Read WIN.INI sections for further variables:

```
item: Read INI Value
  Variable=CCMAILLOC
  Pathname=%WIN%\WIN.INI
  Section=cc:Mail
  Item=ProgramPath
  Default=NOTFOUND
end
item: Read INI Value
  Variable=USER
  Pathname=%WIN%\WIN.INI
  Section=cc:Mail
  Item=User1Name
  Default=NOTFOUND
end
```

Section 4   The fourth section uses the CCMAILLOC variable, set previously, to determine if the default value of NOTFOUND was retained. If the value equals NOTFOUND, this is an indication that cc:Mail is not set up properly on the computer and the utility displays an error message and exits. This adds fault tolerance to the utility.

Check to see that cc:Mail is installed/configured correctly, exit if it is not:

```
item: If/While Statement
  Variable=CCMAILLOC
  Value=NOTFOUND
end
item: Display Message
  Title English=Check Configuration...
  Text English=cc:Mail has not been properly configured
on this computer. Please check the installation before
retrying this operation.
  Text English=
  Text English=The utility will now exit.
  Flags=00101000
end
```

```
item: Exit Installation
end
item: End Block
end
```

Section 5 The fifth section displays a dialog box, shown in Figure 6-13, allowing you to select the operation that will be performed (export or import). The output of the selected radio button determines which path is taken in the logic block. A value of A runs the export; a value of B runs the import. For more information on the way the radio button selections work, see the Custom Dialog script action reference in Chapter 05.

Display user interface to choose import or export procedure:

```
item: Custom Dialog Set
  Name=cc:Mail Export/Import
  item: Dialog
    Title English=cc:Mail Export/Import
    Width=150
    Height=150
    Font Name=Helv
    Font Size=8
    item: Push Button
      Rectangle=100 106 135 121
      Variable=DIRECTION
```

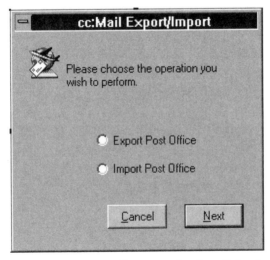

Figure 6-13 *Export/Import selection dialog box.*

```
      Value=N
      Create Flags=01010000000000010000000000000001
      Text English=&Next
    end
    item: Static
      Rectangle=31 18 132 38
      Create Flags=01010000000000000000000000000000
      Text English=Please choose the operation you wish to
perform.
    end
    item: Radio Button
      Rectangle=48 58 116 93
      Variable=RADIO1
      Create Flags=01010000000000010000000000001001
      Text English=Export Post Office
      Text English=Import Post Office
      Text English=
    end
    item: Static
      Rectangle=7 6 31 32
      Action=2
      Create Flags=01010000000000000000000000001011
      Pathname English=D:\PACKAGES\CCEXIMP\CCM.bmp
    end
    item: Push Button
      Rectangle=55 106 90 121
      Action=3
      Create Flags=01010000000000010000000000000000
      Text English=&Cancel
    end
  end
end
```

Section 6 The sixth section prompts for the user's mailbox password (see Figure 6-14). The value is placed into the PASSWORD variable that is used with both the IMPORT and EXPORT command lines.

Display dialog box for entering the user's post office password:

```
item: Custom Dialog Set
  Name=Password
  item: Dialog
    Title English=Password
    Width=150
    Height=150
    Font Name=Helv
    Font Size=8
```

Figure 6-14 *Password dialog box.*

```
item: Push Button
  Rectangle=100 106 135 121
  Variable=DIRECTION
  Value=N
  Create Flags=01010000000000010000000000000001
  Text English=&Next
end
item: Static
  Rectangle=7 6 31 32
  Action=2
  Create Flags=01010000000000000000000000001011
  Pathname English=D:\PACKAGES\CCEXIMP\CCM.bmp
end
item: Push Button
  Rectangle=55 106 90 121
  Action=3
  Create Flags=01010000000000010000000000000000
  Text English=&Cancel
end
item: Static
  Rectangle=35 15 122 34
  Create Flags=01010000000000000000000000000000
  Text English=Please enter the user's cc:Mail
password.
end
item: Editbox
  Rectangle=57 58 130 73
```

```
      Variable=PASSWORD
      Help Context=16711681
      Create Flags=01010000100000010000000100000000
    end
    item: Static
      Rectangle=22 60 53 75
      Create Flags=01010000000000000000000000000000
      Text English=Password:
    end
  end
end
```

Section 7   The seventh section starts the logic block, and based on the RADIO1 value (the Import/Export selection), it either runs the Export or the Import script branch. If the value is A, the script continues. If the value is B, the script moves to the Else Statement functions later in the script. A drive/directory dialog box is presented to the user for the selection of a directory to place the Export files, and then the command line to export the user's e-mail files is run. Also, the MB1DIR directory is copied to the same location as the exported e-mail. This saves the user's specific settings and private mailing list.

If/While block:

```
item: If/While Statement
  Variable=RADIO1
  Value=A
end
item: Browse for Directory
  Variable=EXPDIR
  Flags=3
  Window Name English=Select Export Directory...
  Prompt Description English=Please select the directory
that the exported mailbox should be saved to.
  Prompt Name English=Directory
  Default Value English=D:\TEMP
end
item: Execute Program
  Pathname=%CCMAILLOC%\EXPORT.EXE
  Command Line=localpo %PASSWORD% %CCMAILLOC%\ccdata1
mailbox/"%USER%" @%EXPDIR%\MAIL.EXP
  Default Directory=%CCMAILLOC%
  Flags=00000010
end
```

```
item: Execute Program
  Pathname=%CCMAILLOC%\EXPORT.EXE
  Command Line=localpo %PASSWORD% %CCMAILLOC%\ccdata1 list
@%EXPDIR%\PUBLIC.EXP
  Default Directory=%CCMAILLOC%
  Flags=00000010
end
item: Copy Local File
  Source=%MB1DIRLOC%\*.*
  Destination=%EXPDIR%\MB1DIR\
  Description English=cc:Mail rules and private list...
  Flags=0000000001000010
end
```

Section 8   After the mail is exported and the MB1DIR is backed up, a dialog box, shown in Figure 6-15, prompts to delete the old mailbox. This is helpful when creating a scratch database. If "Yes" is selected, this script action deletes the CCDATA1 directory and its contents. This creates another logic block within the primary logic block and uses radio buttons to determine the outcome.

Figure 6-15 *Post Office deletion dialog box.*

Prompt to delete old mailbox files:

```
item: Custom Dialog Set
  Name=DeletePO
  item: Dialog
    Title English=Old Post Office
    Width=150
    Height=150
    Font Name=Helv
    Font Size=8
    item: Push Button
      Rectangle=100 106 135 121
      Variable=DIRECTION
      Value=N
      Create Flags=01010000000000010000000000000001
      Text English=&Next
    end
    item: Static
      Rectangle=7 6 31 32
      Action=2
      Create Flags=01010000000000000000000000001011
      Pathname English=D:\PACKAGES\CCEXIMP\CCM.bmp
    end
    item: Static
      Rectangle=9 46 137 68
      Create Flags=01010000000000000000000000000000
      Text English=Would you like to go ahead and delete
the old post office on this computer?
    end
    item: Static
      Rectangle=32 13 137 28
      Create Flags=01010000000000000000000000000000
      Flags=0000000000000001
      Name=Arial
      Font Style=-16 0 0 0 700 255 0 0 0 3 2 1 34
      Text English=Delete Old Post Office?
    end
    item: Radio Button
      Rectangle=57 69 92 97
      Variable=RADIO2
      Create Flags=01010000000000010000000000001001
      Text English=Yes
      Text English=No
      Text English=
    end
  end
end
```

Section 9   The ninth section performs the actual deletion of the old post office directory.

Delete the old post office files if selected:

```
item: If/While Statement
  Variable=RADIO2
  Value=A
end
item: Delete File
  Pathname=%CCMAILLOC%\CCDATA1\*.*
  Flags=00000100
end
item: Else Statement
end
item: End Block
end
```

Section 10   When the export procedure is complete, the Export Finished dialog box, shown in Figure 6-16, is displayed.

Display Export Finished dialog box:

```
item: Custom Dialog Set
  Name=Finished
  item: Dialog
    Title English=Finished!
```

Figure 6-16 *Export Finished dialog box.*

```
      Width=150
      Height=150
      Font Name=Helv
      Font Size=8
      item: Push Button
        Rectangle=100 106 135 121
        Variable=DIRECTION
        Create Flags=01010000000000010000000000000001
        Text English=&Finish
      end
      item: Static
        Rectangle=7 6 31 32
        Action=2
        Create Flags=01010000000000000000000000001011
        Pathname English=D:\PACKAGES\CCEXIMP\CCM.bmp
      end
      item: Static
        Rectangle=9 46 137 68
        Create Flags=01010000000000000000000000000000
        Text English=The Export has completed. You will find
the cc:Mail files in the %EXPDIR%\ directory.
      end
      item: Static
        Rectangle=37 14 124 29
        Create Flags=01010000000000000000000000000000
        Flags=0000000000000001
        Name=Arial
        Font Style=-16 0 0 0 700 255 0 0 0 3 2 1 34
        Text English=Process Complete!
      end
    end
  end
end
```

Section 11   The eleventh section is the Else Statement function that is run if the import procedure was selected, instead of the export, from the original dialog box. A drive/directory dialog box allows the selection of a directory where the original export files are stored. Based on the selection, the Lotus Import command is issued.

Run the Import procedure if selected:

```
item: Else Statement
end
item: Browse for Directory
  Variable=IMPDIR
  Flags=1
```

```
  Window Name English=Select Export Directory...
  Prompt Description English=Please select the directory
that the exported mailbox was originally saved to.
  Prompt Name English=Directory
  Flags=00000001
end
item: Execute Program
  Pathname=%CCMAILLOC%\IMPORT.EXE
  Command Line=localpo %PASSWORD% %CCMAILLOC%\ccdata1
@%IMPDIR%\MAIL.EXP
  Default Directory=%CCMAILLOC%
  Flags=00000010
end
item: Execute Program
  Pathname=%CCMAILLOC%\IMPORT.EXE
  Command Line=localpo %PASSWORD% %CCMAILLOC%\ccdata1
directory @%IMPDIR%\PUBLIC.EXP
  Default Directory=%CCMAILLOC%
  Flags=00000010
end
item: Copy Local File
  Source=%IMPDIR%\MB1DIR\*.*
  Destination=%MB1DIRLOC%\
  Description English=cc:Mail rules and private list...
  Flags=0000000001000010
end
item: Delete File
  Pathname=%IMPDIR%\MB1DIR\*.*
  Flags=00000100
end
```

Section 12 The twelfth section displays the Import Finished dialog box, shown in Figure 6-17, when the import process is complete.

Display Import Finished dialog box:

```
item: Custom Dialog Set
  Name=Finished
  item: Dialog
    Title English=Finished!
    Width=150
    Height=150
    Font Name=Helv
    Font Size=8
    item: Push Button
```

Figure 6-17 *Import Finished Dialog Box.*

```
      Rectangle=100 106 135 121
      Variable=DIRECTION
      Create Flags=01010000000000010000000000000001
      Text English=&Finish
   end
   item: Static
      Rectangle=7 6 31 32
      Action=2
      Create Flags=01010000000000000000000000001011
      Pathname English=D:\PACKAGES\CCEXIMP\CCM.bmp
   end
   item: Static
      Rectangle=17 48 126 60
      Create Flags=01010000000000000000000000000000
      Text English=The Import has completed successfully.
   end
   item: Static
      Rectangle=37 14 124 29
      Create Flags=01010000000000000000000000000000
      Flags=0000000000000001
      Name=Arial
      Font Style=-16 0 0 0 700 255 0 0 3 2 1 34
      Text English=Process Complete!
   end
  end
end
```

```
item: End Block
end
```

Real-World Solutions

The following solutions are listed in script format. These scripts
can be typed into a text file and then copied into the SMS
Installer Script window. (For more information on using text files
with SMS Installer see "Sharing Scripts as Plain Text" in Chapter
08.) They are also included on the CD with this book.

The solutions are included to help spur your imagination to
use SMS Installer for more than a repackaging utility. A majority
of the scripts are not feature-complete but only include the necessary items to prove the concept. They can be used in your own
scripts to provide additional functionality. These can be used to
start your own script library.

Setting the Time Zone as a Variable

This script retrieves the computer's time zone from the registry
and places it into a TZ variable that can be used with the remainder of the script.

```
————-Begin Script
item: Get Registry Key Value
  Variable=TZ
  Key=SYSTEM\CurrentControlSet\Control\TimeZoneInformation
Value Name=StandardName
  Flags=00000100
end
item: Edit Registry
  Total Keys=1
  Key=SYSTEM\CurrentControlSet\Control\Session
Manager\Environment
  New Value=%TZ%
  Value Name=TZ
  Root=2
end
————-End Script
```

Setting the PC Clock with a Domain Controller in
Different Time Zones

This script not only sets the time zone for the computer with
the domain controller, it also takes into account the enterprise

environment by adding variables for different time zones across
the United States.

```
───────-Begin Script
item: Get Registry Key Value
  Variable=TIMEZONE
  Key=SYSTEM\CurrentControlSet\Control\TimeZoneInformation
Value Name=StandardName
  Flags=00000100
end
item: If/While Statement
  Variable=TIMEZONE
  Value=Eastern Standard Time
end
item: Execute Program
  Pathname=%SYS%\NET.EXE
  Command Line=TIME \\EasternServerName
  Flags=00000010
end
item: End Block
end
item: If/While Statement
  Variable=TIMEZONE
  Value=Central Standard Time
end
item: Execute Program
  Pathname=%SYS%\NET.EXE
  Command Line=TIME \\CentralServerName
  Flags=00000010
end
item: End Block
end
item: If/While Statement
  Variable=TIMEZONE
  Value=Mountain Standard Time
end
item: Execute Program
  Pathname=%SYS%\NET.EXE
  Command Line=TIME \\MountainServerName
  Flags=00000010
end
item: End Block
end
item: If/While Statement
  Variable=TIMEZONE
  Value=Pacific Standard Time
end
item: Execute Program
  Pathname=%SYS%\NET.EXE
```

```
Command Line=TIME \\PacificServerName
 Flags=00000010
end
item: End Block
end
————-End Script
```

Clearing the Pagefile at Shutdown

For those security-conscious individuals, here is a utility that clears the Win NT Pagefile at shutdown. Clearing the Pagefile keeps the paging data from being available on bootup.

The registry key is HKEY_LOCAL_MACHINE\SYSTEM\ CurrentControlSet\Control\Session Manager\Memory Management

The value is ClearPagefileAtShutdown.

```
————-Begin Script
item: Edit Registry
 Total Keys=1
 Key=SYSTEM\CurrentControlSet\Control\Session Manager\Mem-
ory Management
 New Value=1
 Value Name=ClearPageFileAtShutdown
 Root=2
 Data Type=3
end
————-End Script
```

Creating a Windows NT BootDisk

One of the tougher things to do with SMS Installer is working with the floppy drive. The following script creates an NT boot disk by formatting a diskette in the A: drive, then copying the following files to the floppy drive:

```
NTDETECT.COM
BOOT.INI
NTLDR
```

```
————-Begin Script
item: Set Variable
 Variable=FLOPPYDRV
 Value=A:\
end item: Set Variable
 Variable=FLOPPYDRV
 Value=A:\
end
```

```
item: Execute Program
  Pathname=%SYS32%\FORMAT.COM
  Command Line=a: /u/q
  Flags=00000010
end
item: Search for File
  Variable=NTLDRFILE
  Pathname List=NTLDR
  Flags=00001000
end
item: Search for File
  Variable=BOOTINI
  Pathname List=BOOT.INI
  Flags=00001000
end
item: Search for File
  Variable=NTDETECT
  Pathname List=NTDETECT.COM
  Flags=00001000
end
item: Copy Local File
  Source=%BOOTINI%
  Destination=%FLOPPYDRV%BOOT.INI
  Description English=BOOT.INI...
  Flags=0000000001000010
end
item: Copy Local File
  Source=%NTDETECT%
  Destination=%FLOPPYDRV%NTDETECT.COM
  Description English=NTDETECT.COM...
  Flags=0000000001000010
end
item: Copy Local File
  Source=%NTLDRFILE%
  Destination=%FLOPPYDRV%NTLDR
  Description English=NTLDR...
  Flags=0000000001000010
end
————-End Script
```

Resetting the Admin$ Share on a Windows NT Computer

Some security articles, books, and so on suggest removing the default Win NT Admin$ shares for better security and protection against hackers. While this is a boon for security, running on a default installation of SMS 1.2 can prevent the services from con-

necting to the server and performing their tasks. If you are in a
large organization, some separate offices may incorporate this
feature, causing you to spend hours supporting it and trying to
diagnose the problem.

For Windows NT Server:

```
———-Begin Script
item: Edit Registry
  Total Keys=1
  Key=SYSTEM\CurrentControlSet\Services\LanmanServer\
Parameters
  New Value=1
  Value Name=AutoShareServer
  Root=2
  Data Type=3
end
———-End Script
```

For Windows NT Workstation:

```
———-Begin Script
item: Edit Registry
  Total Keys=1
  Key=SYSTEM\CurrentControlSet\Services\LanmanServer\
Parameters
  New Value=1
  Value Name=AutoShareWks
  Root=2
  Data Type=3
end
———-End Script
```

AutoComplete for the Windows NT Command Line

Did you know that you can get the Win NT command prompt
to auto-enter commands for you? Suppose you want to type
regedt32. If you make a registry modification, you can type reg
and then hit the Tab key to make Win NT complete the command
as long as you are in the directory in which the command resides.

```
———-Begin Script
item: Edit INI File
  Pathname=%WIN%SYSTEM.INI
  Settings=[386Enh]
  Settings=RESTART=
```

```
  Settings=
end
item: Edit Registry
  Total Keys=1
  Key=Software\Microsoft\Command Processor
New Value=0
  Value Name=CompletionChar
  Root=1
  Data Type=3
end
item: Add to SYSTEM.INI
  Device=RESTART=S
end
————-End Script
```

Default File Save Location in MS Word and MS Excel 2000

This script allows you to distribute settings for Word and Excel 2000 that change the default file save location to a common directory.

The registry keys modifies HKEY_CURRENT_USER:

```
Key=Software\Microsoft\Office\9.0\Excel\Options
New Value=C:\MyData
Value Name=DefaultPath
Key=Software\Microsoft\Office\9.0\Word\Options
New Value=C:\MyData
Value Name=DOC-PATH

Key=Software\Microsoft\Office\9.0\Word\Options
New Value=C:\MyData\AutoSave
Value Name=AUTOSAVE-PATH
```

You can modify the registry entry in SMS Installer to change to the default directory that your organization has standardized on.

```
————-Begin Script
item: Edit Registry
  Total Keys=3
  item: Key
    Key=Software\Microsoft\Office\9.0\Excel\Options
  New Value=C:\MyData
  Value Name=DefaultPath
  Root=1
end
item: Key
  Key=Software\Microsoft\Office\9.0\Word\Options
```

```
    New Value=C:\MyData
    Value Name=DOC-PATH
    Root=1
end
item: Key
  Key=Software\Microsoft\Office\9.0\Word\Options
  New Value=C:\MyData\AutoSave
  Value Name=AUTOSAVE-PATH
  Root=1
 end
end
———-End Script
```

Troubleshooting High-Performance Video Problems

Do you think that you are having trouble with your high-performance video card? Several things will show evidence of this, including:

1. The PC locks up when you drag-and-drop files to the floppy drive.

2. SMS remote control causes the PC to lock up.

These items generally indicate a conflict with the high-performance video card you have installed and the PC BIOS (basic input/output system). To troubleshoot this problem, you can add an NT Registry key name called DisableUSWC (leave the class empty) to the following key:

LOCAL_MACHINE\SYSTEM\CurrentControlSet\Control\ GraphicsDrivers

```
———-Begin Script
item: Edit Registry
  Total Keys=1
  Key=SYSTEM\CurrentControlSet\Control\GraphicsDrivers\
DisableUSWC
  Root=66
  Data Type=5
end
———-End Script
```

Personalize the Title of Internet Explorer 4.0 or 5.0

Some organizations like to personalize the title of Internet Explorer 4.0 or 5.0. This script, once modified and compiled, can

be distributed to the end user to change the IE title. Change
Value Name to the IE window title you want to display.

```
--------Begin Script
item: Edit Registry
  Total Keys=1
  Key=SOFTWARE\Microsoft\Internet Explorer\Main
New Value=IE Title Change
  Value Name=Window Title
  Root=2
end
--------End Script
```

Setting a Company-Default Internet Explorer Search Page

It is wise to establish a company default Internet Explorer
search page. These reasons include standardizing across the organization, sending users to a corporate intranet search page, or
even controlling which search page is accessed based on Web
page advertisements or content that could lead to an unproduc-
tive employee. Modify the New Value line and insert the search
page you want IE to offer.

```
--------Begin Script
item: Edit Registry
  Total Keys=3
  item: Key
  =Software\Microsoft\Internet Explorer\Main
    New Value=http://www.ThisIsMySearchPage.com
Value Name=Search Bar
    Root=1
  end
  item: Key
    Key=Software\Microsoft\Internet Explorer\Main
New Value=http://www.ThisIsMySearchPage.com
    Value Name=Use Custom Search URL
    Root=1
  end
  item: Key
    Key=SOFTWARE\Microsoft\Internet Explorer\Search
New Value=http://www.ThisIsMySearchPage.com
    Value Name=SearchAssistant
    Root=2
  end
end
--------End Script
```

Adding a Legal Notice to the Windows NT Logon

Modifying a Win NT Registry value will allow a text box to be displayed every time a user logs in to a Win NT workstation or server. This text box could be used for a number of purposes: legal notice, organization policy, information on user default policies, or even a help desk phone number to call for help with logging into the PC. It also adds an additional layer of security when logging into the domain, because the text box must be acknowledged before the user continues to log in.

Modify New Value and the legal notice to display upon Windows NT logon. This field can support up to 256 characters.

```
————-Begin Script
item: Edit Registry
  Total Keys=1
  Key=SOFTWARE\Microsoft\Windows NT\CurrentVersion\Winlogon
  New Value=Enter LegalNoticeText Here
  Value Name=LegalNoticeText
  Root=2
end
————-End Script
```

Setting Windows NT with SP4 to Allow a Quick Reboot

With the release of Windows NT Service Pack 4, Microsoft included additional functionality to allow a quick reboot of a Windows NT computer. You can accomplish this by pressing SHIFT-CTRL-ALT-DELETE after you have modified this registry value.

```
————-Begin Script
item: Edit Registry
  Total Keys=1
  Key=SOFTWARE\Microsoft\Windows NT\CurrentVersion\Winlogon
  New Value=1
  Value Name=EnableQuickReboot
  Root=2
end
————-End Script
```

Adding a Password Expiration Warning for Network Users

If you've ever worked at a help desk, you know that remembering to change the network password is probably the most difficult task for the user population to accomplish. Use this script to add the PasswordExpiryWarning registry key to inform users how many days remain until their password expires (giving them an extra push to get it taken care of).

To do this, change `New Value` to indicate the number of days before the password expires to warn the user.

```
————Begin Script
item: Edit Registry
  Total Keys=1
  Key=SOFTWARE\Microsoft\Windows NT\CurrentVersion\Winlogon
  New Value=20
  Value Name=PasswordExpiryWarning
  Root=2
  Data Type=3
end
————End Script
```

Setting Programs to Run from the Registry

Your company may require certain apps to be run when the computer starts up. You may have deployed pieces of software that automatically start when the computer is booted. You probably place these items in the Startup folder. Unfortunately, placing the software in the Startup folder is a sure bet that the software will be easily removed should the user not like having the application or service starting when the computer is turned on.

To help prevent this, simply replace the `Pathname List` with your required application executable and the `Value` with the name of the application.

```
————Begin Script
item: Search for File
  Variable=APPLOC
  Pathname List=yourfile.exe
end
item: Set Variable
  Variable=APPNAME
  Value=Your App Name
end
item: Edit Registry
  Total Keys=1
  Key=Software\Microsoft\Windows\CurrentVersion\Run
New Value=%APPLOC%
  Value Name=%APPNAME%
```

```
   Root=1
end
————-End Script
```

Dynamic Remote Control Logging on
the SMS 2.0 Client

By default, logging for the Remote Control function is enabled, but it is not dynamic. The standard log is located at %windir%\MS\SMS\LOGS\RemCtrl.log.

Creating an additional registry value can enable a more robust and dynamic log to help troubleshoot remote control problems. The registry key is created at HKEY_LOCAL_MACHINE\Software\Microsoft\SMS\Client\Client Components\ Remote Control.

Insert a REG_DWORD value of LogToFile (case is important), and set it to 1. Because WUSER32 runs as a Windows NT service, the registry change takes place dynamically. On Windows 95 and 98 machines, the PC must be rebooted for the change to take effect.

The new log file is located at %windir%\MS\SMS\LOGS\ RemCtrl.log.

```
————-Begin Script
item: Edit Registry
  Total Keys=1
  Key=SOFTWARE\Microsoft\SMS\Client\Client
Components\Remote Control
  New Value=1
  Value Name=LogToFile
  Root=2
  Data Type=3
end
item: Check Configuration
  Flags=10000000
end
item: Edit INI File
  Pathname=%WIN%\SYSTEM.INI
  Settings=[386Enh]
  Settings=RESTART=
  Settings=
end
item: Add to SYSTEM.INI
  Device=RESTART=S
end
item: Else Statement
```

```
end
item: End Block
end
———-End Script
```

Removing the SMS 1.2 Client from Win 9x Workstations

Within some organizations, SMS may not be utilized completely. Users transfer from office to office, sometimes taking their PCs with them. If the user transfers to an office that does not currently utilize SMS, the client components that are installed cause the user to be prompted to continue looking for an SMS logon server.

At around 84 KB, the compiled script can be sent via e-mail to the user to remove the SMS client components. Or, you can use the utility for troubleshooting, quickly removing the client files and entries. The utility does the following:

1. Pulls the SMS client location from the SMS.INI

2. Deletes the SMS-specific files from the %WIN% directory

3. Deletes the \MS\SMS directory structure (except for the open files, PCM16R.DLL and PCMWIN16.BIN)

4. Removes the C:\MS\SMS\DATA\client.bat from the Autoexec.bat

5. Deletes the SMS.INI

6. Removes the SMS Load line from the WIN.INI

7. Comments-out the VUser.386 device from the System.ini

8. Removes the icons and the group associated with the SMS client

```
———-Begin Script
item: Search for File
  Variable=SMSINILOC
  Pathname List=SMS.INI
  Flags=00001000
end
item: Set File Attributes
  Pathname=%SMSINILOC%
end
item: Read INI Value
```

```
        Variable=SMSLOC
        Pathname=%SMSINILOC%
        Section=SMS
        Item=SMSPATH
    end
    item: Rename File/Directory
        Old Pathname=%SMSLOC%\PCM16R.DLL
        New Filename=PCM16R.BAK
    end
    item: Rename File/Directory
        Old Pathname=%SMSLOC%\PCMWIN16.EXE
        New Filename=PCMWIN16.BIN
    end
    item: Delete File
        Pathname=%SMSLOC%
        Flags=00001100
    end
    item: Delete File
        Pathname=%WIN%\smscfg.ini
    end
    item: Delete File
        Pathname=%WIN%\ISMIF16.DLL
    end
    item: Delete File
        Pathname=%WIN%\ISMIF32.DLL
    end
    item: Delete File
        Pathname=%WIN%\ACMEWKS_.DLL
    end
    item: Delete File
        Pathname=%SMSINILOC%
    end
    item: Add to AUTOEXEC.BAT
        New Text=REM *** SMS Client line removed from this
    position ***
        Search Text=C:\MS\SMS\DATA\client.bat
        Line Number=0
        Flags=00101110
    end
    item: Edit INI File
        Pathname=%WIN%\WIN.INI
        Settings=[windows]
        Settings=load=
        Settings=
    end
    item: Remove from SYSTEM.INI
        Device=device=C:\WINDOWS\VUser.386
    end
```

```
item: Delete File
  Pathname=%STARTMENUDIR%\Programs\SMS Client
  Flags=00001100
end
item: Delete File
  Pathname=%STARTMENUDIR2%\Programs\SMS Client
  Flags=00001100
end
————-End Script
```

Rescanning the SMS 1.2 Client

Sometimes, for a multitude of reasons, a PC will stop performing the regular SMS scans, usually because of a corrupt SMS ID or corrupt client files. The client PC shows in the SMS inventory. After a quick look you see the client files are installed on the PC, but the PC still has not inventoried in a long time. You also notice that when sending an RCW (Run Command on Workstation job), the package distribution fails.

Forget about trying to determine the cause for the corruption. It happens. Most often, it is a user problem. It results from a user shutting the PC down incorrectly, accidentally deleting files, or installing some strange "must-have" application the user found on the Internet. Even worse, sometimes a technical support staff person in another office who is uneducated in the ways of SMS causes it. Forgive them and move on.

The script does the following:

1. Searches for SMS.INI

2. Pulls logon server from the SMS.INI and places it in a variable

3. Checks for an existing network connection (exits if none available)

4. If the OS is Windows 95, detects the PNP (primary network provider) from the registry

   a. If the PNP is NetWare, runs the RUNSMS.BAT from F:\SMS\LOGON.SRV

   b. If the PNP is Microsoft, maps a drive to Q:\%LOGON-SERVER%\SMS_SHR and runs RUNSMS.BAT

5. If the OS is WinNT, maps a drive to Q:\%LOGON-SERVER%\SMS_SHR and runs RUNSMS.CMD

6. After the scans are complete, deletes the drive mapping.

```
————Begin Script
item: Open/Close INSTALL.LOG
end
item: Check Disk Space
  Component=COMPONENTS
end
item: Wizard Block
  Direction Variable=DIRECTION
  Display Variable=DISPLAY
  Bitmap Pathname=E:\packages\smsclnt\check2.bmp
  X Position=0
  Y Position=0
  Filler Color=0
  Flags=00000010
end
item: Custom Dialog Set
  Name=Hardware/Software Scan
  Display Variable=DISPLAY
  item: Dialog
    Title English=SMS: Hardware/Software Scan
    Width=150
    Height=125
    Font Name=Helv
    Font Size=8
    item: Static
      Rectangle=21 31 142 83
      Create Flags=01010000000000000000000000000000
      Text English=This program will scan your computer's
hardware and software utilizing Microsoft Systems Manage-
ment Server. The scan will take no longer than 15 seconds.
Click Next to continue.
    end
    item: Push Button
      Rectangle=25 89 70 103
      Variable=DIRECTION
      Action=3
      Create Flags=01010000000000010000000000000000
      Text English=&Cancel
    end
    item: Push Button
      Rectangle=88 89 133 104
      Variable=DIRECTION
      Value=N
      Create Flags=01010000000000010000000000000001
      Text Danish=&Nëste >
      Text Dutch=&Volgende >
```

```
      Text English=&Next >
      Text Finnish=&Seuraava >
      Text French=&Suivant >
      Text German=&Weiter >
      Text Italian=&Avanti >
      Text Norwegian=&Neste >
      Text Portuguese=&Avanáar >
      Text Spanish=&Siguiente >
      Text Swedish=&NÑsta >
    end
    item: Static
      Rectangle=26 4 141 26
      Create Flags=0101000000000000000000000000000000
      Flags=0000000000000001
      Name=Georgia
      Font Style=-13 0 0 0 700 255 0 0 0 3 2 1 18
      Text English=Microsoft Systems Management Server
     end
   end
end
item: Search for File
  Variable=SMSINILOC
  Pathname List=SMS.INI
  Flags=00001000
end
item: Read INI Value
  Variable=LOGONSERVER
  Pathname=%SMSINILOC%
  Section=SERVERS
  Item=CurrentLogonServer
end
item: Check if File/Dir Exists
  Pathname=F:\
  Message English=This PC is not currently logged into the
network. You must be correctly logged into the network for
this scan to run. Verify the physical network connections,
restart your PC, and try logging in again. Then, rerun this
program. This program will now exit.
  Title English=Network Check
  Flags=00000011
end
item: End Block
end
item: Check Configuration
  Flags=10111001
end
item: Get Registry Key Value
  Variable=95NETPROVIDER
```

```
      Key=Network\Logon
      Value Name=PrimaryProvider
      Flags=00000100
   end
   item: If/While Statement
      Variable=95NETPROVIDER
      Value=NetWare
      Flags=00000100
   end
   item: Execute Program
      Pathname=F:\SMS\LOGON.SRV\RUNSMS.BAT
      Flags=00000010
   end
   item: Else Statement
   end
   item: Execute Program
      Pathname=NET
      Command Line=USE Q: \\%LOGONSERVER%\SMS_SHR
      Flags=00000010
   end
   item: Execute Program
      Pathname=Q:\RUNSMS.BAT
      Flags=00000010
   end
   item: Execute Program
      Pathname=NET
      Command Line=USE Q: /DELETE
      Flags=00000010
   end
   item: End Block
   end
   item: End Block
   end
   item: Check Configuration
      Flags=10100000
   end
   item: Execute Program
      Pathname=NET
      Command Line=USE Q: \\%LOGONSERVER%\SMS_SHR
      Flags=00000010
   end
   item: Execute Program
      Pathname=Q:\RUNSMS.CMD
      Flags=00000010
   end
   item: Execute Program
      Pathname=NET
      Command Line=USE Q: /DELETE
      Flags=00000010
```

```
end
item: End Block
end
item: Wizard Block
  Direction Variable=DIRECTION
  Display Variable=DISPLAY
  X Position=0
  Y Position=0
  Filler Color=0
  Flags=00000010
end
item: Custom Dialog Set
  Name=Hardware/Software Scan
  Display Variable=DISPLAY
item: Dialog
  Title English=SMS: Hardware/Software Scan
  Width=150
  Height=120
  Font Name=Helv
  Font Size=8
  item: Push Button
    Control Name=Finished
    Rectangle=97 84 132 99
    Variable=DIRECTION
    Value=N
    Create Flags=01010000000000010000000000000001
    Text English=&Finish
  end
  item: Static
    Rectangle=26 28 131 74
    Create Flags=01010000000000000000000000000000
    Text English=The Hardware/Software of this PC has
completed successfully. To complete, click the Finish
button.
  end
  item: Static
    Rectangle=31 2 145 24
    Create Flags=01010000000000000000000000000000
    Flags=0000000000000001
    Name=Georgia
    Font Style=-24 0 0 0 700 255 0 0 0 3 2 1 18
    Text English=Scan Complete!
  end
  item: Static
    Rectangle=0 0 19 19
    Action=2
    Create Flags=01010000000000000000000000001011
    Pathname English=E:\packages\smsclnt\check2.bmp
  end
```

```
   end
end
item: End Block
end
———-End Script
```

Disabling the PCM Countdown Timer

If an SMS 1.2 distribution is set to mandatory, the Package Command Manager displays a countdown timer that waits 5 minutes before the mandatory package installation starts. You can disable the countdown timer and force the package to start immediately by using the following script:

```
———-Begin Script
item: Set Variable
  Variable=CDRIVE
  Value=C:
end
item: Edit INI File
  Pathname=%WIN%\SYSTEM.INI
  Settings=[386Enh]
  Settings=
  Settings=RESTART=
  Settings=
end
item: Set File Attributes
  Pathname=%CDRIVE%\SMS.INI
end
item: Edit INI File
  Pathname=%CDRIVE%\SMS.INI
  Settings=[Local]
  Settings=
  Settings=DisablePCMCountdown=TRUE
  Settings=
end
item: Set File Attributes
  Pathname=%CDRIVE%\SMS.INI
  Flags=00000011
end
item: Edit INI File
  Pathname=%WIN%\SYSTEM.INI
  Settings=[386Enh]
  Settings=
  Settings=RESTART=S
  Settings=
end
———-End Script
```

Windows 95 Spool32 Errors

In Win 9x, a common printing problem is the Spool32 error. Evidence of this can be seen in the following error messages when printing on a network:

```
SPOOL32 caused a General Protection Fault in module Ker-
nel32.dll at <address>.
```

or:

```
SPOOL32 caused an Invalid Page Fault in module Kernel32.dll
at <address>.
```

or:

```
SPOOL32 caused a Stack Fault in module Kernel32.dll at
<address>.
```

A clever solution to help alleviate this error is to load the Spool32.exe command into memory when the OS loads. Based on Microsoft's Knowledge Base Article Q191949, this SMS Installer script places the command C:\WINDOWS\SPOOL32.EXE in the RUN line of the WIN.INI.

```
———-Begin Script
item: Edit INI File
  Pathname=%WIN%\WIN.INI
  Settings=[windows]
  Settings=load=C:\WINDOWS\SYSTEM\SPOOL32.EXE
  Settings=
end
item: Add to SYSTEM.INI
  Device=RESTART=S
end
———-End Script
```

Setting the Desktop Icons Back to Default

Users will sometimes change the default icons on their desktop to other local icons or even pictures downloaded from the Internet. This script sets all the icons back to their default.

```
———-Begin Script
item: Edit INI File
  Pathname=%WIN%\SYSTEM.INI
  Settings=[386Enh]
  Settings=
  Settings=RESTART=
  Settings=
```

```
end
item: Edit Registry
  Total Keys=6
  item: Key
    Key=CLSID\{20D04FE0-3AEA-1069-A2D8-
08002B30309D}\DefaultIcon
    New Value=%WIN%\explorer.exe,0
  end
  item: Key
    Key=CLSID\{208D2C60-3AEA-1069-A2D7-
08002B30309D}\DefaultIcon
    New Value=%SYS32%\shell32.dll,17
  end
  item: Key
   ·Key=CLSID\{645FF040-5081-101B-9F08-
00AA002F954E}\DefaultIcon
    New Value=%SYS32%\shell32.dll,31
  end
  item: Key
    Key=CLSID\{645FF040-5081-101B-9F08-
00AA002F954E}\DefaultIcon
    New Value=%SYS32%\shell32.dll,31
Value Name=Empty
  end
  item: Key
    Key=CLSID\{645FF040-5081-101B-9F08-
00AA002F954E}\DefaultIcon
    New Value=%SYS32%\shell32.dll,32
Value Name=Full
  end
  item: Key
    Key=CLSID\{85BBD920-42A0-1069-A2E4-
08002B30309D}\DefaultIcon
    New Value=%SYS32%\syncui.dll,0
  end
end
item: Add to SYSTEM.INI
  Device=RESTART=S
end
———-End Script
```

Associating Unknown File Types with Notepad

This script associates files with no extension to open in Windows Notepad.

```
———-Begin Script
item: Edit Registry
  Total Keys=1
```

```
Key=Unknown\shell\open\command
New Value=notepad.exe %1
Data Type=1
end
————-End Script
```

Resetting the License Logging Service

SMS uses a client license every time it issues a unique SMS ID. Due to the constant upgrading to new computers and reimaging PCs (thereby assigning new SMS IDS), the Windows NT License Service can run out of licenses. When this happens, the License Service reports information in the Windows NT Event Log. Because it reports this information very frequently, the SMS server performance can degrade. You can reset the License Logging Service by using the following script:

```
————-Begin Script
item: Start/Stop Service
  Service Name=LICENSE LOGGING SERVICE
  Flags=00000001
end
item: Delete File
  Pathname=%SYS32%\CPL.CFG
end
item: Delete File
  Pathname=%SYS32%\LLS\LLSMAP.LLS
end
item: Delete File
  Pathname=%SYS32%\LLS\LLSUSER.LLS
end
item: Start/Stop Service
  Service Name=LICENSE LOGGING SERVICE
end
————-End Script
```

Shutting Down Windows NT

When NT shuts down, it sends shutdown requests to all running processes. Most applications have no trouble honoring the requests. Some older 16-bit apps, running in the virtual DOS machine (VDM), often hang and will not shut down properly. When this happens, NT prompts you with a dialog box asking if you want to kill the task, wait for the task, or cancel the shutdown. By modifying the registry, the process can be automated.

You can force NT to kill all running processes automatically, resulting in a more efficient, quicker shutdown. The following registry key is modified:

HKEY_CURRENT_USER\Control Panel\Desktop\AutoEndTasks
Value: 1

The script is as follows:

```
————-Begin Script
item: Edit Registry
  Total Keys=2
  item: Key
    Key=Control Panel\Desktop
    New Value=1
    Value Name=AutoEndTasks
    Root=1
  end
  item: Key
    Key=S-1-5-21-11087255-1280516441-903097961-1025\Control
Panel\Desktop
    New Value=1
    Value Name=AutoEndTasks
    Root=3
  end
end
————-End Script
```

Don't Display Last Logged-on Username

By default, Windows NT places the name of the last user to log on in the Username field of the Logon dialog box. While this is a convenience for logging into a system, it can be a potential security risk. The following utility keeps the username from appearing in the Logon dialog box:

```
————-Begin Script
item: Edit Registry
  Total Keys=1
  Key=SOFTWARE\Microsoft\Windows NT\CurrentVersion\Winlogon
  New Value=1
  Value Name=DontDisplayLastUserName
  Root=2
end
————-End Script
```

Turning On/Off Verbose SMS 2.0 Client Logging

Client logging is an indispensable tool when diagnosing SMS 2.0 client problems. Microsoft included a series of utilities on the SMS 2.0 CD in the SUPPORT directory. One of these utilities allows you to turn verbose logging on at the client and set the client log's threshold to 5 MB. The client logging, by default, captures a considerable amount of data. Enabling the increased logging can help pinpoint the difficulty when normal logging fails to capture the problem. See Table 6-1 for a list of the client logs.

It is important to remember to turn off the additional client logging after you have diagnosed the problem. The amount of information that is input into the log files is vast, taking up valuable processor time on the client and causing a noticeable performance loss.   **Note**

The following script turns on the verbose logging:

```
————Begin Script
item: Edit Registry
  Total Keys=3
  item: Key
    Key=SOFTWARE\Microsoft\NAL\Logging
    New Value=7
    Value Name=Verbosity
    Root=2
    Data Type=3
  end
  item: Key
    Key=SOFTWARE\Microsoft\NAL\Logging
    New Value=3
    Value Name=Log To
    Root=2
    Data Type=3
  end
  item: Key
    Key=SOFTWARE\Microsoft\SMS\Client\Configuration\Client
Properties
    New Value=5000
    Value Name=Log File Size for Debugging
    Root=2
    Data Type=3
  end
```

```
end
———-End Script
```

The following script turns off verbose logging:

```
———-Begin Script
item: Edit Registry
  Total Keys=1
  Key=SOFTWARE\Microsoft\NAL\Logging
  New Value=1
  Value Name=Verbosity
  Root=2
  Data Type=3
end
———-End Script
```

Mapping a Network Drive

Since you can use SMS Installer to execute external commands, it is easy to use SMS Installer to map network drives using the old standby Windows NT command NET.EXE.

This portion of script maps a permanent network drive:

```
———-Begin Script
item: Execute Program
  Pathname=%sys32%\net.exe
  Command Line=use z: \\server\share /persistent:yes
  Flags=00000110
end
———-End Script
```

This portion will temporarily map a network drive and then delete it, allowing you to execute some network commands in between:

```
———-Begin Script
item: Execute Program
  Pathname=%sys32%\net.exe
  Command Line=use z: \\server\share
  Flags=00000110
end
item: Execute Program
  Pathname=%sys32%\net.exe
  Command Line=use z: /delete
  Flags=00000110
end
———-End Script
```

Table 6-1   *Client logs*

Thread	Log File
Advertised Programs Manager Win 9x and Win NT)	\%winroot%\MS\SMS\Logs\ SMSapm32.log
CCIM32 Client Maintenance (32-bit client)	%windir%\MS\SMS\Logs\Ccim32.log
Client Component Installation Manager	%windir%\MS\SMS\Logs\Ccim32.log
Client Service (CliSvcl)	%windir%\MS\SMS\Logs\Clisvc.log
Copy Queue	%windir%\MxS\SMS\Logs\ Cqmgr32.log
Core Client Installation Process (16-bit client)	MS\SMS\Logs\Clicore.log \
	\MS\SMS\Logs\Install.log
Core Client Installation Process (32-bit client)	\MS\SMS\Logs\Clicore.log
Hardware Inventory Agent	%windir%\MS\SMS\Logs\Hinv32.log
Individual Component Installation	\MS\SMS\Logs\individual logs
Installing Core Component (32-bit client)	\MS\SMS\Logs\Ccim32.log
Installing Optional Components (16-bit client)	\MS\SMS\Logs\Cliex16.log
Installing Optional Components (32-bit client)	\MS\SMS\Logs\Ccim32.log \MS\SMS\Logs\SMSapm32.log
Launch16 Process (16-bit client)	\MS\SMS\Logs\Launch16.log
Launch32 Process (32-bit client)	\MS\SMS\Logs\Launch32.log
License Metering Client Component	%windir%\MS\SMS\Logs\Liccli.log

Table 6-1 *Client logs (Continued).*

Thread	Log File
Remote Control Client Component	%windir%\MS\SMS\Logs\Remctrl.log
SMSBoot1/Boot16wn (16-bit client)	\MS\SMS\Logs\WN_logon.log
SMSBoot1/Boot32WN (32-bit client)	\MS\SMS\Logs\WN_logon.log
Software Inventory Agent	%windir%\MS\SMS\Logs\Sinv32.log
Windows System Offer Data Provider (Win 9x and Win NT)	\%winroot%\MS\SMS\Logs\ Odpsys32.log
Windows User Group Offer Data Provider (Win 9x)	\%winroot%\MS\SMS\Logs\ Odpwnt9x.log
Windows User Group Offer Data Provider (Win NT)	\%winroot%\MS\SMS\Logs\ Odpwnt32.log
Windows User Offer Data Provider (Win 9x)	\%winroot%\MS\SMS\Logs\ Odpusr9x.log
Windows User Offer Data Provider (Win NT)	\%winroot%\MS\SMS\Logs\ Odpusr32.log

Removing the Overlay on Shortcuts

The Overlay utility removes the arrow on the program short-cuts. It modifies two registry values:

For Win shortcuts:

```
HKEY_LOCAL_MACHINE\SOFTWARE\Classes\lnkfile
Value Name=IsShortcut
```

For CMD shortcuts:

```
HKEY_LOCAL_MACHINE\SOFTWARE\Classes\piffile
Value Name=IsShortcut
```

The script is as follows:

```
————-Begin Script
item: Edit Registry
  Total Keys=2
  item: Key
    Key=SOFTWARE\Classes\lnkfile
    Value Name=IsShortcut
    Root=194
  end
  item: Key
    Key=SOFTWARE\Classes\piffile
    Value Name=IsShortcut
    Root=194
  end
end
————-End Script
```

Stopping SMS 2.0 Remote Control

Occasionally, to help with troubleshooting client problems, you may want to turn off the Remote Control Agent. On Windows NT clients, you just shut down the Wuser32 service. On Windows 95 and Windows 98 clients, you have to run the following command line:

```
%WINDIR%\MS\SMS\Clicomp\RemCtrl\WUSER32.EXE /X
```

To help with this, following is the StopRC utility for download. Written with SMS Installer, the utility determines the OS and applies the appropriate method listed above. The utility can be sent to the PC via an SMS package, e-mailed, or installed on the PC at configuration time.

```
————-Begin Script
item: Display Message
  Title English=Shutting down Remote Control Agent...
  Text English=Click OK to Continue.
  Flags=00000100
end
item: Check Configuration
  Flags=10100000
end
item: Start/Stop Service
  Service Name=Wuser32
  Flags=00000001
end
item: End Block
end
```

```
item: Check Configuration
  Flags=10000000
end
item: Execute Program
  Pathname=%WIN%\MS\SMS\CLICOMP\REMCTRL\WUSER32.EXE
  Command Line=/X
  Flags=00000110
end
item: End Block
end
item: Display Message
  Title English=Shutdown complete!
  Text English=Click OK to finish.
  Flags=00001000
end
————-End Script
```

Starting SMS 2.0 Remote Control

Occasionally, to help with troubleshooting client problems, you may want to turn off the Remote Control Agent. See the previous section, "Stopping SMS 2.0 Remote Control," for a utility to do this.

After the troubleshooting you may want to restart the Remote Control Agent. Or you may want to start the Remote Control Agent if you have your SMS site set not to load the component automatically without manual input from the user.

On Windows NT clients, you just restart the Wuser32 service. On Windows 95 and Windows 98 clients, you have to run the following command line:

```
%WINDIR%\MS\SMS\Clicomp\RemCtrl\WUSER32.EXE
```

To help with this, following is the StartRC utility for download. Written with SMS Installer, the utility determines the OS and applies the appropriate method listed above. The utility can be sent to the PC via an SMS package, e-mailed, or installed on the PC at configuration time.

```
————-Begin Script
item: Display Message
  Title English=Starting the Remote Control Agent...
  Text English=Click OK to Continue.
  Flags=00000100
end
```

```
item: Check Configuration
  Flags=10100000
end
item: Start/Stop Service
  Service Name=Wuser32
end
item: End Block
end
item: Check Configuration
  Flags=10000000
end
item: Execute Program
  Pathname=%WIN%\MS\SMS\CLICOMP\REMCTRL\WUSER32.EXE
  Flags=00000110
end
item: End Block
end
item: Display Message
  Title English=Remote Control Restarted!
  Text English=Click OK to finish.
  Flags=00001000
end
———-End Script
```

Preloading SMS 2.0 Client Components

Some of the SMS 2.0 core client components can be loaded on the computer even before the computer has been inventoried. The initial client components are about 12 MB in size, and preloading them saves a tremendous amount of network bandwidth the first time the client is inventoried. Computers can be "imaged" with the core components when you are distributing computers to new users. The following script contains the preinstallable file list:

```
———-Begin Script
item: Get Environment Variable
  Variable=WINDIR
  Environment=WINDIR
  Default=c:\windows
end
item: Create Directory
  Pathname=%WINDIR%\MS\SMS\BIN
end
item: Check Configuration
  Flags=10111010
end
item: Install File
```

```
   Source=%SMSLOGON%\%PROCESSOR%.BIN\clicore.exe
   Destination=%WINDIR%\MS\SMS\CORE\BIN\clicore.exe
   Description English=Client infrastructure core components
   Flags=0000000000000010
end
item: Install File
   Source=%SMSLOGON%\%PROCESSOR%.BIN\slwnt32.exe
   Destination=%WINDIR%\MS\SMS\CORE\BIN\slownet.exe
   Description English=Slow network detection component
   Flags=0000000000000010
end
item: Install File
   Source=%SMSLOGON%\%PROCESSOR%.BIN\boot32wn.exe
   Destination=%WINDIR%\MS\SMS\CORE\BIN\boot32wn.exe
   Description English=Client infrastructure bootstrap
components
   Flags=0000000000000010
end
item: Install File
   Source=%SMSLOGON%\%PROCESSOR%.BIN\smsboot1.exe
   Destination=%WINDIR%\MS\SMS\CORE\BIN\smsboot1.exe
   Description English=Client infrastructure bootstrap
components
   Flags=0000000000000010
end
item: Install File
   Source=%SMSLOGON%\%PROCESSOR%.BIN\00000409\smsman.exe
   Destination=%WINDIR%\MS\SMS\CORE\BIN\00000409\smsman.exe
   Description English=Manual installation component
   Flags=0000000000000010
end
item: Else Statement
end
item: Check Configuration
   Flags=10011010
end
item: Install File
   Source=%SMSLOGON%\%PROCESSOR%.BIN\clicor16.exe
   Destination=%WINDIR%\MS\SMS\CORE\BIN\clicor16.exe
   Description English=Client infrastructure core components
   Flags=0000000000000010
end
item: Install File
   Source=%SMSLOGON%\%PROCESSOR%.BIN\slwnt16.exe
   Destination=%WINDIR%\MS\SMS\CORE\BIN\slownet.exe
   Description English=Slow network detection component
   Flags=0000000000000010
end
```

```
item: Install File
  Source=%SMSLOGON%\%PROCESSOR%.BIN\boot16wn.exe
  Destination=%WINDIR%\MS\SMS\CORE\BIN\boot16wn.exe
  Description English=Client infrastructure bootstrap
components
  Flags=0000000000000010
end
item: Install File
  Source=%SMSLOGON%\%PROCESSOR%.BIN\smsboot1.exe
  Destination=%WINDIR%\MS\SMS\CORE\BIN\smsboot1.exe
  Description English=Client infrastructure bootstrap
components
  Flags=0000000000000010
end
item: Install File
  Source=%SMSLOGON%\%PROCESSOR%.BIN\00000409\smsman16.exe
  Destination=%WINDIR%\MS\SMS\CORE\BIN\00000409\
smsman16.exe
  Description English=Manual installation component
  Flags=0000000000000010
end
item: End Block
end
item: End Block
end
─────-End Script
```

Resetting the SMS 1.2 Client

With the advent of drive imaging for deployment, a critical issue was created for those images that included the SMS.ini file. The SMS.ini was duplicated around the enterprise, creating an issue with Microsoft SMS and duplicate SMS IDs. SMS allocates a unique ID for each client that SMS software is installed on. The same ID on multiple machines can confuse SMS because it views each of those computers as the same computer.

The attempt to deploy the software can fail on the computers with the same SMS ID, because once a program is installed successfully on an ID, the client reports back that the distribution was successful, and it goes no further. Sending to multiple clients fails because SMS believes the software has installed correctly, and it does not see past the original successful deployment.

In SMS Service Pack 4, Microsoft has included utilities to address the duplicate SMS ID at the server or SQL database level. This is fine as long as each client computer can be visited person-

ally and the SMS ID removed by a support person. When the
client logs back in to the network the next time, it will be scanned
by SMS and a good ID will be allocated. For enterprise sites,
where the client population is very large, it is almost impossible
to visit each and every PC and remove the SMS.ini file. You could
send an e-mail or voice mail and have the user of the PC change
the attribute on the SMS.ini file and have them delete the file
manually. But what technical support person really wants the user
to know where the SMS.ini file exists and how to delete it?

I believe every organization that utilizes SMS and has done
some drive imaging has experienced this problem. In fact, our
organization has experienced this problem and continues to experience it from time to time. We have created a script using the
SMS Installer that finds the SMS.INI, changes the attribute, and
deletes it. Compiled, it is very small, making it easy to distribute
to the user via e-mail.

Before sending the compiled script to users, you must first
know which users are affected. As mentioned, SMS Service Pack
4 includes utilities that assist in duplicate IDs on the server side.
When run, one of the utilities, SMSIDDUP, will produce a log listing the users who are affected by duplicated IDs.

The compiled script presents the user with a Start and Finish
interface, much like any other utility. The script searches for the
SMS.ID, places the location in a variable, and then deletes the
variable. Fully compiled, the utility is about 90 KB, making it an
easy e-mail attachment for most electronic post offices to handle.

```
————-Begin Script
item: Wizard Block
  Direction Variable=DIRECTION
  Display Variable=DISPLAY
  X Position=0
  Y Position=0
  Filler Color=0
end
item: Custom Dialog Set
  Name=Inventory Reset
  Display Variable=DISPLAY
  item: Dialog
    Title English=SMS Reset
    Width=150
    Height=114
```

```
    Font Name=Helv
    Font Size=8
    item: Push Button
      Rectangle=37 74 82 88
      Variable=DIRECTION
      Action=3
      Create Flags=01010000000000010000000000000000
      Text English=&Cancel
    end
    item: Push Button
      Rectangle=93 74 138 89
      Variable=DIRECTION
      Value=N
      Create Flags=01010000000000010000000000000001
      Text Danish=&Nëste >
      Text Dutch=&Volgende >
      Text English=&Next >
      Text Finnish=&Seuraava >
      Text French=&Suivant >
      Text German=&Weiter >
      Text Italian=&Avanti >
      Text Norwegian=&Neste >
      Text Portuguese=&Avanáar >
      Text Spanish=&Siguiente >
      Text Swedish=&NÑsta >
    end
    item: Static
      Rectangle=39 25 132 43
      Create Flags=01010000000000000000000000000000
      Text English=The inventory information of this PC is
invalid and it must be reset.
    end
    item: Static
      Rectangle=39 57 128 67
      Create Flags=01010000000000000000000000000000
      Text English=Please click NEXT to continue...
    end
    item: Static
      Rectangle=5 5 27 29
      Action=2
      Create Flags=01010000000000000000000000001011
      Pathname English=E:\packages\delini\laptop.bmp
    end
    item: Static
      Rectangle=40 5 135 23
      Create Flags=01010000000000000000000000000000
      Flags=0000000000000001
      Name=Georgia
      Font Style=-21 0 0 0 700 255 0 0 0 3 2 1 18
```

```
            Text English=Resetting SMS
          end
        end
    end
    item: Search for File
      Variable=SMSINILOC
      Pathname List=SMS.INI
      Flags=00001000
    end
    item: Set File Attributes
      Pathname=%SMSINILOC%
      Flags=00010000
    end
    item: Delete File
      Pathname=%SMSINILOC%
    end
    item: End Block
    end
    item: Wizard Block
      Direction Variable=DIRECTION
      Display Variable=DISPLAY
      X Position=0
      Y Position=0
      Filler Color=0
    end
    item: Custom Dialog Set
      Name=Finished
      Display Variable=DISPLAY
      item: Dialog
        Title English=Finished
        Width=150
        Height=131
        Font Name=Helv
        Font Size=8
        item: Push Button
          Control Name=Finished
          Rectangle=101 94 136 109
          Variable=DIRECTION
          Value=N
          Create Flags=01010000000000010000000000000001
          Text English=&Finish
        end
        item: Static
          Rectangle=25 31 138 71
          Create Flags=01010000000000000000000000000000
          Text English=This PC has been reset. The next
time the PC is logged into the network, the hardware and
software scans will run successfully.
        end
```

```
      item: Static
        Rectangle=58 80 134 94
        Create Flags=01010000000000000000000000000000
        Text English=Click Finish to continue.
      end
      item: Static
        Rectangle=3 4 25 28
        Action=2
        Create Flags=01010000000000000000000000001011
        Pathname English=E:\packages\delini\laptop.bmp
      end
      item: Static
        Rectangle=27 5 141 25
        Create Flags=01010000000000000000000000000000
        Flags=0000000000000001
        Name=Georgia
        Font Style=-24 0 0 0 700 255 0 0 0 3 2 1 18
        Text English=Reset Complete!
      end
    end
  end
end
item: End Block
end
————-End Script
```

Turning Numlock on at Bootup

Some PCs running Windows NT SP3 will not turn on the numlock at bootup, even though the system BIOS option has been set. This utility makes a Windows NT Registry change that forces NT to turn the numlock on. It can be distributed via SMS with the /s (silent switch) when a user complains about this problem.

Upgrading to Windows NT SP4 also fixes this problem.   **Note**

```
————-Begin Script
item: Edit Registry
  Total Keys=2
  item: Key
    Key=Control Panel\Keyboard
    New Value=2
    Value Name=InitialKeyboardIndicators
    Root=1
  end
  item: Key
    Key=S-1-5-21-11087255-1280516441-903097961-1025\Control
Panel\Keyboard
    New Value=2
```

```
        Value Name=InitialKeyboardIndicators
        Root=3
    end
end
────-End Script
```

Turning CD AutoRun On and Off

The AutoRun feature of Win NT is a nice feature, but it can be annoying at times. You can turn the feature on or off with a registry modification.

The registry key is HKEY_LOCAL_MACHINE\SYSTEM\CurrentControlSet\Services\Cdrom. The value is Autorun.

A string of 0 turns off the AutoRun feature, while a string of 1 turns it on.

Note The PC must be restarted for the change to take effect. The SMS Installer scripts below are scripted to restart the PC.

Turning AutoRun Off:

```
────-Begin Script
item: Edit INI File
  Pathname=%WIN%\SYSTEM.INI
  Settings=[386Enh]
  Settings=RESTART=
  Settings=
end
item: Edit Registry
  Total Keys=1
  Key=SYSTEM\CurrentControlSet\Services\Cdrom
  New Value=0
  Value Name=Autorun
  Root=2
  Data Type=3
end
item: Add to SYSTEM.INI
  Device=RESTART=S
end
────-End Script
```

Turning AutoRun On:

```
────-Begin Script
item: Edit INI File
  Pathname=%WIN%\SYSTEM.INI
```

```
   Settings=[386Enh]
   Settings=RESTART=
   Settings=
end
item: Edit Registry
   Total Keys=1
   Key=SYSTEM\CurrentControlSet\Services\Cdrom
   New Value=1
   Value Name=Autorun
   Root=2
   Data Type=3
end
item: Add to SYSTEM.INI
   Device=RESTART=S
end
———-End Script
```

Turn Off RAS Password Saving

NT's Dial-Up Networking (DUN) has a convenient setting that allows users to save their dial-in password. While this is convenient for the user, it poses a large security risk to the network. The RASPass utility adds a registry key to the NT workstation that disables the saving of RAS passwords.

The registry key is HKEY_LOCAL_MACHINE\SYSTEM\ CurrentControlSet\Services\RasMan\Parameters. The value added is DisableSavePassword.

Send or advertise the utility via SMS with the /s (silent switch).

```
———-Begin Script
item: Edit Registry
   Total Keys=1
   Key=SYSTEM\CurrentControlSet\Services\RasMan\Parameters
   New Value=0
   Value Name=DisableSavePassword
   Root=2
   Data Type=3
end
———-End Script
```

Checking Video Configuration

Some applications require certain video settings before an installation. If doing a repackage of an application, SMS Installer will not check for these requirements. You will need to manually script a section of script to handle this requirement.

For 1024 × 768 or better:

```
-------Begin Script
item: Check Configuration
  Flags=00001100
end
item: Display Message
  Title English=Video mode not supported...
  Text English=This computer does not have the necessary
video requirements to install and run this program. Please
upgrade your computer's video settings and rerun the
installation.
  Flags=00001000
end
item: Exit Installation
end
item: Else Statement
end
-------End Script
```

For 800 × 600 or better:

```
-------Begin Script
item: Check Configuration
  Flags=00001011
end
item: Display Message
  Title English=Video mode not supported...
  Text English=This computer does not have the necessary
video requirements to install and run this program. Please
upgrade your computer's video settings and rerun the
installation.
  Flags=00001000
end
item: Exit Installation
end
item: Else Statement
end
-------End Script
```

Disabling the Windows NT Logoff Button

The following script disables the Logoff button on the Windows Security dialog box that displays when Ctl-Alt-Delete is pressed. The registry root key is HKEY_CURRENT_USER.

```
-------Begin Script
item: Edit Registry
  Total Keys=1
```

```
Key=Software\Microsoft\Windows
New Value=1
Value Name=NoLogoff
Root=1
Data Type=3
end
————-End Script
```

Changing the Registry Limit Size

The registry size is set by default when Windows NT is installed. Whenever the registry is modified, the size increases. It may be critical to increase the size of the registry limit to accommodate these modifications. If the registry reaches or tries to go beyond the set limit, the registry could become corrupt. The value for the RegistrySizeLimit in the script below is set for 28 MB, or 1900000 in hex.

```
————-Begin Script
item: Edit Registry
  Total Keys=1
  Key=SYSTEM\CurrentControlSet\Control
  New Value=1900000
  Value Name=RegistrySizeLimit
  Root=2
  Data Type=3
end
————-End Script
```

Viewing Super Hidden Files in Windows 2000

Windows 2000 incorporates a new security type on certain OS files. These files are called *super hidden files*. Even if the option is turned on to view hidden files, these will remain hidden. These are critical files, such as the Windows 2000 OS recovery information. The super hidden files can be viewed by modifying the registry.

```
————-Begin Script
item: Edit Registry
  Total Keys=1
  Key=SOFTWARE\Microsoft\Windows\CurrentVersion\Explorer
  New Value=1
  Value Name=ShowSuperHidden
  Root=2
  Data Type=3
end
————-End Script
```

Determining Windows NT OS Type

When scripting with SMS Installer, you may be required to determine if the Windows NT target machine is a workstation or a server to install specific components for each within the same script. The Windows NT registry key HKEY_LOCAL_ MACHINE\System\CurrentControlSet\Control\ProductOptions holds the ProductType value. If the computer has Windows NT Workstation, the value will be WinNT. If the computer is a Windows NT Server, the value will be LanmanNT. This information can be used to perform If/Then logic statements to separate installation components on the different OS types.

The following script retrieves this value, places it into the OSTYPE variable, and writes the information to a TEST.TXT file in the root directory of the C: drive for testing:

```
————-Begin Script
item: Set Variable
  Variable=ROOT
  Value=C:\
end
item: Check Disk Space
end
item: Get Registry Key Value
  Variable=OSTYPE
  Key=HKEY_LOCAL_MACHINE\System\CurrentControlSet\Control\
ProductOptions
  Default=WinNT
  Value Name=ProductType
  Flags=00000100
end
item: If/While Statement
  Variable=OSTYPE
  Value=WinNT
end
item: Insert Line into Text File
  Pathname=%ROOT%TEST.TXT
  New Text=%OSTYPE%
  Line Number=0
end
item: Else Statement
end
item: Insert Line into Text File
  Pathname=%ROOT%TEST.TXT
  New Text=%OSTYPE%
```

```
  Line Number=0
end
item: End Block
end
——–End Script
```

Shutting Down without Logging On

Windows NT by default disables the Shut Down button on the logon screen. Setting a registry key value can turn this on

Key:

HKEY_LOCAL_MACHINE\SOFTWARE\Microsoft\Windows NT\CurrentVersion\Winlogon.

Value: ShutdownWithoutLogon

Type: REG_SZ

Data: 0 = Off, 1 = On

```
——–Begin Script
item: Edit Registry
  Total Keys=1
  Key=SOFTWARE\Microsoft\Windows NT\CurrentVersion\
Winlogon
  New Value=1
  Value Name=ShutdownWithoutLogon
  Root=2
end
——–End Script
```

Turning Off Printer Notification

When a network job prints, the printer can be set up to notify the user when the job is complete. This may become annoying to some users. It can therefore be turned off in the advanced properties of the printer, or you can create an SMS Installer utility with the following script.

Key:

HKEY_LOCAL_MACHINE\SYSTEM\CurrentControlSet\ Control\Print\Providers

Value: NetPopup

Type: REG_DWORD

Data: 0

```
————-Begin Script
item: Edit Registry
  Total Keys=1
  Key=SYSTEM\CurrentControlSet\Control\Print\Providers
  New Value=0
  Value Name=NetPopup
  Root=2
  Data Type=3
end
————-End Script
```

Determining OS Revision Type

The following script pulls the OS revision information from the computer's registry and writes the information to a text file. Listed are examples of some OS version parameters:

Windows 2000 Build 2128 = 5.0.2128

Windows 95A = 4.0.950

Windows 95B = 4.0.1212

Windows 98 = 4.10.1998

Windows 98 Second Edition = 4.10.2222 A

```
————-Begin Script
item: Set Variable
  Variable=ROOT
  Value=C:\
end
item: Check Disk Space
end
item: Get System Information
  Variable=OSTYPE
  Flags=00000001
end
item: Insert Line into Text File
  Pathname=%ROOT%test.txt
  New Text=%OSTYPE%
  Line Number=0
end
————-End Script
```

Retrieving Environment Variable Information

The following script retrieves the computer's environment variable information. It sends the output of the SET command to a text file, which is displayed in a dialog box window using the

Display Readme File script action. The information can be used to determine a local environment variable to place into an SMS Installer script variable. This runs on Windows NT only.

```
————-Begin Script
item: Check Disk Space
end
item: Set Variable
  Variable=ROOT
  Value=C:\
end
item: Execute Program
  Pathname=%SYS32%\CMD.EXE
  Command Line=/c SET >%ROOT%ENVVAR.TXT
  Flags=00000110
end
item: Display ReadMe File
  Pathname=%ROOT%ENVVAR.TXT
  Title English=Environment Variables...
  Description English=The list shows the environment
variables that are currently defined on the computer.
end
————-End Script
```

Retrieving Client TCP/IP Information

The following script checks the local operating system. If the operating system is Windows NT, the external program IPCONFIG is called. The IPCONFIG information is passed to a text file in the root of the C: drive. The user is presented with a dialog box containing the computer's current TCP/IP information. If the operating system is not Windows NT, an error message is displayed stating that the utility only runs on Windows NT and that the utility will exit.

```
————Begin Script
item: Check Disk Space
end
item: Set Variable
  Variable=ROOT
  Value=C:\
end
item: Check Configuration
  Flags=10100000
end
item: Execute Program
  Pathname=%SYS32%\CMD.EXE
```

```
   Command Line=/c %SYS32%\ipconfig.exe >c:\IPINFO.txt
   Flags=00000110
end
item: Display ReadMe File
  Pathname=%ROOT%IPINFO.TXT
  Title English=Windows NT TCP/IP Configuration
  Description English=The information listed is the most
current TCP/IP settings for this computer.
end
item: Allow Floppy Disk Change
end
item: Else Statement
end
item: Display Message
  Title English=Unsupported Operating System...
  Text English=This utility only runs with Windows NT. The
program will now exit...
  Flags=00110000
end
item: End Block
end
————-End Script
```

Forcing SMS 2.0 Client Hardware Inventory

```
————-Begin Script
item: Get Registry Key Value
  Variable=SMSLOC
  Key=SOFTWARE\Microsoft\SMS\Client\Configuration\Client
Properties
  Default=NOTFOUND
  Value Name=Local SMS Path
  Flags=00000100
end
item: Execute Program
  Pathname=%SMSLOC%\clicomp\hinv\hinv32.exe
  Default Directory=%SMSLOC%\Core\Bin
  Flags=00000100
end
————-End Script
```

Forcing SMS 2.0 Client Software Inventory

```
————-Begin Script
item: Get Registry Key Value
  Variable=SMSLOC
  Key=SOFTWARE\Microsoft\SMS\Client\Configuration\Client
Properties
```

```
  Default=NOTFOUND
  Value Name=Local SMS Path
  Flags=00000100
end
item: Execute Program
  Pathname=%SMSLOC%\clicomp\sinv\sinv32.exe
  Default Directory=%SMSLOC%\Core\Bin
  Flags=00000100
end
————-End Script
```

SysRead

The following script/utility is similar to the Windows `Sysedit` command. It displays the computer's configuration files, but it displays them in read-only format. Also, it will display different files based on the computer's operating system. It can't be installed on a computer or sent to a remote user to help isolate configuration problems that can arise from unknown software installations.

For Windows NT, it displays these files:

1. Autoexec.bat

2. Config.sys

3. Autoexec.NT

4. Config.NT

5. Win.ini

6. System.ini

7. Boot.ini

For Windows 9x, it displays these files:

1. Autoexec.bat

2. Config.sys

3. Win.ini

4. System.ini

5. Bootlog.txt

```
————-Begin Script
item: Set Variable
  Variable=ROOT
```

```
    Value=C:
  end
  item: Set Variable
    Variable=AUTO
    Value=%ROOT%\Autoexec.bat
  end
  item: Set Variable
    Variable=CONFIG
    Value=%ROOT%\Config.sys
  end
  item: Set Variable
    Variable=WININI
    Value=%WIN%\WIN.INI
  end
  item: Set Variable
    Variable=BOOT
    Value=%ROOT%\BOOT.INI
  end
  item: Set Variable
    Variable=SYSTEMINI
    Value=%WIN%\SYSTEM.INI
  end
  item: Set Variable
    Variable=AUTONT
    Value=%SYS32%\AUTOEXEC.NT
  end
  item: Set Variable
    Variable=CONFIGNT
    Value=%SYS32%\CONFIG.NT
  end
  item: Set Variable
    Variable=BOOTLOG
    Value=%ROOT%\BOOTLOG.TXT
  end
  item: Check Configuration
    Flags=10000000
  end
  item: Custom Dialog Set
    Name=MySysEdit
    item: Dialog
      Title English=SysRead
      Width=411
      Height=419
      Font Name=Helv
      Font Size=8
      item: Editbox
        Rectangle=5 18 183 142
        Value=%AUTO%
```

```
    Help Context=16711681
    Create Flags=010100001011000000000100000000100
end
item: Editbox
  Rectangle=5 166 184 270
  Value=%CONFIG%
  Help Context=16711681
  Create Flags=010100001011000000000100000000100
end
item: Editbox
  Rectangle=199 18 397 142
  Value=%WININI%
  Help Context=16711681
  Create Flags=010100001011000000000100000000100
end
item: Editbox
  Rectangle=198 166 396 274
  Value=%SYSTEMINI%
  Help Context=16711681
  Create Flags=010100001011000000000100000000100
end
item: Static
  Rectangle=6 4 63 14
  Create Flags=01010000000000000000000000000000
  Flags=0000000000000001
  Name=Arial
  Font Style=-13 0 0 0 700 0 0 0 0 3 2 1 34
  Text English=AUTOEXEC.BAT
end
item: Static
  Rectangle=4 154 61 164
  Create Flags=01010000000000000000000000000000
  Flags=0000000000000001
  Name=Arial
  Font Style=-13 0 0 0 700 0 0 0 0 3 2 1 34
  Text English=CONFIG.SYS
end
item: Static
  Rectangle=199 6 256 16
  Create Flags=01010000000000000000000000000000
  Flags=0000000000000001
  Name=Arial
  Font Style=-13 0 0 0 700 0 0 0 0 3 2 1 34
  Text English=WIN.INI
end
item: Static
  Rectangle=198 154 255 164
  Create Flags=01010000000000000000000000000000
```

```
            Flags=0000000000000001
            Name=Arial
            Font Style=-13 0 0 0 700 0 0 0 3 2 1 34
            Text English=SYSTEM.INI
          end
          item: Push Button
            Rectangle=363 378 398 393
            Variable=DIRECTION
            Value=N
            Create Flags=0101000000000001000000000000001
            Text English=&OK
          end
          item: Editbox
            Rectangle=4 290 185 398
            Value=%BOOTLOG%
            Help Context=16711681
            Create Flags=01010000101100000000100000000100
          end
          item: Static
            Rectangle=5 274 62 284
            Create Flags=0101000000000000000000000000000000
            Flags=0000000000000001
            Name=Arial
            Font Style=-13 0 0 0 700 0 0 0 3 2 1 34
            Text English=BOOTLOG.TXT
          end
          item: Static
            Rectangle=246 289 322 370
            Action=2
            Create Flags=01010000000000000000000000001011
            Pathname English=E:\Folders\packages\MySysEdit\
        monitor.bmp
          end
        end
      end
    end
    item: Else Statement
    end
    item: Custom Dialog Set
      Name=MySysEdit
      item: Dialog
        Title English=SysRead
        Width=579
        Height=426
        Font Name=Helv
        Font Size=8
        item: Editbox
          Rectangle=5 18 183 142
          Value=%AUTO%
```

```
      Help Context=16711681
      Create Flags=010100001011000000001000000000100
    end
    item: Editbox
      Rectangle=5 166 184 270
      Value=%CONFIG%
      Help Context=16711681
      Create Flags=010100001011000000001000000000100
    end
    item: Editbox
      Rectangle=190 18 367 142
      Value=%WININI%
      Help Context=16711681
      Create Flags=010100001011000000001000000000100
    end
    item: Editbox
      Rectangle=190 166 368 270
      Value=%SYSTEMINI%
      Help Context=16711681
      Create Flags=010100001011000000001000000000100
    end
    item: Static
      Rectangle=6 4 63 14
      Create Flags=010100000000000000000000000000000
      Flags=0000000000000001
      Name=Arial
      Font Style=-13 0 0 0 700 0 0 0 0 3 2 1 34
      Text English=AUTOEXEC.BAT
    end
    item: Static
      Rectangle=4 154 61 164
      Create Flags=010100000000000000000000000000000
      Flags=0000000000000001
      Name=Arial
      Font Style=-13 0 0 0 700 0 0 0 0 3 2 1 34
      Text English=CONFIG.SYS
    end
    item: Static
      Rectangle=190 5 247 15
      Create Flags=010100000000000000000000000000000
      Flags=0000000000000001
      Name=Arial
      Font Style=-13 0 0 0 700 0 0 0 0 3 2 1 34
      Text English=WIN.INI
    end
    item: Static
      Rectangle=190 153 247 163
      Create Flags=010100000000000000000000000000000
```

```
        Flags=0000000000000001
        Name=Arial
        Font Style=-13 0 0 0 700 0 0 0 3 2 1 34
        Text English=SYSTEM.INI
     end
     item: Push Button
        Rectangle=523 378 558 393
        Variable=DIRECTION
        Value=N
        Create Flags=01010000000000010000000000000001
        Text English=&OK
     end
     item: Editbox
        Rectangle=4 290 185 398
        Value=%BOOT%
        Help Context=16711681
        Create Flags=01010000101100000000100000000100
     end
     item: Static
        Rectangle=5 274 62 284
        Create Flags=01010000000000000000000000000000
        Flags=0000000000000001
        Name=Arial
        Font Style=-13 0 0 0 700 0 0 0 3 2 1 34
        Text English=BOOT.INI
     end
     item: Static
        Rectangle=439 238 515 319
        Action=2
        Create Flags=01010000000000000000000000001011
        Pathname
English=E:\Folders\packages\MySysEdit\monitor.bmp
     end
     item: Editbox
        Rectangle=190 290 370 398
        Value=%AUTONT%
        Help Context=16711681
        Create Flags=01010000101100000000100000000100
     end
     item: Static
        Rectangle=190 277 247 287
        Create Flags=01010000000000000000000000000000
        Flags=0000000000000001
        Name=Arial
        Font Style=-13 0 0 0 700 0 0 0 3 2 1 34
        Text English=AUTOEXEC.NT
     end
     item: Editbox
```

```
        Rectangle=377 18 566 141
        Value=%CONFIGNT%
        Help Context=16711681
        Create Flags=01010000101100000000100000000100
      end
      item: Static
        Rectangle=378 4 435 14
        Create Flags=01010000000000000000000000000000
        Flags=0000000000000001
        Name=Arial
        Font Style=-13 0 0 0 700 0 0 0 0 3 2 1 34
        Text English=CONFIG.NT
      end
    end
  end
end
item: End Block
end
──────-End Script
```

InstSend

The following script/utility gives a graphical interface to the Windows NT NET SEND command:

```
──────-Begin Script
item: Set Variable
  Variable=EXIT
end
item: If/While Statement
  Variable=EXIT
  Flags=00010000
end
item: Custom Dialog Set
  Name=WinNetSend
  item: Dialog
    Title English=WinNetSend
    Width=150
    Height=150
    Font Name=Helv
    Font Size=8
    item: Editbox
    Rectangle=7 38 136 85
    Variable=TEXT
    Help Context=16711681
    Create Flags=01010000100000010000000000000100
  end
  item: Editbox
    Rectangle=55 92 137 107
    Variable=USER
```

```
      Help Context=16711681
      Create Flags=01010000100000010000000000000000
    end
    item: Push Button
      Rectangle=102 114 137 129
      Variable=DIRECTION
      Value=N
      Create Flags=01010000000000010000000000000000
      Text English=&Send
    end
    item: Static
      Rectangle=3 24 36 36
      Create Flags=01010000000000000000000000000000
      Flags=0000000000000001
      Name=Arial
      Font Style=-11 0 0 0 700 0 0 0 0 3 2 1 34
      Text English=Message:
    end
    item: Static
      Rectangle=13 94 54 108
      Create Flags=01010000000000000000000000000000
      Flags=0000000000000001
      Name=Arial
      Font Style=-11 0 0 0 700 0 0 0 0 3 2 1 34
      Text English=User Name:
    end
    item: Static
      Rectangle=110 5 136 29
      Action=2
      Create Flags=01010000000000000000000000001011
      Pathname English=E:\Folders\McGraw Hill\Scripts\Chapter
Six\InstSend\send256.bmp
    end
  end
end
item: Execute Program
  Pathname=%SYS32%\NET.EXE
  Command Line=SEND %USER% %TEXT%
  Flags=00000110
end
item: Custom Dialog Set
  Name=WinNetSend
  item: Dialog
    Title English=WinNetSend
    Width=150
    Height=150
    Font Name=Helv
    Font Size=8
```

```
    item: Push Button
    Rectangle=48 112 94 127
    Variable=DIRECTION
    Value=N
    Create Flags=01010000000000010000000000000000
    Text English=&Send Another
    end
    item: Push Button
    Rectangle=101 112 136 127
    Variable=EXIT
    Value=X
    Create Flags=01010000000000010000000000000000
    Text English=E&xit
    end
    item: Static
    Rectangle=11 42 131 58
    Create Flags=01010000000000000000000000000000
    Flags=0000000000000001
    Name=Arial
    Font Style=-16 0 0 0 700 255 0 0 0 3 2 1 34
    Text English=Message sent successfully!
    end
    item: Static
    Rectangle=110 5 136 29
    Action=2
    Create Flags=01010000000000000000000000001011
    Pathname English=E:\Folders\McGraw Hill\Scripts\Chapter
Six\InstSend\send256.bmp
    end
    end
end
item: End Block
end
————-End Script
```

LockWorkstation

The LockWorkstation script uses the Call DLL function script action to lock a Windows NT workstation. This script could be useful when a user's employment is terminated. The compiled script can be sent via SMS to lock down the workstation before the user even arrives back at his or her desk and finds his or her network account has been deleted.

```
————-Begin Script
item: Call DLL Function
  Pathname=%SYS32%\user32.dll
```

```
Function Name=LockWorkStation
Return Variable=0
Flags=00100000
end
———-End Script
```

07

Related Technologies

549

In this chapter, we will look at some of the technologies and methodologies discussed with SMS Installer. Understanding these topics is key in working with SMS Installer and its various functions and components.

The Methodology of Software Creation/Distribution

Software distribution has to be the most anticipated component when a company is determining the requirements for purchasing and implementing a management system. It is the piece that technical support counts on; seemingly, second only to the HelpDesk function as a way of minimizing cost. You can almost see the IT manager maniacally rubbing his hands together with a knowing scowl on his face. Proper software distribution can be a boon to the way upgrades, patches, and new installations are distributed.

Cost of Poor Distributions

The emphasis is on "proper" software distribution. A poorly distributed application can cause more trouble than it is worth in the following readily evident areas:

1. The client PC (missing software components, failed installations)
2. The distribution servers (performance problems)
3. Network staff (diagnosing stuck packages)
4. Help desk staff (increased volume of calls to the company help desk)

It also impacts the following more obscure but important areas:

1. Associated costs (a poor distribution can negate any cost savings)
2. Confidence in support (repeated unsuccessful distributions would solicit the "critical eye")
3. Confidence in support management (guilt by association)

Basic Distribution Workflow

To secure successful software distribution, there are several basic steps that must be followed. These are outlined in the workflow flowchart shown in Figure 7-1. Some companies add more to the workflow, but the flowchart shows the necessities. Because we're dealing with SMS Installer, the flowchart is based on the deployment of Microsoft Systems Management Server, but it can be used as a methodology for any application distribution system. Replace "SMS" with your software distribution mechanism.

Phases Defined

Determination Phase

This is the phase that will have the most diversified results but is ultimately the most important. Each company must create their own *Software Distribution Compliance Policy (SDCP)*. The SDCP consists of a unified theory of how software should be distributed to the client PCs in the company. Adhering to the communicated policy is critical and will impact all the other steps. A few factors should be considered when creating this policy:

1. Experience of user base

2. Importance of companywide standards

3. Distribution standards

The idea behind software distribution is to make the distribution as easy and painless as possible. Easy and painless for the user base means that the fewer decisions the user has to make and the fewer screens the user has to click through, the more successful the installation will be. If all software has been installed with the same options on each PC, supporting the user base from the help desk access point makes the support similar in all cases. This results in a happier user population, a happier help desk support staff, and ultimately happier management because there will be fewer user complaints.

The distribution standard generally depends on what product is being used to do the scripting. Most products will compile the script and application files into a one-file executable, while others actually copy the whole directory structure, uncompressed, to a

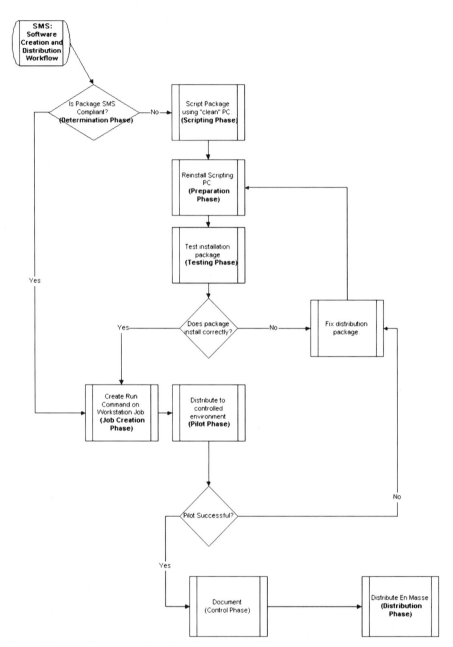

Figure 7-1 *Package creation/distribution workflow.*

point on the network. The one-file method means there is less to copy to the distribution servers, so there can be better efficiency and better utilization of bandwidth across the LAN and WAN.

Some software manufacturers already provide SMS-compliant installations or installations that would fall under your SDCP. Be sure to check these out. Doing so could save a lot of scripting time.

Also, make sure the SDCP is documented as a standard in a memo or technical pronouncement format. It is easier to enforce the policy if it is a communicated document as part of an employee guide or affirmation.

Scripting Phase

A successful scripting phase is dependent upon a good scripting environment. The scripting environment consists of a good scripting program, such as SMS Installer or Wise Installer, and a "clean" PC. A clean PC means a low-end computer that is a nominal (lowest common denominator) installation of the company's standard OS. Nothing else should be installed—only the bare necessities of the standard OS with the minimal amount of components. Once the final clean PC is finalized for your environment, use the imaging product of your choice to make a copy of the clean environment. You will use this image later in the process.

This phase is also dependent on a qualified scripting person. In large enterprise environments, scripting can be a full-time job. Hiring a person specifically to script distributions is wise in this type of situation. Once the script is complete, the functional groups can sign off on the final product or send it back to the drawing board.

Preparation Phase

After the script is complete and compiled into an executable, the scripting machine should be put back into "clean" shape. To some this would be common sense, but giving this step its own phase serves as a reminder.

Testing Phase

Once the PC is back to "pristine" condition, run through the entire installation as the user would, then run the installed application. Run through every component of the installed application to make sure everything works. For instance, open files, open multiple files at once, close files, save files, print files, and so on. Obviously, it is important that the installed application function properly.

Job Creation Phase

The SMS administrator in charge of creating packages should handle this phase. This person will have a repository already defined, somewhere on the network, where the package source is stored and where the Run Command on Workstation job is created.

Pilot Phase

Select some individuals from the user population based on varying levels of experience and distribute the job to them. The theory here is that if the least technical user can install the package with no problems, then the rest of the user population should have no problems.

Also, keep in mind that it is a smart practice to also include the help desk staff in this distribution, as they will be the ones supporting the installation via phone calls and the SMS Remote Control function. They will know how the installation works, making it easier to help users through it, should there be issues with the installation.

Control Phase

Documentation of any project is critical to its operation, even if it is just an e-mail. If there are specifics about the distribution package, these should be identified here. Documentation also provides security in case the person who created the package goes on vacation or leaves the company.

Distribution Phase

This is the final phase—the completion phase. If the steps above were followed correctly and efficiently, the distribution should be successful.

Authenticode Technology

When a person buys computer software in a store, there is a feeling of assurance because the source of the software is physical. The person can see the software, hold it in his or her hands, tell whether or not it's been opened, read about the software on the box, and purchase it in the checkout line. If something is wrong with the software when it is taken home and installed on the computer, the person has a point of reference to take the software back and exchange it.

When software is downloaded from the Internet, the same rules do not apply. The Internet lacks that certain assurance people are used to when they browse the software titles at the local software store. Without this feeling, it is hard to determine if the software downloaded and installed from the Internet is safe or worthy of trust. Every time a software link is clicked, the potential for disaster increases. Internet software could contain viruses, bugs, and Trojan horses capable of wiping out the entire data store on the computer. The file could be corrupt and cause the PC to lock up, increasing the potential to lose critical data.

Microsoft's solution to these issues is Authenticode. In simple terms, Authenticode Technology is a Microsoft technology to ensure software is from a trusted source and has not been tampered with. Authenticode, along with digital signatures, gives software developers the ability to incorporate their information and their software code with their programs.

When Authenticode is used, the end user can rest assured that the software really comes from the publisher who signed it and it has not been altered or corrupted since it was signed. It also adds an extra level of accountability. If the software doesn't perform as touted or it causes problems with the computer, action can be taken against the publisher.

Authenticode and SMS Installer

Authenticode was specifically developed for the Internet but can be incorporated into SMS Installer packages. Signing SMS Installer packages is not a must, but there are a few benefits to doing so. Adding Authenticode signing to SMS Installer packages for distribution via SMS gives the same level of assurance to the end user that the Authenticode gives to Internet-based software. It adds an extra level of company ownership for the distribution packages and gives end users the impression that the package they receive is company-sanctioned and installing it is critical.

SMS Installer packages can be placed on intranet and Internet sites, as well as distributed via the SMS system. Signing an SMS Installer package that is distributed via a Web-based distribution method gives the package the same look and feel the user is accustomed to.

Certificate File Details

When a new certificate is accessed and downloaded, a security warning, shown in Figure 7-2, prompts the user. The security warning displays information about the certificate provider and allows you to choose to always trust the source.

Each certificate file contains information about the certificate file itself. You can access the information by right-clicking on the certificate icon and choosing properties.

The General tab, shown in Figure 7-3, displays quick information about the certificate, such as who the certificate was

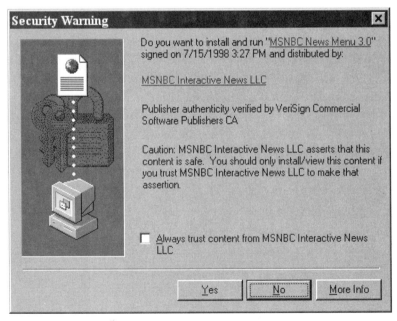

Figure 7-2 *Certificate Security Warning.*

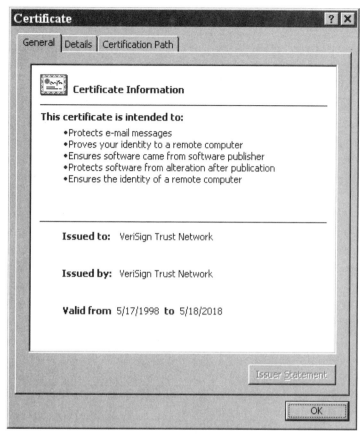

Figure 7-3 *Certificate General tab.*

issued to, what the certificate does, and the date the certificate is valid.

The Details tab, shown in Figure 7-4, displays more details about the certificate.

The Certification Path tab, shown in Figure 7-5, checks the status of the certificate and displays a message indicating if the certificate is still good or whether it has expired.

Importing a Certificate

Certificate files can be imported into the current configuration. This allows you to distribute certificates through any means.

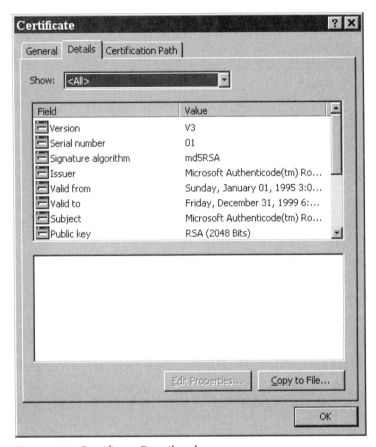

Figure 7-4 *Certificate Details tab.*

If you right-click on the certificate icon, you choose the Install Certificate option. See Figures 7-6 and 7-7. The Certificate Manager Import Wizard appears, as shown in Figure 7-8.

If you accept the default, the certificate will be stored based on its type. You can also select the specific certificate store location, as shown in Figures 7-9 and 7-10.

Upon completing the process, the dialogs in Figures 7-11 and 7-12 appear.

Common Authenticode Terms

1X.509 Certificate   The X.509 Certificate is a "cryptographic" certificate that contains a vendor's unique name and the vendor's public key.

Figure 7-5 *Certificate Certification Path tab.*

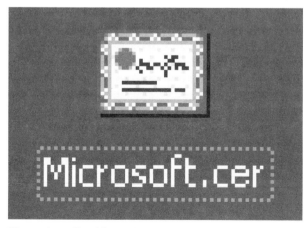

Figure 7-6 *Certificate icon.*

Figure 7-7 *Install Certificate option.*

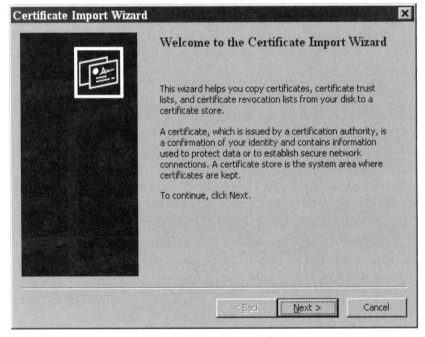

Figure 7-8 *Certificate Manager Import Wizard.*

PKCS #7 Signed Data   PKCS #7 is a Public Key Certificate Standard #7.

Certification authority (CA)   The CA is a trusted standards entity that identifies the authenticity of another certificate.

Local Registration Authority (LRA)   The LRA is the "middle man" between a publisher and a CA. The LRA can verify a publisher's credentials before sending them to the certification authority.

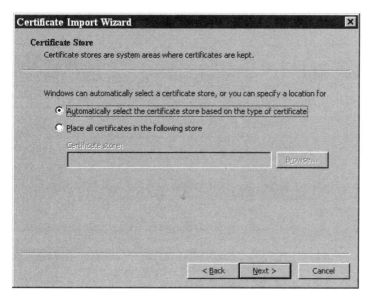

Figure 7-9 *Selecting Certificate Store.*

Figure 7-10 *Custom Certificate Store.*

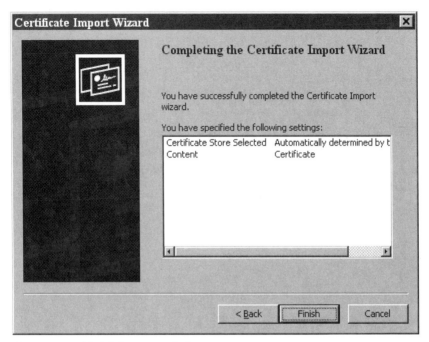

Figure 7-11 *Finish Import window.*

Figure 7-12 *Import successful.*

Portable Executable (PE) Image   PE Image is the standard Win32 executable format.

Software Publishing Certificate (SPC)   A PKCS #7 signed-data object containing X.509 certificates.

Trust provider   The software that runs to decide whether the file is trusted. The trust provider acts on the certificate associated with the file.

WIN_CERTIFICATE   A Win32-specific data structure that contains either a PKCS #7 signed-data object or an X.509 certificate.

Authenticode Resources

Microsoft
http://msdn.microsoft.com/isapi/msdnlib.idc?theURL=/library/sdkdoc/crypto/cryptotools_1751.htm

RSA Laboratories
http://www.rsa.com

Thawt
http://www.thawte.com/certs/developer/msauthenticode.html

VeriSign
http://www.verisign.com/

Registry Overview

The registry can be an unmanageable beast if it is not understood. At first glance, the registry makes little sense. Some of the information and names contained inside are familiar, related to specific installed hardware and software, but understanding its depth takes a bit of time.

The Windows Registry is a centralized, hierarchal database of settings, configurations, application information, hardware information, security settings, and preferences. The registry consists of five *subtrees*:

1. HKEY_CLASSES_ROOT

2. HKEY_CURRENT_USER

3. HKEY_LOCAL_MACHINE

4. HKEY_USERS

5. HKEY_CURRENT_CONFIG

HKEY_CLASSES_ROOT
The HKEY_CLASSES_ROOT contains two types of data:

1. Data to associate file types with applications

2. Configuration information for COM objects

It provides backward-compatibility with Windows 3.x for OLE (Object Linking and Embedding) and DDE (Dynamic Data Exchange) support.

HKEY_CURRENT_USER

The HKEY_CURRENT_USER is similar to what the name implies. This subtree contains user-specific information for the user who is currently logged on to the computer. It contains the profile settings for each person who is logged on and creates a new profile for each person who logs on in the future. It contains items such as environment variables, personal program groups and icons, desktop settings, network connections, specific printers, and application properties and preferences.

HKEY_LOCAL_MACHINE

The HKEY_LOCAL_MACHINE contains the information about the computer itself. Items include memory, hard disk, operating system information, device drivers lists, service, and so on. The hardware information is non-user-specific, meaning the information is specific to the computer itself regardless of who is logged on.

HKEY_USERS

HKEY_USERS contains the profiles for all actively logged-on users, and any user who has logged on to the computer.

HKEY_CURRENT_CONFIG

The HKEY_CURRENT_CONFIG contains the information on the current hardware profile. Underneath the subtrees are *keys*, *subkeys*, and *values*. An example of this structure would be as follows:

```
HKEY_LOCAL_MACHINE = subtree
System = key
CurrentControlSet = (active) subkey
Services = subkey of CurrentControlSet
Schedule = subkey of Services
DisplayName = value
```

The convention for describing this registry key structure would be as follows:

HKEY_LOCAL_MACHINE\System\CurrentControlSet\
Services\Schedule\DisplayName

The registry is described in the form of a map in much the same way a directory and file structure is described. For instance, a directory structure could be the following:

```
C:\ = subtree
WINNT = key
SYSTEM32 = subkey
CMD.EXE = value
```

Hence, C:\WINNT\SYSTEM32\CMD.EXE is the directory path to the Windows NT Command Interpreter file. This similar convention simplifies the registry, making it easier to navigate and easier to understand its structure.

As mentioned, the registry stores computer- and user-specific information. It stores this information in values. Values can have one of six different data types:

1. REG_MULTI_SZ

2. REG_BINARY

3. REG_SZ

4. REG_DWORD

5. REG_EXPAND_SZ

6. REG_FULL_RESOURCE_DESCRIPTOR

REG_MULTI_SZ

Data is stored in multiple string values. Most values are stored in a readable format, instead of hex or binary.

> A *string* is a set of alphabetic characters that relates to any type of text. **Note**

REG_BINARY

Data is stored in binary format. This usually indicates hardware component information. Since it is binary, having vendor-specific information about the binary variables is a must before making any modifications.

Note   Binary is a set of hexadecimal digits (base 16) within the scope of 0-9 and A-F. To convert binary to hexadecimal:

1. Start the Calculator program that comes with the Windows operating system (calc.exe).
2. Change to the Scientific view by clicking on the View menu.
3. Click on the *Bin* radio button, and then set the data type radio button to Dword.
4. Input the binary string. (When in this mode you will notice that only the 0 and 1 on the keypad is available. Binary is base 2, and each digit can only be 0 or 1.)
5. Click on the *Hex* dialog button, and your binary number is automatically converted to hex.

REG_SZ

Data is stored in strings of information. This data type is usually Standard English entries indicating information stored in an easily readable format. Hence, this data type is easy to understand and the easiest to modify.

REG_DWORD

DWORD, or double word, is data stored in 4 bytes. This data type can be viewed in hexadecimal, binary, or decimal and usually indicates things such as memory addresses, interrupt settings, and device factors.

Note   The double-word value is a 32-bit value broken down into 8 hexadecimal digits.

REG_EXPAND_SZ

REG_EXPAND_SZ is a data type that is contained in variables. These variables are queried by applications and installations.

REG_FULL_RESOURCE_DESCRIPTOR

This data type contains hardware device information that is stored in the HKEY_LOCAL_MACHINE\HARDWARE key.

Before the registry, there were INI files. These INI files contain much of the same information contained in the registry. The main reason the registry was created was to replace these files. INI files create a complex problem for administration of these settings. First of all, INI files can be placed anywhere on the PC, making it hard to centralize settings and making it even harder to find the files should the need arise to modify them. Second, INI files are just simple text files in the directory structure that can be easily deleted either on purpose or by accident. They are just as easy to open in any text editor, and the unsuspecting user can make modifications that could keep his or her application from running correctly or not at all. Third, files like the original Windows 3.x files (WIN.INI, SYSTEM.INI PROGMAN.INI, CONTROL.INI, and WINFILE.INI) were hard to manage because when applications were removed from the computer, the application information remained in the INI files. Not only would these files become large over time, they would also contain a lot of old information that was hard to clean without the possibility of removing settings pertinent to another application. Incorporating all these settings into the Windows Registry keeps the settings safe and gives the application vendor a central location from which to remove the settings during an uninstall.

Warning!

Microsoft always displays warnings that editing the registry is a potentially dangerous procedure, yet most of the fixes and workarounds issued by Microsoft involve modifying the registry. There are some important safeguards to follow when editing the registry:

1. *Read-only*   In the registry editor REGEDT32, turn on the Read-only Option.

2. *Backup*   First, make sure the registry is backed up with your normal backups. Second, make sure to back up the registry or hive you are working with before making any changes.

For a quick reference of helpful registry keys for use with SMS Installer, see Chapter 10.

Table 7-1 *Common User Profile directories.*

Folder name	Contents
Desktop	Directory used to store physical file objects on the desktop
Favorites	Directory containing shortcuts to favorite items such as Internet shortcuts
NetHood	Directory containing objects that appear in the Network Neighborhood
Personal	Directory that holds user-specific common documents
PrintHood	The printers folder containing shortcuts to printers
Recent	Directory that contains user's most recently accessed documents
SendTo	Directory that contains Send To menu items
START menu	Directory containing Start menu items
Programs	Directory that contains the user's program groups
StartUp	Directory that relates to the user's Startup program group

Profiles Overview

On Windows systems, there are two types of profiles: computer profiles and user profiles. The computer profile relates to the computer itself, with all the computer-specific settings, drivers, software information, and so on. The user profile relates to the user-specific settings and preferences. A different user profile is created for each person who logs onto the computer.

The directory structure for computers using user profiles is different. If you look at the directory structure under the C:\WINDOWS (for Windows computers) or C:\WINNT (for Windows NT computers), you'll see a PROFILES directory. Underneath this directory, separate directories for each user account are created when the specific user account logs on to the computer for the first time. The Profiles directories are stored here for each time the person logs on to this computer. Each Profiles directory has its own Start menu, Application Data, Desktop directory, and so on. Because each has its own directory structure, each user will see different icons and settings when the user logs on. Based on the username (correct password) that is entered when the computer boots, the operating system is directed to that Profiles directory. If the directory does not exist, one is created. Anything that is placed in the Common section will be available to the new user profile. If any other piece of software is needed, it will only be available if it is installed, even if the application already exists somewhere in the computer's directory structure.

Some common user profile directories are shown in Table 7-1.

QuickTips

This chapter covers some quick tips not included previously for using SMS Installer.

The RESTART Variable

The RESTART variable seems to cause some confusion. Below are the guidelines for using this variable.

Variable Options

The variable RESTART can be set to any of the following values:

- W   A restart of Windows will be performed. The Windows interface (Explorer.exe) is shut down and restarted.

- S   A warm boot of the system will be performed.

- E <*MS-DOS program name*>   An MS-DOS program is identified that will be executed during the restart.

Automatic Restart

By adding the following script items to the script (either automatically through a repackage or manually), the RESTART variable is set automatically:

- Add to Autoexec.bat (see Figure 8-1).

- Add to Config.sys (see Figure 8-2).

- Add Device to SYSTEM.INI (see Figure 8-3).

In addition, the RESTART variable is automatically set if files in use are replaced during the installation. When files in use are replaced, SMS Installer does the following:

1. It copies the new version of the file into the directory with a temporary filename.

2. Upon system restart, the original file is deleted and the temporary file is renamed.

For troubleshooting purposes, you can find out which file(s) is causing the RESTART variable to be set. Place a Display Message %RESTART% script item after each system file that is installed. If an "S" is displayed, the file has been marked for replacement on restart because it is in use. See Figure 8-4.

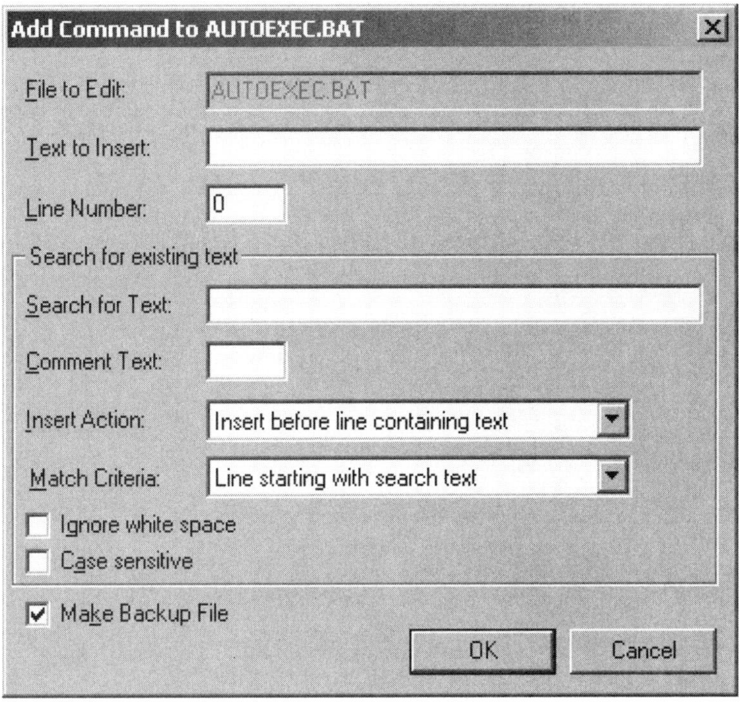

Figure 8-1 *Add to AUTOEXEC.BAT.*

To keep the PC from rebooting altogether, include a Set Variable script item at the bottom of the script:

```
Variable:    RESTART
New Value:   (leaving it blank will set it to NULL)
Operation:   Nothing
```

See Figure 8-5.

Layman's Terms

Here is a procedure that works very well when you need to cause the computer to restart:

1. At the beginning of each script, put in an Edit INI File script item with the parameters shown in Figure 8-6.

   This inserts (if not already present from a previous installation) the RESTART variable into the 386 Enhanced section of the SYSTEM.INI with a blank line. Do this in the event the

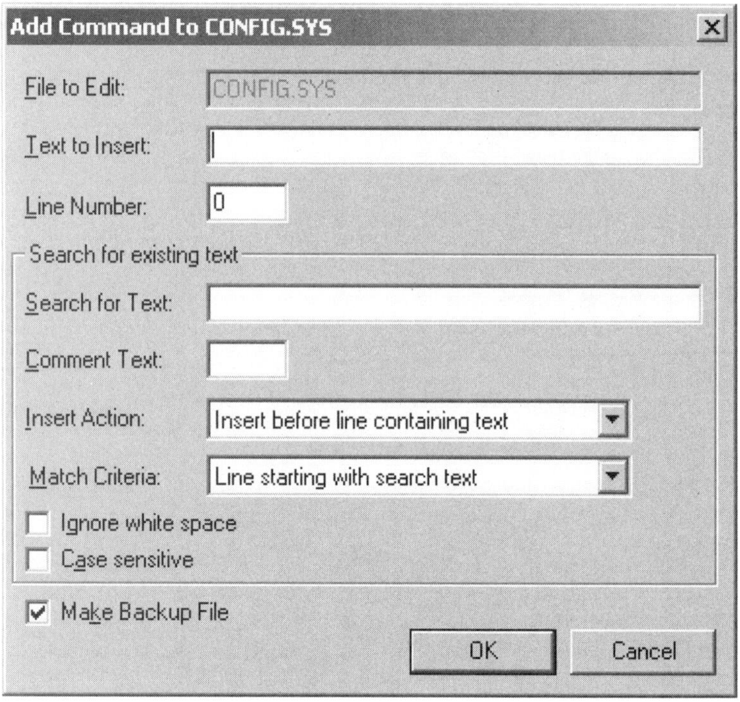

Figure 8-2 *Add to CONFIG.SYS.*

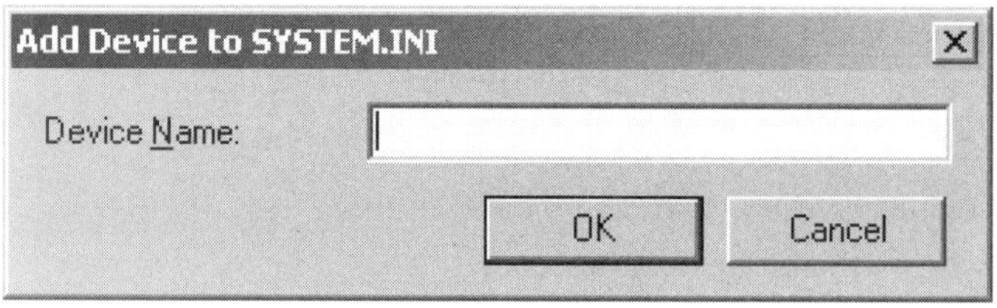

Figure 8-3 *Add Device to SYSTEM.INI.*

RESTART variable has been used before and the value for RESTART is already set to "S" or "W," as mentioned above.

2. Then, at the end of the script, put in an Add Device to SYSTEM.INI script item, shown in Figure 8-7.

   As mentioned above, this script item forces a reboot of the computer. The variable is set based on preference or requirement of the application. If changes have been made to the

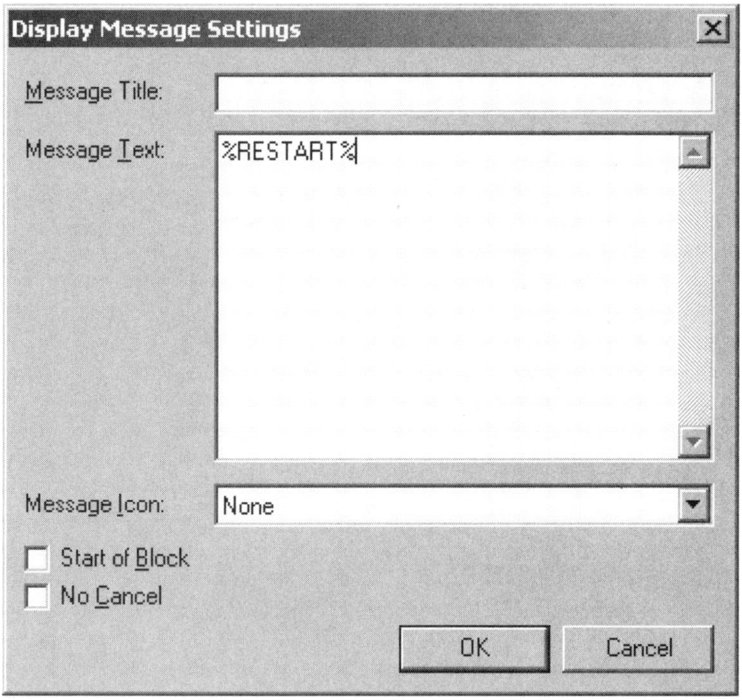

Figure 8-4 *Display RESTART Message.*

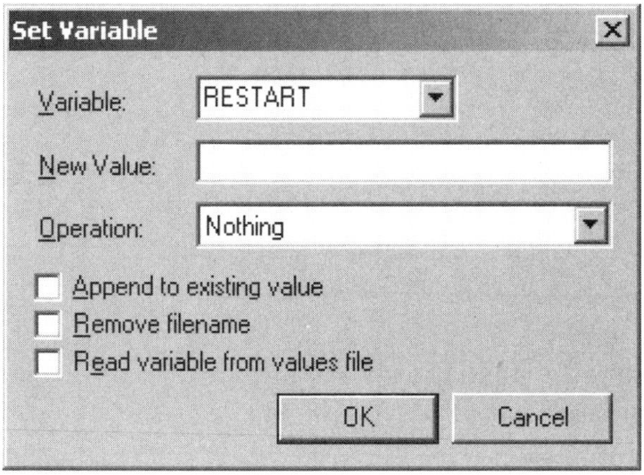

Figure 8-5 *Set Variable RESTART.*

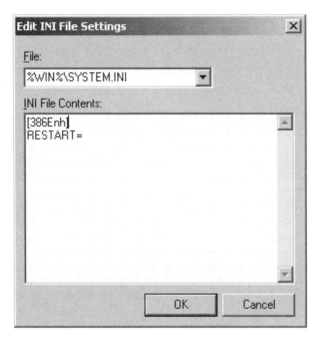

Figure 8-6 *Edit SYSTEM.INI.*

Figure 8-7 *Add Device RESTART to SYSTEM.INI.*

Autoexec.bat or the Config.sys, or files in use are replaced, a complete reboot will be required—so use the S parameter.

Why Force a Restart?

Because vendors still refuse to write installations that are completely MS-compliant, sometimes a forced reboot is required for the installation to be successful. A correctly written installation will make calls to the Win APIs for the reboot, and SMS Installer will pick it up during a repackage. A poorly written installation will incorporate its own restart routines, and SMS Installer (or any other repackaging utility for that matter) will have a hard time realizing a restart is needed.

Also, some installations will replace in-use files on the fly, not requiring a reboot. SMS Installer does not work this way. For in-use files to be replaced, if the installation has been repackaged with SMS Installer, you must include script items to force a reboot even though the original installation does not.

Other Ways to Restart

As you should now know, SMS Installer provides a way to run external commands during the script. Along with the Execute Program script action, the following information can be used to perform special restart procedures.

Rundll32.exe

Rundll32.exe is a utility included with Windows 9x and Windows NT. On Windows 9x computers it is located in the C:\WINDOWS directory; on Windows NT, it is located in the C:\WINNT\SYSTEM32 directory. Rundll32 automates the exporting of functions of other DLL files.

Using the Rundll32 utility, you can use a function of the SHELL32.DLL file to perform different reboots of the computer.

Syntax:

```
rundll32.exe shell32.dll,SHExitWindowsEx n
```

The *n* is a number variable related to Table 8-1.

In SMS Installer, using the Execute Program script action, the command would look like Figure 8-8.

The displayed option forces the computer to shut down. The following is how the script will look:

```
————-Begin Script
item: Execute Program
  Pathname=%WIN%\rundll32.exe
  Command Line=shell32.dll,SHExitWindowsEx 4
end
————-End Script
```

Table 8-1   *Function variables.*

Variable	Function	Description
0	LOGOFF	Shuts down all running processes and logs the user off the computer or network.
1	SHUTDOWN	Prepares the computer to be powered off. It shuts down all running processes and flushes all file buffers to save data.
2	REBOOT	Performs a restart of the computer.
4	FORCE	Forces the computer to shut down even if applications and processes are still running.
8	POWEROFF	Shuts down the system and turns off the power.

RunOnce.exe

RunOnce.exe is a utility included with Windows 9x and Windows NT. This utility enters information into the registry for programs to run once when the computer boots. After the computer has booted and the command has run, the registry entry is removed so it will not be run at next boot.

Using the Execute Program script action in the Script Editor, RunOnce can be run as an external program to reboot the com-

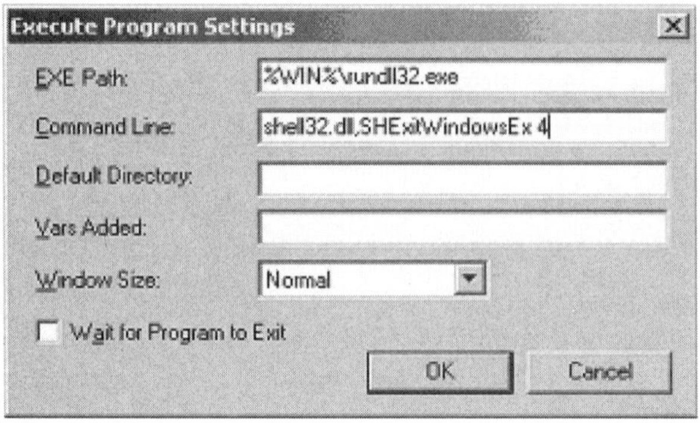

Figure 8-8 *Execute Rundll32.exe.*

puter. The -q command-line switch restarts the computer after a
15-second delay.

Syntax:

```
RunOnce.exe -q
```

The Execute Program script action would look like Figure 8-9.
And the script would look like this:

```
———-Begin Script
item: Execute Program
  Pathname=%WIN%\runonce.exe
  Command Line=-q
end
———-End Script
```

Suppressing the Restart

Even if the restart requirements have been set in the SMS
Installer script, you may not want to force the user to reboot the
computer after the installation. Although you may have created
an installation that you want to be completely silent, perhaps a
device gets added to the SYSTEM.INI in the process that prompts
the user to restart the computer at the end of the installation. To
avoid this, you can put a line at the end of the SMS Installer
script that will suppress the restart altogether.

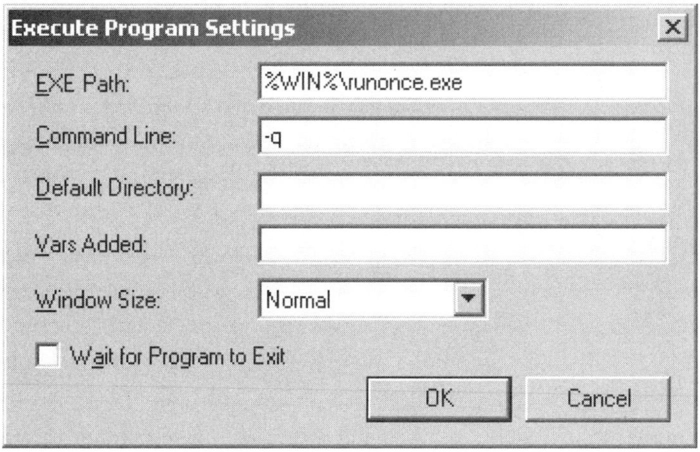

Figure 8-9 *Executing RunOnce.*

At the very end of the script, in the Script Editor, add a Set Variable script item. Name the new variable RESTART and click on *OK*. Leave the New Value line blank, and keep the Operation at Nothing. See Figure 8-10.

Note   Be careful using this method. During the script's file installation procedure, files that are in use (open) are marked for replacement when the computer is restarted. When you are using the procedure of suppressing the restart, the file replacement procedure is skipped.

Creating a Silent Uninstall

In some instances, it may make sense to run a silent uninstall of a particular software application that was installed using an SMS Installer installation file. There are two ways to accomplish this: by using an Edit Registry script action and by modifying the UNINSTAL.IPF file.

Use an Edit Registry Script Action.   When you look at the Add/Remove list in the Control Panel applet, you see all the applications that have Uninstall support. When an application with uninstall support installs, it adds its uninstall information to

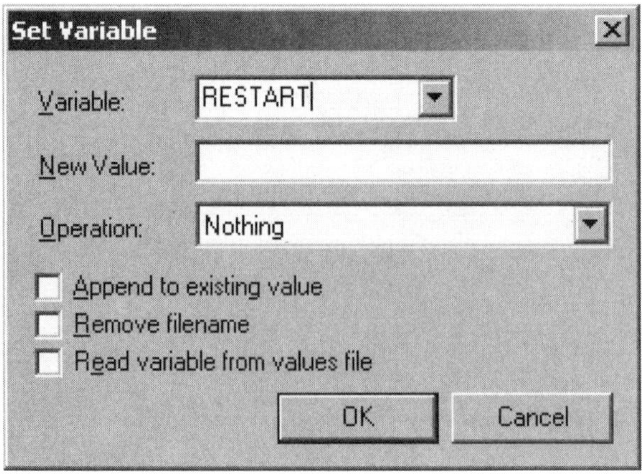

Figure 8-10 *Set Variable RESTART to Blank.*

a registry key. For this instance, we'll look at the Microsoft SMS Installer uninstall information.

Key:
HKEY_LOCAL_MACHINE\SOFTWARE\Microsoft\Windows\
CurrentVersion\Uninstall\Microsoft SMS Installer

Value0: DisplayName

Type: REG_SZ

Data: Microsoft SMS Installer

Value1: UninstallString

Type: REG_SZ

Data: "e:\Program Files\Microsoft SMS Installer\
UNINSTAL.EXE" "e:\Program Files\Microsoft SMS Installer\
INSTALL.LOG" "Microsoft SMS Installer Uninstall"

The DisplayName data string is the actual program name you see in the Add/Remove programs list. The UninstallString data is the path, filename, and commands that uninstall SMS Installer from the computer.

To create a silent uninstall for SMS Installer, you insert a /S switch after the UNINSTAL.EXE command in the data value command line. The command line would become: "e:\Program Files\Microsoft SMS Installer\UNINSTAL.EXE /S" "e:\Program Files\Microsoft SMS Installer\INSTALL.LOG" "Microsoft SMS Installer Uninstall."

The Edit Registry script action would look like this:

```
———-Begin Script
item: Edit Registry
  Total Keys=1
  Key=SOFTWARE\Microsoft\Windows\CurrentVersion\Uninstall\
Microsoft SMS Installer
  New Value="e:\Program Files\Microsoft SMS Installer
\UNINSTAL.EXE /S" "e:\Program Files\Microsoft SMS
Installer\INSTALL.LOG" "Microsoft SMS Installer Uninstall"
  Value Name=UninstallString
  Root=2
end
———-End Script
```

```
/* Rem Create Icon/Register uninstall

If APPTITLE Not Equal "" then
  If System Has Windows 95 Shell Interface Start Block
    Registry Key Software\Microsoft\Windows\CurrentVersion\Uninstall\%APPTITLE% = %APPTITLE%
    Registry Key Software\Microsoft\Windows\CurrentVersion\Uninstall\%APPTITLE% = "%UNINSTALL_PATH%
```

Figure 8-11 *Create Icon/Register Uninstall.*

Now, when the application is selected to uninstall, it will be completely silent.

Modify the UNINSTAL.IPF File.   To create a silent uninstall for the package at the original compile time of the SMS Installer executable, you can modify the UNINSTAL.IPF file located in the Microsoft SMS Installer directory under the Include folder. Open the UNINSTAL.IPF file in the Script Editor.

Note   Be sure to back up the original UNINSTAL.IPF file. When this file is modified, all subsequent compilations will be created with a silent uninstall. Just copy the silent IPF and the normal IPF back and forth into the Include directory as needed.

At the bottom of the UNINSTAL.IPF file, there is a section with the comment: `Create Icon/Register uninstall`, as shown in Figure 8-11.

On the second `Registry Key Software...` line, change:

```
————-Begin Script
item: Edit Registry
  Total Keys=1
  Key=Software\Microsoft\Windows\CurrentVersion\
Uninstall\%APPTITLE%
  New Value="%UNINSTALL_PATH%" "%_LOGFILE_PATH_%"
"%APPTITLE% Uninstall"
  Value Name=UninstallString
  Root=2
end
————-End Script
```

to:

```
————-Begin Script
item: Edit Registry
  Total Keys=1
```

```
  Key=Software\Microsoft\Windows\CurrentVersion\
Uninstall\%APPTITLE%
  New Value="%UNINSTALL_PATH%" /S "%_LOGFILE_PATH_%"
"%APPTITLE% Uninstall"
  Value Name=UninstallString
  Root=2
end
————-End Script
```

If you save the UNINSTAL.IPF file, then all SMS Installer scripts that use this modified IPF file will be created with silent uninstalls.

Simplifying the Repackage

Suppose you already know what changes will be made when a package is installed, which directories are modified, and which registry keys are manipulated. Or maybe you just want to track registry changes and nothing else. You can customize the SMS Installer repackage process to work for you.

To do so:

1. After clicking on the Repackage button in the Installation Expert, click on the *Change* button, shown in Figure 8-12.

2. At the next screen, shown in Figure 8-13, you can change the directory to scan during the repackage. For instance, if you know that C:\BATCH is the only directory modified, delete the default C:\ directory and replace it with C:\BATCH (see Figure 8-14). If you only want to track registry modifications, select a directory that you know will not be modified at all.

3. On the Registry Keys tab, you can select any registry key to watch during the repackage. You can select all the way down to a particular registry value. The example in Figure 8-15 only watches changes to the HKEY_CURRENT_USER\Software\Microsoft\Command Processor\CompletionChar value.

Case-Sensitive Registry

When manually adding, modifying, and deleting registry keys, make sure to match the letter case. If you miss one letter case, the

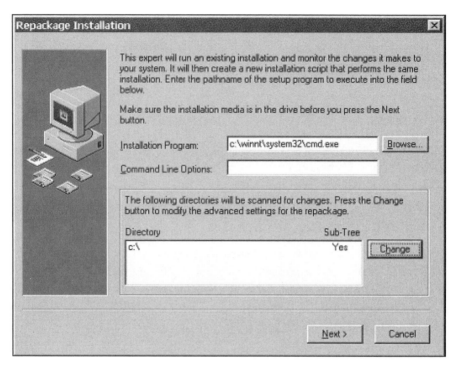

Figure 8-12 *Repackage window.*

registry changes will not take place. For instance, in Figure 8-16, if you take a look at HKEY_CURRENT_USER, the software key is `Software`. If you look above at HKEY_LOCAL_MACHINE, the software key is `SOFTWARE`.

Tracking Changes

Not really familiar or comfortable with the scripting side of SMS Installer yet? You can run a repackage in SMS Installer and track changes to the PC without running a full software installation. Here's how:

1. In SMS Installer, in the Installation Expert, click on the *Repackage* button, shown in Figure 8-17.

2. When the Wizard asks for an installation program, select the OS command interpreter. In Figure 8-18, the NT command interpreter is used (C:\WINNT\SYSTEM32\CMD.EXE). Click on *Next* to start the preinstallation system check.

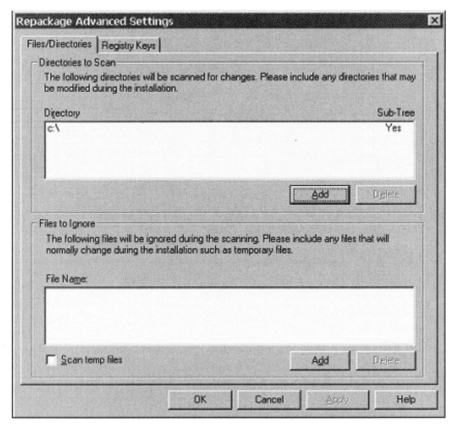

Figure 8-13 *Repackage Advanced Settings.*

3. After SMS Installer has "photographed" your preinstallation
   PC, the command interpreter is run and a DOS box opens, as
   shown in Figure 8-19. Close the DOS box, and make changes
   to the PC. Any kind of change is acceptable (e.g., registry
   additions/changes/deletions, INI file modifications, file addi-
   tions/copies/deletions, shortcut creations/deletions, environment changes, and so on).

4. After you have made your changes, click on the *Next* button,
   shown in Figure 8-20, to have SMS Installer compare the preinstallation image to the current image.

5. After it completes, click on the *Finish* button, shown in Figure
   8-21, to return to the Installation Expert screen.

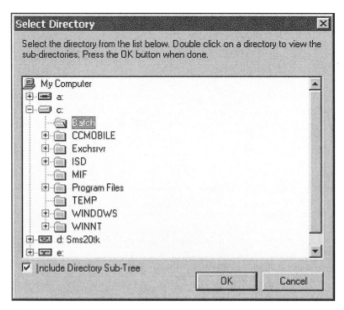

Figure 8-14 *Select Directory.*

For this example, a registry modification is made to HKEY_LOCAL_MACHINE\SOFTWARE\Microsoft\ Windows NT\CurrentVersion\Winlogon\LegalNoticeCaption, and the line `This is a test for SMS Installer` is added.

6. Figure 8-22 shows the User Configuration window as having one registry key modified.

   If you double-click on the Registry Keys icon, the screen in Figure 8-23 is displayed. Notice how SMS Installer captured the change made to the registry.

   If you double-click on the LegalNoticeCaption, the screen in Figure 8-24 is displayed.

   Switching to the Script Editor view, toward the bottom of the screen (registry changes are placed at the bottom of the script by default), the line shown in Figure 8-25 has been inserted into the script.

   Double-clicking on the line displays the screen shown in Figure 8-26. Notice how similar the information is to the Installation Expert information.

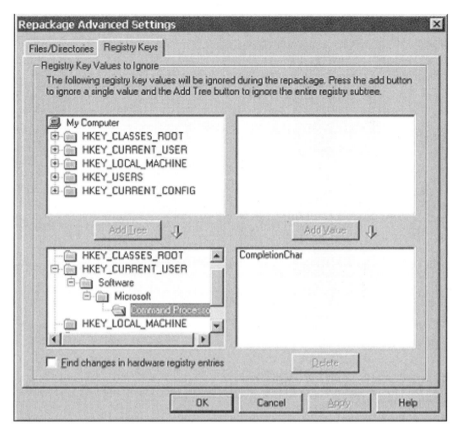

Figure 8-15 *Repackage Advanced Settings.*

7. You can save the SMS Installer script and compile it at this point.

Sharing Scripts as Plain Text

Not only can you attach the IPF file to an e-mail or other means of distribution, you can send SMS Installer scripts as plain text that can easily import into SMS Installer.

With a script open to the scripting facility, highlight the entire script by using the common Windows feature of clicking the first line, holding down the Shift key, then clicking on the last line of the script.

Next, select *Edit|Copy*, as shown in Figure 8-27. This copies the script into the clipboard.

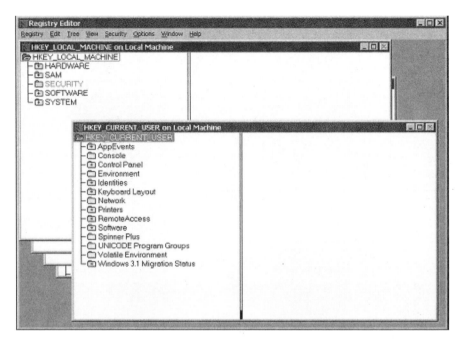

Figure 8-16 *Registry Editor window.*

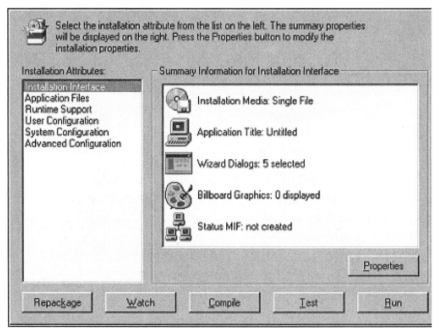

Figure 8-17 *Installation Expert.*

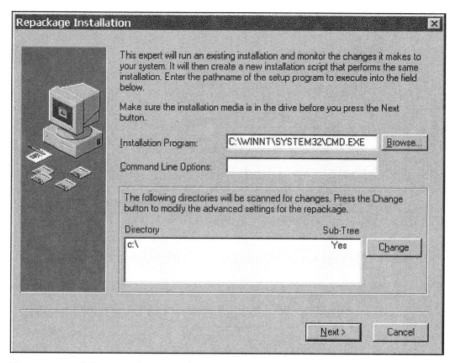

Figure 8-18 *Selecting Command Interpreter.*

Now you have several options of what you would like to do with the contents of the Windows clipboard. You can both copy the contents into any text editor such as Notepad and attach the text file to an e-mail message (shown in Figure 8-28).

Or you can copy the contents into your favorite e-mail program and send the SMS Installer script as the text of the e-mail. (See Figure 8-29.)

Once recipients receive copies of the script, they just copy and paste them into SMS Installer. SMS Installer automatically reformats the plain text into readable script.

Shutting Down Antivirus Packages

Before repackaging an application or even watching an application with SMS Installer, make sure to shut down any packages, services, or TSRs related to an antivirus program. Because of the aggressive file scanning of antivirus programs, files can be left

Figure 8-19 *MS-DOS window.*

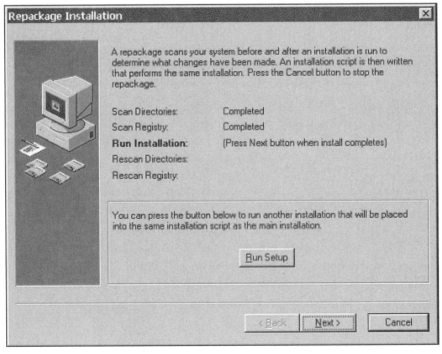

Figure 8-20 *Completed first scan.*

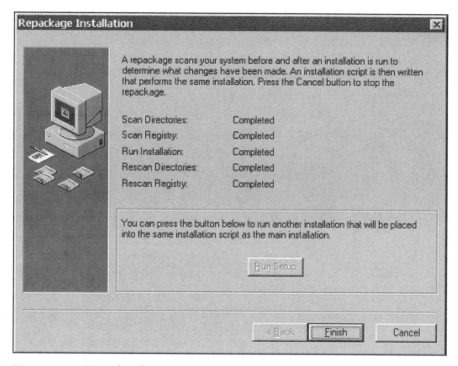

Figure 8-21 *Completed second scan.*

open that could keep a package creation from being successful. If you know the command to shut down or temporarily disable the antivirus package, you may want to include this command in each script.

SMS Client on SMS Installer Computers

Do not run a repackage or watch operation on a computer that has the SMS 1.2 or 2.0 client installed. If the SMS 1.2 client happens to be making changes to the SMS.INI file, this file could be collected during the final snapshot and then distributed to all other computers that receive the repackaged installation. This will cause duplicate SMS IDs to show up in the SMS 1.2 database, causing problems with distributing future applications and retrieving accurate inventory.

If the SMS 2.0 client is doing a hardware or software inventory or writing a DDR (Data Discovery Record), this information will

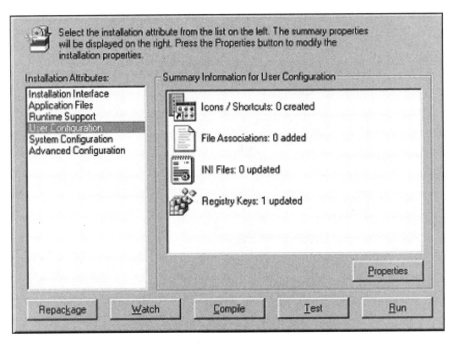

Figure 8-22 *Installation Expert changes.*

be included in the repackage. Other things that could inadvertently be included in the repackage are the client logs. SMS 2.0 writes a lot of information to the client logs for troubleshooting purposes. If these logs are changed during a repackage, these files will be included because SMS Installer sees the changes.

16 bit vs. 32 bit

SMS Installer includes support for distribution to 16-bit operating systems. Make sure that if a package will be distributed to a 32-bit operating system only, such as Windows NT, select the 32-bit Windows option, as shown in Figure 8-30. Running a 16-bit installation on Windows NT can cause errors.

Giving the Install.log File a Home

Even when just creating utilities with SMS Installer and including uninstall support, make sure you go back to the Advanced Configuration window and give your script a path for the install.log

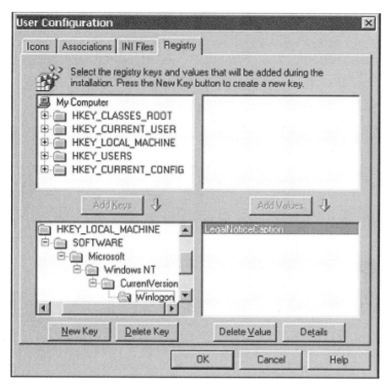

Figure 8-23 *Registry changes.*

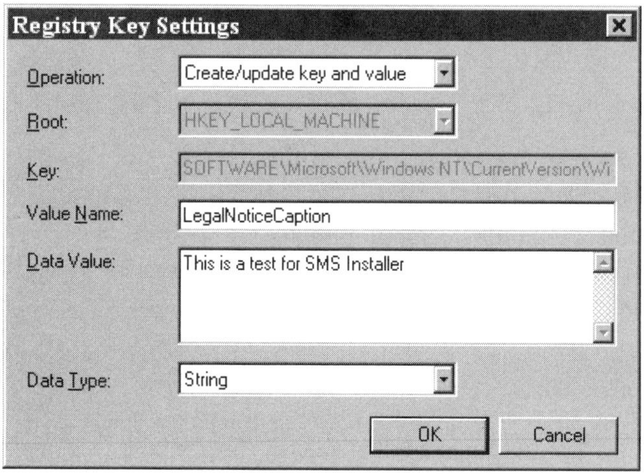

Figure 8-24 *LegalNoticeCaption Registry dialog box.*

Registry Key SOFTWARE\Microsoft\Windows NT\CurrentVersion\Winlogon = This is a test for SMS Installer

Figure 8-25 *Script Editor registry changes.*

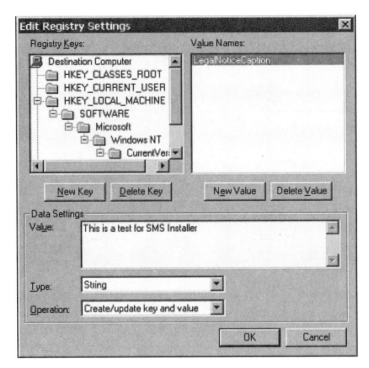

Figure 8-26 *Script Registry information.*

file (see Figure 8-31). If you forget to specify a path for the
Install.log, it could be installed to the root of the C: drive. And
each time you forget to do this, the current Install.log file is overwritten, destroying the information for future uninstalls of previous installations.

Style Log Names

When naming your Install.log files, make sure to use the standard
8.3 naming convention to make them compatible across multiple
platforms.

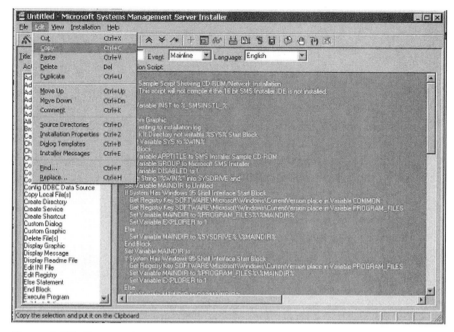

Figure 8-27 *Copy script.*

Compiling Your IPF

It would be a real disaster if you lost or deleted your IPF file for a particular package. To keep from losing the IPF for a package, compile the IPF file with your SMS Installer package. Later, you can use the / x parameter to extract the compiled IPF or make the compile executable Zip-compatible through the Advanced Configuration screen.

Testing Your Variables

If your script does not work, it could be that the custom variable information is not being picked up. To test your variables, pipe the variable information to a text file by adding an Insert Line into Text File script item.

For example, here is a quick script that pulls the Windows Logon Name and then writes the retrieved information to a text file:

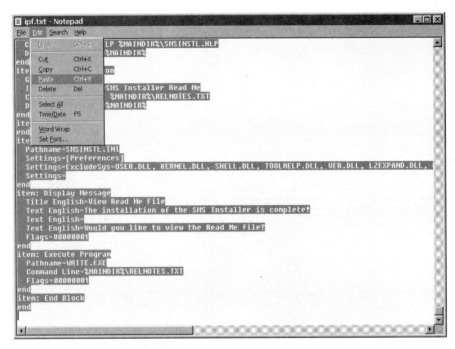

Figure 8-28 *Script in text file.*

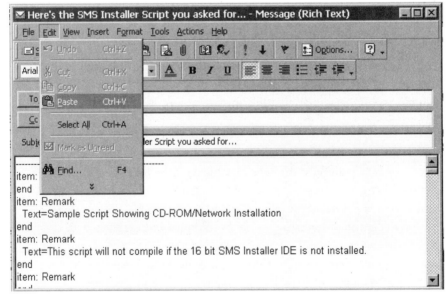

Figure 8-29 *Script in e-mail message.*

Figure 8-30 *16-bit/32-bit selection.*

Figure 8-31 *Install.log pathname.*

```
Check free disk space
Set Variable ROOT to C:\
Get Registry Key Hardware\Devicemap\Video place in Variable VIDDRIVER
Insert line "Video Hardware Key:  %VIDDRIVER%" into text file %ROOT%Video.txt.
Parse String "%VIDDRIVER%" into BEFORE and AFTER
Insert line "First Parse Variable:  %BEFORE%" into text file %ROOT%video.txt.
Insert line "2nd Parse Variable: %AFTER%" into text file %ROOT%video.txt.
Parse String "%AFTER%" into VIDBEFORE and VIDAFTER
Insert line "Final Output/Video Driver Name:  %VIDBEFORE%" into text file %ROOT%video.txt.
Get Registry Key System\CurrentControlSet\Services\%VIDBEFORE%\Device0 place in Variable CHIPSETNAME
Insert line "Video Driver Manufacturer Name:  %CHIPSETNAME%" into text file %ROOT%Video.txt.
```

Figure 8-32 *Script output.*

```
--------Begin Script
item: Get System Information
  Variable=WINNAME
  Flags=00010001
end
item: Insert Line into Text File
  Pathname=C:\TEMP.TXT
  New Text=%WINNAME%
  Line Number=0
end
--------End Script
```

The output is shown in Figure 8-32.

Now go back and test the next variable with the following script items:

```
--------Begin Script
item: Set Variable
  Variable=RECENTDIR
  Value=%WIN%\PROFILES\%WINNAME%\RECENT
end
item: Insert Line into Text File
  Pathname=C:\TEMP.TXT
```

```
   New Text=%RECENTDIR%
   Line Number=0
end
      --End Script
```

The output of the new action is displayed in Figure 8-33.

Next, go down the line until all the custom variables have been tested. When you know the variables are being recorded correctly, you can look elsewhere in my script for the answer to the problem.

Using Temporary Scripts

Starting with the Script Editor and then switching to the Installation Expert will cause the current script to be deleted. Some items are only available in the Installation Expert, so on some occasions, you have to switch to make modifications. Before switching, save the current script to a temporary file, then copy and paste the file into the script after switching back to the Script Editor.

Creating a Script Library

You may find that you will reuse a lot of script item procedures. Copy these common procedures out of the successful scripts into smaller scripts. When you are scripting in the future and you find you need a similar procedure that you have written before, copy it into the current script. These "scriplets" can save a lot of time.

Creating Command-Line Switches

You can incorporate your own command-line switches into your compiled SMS Installer utilities. First, set the CMDLINE variable. Then, insert an If/While statement that looks for the CMDLINE

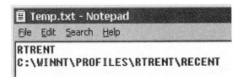

Figure 8-33 *New script output.*

value that has been entered, and act on the value. In the following script, the / ? command-line switch is defined as the value. When this switch is used, a dialog box is presented that gives a simple Help dialog box.

```
————-Begin Script
item: Set Variable
  Variable=CMDLINE
  Value=%CMDLINE%
  Flags=00011100
end
item: If/While Statement
  Variable=CMDLINE
  Value=/?
  Flags=00000010
end
item: Display Message
  Title English=Help Screen
  Text English=You have entered the command line switch:
/?. This switch brings up this help screen. It describes
the other switches that are available for this command.
  Flags=00100100
end
item: Exit Installation
end
item: End Block
end
————-End Script
```

Printing the SMS Installer Script

Choosing File|Print from the SMS Installer may not produce the results you require. Copying and pasting portions of the script into a simple text file may provide more information.

Using the RunOnce Utility

As mentioned earlier in the chapter, RunOnce.exe, included with Windows 9x and Windows NT, is a great utility used in conjunction with SMS Installer. Some scripts you code may require a restart before finishing. This can be accomplished using the RunOnce.exe utility (and the RunOnce registry keys covered next). You just include an SMS Installer compiled executable in the File Copy section of the current script, then use the

RunOnce.exe utility to place the path and command in the registry to run on bootup. Once the command has been run one time, it is removed from the registry, so it will not run again on any subsequent boots.

Using the RunOnce Registry Keys

As with using the RunOnce utility, the RunOnce registry keys can be modified to run programs after the computer is rebooted. The registry keys can be modified directly during a script using the Edit Registry script action in the Script Editor. You can add commands to these registry keys that will run when the computer is restarted (either through the use of the RESTART variable in SMS Installer or by a manual restart by the user).

The RunOnce registry keys are as follows:

HKEY_LOCAL_MACHINE\Software\Microsoft\Windows\ CurrentVersion\RunOnce

HKEY_CURRENT_USER\Software\Microsoft\Windows\ CurrentVersion\RunOnce

Note   HKEY_LOCAL_MACHINE affects all users of the computer; HKEY_CURRENT_USER affects just the current user's profile.

The following script places the information in the HKEY_LOCAL_MACHINE registry key (in this case the TEST.EXE file is copied to the C:\WINNT\SYSTEM32 directory and then placed into the RunOnce key):

```
————-Begin Script
item: Copy Local File
  Source=C:\Documents and Settings\rtrent\Desktop\TEST.EXE
  Destination=%SYS32%\TEST.EXE
  Local Path=C:\Documents and
Settings\rtrent\Desktop\TEST.EXE
  Flags=0000000001000010
end
item: Edit Registry
  Total Keys=1
  Key=Software\Microsoft\Windows\CurrentVersion\RunOnce
  New Value=C:\WINNT\SYSTEM32\TEST.EXE
  Value Name=Test Application
```

```
   Root=2
end
--------End Script
```

Using the Latest Version of SMS Installer

SMS Installer is updated on a fairly regular basis. It is generally updated to fix bugs but sometimes includes enhancements and feature additions. Always use the latest version. You can check for updated versions at http://www.microsoft.com/smsmgmt/default.asp. In addition, you can find notifications of new versions and information on bugs and added features at http://www.swynk.com/trent.

Valid Temp Directory

On both the reference and target computers, always verify that a Temp directory is defined in the environment variable and also verify that the Temp directory actually exists. The user could have inadvertently deleted this directory. Some application installations use the Temp directory for storing temporary files that are deleted after the installation is complete. If the Temp directory is not present, the installation could fail or display an error message.

Use the Get Environment Variable script action, as shown below. The script action prompts for the environment variable (in this case, the environment variable is commonly named TEMP) and prompts for a new SMS Installer variable name to place the information into. See Figure 8-34.

```
--------Begin Script
item: Get Environment Variable
  Variable=TEMPDIR
  Environment=TEMP
end
--------End Script
```

Do Not Repackage Device Drivers of Service Packs

Device drivers are enumerated differently from computer to computer because of dissimilarity between the hardware settings. For

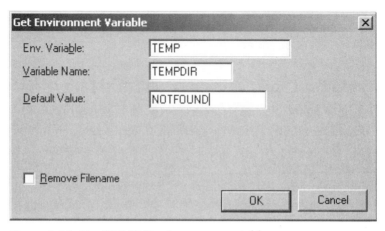

Figure 8-34 *Get TEMP Environment variable.*

this reason, do not repackage device drivers. Similarly, do not repackage service packs, because they generally contain device drivers.

Do Not Repackage Windows Installer Installations

Windows Installer technology replaces the need to repackage installations. Repackaging a Windows Installer installation with SMS Installer will not register the application correctly with the Windows Installer service. This will hinder the Windows Installer service from performing the auto-healing procedure. See Chapter 09, "The Future of Installer Technology," for more information.

The Future of Installer Technology

Windows Installer Technology

With Windows 2000 approaching its release date, Microsoft has changed the way it distributes and installs applications. This helps Microsoft approach their aim of further lowering the total cost of ownership through the *ZAW* (Zero Administration Windows) initiative (described in the next section). The old way of installing applications through a Setup.exe or executable file is being retired. Microsoft's new Windows Installer technology is replacing the old way in hopes of simplifying installations, adding better manageability, and incorporating software repair procedures. See Figure 9-1.

Instead of executables for installing software, new MSI files are used. The MSI files contain all the information for installing the software, making modifications to the computer such as registry changes, and icon and shortcut installations. Microsoft requires other software vendors to use the new Windows Installer technology for their application installations. Without a Windows Installer path, Microsoft will not certify the application for use on Windows 2000 and will not grant the Windows 2000 Gold Logo authorization.

For more information on the Win2000 logo certification, see http://msdn.microsoft.com/certification/description.asp.

The installer organizes installations around the concept of components and features, and stores all information about the installation in a relational database. Each installation package includes an MSI file, organized as COM-structured storage, containing an

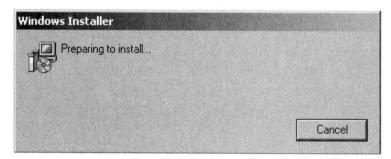

Figure 9-1 *Windows Installer service.*

installation database, a summary information stream, and data streams for various parts of the installation. The MSI file can also contain one or more *transforms*, internal source files, and external source files or cabinet files required by the installation.

Windows Installer is a computer service that runs the MSI files and watches the installation. The Windows Installer service is built into Windows 2000 but is available for Windows 95, Windows 98, and Windows NT 4.0 (see Figure 9-2).

Windows Installer views all applications as having three "building blocks": components, features, and products.

Components

Components can be described as a collection of files, registry keys, and other resources that are all installed as a group or unit. Resources are managed on the component level rather than on a file level, allowing the Windows Installer to accurately track the files, registry keys, and shortcuts that are shared by multiple applications. For instance, if an application that uses a shared component such as a DLL is uninstalled, the DLL will not be removed unless there are no other applications using the component.

Features

Features are the options or user preferences that can be selected during a software installation.

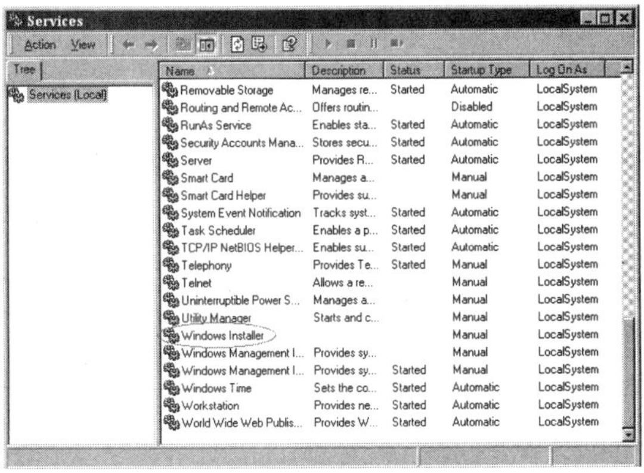

Figure 9-2 *Windows Installer Windows NT service.*

Products

Products are described as single applications, such as Microsoft Office 2000. A product is a collective group of features. A Windows Installer package file (MSI file) contains information that describes the product. The package file itself is the relational database that is optimized for installation performance. When installation is started, the Windows Installer service opens the package file and uses the information to determine the installation operations that must be performed for that product.

Windows Installer technology will seek to end "DLL hell," meaning applications in the market that do not follow any logical procedures for installations. Such applications include the files *they* want to install and totally disregard that other applications are needed to provide additional solutions, resulting in DLL files being overwritten needlessly and versions being changed, and causing other installed software to stop functioning or to stop functioning correctly.

Windows Installer tracks all the software components that are installed, identifies the ones that are shared by multiple applications, and marks the correct versions. Because of the tracking through the relational database, Windows Installer can locate missing files and even determine when files are corrupt. This will alert the Windows Installer service to start, whereupon it will prompt the user to repair the software installation. As long as the installation source is available, Windows Installer will "fix" the software.

Windows Installer also allows for "Install-On-Demand," meaning users can install the components they know they will need now and (because of the relational database) will be able to automatically install the other components later just by clicking on it. For instance, not every user uses the Clip Art feature of Microsoft Office products. Choosing not to install the clip art saves hard disk space. The business need for a particular user might change in the future. Clip art may become a critical component. Just by clicking on the File Menu reference will cause Windows Installer to start the installation of the clip art automatically.

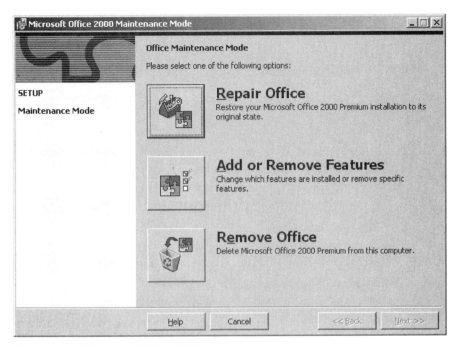

Figure 9-3 *Microsoft Office 2000.*

Microsoft Office 2000, shown in Figure 9-3, introduced some of the first Windows Installer installations.

Windows Installer technology will be incorporated into Windows 2000 as an admin tool for distributing applications via the Microsoft Management Console (MMC). Windows 2000 uses the Microsoft Active Directory (AD) structure to distribute installations to the local Windows NT domain. AD software installations will be targeted toward users and groups within the local Windows NT domain, while SMS will remain to support software distribution through enterprise environments.

Table 9-1 lists some current Installer products and the availability of Microsoft Installer formats.

Windows Installer Step-up Utility

As noted in Table 9-1, SMS Installer does not currently support the Microsoft Installer technology. Microsoft's MSI tools will allow the conversion of IPF files into the MSI format. It will

Table 9-1   *Installer products and formats.*

	Current Package Format	Currently Supports Microsoft Installer Technology?
Wise InstallManager	*.WSE	Yes
SMS Installer	*.IPF	No
InstallShield		Yes
WinInstall and Winstall LE	*.NAI	Yes

import the software installation information only, such as files installed and computer modifications. It will not support importing of SMS Installer customizations such as dialogs and graphics.

The tool to provide this conversion is the Windows Installer Step-up utility. This tool will provide the ability to convert SMS Installer scripts to Microsoft Installer, helping to preserve the investment that companies have made in the SMS Installer tool for software distributions. The Step-up utility is a command-line tool. It can be used in batch mode to migrate many SMS Installer setup packages at once from a directory tree. The Step-up utility works by looking at the executables created by SMS Installer, re-creating the scripts, extracting the data file, and then migrating the new script information to the Windows Installer format. Step-up will also create the Windows Installer files from the original SMS Installer script file (IPF), but this is not necessary. The custom scripts created with SMS Installer can also be converted, but the output cannot be used on 16-bit operating systems or distributed via floppy disks.

Visual Studio Installer

Visual Studio Installer is a Microsoft tool that creates MSI installs. It is available free of charge for Visual Studio customers on CD and for download as part of the Windows 2000 Developer's Readiness Kit. It seamlessly integrates into the Visual Studio shell and automatically handles file dependencies. It does not support custom installation dialogs, user interfaces, or testing facilities. If you want to be able to test your scripts, you need a tool like Install Shield for Windows Installer or Wise for Windows Installer.

Visual Studio Installer Resource is available at http://msdn.microsoft.com/vstudio/downloads/vsi/default.asp. Install Shield for Windows Installer is at http://www.install-shield.com/iswi/. Wise for Windows Installer is at http://www.wis-esolutions.com/wisewin.htm. In addition, there is a Windows Installer redistributable component available for download, at http://www.microsoft.com/msdownload/platformsdk/instmsi.htm.

ZAW (Zero Administration Windows)

The Zero Administration Windows initiative is a Microsoft strategic vision for continuing to lower the total cost of ownership through the use of new technologies. The tools are readily available for use in organizations. These should enable administrators to centrally manage and update software distributions and installations on computers connected to a LAN and WAN. The theory behind ZAW is that computers are too expensive to set up, deploy, maintain, upgrade, and replace. Certain costs associated with computers can never be reclaimed; for instance, the cost of the PC itself and the cost of break-fix and downtime. But there are certain parts of the costs that can be reclaimed by streamlining the technologies that are used to support them. These technologies include the components shown in Table 9-2.

Table 9-2 *ZAW components.*

Component	Explanation
Windows Driver Model	Unified driver for Windows 95 and Windows NT devices.
OnNow	Powers down some parts of PC, enabling five-second bootup time; maintains LAN connection for off-hours maintenance.

Table 9-2 *ZAW components (Continued).*

Component	Explanation
Automatic System Update	Checks server for changes on bootup; installs operating system or application changes automatically.
NetPC	Sealed case design keeps users from adding or removing software or hardware.
Server-based control	Enables operating system, applications, and configurations to be stored on server while updates are made centrally. Lets users roam from system to system while server replicates settings.
IntelliMirror	The ability to distribute applications and updates to a LAN environment using the Microsoft Active Directory. IntelliMirror technology is part of Windows 2000.
DMI 2.0	Allows remote management of DMI-compliant systems.

Index

About the Author

Rod Trent is a network engineer at Deloitte & Touche with over 5 years' experience in training, implementation, and support of Microsoft Systems Management Server (SMS). He writes SMS technical articles for www.swynk.com and is the section manager for SMS. His 14 years of experience in the computing industry include certifications such as MCP, MCSE, CNE, and A+.

SOFTWARE AND INFORMATION LICENSE

The software and information on this diskette (collectively referred to as the "Product") are the property of The McGraw-Hill Companies, Inc. ("McGraw-Hill") and are protected by both United States copyright law and international copyright treaty provision. You must treat this Product just like a book, except that you may copy it into a computer to be used and you may make archival copies of the Products for the sole purpose of backing up our software and protecting your investment from loss.

By saying "just like a book," McGraw-Hill means, for example, that the Product may be used by any number of people and may be freely moved from one computer location to another, so long as there is no possibility of the Product (or any part of the Product) being used at one location or on one computer while it is being used at another. Just as a book cannot be read by two different people in two different places at the same time, neither can the Product be used by two different people in two different places at the same time (unless, of course, McGraw-Hill's rights are being violated).

McGraw-Hill reserves the right to alter or modify the contents of the Product at any time.

This agreement is effective until terminated. The Agreement will terminate automatically without notice if you fail to comply with any provisions of this Agreement. In the event of termination by reason of your breach, you will destroy or erase all copies of the Product installed on any computer system or made for backup purposes and shall expunge the Product from your data storage facilities.

LIMITED WARRANTY

McGraw-Hill warrants the physical diskette(s) enclosed herein to be free of defects in materials and workmanship for a period of sixty days from the purchase date. If McGraw-Hill receives written notification within the warranty period of defects in materials or workmanship, and such notification is determined by McGraw-Hill to be correct, McGraw-Hill will replace the defective diskette(s). Send request to:

Customer Service
McGraw-Hill
Gahanna Industrial Park
860 Taylor Station Road
Blacklick, OH 43004-9615

The entire and exclusive liability and remedy for breach of this Limited Warranty shall be limited to replacement of defective diskette(s) and shall not include or extend to any claim for or right to cover any other damages, including but not limited to, loss of profit, data, or use of the software, or special, incidental, or consequential damages or other similar claims, even if McGraw-Hill has been specifically advised as to the possibility of such damages. In no event will McGraw-Hill's liability for any damages to you or any other person ever exceed the lower of suggested list price or actual price paid for the license to use the Product, regardless of any form of the claim.

THE McGRAW-HILL COMPANIES, INC. SPECIFICALLY DISCLAIMS ALL OTHER WARRANTIES, EXPRESSED OR IMPLIED, INCLUDING BUT NOT LIMITED TO, ANY IMPLIED WARRANTY OF MERCHANTABILITY OR FITNESS FOR A PARTICULAR PURPOSE. Specifically, McGraw-Hill makes no representation or warranty that the Product is fit for any particular purpose and any implied warranty of merchantability is limited to the sixty day duration of the Limited Warranty covering the physical diskette(s) only (and not the software or information) and is otherwise expressly and specifically disclaimed.

This Limited Warranty gives you specific legal rights; you may have others which may vary from state to state. Some states do not allow the exclusion of incidental or consequential damages, or the limitation on how long an implied warranty lasts, so some of the above may not apply to you.

This Agreement constitutes the entire agreement between the parties relating to use of the Product. The terms of any purchase order shall have no effect on the terms of this Agreement. Failure of McGraw-Hill to insist at any time on strict compliance with this Agreement shall not constitute a waiver of any rights under this Agreement. This Agreement shall be construed and governed in accordance with the laws of New York. If any provision of this Agreement is held to be contrary to law, that provision will be enforced to the maximum extent permissible and the remaining provisions will remain in force and effect.